AGAINST ETHICS

Studies in Continental Thought

John Sallis, general editor

AGAINST ETHICS

*Contributions to a Poetics of Obligation
with Constant Reference to
Deconstruction*

JOHN D. CAPUTO

INDIANA UNIVERSITY PRESS
Bloomington and Indianapolis

Grateful acknowledgment is made to Persea Books for permission to reprint Paul Celan's "Todesfuge," from *Poems of Paul Celan*, translated by Michael Hamburger, copyright © 1988 by Michael Hamburger; and "Todnauberg," from *Poems of Paul Celan*, translated by Michael Hamburger, copyright © 1988 by Michael Hamburger. Reprinted by permission of Persea Books.

The paper used in this publication meets the minimum requirements of American National Standards for Information Sciences—Permanence of Paper for Printed Library Materials, ANSI Z39.48-1984.

Manufactured in the United States of America

Library of Congress Cataloging-in-Publication Data

Caputo, John D.
    Against ethics : contributions to a poetics of obligation with constant reference to deconstruction / John D. Caputo.
        p.   cm. — (Studies in Continental thought)
    Includes bibliographical references and index.
    ISBN 0-253-31313-9 (alk. paper). — ISBN 0-253-20816-5 (pbk. : alk. paper)
    1. Ethics. I. Title. II. Series.
BJ1012.C316   1993
170—dc20   92-41567

3   4   5   99

To Paul,
For your golden laughter

CONTENTS

ACKNOWLEDGMENTS

This is a book with many obligations. My thanks to my students and colleagues at Villanova who have had to listen to this in its various stages and who have reacted with patience and acumen. In particular my thanks to my assistants Matthew Pacholec and Matthew Volta, who read earlier drafts of this study with care and made numerous helpful suggestions. I owe a great deal to Jacqueline Brogan, Walter Brogan, Thomas Busch, Drucilla Cornell, Thomas Sheehan, Mark Taylor, and Edith Wyschogrod for their insightful comments on the penultimate draft. John Tich has been my classical languages consultant.

I gratefully acknowledge the help of Jacques Derrida in loosening my tongue. My reference to Derrida's work would have been even more constant had not his essay on Kierkegaard and the story of Abraham, *"Donner la mort,"* in *L'éthique du don: Jacques Derrida et la pensée du don* (Paris: Métailié, 1992), appeared only after the completion of this book; this deferred gift, which also instructs Levinas on how to read Kierkegaard, confirms my premonition that for Derrida, as for Kierkegaard, ethics ought to be sacrificed in the name of obligation.

An earlier version of chapter 1 appears in *Joyful Wisdom: A Journal for Post Modern Ethics*, 2 (1992), and I thank Joyful Wisdom Publishing Limited for permission to use parts of this study. The permission of Persea Books to cite Michael Hamburger's translation of Paul Celan's "Todesfuge" and "Todtnauberg" is gratefully acknowledged.

I am indebted to a National Endowment of the Humanities Fellowship for College Teachers, 1991–1992, which made possible the sustained work that a book of this sort requires. I owe more than I can say to Rev. Lawrence Gallen, O.S.A., Vice-President of Academic Affairs, Villanova University, whose generous support of my work, now and in the past, exceeds my ability to thank him. Above all, I thank my wife, Kathy, whose patience with my work knows no bounds, who did the artwork for the cover.

ONE

Against Ethics

LOSING A GOOD NAME

I have for some time now entertained certain opinions that I have been reluctant to make public. But I have at length concluded that the time has
come to air my views, clearly and without apology, and to suffer whatever
consequences come my way.

I am against ethics.

Here I stand. I cannot do otherwise.

But, surely, there is enough immorality in the world, enough unethical
conduct in public and private life, without the philosophers coming out
against ethics! Would it not be a better and more salutary undertaking, and
certainly more in the public interest, to defend ethics against its detractors
instead of implicating oneself in damaging its good name?

Against ethics? Does not the ground open up before us? Does one not
shudder from the thought? Is one not visited by the worst fear and trembling?[1]

I confess to certain misgivings. I have up to now always tried to strike a
more respectable pose. Having consorted in the past chiefly with mystics[2] and
saints,[3] I have always made it my business to defend ethics, a more originary
ethics, an ethics of *Gelassenheit* and letting be, an ethics of dissemination, a veritable postmodern ethics.[4] I have always protested that if I traffic with anarchy, it is with a very responsible anarchy.[5] Who, after all, wants to be found
wanting in the matter of ethics? Who wants to risk having no ethics, or questioning its good name? I am, I have been—until now, when I found my nerve
(or lost my senses)—quite intimidated by the word "ethics." Its discursive
prestige has been too much for me. When I saw it coming down the street, I
always greeted it with my very best smile, tipped my hat and bowed in the
most courteous way, offering it my warmest salutations. That halcyon time is
over now. I will no longer be able to perpetrate this ruse. My neighbors will
soon know that I am registered in the opposing party.

Still, unlike Abraham, I am no hero,[6] no fearless explorer of unknown
lands, no swaggering venturer on uncharted seas. I think of myself rather
as rowing a small boat some distance behind, sticking close to the shores in
case a storm blows up, in waters where great and mighty vessels have first
shown the way. Up ahead, at the front of the fleet, I see the great
Heidegger, a master of thinking, an admirable admiral of bottomless seas
and groundless grounds, giving us our "heading" (*cap*) and setting our
course, giving European philosophy the direction it has taken today.[7] It

was Heidegger who first put this idea in my head and, if I am charged with impropriety, I will shamelessly blame a great deal on him while pleading for mercy for myself. It was Heidegger who first filled my mind with these impious thoughts about ethics, who first tempted me to consider the idea that we do not need ethics, that there is something to be said for getting beyond ethics, or even taking a stand against ethics:

> . . . Along with "logic" and "physics," "ethics" appeared for the first time in the school of Plato. These disciplines arose at a time when thinking was becoming "philosophy," philosophy, *episteme* (science), and science itself a matter for schools and academic pursuits. In the course of a philosophy so understood, science waxed and thinking waned. Thinkers prior to this period knew neither a "logic" nor an "ethics" nor "physics." Yet their thinking was neither illogical nor immoral. . . . The tragedies of Sophocles—provided such a comparison is at all permissible—preserve the *ethos* in their sagas more primordially than Aristotle's lectures on "ethics."[8]

In Heidegger, this disturbing of ethics is all very beautiful and even oddly reassuring. The task of stepping back from ethics or metaphysics, of overcoming metaphysics or ethics, is undertaken in the name of something more primordial and originary (*ursprünglicher*), something that happened once, long ago, in a time of radiant splendor, a brief but magnificent time, as opposed to the present time of need.[9] For Heidegger, to be against ethics is just as much to be for something more primordial, a more originary ethics, so that one can show one is not being immoral or illogical. That would make it easier to save one's reputation and salvage one's good name.

But the time has also come for me to confess something else, to make a clean breast of everything that has been going on inside me.

I am also against "originary ethics."

I confess to having lost all contact with the First Beginning and everything Originary. I have given up hope of catching a glimpse of the last god's passing by in this end-time when the first gods have flown.[10] I do not expect to be on hand for the Other Beginning, which can be granted if and only if one can maintain communications with the First Beginning. I have in short been abandoned, become a part of and a party to the very *Seinsverlassenheit* against which Heidegger has at length warned us all. Though I wait daily by my phone, though I keep my ear close to the ground, I cannot, for the life of me, hear the call of Being. I have been forsaken.[11] (I think that Being has discovered I am American and that I use a computer. I suspect an informer.)

So I am denied the Heideggerian saving leap, the leap beyond ethics and metaphysics, to the Saving Event, to a Sophocles beyond Aristotle, a Thinking beyond ethics. By the same token, it would be shameless of me to turn to the Aristotelians for help. They will turn me out as well, and with every right, I who have chosen to speak against ethics and who have contributed modestly to numerous campaigns to overcome metaphysics.

What I have in mind by saying that I am against ethics is, unhappily, not a matter of unconcealing something more originary than ethics. It is a little more like confessing that the ground on which I stand tends to shift, that something that hitherto seemed to me firm and fixed is given to drift. My situation is to be compared to a man who discovers that the ground he hitherto took to be a *terra firma* is in fact an island adrift in a vast sea, so that even if he stands absolutely firm he is in fact constantly in motion. Add to this the thought that the sea is endless, the sky starless, and the island's drift aimless, and you gain some measure of the level of my consternation.

What I have to offer my readers is not a deep *Wiederholung*, a retrieval of something More Primordial, and this by way of having purchased myself a seat on the great Greco-Germanic shuttle that runs the Truth of Being back and forth between the great Beginnings. I have turned in my Greco-Euro-pass. I have chosen to speak instead of a *déconstruction*, in the French, a Romance language, in which it is openly confessed one cannot think, so that if, at some later time, it should be decided that one wants to think, one would have to switch to German.[12] My project is more Thought-less and Latinate, conducted in good English, with the help of Romance tongues — but it is not, I trust, too romantic. On the contrary, it is part of my present heretical state of mind to think that the Big Story, the *grand récit*, of Being's bends and turns, the *Seinsroman* of the great Beginnings, which assure us of Something Saving, is where romanticism makes its nest.

It would, as Derrida says, be a very "congenial"[13] undertaking to rally to the defense of ethics so that we could assure everyone of the good name of deconstruction, particularly those detractors of deconstruction, the "officials of anti-deconstruction," who protest loudly their love of the Good and the True and who thank God daily in their temple that they are not like the deconstructionists. For the names of "ethics," "morality," and "responsibility" are "fine names," and we regret losing them. But however congenial a task, the "remoralization of deconstruction" is too easy, too hasty a project. One needs to avoid generating

> a consensual euphoria or, worse, a community of complacent deconstructionists, reassured and reconciled with the world in ethical certainty, good conscience, satisfaction of service rendered, and the consciousness of duty accomplished (or, more heroically still, yet to be accomplished).

From a deconstructive point of view, declining the good name of ethics is an operation aimed at appreciating that tenuous and delicate situation of judgment which is addressed by the name "undecidability." Unhappily, "undecidability" has gotten a bad name, a very notorious one, proof positive for the officials of anti-deconstruction that deconstruction must be irresponsible, must itself be very bad.[14]

A deconstruction is thus a less nostalgic, less reassuring undertaking than ethics or Originary Ethics, one in which sound principles or Saving

Events do not at all figure. On the contrary, to speak of being against ethics and of deconstructing ethics is to own up to the lack of safety by which judging is everywhere beset. The thing that concerns me, and that I name under the not very protective cover of deconstruction, is the loss of the assurance, the lack of the safe passage, that ethics has always promised. Ethics makes safe. It throws a net of safety under the judgments we are forced to make, the daily, hourly decisions that make up the texture of our lives. Ethics lays the foundations for principles that force people to be good; it clarifies concepts, secures judgments, provides firm guardrails along the slippery slopes of factical life. It provides principles and criteria and adjudicates hard cases. Ethics is altogether wholesome, constructive work, which is why it enjoys a good name.

The deconstruction of ethics, on the other hand, cuts this net. Or rather, since deconstruction is not some stealthy, cunning agent of disruption, is not an agent at all, is in a sense nothing at all, it is much more accurate to say that a deconstructive analysis shows that the net is already torn, is "always already" split, all along and from the start. The deconstruction of ethics is ethics' own doing, ethics' own undoing, right before our eyes. It is something that happens to ethics and in ethics, something going on in ethics, with or without Jacques Derrida. In any possible deconstruction of ethics, one would be simply passing the word along that one is rather more on one's own than one likes to think, than ethics would have us think.

Deconstruction shows how a film of undecidability creeps quietly over the clarity of decisions, on cat-soft paws, clouding judgment just ever so much, so that we cannot quite make out the figures all around us. But do not be mistaken. Deconstruction offers no excuse not to act. Deconstruction does not put up a stop sign that brings action to a halt, to the full stop of indecision; rather, it installs a flashing yellow light, warning drivers who must in any case get where they are going to proceed with caution, for the way is not safe. Undecidability does not detract from the urgency of decision; it simply underlines the difficulty. Deconstruction takes as its subject matter the task of making one's way along an aporia, along an almost impassable road, where the ground may at any moment shift beneath our feet. Deconstruction issues a warning that the road ahead is still under construction, that there is blasting and the danger of falling rock. Ethics, on the other hand, hands out maps which lead us to believe that the road is finished and there are superhighways all along the way.

The risky thought I have been cultivating, the little bit of heresy that I have been privately nurturing under my little shibboleth "against ethics," is the idea that "obligation" is not safe, that ethics cannot make it safe, that it is not nearly as safe as ethics would have us believe. Life in general, and the life of obligation in particular, is a rather more difficult, risky business than ethics would allow. That is one way to gloss Heidegger's statement above that a Greek tragedy has more to say about the *ethos*—about the difficulty of life[15]—than does a philosophical treatise on ethics. That is true.

(But I do not think that Heidegger has quite taken this tragic message to heart; he tends to assimilate tragic Greeks and tragic poets into a pregiven History of Being, a *Seinsroman*, which blunts their tragic tip.)[16]

By "obligation" I do not mean anything profound. Like Johannes de Silentio, whom I have taken as a certain mentor, I have no such "prodigious head" for profundity.[17] It is all I can do to get through the days and nights of everydayness; the superficial world is already more than I can handle. Obligation does not mean answering the call of Being, or of the History of Being, or of the History of Spirit, or of the Voice of God. I have, I repeat, lost all communications from On High. My satellite has been knocked out. I have in mind instead a very earthbound signal, a superficial-horizontal communication between one human being and another, a certain line of force that runs along the surface upon which you and I stand: the obligation I have to you (and you to me, but this is different) and the both of "us" to "others." Even the notion of "others" must be spread out and disseminated, so as to include not only other human beings but what is other than human—animals, e.g., or other living things generally, and even the earth itself (which would give Heidegger an entrée). I mean the feeling that comes over us when others need our help, when they call out for help, or support, or freedom, or whatever they need, a feeling that grows in strength directly in proportion to the desperateness of the situation of the other. The power of obligation varies directly with the powerlessness of the one who calls for help, which is the power of powerlessness.

To be sure, the oldest and most honorable work of ethics has been to defend and honor obligation, to make obligation safe. But my impious thought is that obligation is not safe and so, in the shameless deconstructionist view I espouse, that it is just in virtue of obligation that ethics comes unstuck. That at least is what I will try to show; that will be a part of the point of the analysis to follow. Obligation, I will hold, is a kind of *skandalon* for ethics, which makes ethics blush, which ethics must reject or expel in order to maintain its good name, for ethics is "philosophy," a certain *episteme*. Ethics contains obligation, but that is its undoing (deconstruction). Ethics harbors within itself what it cannot maintain, what it must expel, expectorate, exclude. Ethics, one might say, cannot contain what it contains.[18]

The deconstruction of ethics sets obligation loose from its containment or confinement or, better, lets that being-set-loose be seen, even as it exposes the vulnerability, the frailty and fragility of obligation. It lets obligation be even as it lets it in for trouble, exposing it to disaster.

A DISASTER

I have confessed that my satellite is out, that I receive no heavenly communications, no messages from the starry sky above. I have often recalled with fondness and admiration what Kant has said about ethics and the stars. Nothing so filled Kant with awe than the starry skies above and the moral law within, the stars being for Kant (and for Aristotle too) obedient to the highest and most surpassing lawfulness, and the Law being for Kant a kind of star to guide us through the swirl of appearances.[19] That is very beautiful. It is further testimony to the unhappy condition into which I have declined that, were I pressed to pursue this metaphor, I myself would have to say that I have for some time now contemplated the unpleasant prospect that life is a disaster. I am not trying to be romantic, to write a new chapter in the history of Being's withdrawal. I mean nothing World-historical or Being-historical. I speak *ad literam*. To suffer a disaster is to lose one's star (*dis-astrum*), to be cut loose from one's lucky or guiding light. For me, the stars above twinkle in a void, without concern for mere mortals down below. Laying claim to neither the *logos* nor the *nomos* of the stars, I suffer a disastronomic, disastrological, deconstructive setback. That is why I have been reluctant to be forthcoming about these matters.

What else does it mean to say that one has lost one's faith in *grands récits*, that one responds with disbelief to sweeping narratives, that one declines fine names like Ethics and Metaphysics, Science and Religion, that one refuses to crown anything with capital letters, that Being, presence, *ousia*, the transcendental signified, History, Man—the list goes on—have all become dreams? Is not this so called postmodern condition[20] a disastrous condition? The name of my report on knowledge would have been *La condition désastreuse*. Is that not what a disaster means? That the star-guide stories that take us by the hand through the storms and tempests of factical life have lost their credibility? Not having been commissioned to speak on behalf of the Spirit of the Age or the Destiny of Being, and speaking for myself, I feel forsaken by such starry guides. It is not a question of knowing what to put in their place, but of just getting along without such a place, of conceding that things are just "decentered," "disseminated," "disastered."

I would say that we are in a fix, except that even to say "we" is to get into a still deeper fix. We are in the fix that we cannot say "we."[21]

Still, I would say, obligation happens, the obligation of me to you and of both of us to others. It is all around us, on every side, constantly tugging at our sleeves, calling upon us for a response.

In the midst of a disaster.

A FACT AS IT WERE

Obligation happens.

That is where I start, not because it is my *fundamentum inconcussum*, but because I do not know where else to begin. I begin wherever I am,[22] in the midst of multiple obligations, in the plural and the lowercase, nothing capitalized or from on high.

Es gibt: there is obligation (Heidegger). *Il arrive*: it happens (Lyotard). Obligation is a fact, as it were (Kant). Here I am (*me voici*), on the receiving end of an obligation (Levinas).[23]

I am not announcing anything world-historical here but simply pointing to a fact (as it were), which surrounds us on every side: Obligations constantly happen, wherever we turn. Innumerable obligations, too many to deal with, sometimes in conflict with one another, often very difficult to sort out, although sometimes clear and pressing. Obligations belong to the most elemental condition of what the young Heidegger called the situation of "factical life," the condition of our "facticity." As soon as we come to be we find ourselves (*sich befinden*) enmeshed in obligations.[24] The "ought" is, in fact, one of the most common features of what "is," of what is happening.

To say that obligations "happen" is to say that obligation is not anything I have brought about, not anything I have negotiated, but rather something that happens to me. Obligations do not ask for my consent. Obligation is not like a contract I have signed after having had a chance first to review it carefully and to have consulted my lawyer. It is not anything I have agreed to be a party to. It binds me. It comes over me and binds me. That is why Lyotard calls obligation a "scandal"—to the "I," to "philosophy," to "autonomy."[25] Ethics, which is philosophy, would just as soon keep this or any other scandal, any stumbling block to reason and intelligibility, at a safe remove. Ethics wants to keep its good name, to keep its house in order.

It binds me. It, *das Es*, binds me. There is/it gives (*es gibt*) obligation. But *what* binds me? What is the *origin* of obligation? I do not know. I have already owned up to being cut off from origins and beginnings. I am always too late for origins. I never arrive in time. By the time I get to the scene of obligation a crowd has already gathered. I do not know the origin of obligation any more than I know the origin of the work of art. Obligation happens before I reach the scene. *Il arrive*: it happens before I get there, has always already happened, without my even being there at all.

You begin to see the effect of the deconstruction of ethics, the double effect of liberating obligation from ethics, of setting it loose from ethics, or rather of watching it twist free from ethics (since this is not anything anyone is doing). Obligation becomes a fact (as it were), but a shaky one, with emphasis on the *as it were*. For I do not know its origin, its whence or its whither. I am not its judge, its law, its personal doorkeeper, charged with checking its papers, its authorizing, legitimating credentials. I feel its force but I can prove nothing of its provenance. Obligation is a feeling, the feeling of being bound (*ligare*, *ob-ligare*, *re-ligare*), an element of my feeling *Befindlichkeit*, but I cannot get on top of it, scale its heights, catch a glimpse of its rising up. It comes at me, comes over me, overtakes me, seizes hold of me. As soon as I come to be I am already in its grasp. I have neither the will nor the means to deny it. When I am obliged I do not know by what dark powers I am held. I only know/feel/find myself caught up, in the midst of obligation, in its snare, in the scandal, in a panic—perhaps even blinded.[26]

Something demands my response, I know not what (although I have a few opinions). Something moves me to respond and to feel obligation, but how am I to know what? I do not know the Name of the Origin of the Law. I have been cut off from all such capitals, de-capitated. For me, decapitation is particularly disastrous, a personal autographic disaster, a disastrous autography, destroying my good name.

All that I know about obligation, all that I can say, is that I am taken hold of from without, seized by something else, something other, *je ne sais quoi*. The otherness of this something other, the heteronomic force of the other, is the dislocating locus or site—I do not say the origin—of obligation. It is the alterity or otherness of the other, the heteronomy, that disrupts me, that is visited upon me, that knocks me out of orbit.

Obligation has a kind of impenetrability and density that I cannot master, that neither my knowledge nor my freedom can surmount, that prevents me from getting on top of it, on the other side of it. Obligation transcends me; it is not one of my transcendental projects. If an obligation is "mine" it is not because it belongs to me but because I belong to it. Obligation is not one more thing I comprehend and want to do, but something that intervenes upon and disrupts the sphere of what the I wants, something that troubles and disturbs the I, that pulls the I out of the circle of the same, as Levinas would say.

I do not know what if any hidden forces I obey when I give heed to this otherness, by what forces I am bound over. Is it the voice or face of God? Or the deep momentum of a network of laws embedded in the "tradition," of what is handed down to me by the ages?[27] Or some still darker law of the unconscious, some blind repressed event that keeps repeating itself on me? Or even some evolutionary survival mechanism aimed at keeping the species going?[28] I cannot say. I am always too late for origins, although I will be grateful for any eyewitness reports, which I ask be mailed to me directly, by express mail.

I would like to say that obligation is safe. I would like to defend it, to fend off its enemies and detractors, to build a high wall around it and keep it safe. That would be a very honorable thing to do and it would, I am sure, restore the good name of deconstruction. That is the gesture of "ethics," but alas, it is a part of my unhappy condition that I am against ethics. Try as I might, I always end up leaving obligation undefended and vulnerable. But it is what I would defend were my luck to change for the better, were my satellite to be put back in repair, were I able to get as far as ethics, which I fear might take many years of preparation and more time than I have available.

A EULOGY TO AN UGLY MAN

Far be it from me to make ethics tremble. I tremble even at the prospect that I will be found guilty of spreading the word that the pants of the great man are split. For that I have already prepared a defense aimed at exonerating me of all responsibility. I follow others. I am following (*je suis*), in fear and trembling, in the wake of others. Of Heidegger, whom I am ready to blame in case of trouble, although he was himself only answering the call of Being. Of Derrida, who put this idea of deconstruction in my head. Of Lyotard, who did not himself have a heart for venturing alone into dangerous seas, but rather "like[d] to speak under the authority and protection of him whom, under the name of Abraham, the young Hegel attacks with the well-known, truly anti-Semitic bitterness in *The Spirit of Christianity*."[29] And of Johannes de Silentio, who was himself a follower of Abraham (who was himself only following orders).

The result is that it will be very hard to identify the guilty party, to find anyone who is singularly responsible, if we are all rounded up by the police and charged with inciting a riot against ethics.

The first line of defense I have devised if the police come knocking at my door is to blame everything on Abraham. He will mind it the least, being the most used to incomprehensible fates.

That is why I begin by offering a eulogy to Abraham. I want to get on the good side of him who is the paradigm and paradox of obligation and answering calls. Abraham is the father of all of those who dare raise their voice against ethics. The story of Abraham is, however, a slightly elusive tale that admits of numerous tellings.[30] Hegel took it to be the story of an ugly man who was alienated from the infinite, and who was unable to make the movement beyond faith to systematic thought. Johannes de Silentio, on the other hand, was convinced that he could never get as far as Abraham, let alone surpass him and raise faith up a notch to the reconciling beauty of knowledge. For de Silentio, this is the story of a daring teleological suspension of ethics, of suspending understanding and hanging ethical knowledge out to dry, of lifting the force of the universal and putting it in *epochē*. For Johannes it is a story not about the suspension of obligation but about the suspension of the fine name of ethics in the name of obligation, about suspending the fine name of universality in the name of the heterogeneity and incommensurability of the singular individual and of going one on one with the Absolute.[31] I myself am following Johannes de Silentio, trying to turn this story into a little deconstructionist narrative, a *petit récit, en bon Français*, about fragments and incommensurables, about ugly singularities. I am less alarmed over what is ugly than over the power and prestige of what is beautiful.

The story of Abraham poses a scandal for ethics. It belongs to the "sacred scriptures" but it seems to tell quite an unholy tale about how it is permissible to commit murder, provided the right conditions are met. Lyotard has put this scandal—the scandal caused to ethics by the story of Abraham, which is the scandal of obligation—in the form of a dilemma, a cognitive form which ethics, which is philosophy, can appreciate. If I understand an obligation, if it is a universal and intelligible principle, then I have made it mine, one of my projects, something I have appropriated and made my

own, and so not an obligation at all, but another bit of my freedom, another
good idea I have and want to pursue. If I do not understand an obligation,
then it is arbitrary; and then I am unable to distinguish among obligations,
to distinguish, say, the command that Yahweh gave to Abraham ("that
Isaac die") from the command issued to the Nazis guards ("that the Jews
die").[32]

That brings the scandal home—by lining up father Abraham with the
most heinous slaughter of the children of Abraham (and of quite a few
other children, too). It is from a salutary fear and trembling before such di-
lemmas as this that we have always wanted to have an ethics, and the exposure to such a dilemma is part of the trouble we purchase, part of the
anxiety we assume, with the deconstruction of ethics.

That is why I start, like Johannes de Silentio, with a eulogy to Abraham,
an ugly man.[33] Some people become great by expecting what is possible
and doing it; it is hard to do and difficult to understand, but possible. Some
people, however, become great by struggling with the eternal, which is
even more difficult. But one man became great by expecting what is impossible, by struggling with God himself, in virtue of a power that is powerlessness, of a wisdom that is foolishness, of a hope that was madness, and
of a love that was hatred to oneself. That man is father Abraham.

Johannes offers a very beautiful eulogy to Abraham, which clearly shows
the beauty of Abraham's faith. Is it then not the case that Abraham is very
beautiful just in virtue of what Hegel calls his ugliness, in which case to
speak of Abraham as an ugly man would be to speak ironically, parodi-
cally? Is it not the case that beauty and ugliness mean many things, too
many to master, and that it is only in virtue of certain beauty that Abraham
is ugly to Hegel?[34] Does Hegel have an eye only for a certain beauty, while
lacking an eye for certain other kinds of beauty? Did Hegel's eagle have an
eye too few? Could we not, in another context, one in which we are not
making trouble for ethics, make a great deal of the beauty of Abraham, and
the beauty of obligation? Would it not be possible to tell very beautiful stories about obligation, to have a kind of poetics of obligation, which would
turn on something otherwise than what Hegel calls beauty, and in which it
would be impossible to differentiate the aesthetical, the ethical, and the religious; or the beautiful and the sublime? Then it would turn out that obligation does not oblige us to renounce poetics, but to poetize differently.

Still, it is quite a mad call that Abraham hears, quite an incomprehensible
command he must obey: to destroy the very seed given to him who was at
the same time called upon to plant the seeds of a new generation, and this
at a time when he and Sarah had reached, let us say, a venerable age.

"Abraham!" The Lord called.

"*Me voici,*" answered Abraham.

The French is very instructive here. If Abraham had spoken Greek, we
would have been forced to translate this into German. As it stands, since
Abraham never studied Greek, we are free to employ the French. Besides,

we are not claiming to get as far as "thinking." As to whether there might be some inner spiritual kinship between Hebrew and French, I have no special information. I am content to treat the whole thing as a matter of good luck and not to think about it too much, since I have other things on my mind. The French puts Abraham in the accusative. *Me voici*: here I am; behold (the) me; here you will find me, *me*, in the accusative, the addressee of an address.[35] Structurally, one is always on the receiving end of an obligation. Abraham does not try to assume the position of the author, the addressor, the transcendental sender, which in this case—where there is question of a message from On High—would be a very dangerous, pretentious gesture on his part. Abraham does not try to get on top of this command, to penetrate it, to see through it, to mount and surmount the word that comes crashing down on him. He just takes it, in the accusative, receives it, accepts it, stands under it, allows it its opacity and impenetrability. This command is not Abraham's idea but an intervention upon Abraham, something that shatters his circle of self-interest.

Hegel thinks that this makes Abraham very ugly, not just one more ugly Jew, but the patriarch and paradigm of ugly Jews. For Hegel, the Jew is someone who must destroy everything he loves, who rips himself up from his native land and sets himself adrift, wandering, without a *Heimat*. "He was a stranger on the earth, a stranger to the soil and to men alike."[36] He took the whole world to be his opposite. Love eluded him but "even the one love he had, his love for his son, even his hope of posterity . . . even this love he once wished to destroy; and his heart was quieted only through the certainty of the feeling that this love was not so strong as to render him unable to slay his beloved son with his own hand."[37] If Abraham loves his son, then he must, in accordance with the law of the cut, prove that he is willing to destroy his son, to cut his heart loose from his son, and this just because he loves his son. For the Jews, Hegel says, God is not a truth but a command, not a friend but a master for their servile spirit. Truth is beauty, but "how can they have an inkling of beauty who saw in everything only matter," not spirit?[38] The tragedy of the Jew is not Greek tragedy, for tragedy is what accompanies the fall of "beautiful character." But the Jews are devoid of beauty. They lack the reconciling spirit of love and beauty, the reconciling power of the Spirit itself, which is not Jewish but Greek and Christian (and maybe also a little Prussian and even Hegelian). The Spirit is not Jewish, for the Jew lacks Spirit and lives lifelessly, in alienation, in incisions and circumcisions, dead and ugly.

Hegel, who as we can see is filled with the Spirit of Love, loves ethics very much and he believes that Abraham is a scandal to ethics and to love, that Abraham scandalized the beauty of love with his ugliness. Ethics is *Sittlichkeit*, the concretely embodied sociohistorical ethical life, the outer embodiment of inner law, the living, substantive content of dead and abstract duty. Ethics turns on intelligibility, reconciliation, and beauty. Obligation must be carefully fitted into *Sittlichkeit* so as not to breach the spirit of harmony and reconciliation. This is done by viewing obligation as the embodiment of the Spirit's own progress on the way to its full unfolding, the embodiment of the Spirit itself in the process of becoming itself. The essence of the Spirit is freedom, which means that in truth there is nothing but Spirit, nothing outside Spirit, nothing to limit freedom, nothing but freedom alone, by itself, close to itself (*bei sich sein*). In terms of *Sittlichkeit*, obligation is nothing more than freedom freely exercising itself. Nothing comes from without; nothing finally lays freedom low. Nothing is outside freedom to constrain or bind (*ligare*) freedom the way Isaac is bound by Abraham and the way Abraham is bound by the Lord's command. Obligation is nothing but the Spirit binding itself, so there is no obligation that cuts into freedom, that imposes itself from without. Were the Hegelian Spirit to say "here I am," it would have to be talking to itself. Ethics is a way for the Spirit to be at home; ethics is *bei sich sein*, Spirit's being close to itself—not a matter of being homeless, uprooted, and adrift like Abraham, who hears other voices, indeed the voice of the Other.[39]

Obligation, on the other hand, is ugly, Jewish, Abrahamic. It lacks entirely the spirit of Greek beauty and autonomy, of *harmonia* and reconciliation, and the Christian spirit of love (which is exemplified by Hegel's love of the Jews). Obligation is the ugliness of discord and subjection, of being disrupted and disturbed by a call that comes from without. This dispossession and alienation will not do at all in ethics, which is philosophy. In philosophy, which is Greek, obligation must always be, in one way or another, something I do to myself, just as, in philosophy, truth is something I have or am of myself. "I, Plato, am the truth." That, as Nietzsche said, is philosophy's opening and paradigmatic gesture. The philosopher *is* the truth and he speaks the truth by turning within himself. Abraham, however, is slavishly dependent upon instruction from the Other, upon a Master or Teacher. Philosophy runs autonomously, on the level of immanence, while obligation is constantly being shocked from without, transcendently.[40]

Kant's voice too must be added to this eulogy to Abraham, even though Johannes de Silentio has pitted Abraham against a very Kantian version of the Law. But Kant's Categorical Imperative, I maintain, is the closest Abraham ever gets to wearing philosophical robes (almost). In Kant, the Law, the Categorical Imperative, comes over us like the voice of the Lord that overtakes Abraham. The Law humbles us with the majesty of its uncompromisable, unconditional command. It strikes us down and leaves us speechless—except to say *ich kann* (which is, take note, in the first person). Kant set sail in the turbulent straits that flow between obligation and ethics, between the Law and autonomy, between Jew and Greek. His "metaphysics of morals" is the work of an *Aufklärer* who also loves father Abraham, who loves the Law more than God.[41]

But Kant also wanted to remove the scandal of the Law, to haul away the stumbling block of transcendence and unintelligibility, the shock of heteronomy. Hegel thought that Kant was too servile and Jewish, that Kant too was ugly and lacking in a beautiful, reconciled soul, that he was not enough of a Greek.[42] But Kant proved to be all too Greek, all too much the *Aufklärer*, to let obligation be, to let it happen. In the end, but only after a very powerful defense of the unconditionally commanding power of the imperative of the Law, Kant washed his hands and turned obligation over to philosophy.

The Law comes to us from on high, like a massive fact, as it were, jutting out through the smooth surface of phenomenal time. The Law is a "cognitive monster," as Lyotard says,[43] something that makes a monstrous show (*monstrare*) of itself against the regular succession of the phenomenal world. It admits of no demonstration or deduction but it is itself the monstrous basis of any future practical deductions.

> "Thou shalt," says the Law. (*Du sollst,* in German/Jewish, a little like Moses taking dictation from On High *auf Deutsch.*)
> "I can," says Kant. (*Ich kann,* in the first person.)

Obligation is a spontaneous causality, a cause without antecedent that breaks in upon the unbroken regularity of phenomenal succession, with a power to move heaven and earth. I have found it necessary to move heaven and earth, Kant says in his best German/Jewish, in order to make room for obligation.[44] Obligation is a fact, categorically, unconditionally. The law comes from on high, like the stars above. As it were.

But then Kant blinked. The *Aufklärer* recovered his senses. Ethics, which is philosophy, and philosophy, which is Greek,[45] cannot abide this much alienation and disappropriation, this much *Unheimlichkeit.* The philosopher, who belongs to the true world, must come home.

"Fundamentally the same old sun, but shining through mist and scepticism; the idea grown sublime, pale, northerly, Königsbergian."[46]

The law that reason obeys is reason's own law, so it does not, ultimately, finally, bend its knee to anything "other" (*heteros*) but offers its respects to itself (*autos*), like a man bowing to himself in the mirror. Even when it honors the Other as an end in itself, it does so in virtue of the Law, which is Reason, which is itself; so it respects itself as an end in itself. Reason gives itself its own law—whence the oxymoron "autonomy," whereas *nomos* ought to signify the shock delivered to the *autos* by the *heteros*. Reason is both the author and the subject of the Law, interchangeably both the addressor and the addressee. Kant wants to insert freedom back at the origin of the Law, before the Law, to make freedom older than the Law, the source of the Law. Reason prescribes to itself. Reason is like a man marching on a drilling field all alone, in full uniform, with perfect Prussian military posture, ordering himself around: "About face! To the left, march." While we admire such a man for his ability to stay in step and not to be caught unawares by an unanticipated command, we do not admire him for his ability to take orders. Kant wants freedom to ratify and legitimate the thing that is supposed to seize freedom and take hold of it. It is as if a man were to seize himself by his own lapels and say to himself, "Now see here. This sort of thing must stop!"

That is why we had to send for a rabbi. It took a philosopher-rabbi to restore the Jewish law, to restore obligation to its original, Abrahamic difficulty, to put the *Aufklärer* back in his place, to deliver the best and most eloquent philosophical eulogy of all to Abraham, who was after all an ugly man. Levinas insisted that the position of the addressee is irreversible, incommutable, that when it comes to prescriptives the pragmatic positions of the addressor and the addressee cannot be exchanged. One is always, necessarily, structurally, on the receiving end of a command, dominated by its transcendence, blinded by its power. That is Lyotard's transcription of Levinas:

> And isn't Levinas's exigency the only safeguard against this illusion [Kant's illusion that prescriptives must be like descriptives which authorize the commutability of addressor and addressee], viz. that one can only phrase ethics ethically, that is, as someone obligated . . . ?[47]

Levinas understood the heteronomic structure of obligation, even as ethics, which is philosophy, can subsist only in the element of autonomy, immanence, and freedom. I, Plato, am the Truth. I, Hegel, am the Spirit. I, Kant, am Reason. "We the people" are the truth and the law. "We" speak in the name of the people, in the name of humankind, in the name of God, in the name of nature.[48] Levinas performed a great double gesture. He spoke in the name of "ethics" and of philosophy, but what he called ethics, which is philosophy, is everything that philosophy resists, excludes, expels in the hope of preserving its good name. Levinas loves ethics like a rabbi. He loves the Torah more than he loves God.[49] But everything that Levinas calls ethics and metaphysics—the shock of heteronomy, unfreedom, and transcendence—is what ethics and metaphysics resist. The effect of Levinas's great eulogy to Abraham, of his great *me voici*, is to rock ethics, to shock the immanence and autonomy of philosophy. Even though Levinas thinks that everything is or turns on ethics and that ethics is first philosophy, even though he is very "pious"[50] and loves ethics like a rabbi, and even though, despite his admiration for Derrida's "formidable questioning," he would defend the priority of "ethics before Being," not the "deconstruction" of ethics,[51] despite all this, has not Levinas carried out, in the name of Abraham and his descendants, the greatest deconstruction of ethics since Johannes de Silentio decided to break his silence about the father of faith?

Ethics flourishes in the element of beauty, universality, legitimacy, autonomy, immanence, intelligibility. Ethics abhors the abyss of singularity and ugly incomprehensibility that engulfs Abraham. Obligation is embedded in the density of particularity and transcendence, in a dark groundlessness on which ethics can only gag. Obligation is an ugly, gluey *glas*-like stuff that clogs the gears of ethical reason and jams its judgment. Ethics is attached to eagle-high principles whose mighty sweep protects the space of ethical life, keeping it safe. But Abraham, caught in the claws of transcendence and singularity, is carried off to our horror in a double bind that defies principled adjudication and which sends a shudder down his spine and ours, which leaves him and us in fear and trembling.

AN IMPIETY

Now I must tell you of my impiety. I am no Abraham, who was a hero, no Levinas, who is too pious, no Kierkegaard, whose point of view is too religious.

Obligation happens. It is a fact, as it were, but it is not a necessary truth. Obligation calls, but its call is finite, a strictly earthbound communication, transpiring here below, not in transcendental space (if there is such a thing.)

Obligation calls, and it calls for justice, but the caller in the call is not identifiable, decidable. I cannot make it out. I cannot say that the call is the Voice of God, or of Pure Practical Reason, or of a Social Contract "we" have all signed, or a trace of the Form of the Good stirring in our souls, or the trace of the Most High. I do not deny that these very beautiful hypotheses of ethics would make obligation safe, but my impiety is that I do not believe that obligation is safe.

Johannes de Silentio has stated the case for this impiety very eloquently:

> If a human being did not have an eternal consciousness, if underlying everything there were only a wild, fermenting power that writhing in dark passions produced everything, be it significant or insignificant, if a vast, never appeased emptiness hid beneath everything, what would life be then but despair? If such were the situation, if there were no sacred bond that knit humankind together, if one generation emerged after another like forest foliage, if one generation succeeded another like the singing of birds in the forest, if a generation passed through the world as a ship through the sea, as wind through the desert, an unthinking and unproductive performance, if an eternal oblivion, perpetually hungry, lurked for its prey and there were no power strong enough to wrench that away from it—how empty and devoid of consolation life would be.[52]

There is a considerable passion in Johannes's description, as if he does not speak of a merely abstract hypothesis that he has devised, but from the bitter fruit of a most painful experience. Might this dark vision be the fear and trembling named in the title of his book? I looked eagerly for the resolution Johannes would offer to this terrible spectre, but his response came to me with the thud of a still more terrible disappointment:

> But precisely for that reason it is not so.

Then he goes on to offer his eulogy to Abraham, as if that were the end of it. That is to say, Johannes holds that it is because such a life as he describes would be without consolation that it cannot be so. As if the emptiness and despair described in the passage would constitute too terrible, too unhappy a condition to be endured and thus *on that account* is not true. As if the unhappiness were an obstacle to its truth. Now though I love Johannes de Silentio dearly, though he is an author whom I would dearly love to imitate had I the nerve and the wit, I have to say that this is one of his most disappointing moments. I was reminded immediately of a passage from Nietzsche, who said that happiness is no argument:

> No one is likely to consider a doctrine true merely because it makes happy or makes virtuous. . . . Happiness and virtue are no arguments. . . . Something might be true although harmful and dangerous in the highest degree; indeed, it could pertain to the fundamental nature of existence that a complete knowledge of it would destroy one—so that the strength of a spirit could be measured by how much 'truth' it could take, more clearly, to what degree it *needed* it attenuated, veiled, sweetened, blunted, and falsified.[53]

Nietzsche's words sear the page on which they are printed. I must confess, however much I love him, Nietzsche has, on this point at least, silenced Johannes de Silentio. Indeed, while I was reading what de Silentio wrote about the "wild fermenting power" in which existence is caught up, I had written in the margins of my book "Nietzsche!" My hopes soared that before this fateful paragraph was out I might at last find an answer to Nietzsche, instead of finding Nietzsche's merciless views confirmed still again by the lameness of the rejoinder.

And so I must confess that my impiety is Nietzschean. Nietzsche is for me a very great philosopher of disasters, the most disastrous—in a very precise sense—the most disastronomical of all modern writers. His is a philosophy of stars dancing in endless cosmic nights without a care for us care-filled beings below, of stars twinkling in a void indifferent to the fate of us mortals below. I have never recovered from Nietzsche's terrible beginning of *On Truth and Lying in the Extramoral Sense*, a text he wrote at a very early age—what an extraordinary young man he must have been—although the text can be laid alongside a very late text, the final aphorism from the *Will to Power* (with which it compares very favorably in the terror of its vision, if not in the exuberance of its style):

> Once upon a time, in some out of the way corner of that universe which is dispersed into numberless twinkling solar systems, there was a star upon which clever beasts invented knowing. That was the most arrogant and mendacious minute of "world history," but nevertheless it was only a minute. After nature had drawn a few breaths, the star cooled and congealed, and the clever beasts had to die.[54]

Substitute "obligation" for "knowing" in this passage, and you will see what I mean by impiety and by the disaster. We pass our days on the surface of a little star which drifts aimlessly through endless skies, inventing such fictions as we require to make it through the day and to persuade ourselves of our meaning and significance. Until at last, weary of its peculiar little local experiment, the cosmos draws another breath and moves on. Then we disappear without a trace. "Knowledge," "obligation," "justice" — these are so many obsolete inventions of the little animals, now useless vapors dissipating in interstellar space. That is a spectre, a cosmic disaster, that disturbs my sleep nightly, the source of my fear and trembling, the dark curtain that hangs by a thread over all my enterprises.

Lyotard raises the same spectre in the context of a different question. Our sun, he says, is getting older and will explode in 4.5 billion years, a solar catastrophe that will spell the end of our phenomenology and politics. This solar explosion means "[n]egation without remainder. No self to make sense of it. Pure event. Disaster. . . . Matter asks no questions, expects no answers of us. It ignores us. It made us the way it made all bodies — by chance and according to its laws."[55]

So you see how far fallen from Kant I am, how far removed from his faith in stars I have become. Far from filling me with awe, the starry sky above speaks to me of the frailty of our condition and of the indifference of the stars to our fragile mortal fates. Four and a half billion years from now, when our little star has cooled off and congealed, and has dropped back into the sun, when the solar system itself has dissipated, the call of justice will have sunk into oblivion.[56] You and I, all things, this very moment, this innocent child here who suffers needlessly, these prosperous white upper classes who flourish at the expense of others — that is all so much will to power, so many quanta of force charging and discharging their energy, a veritable monster of energy, decreasing here, increasing there, blessing itself in its sheer innocence.[57] Or, if you prefer, in the equally terrible hypothesis of Johannes de Silentio, it is all a "wild fermenting power," a "vast never appeased emptiness."

Und nichts außerdem.

That is Nietzsche's accounting of the disaster, Nietzsche's disastronomics, supplemented with parallel texts from Lyotard and Johannes de Silentio. You and I stand on the surface of the little star and shout, "racism is unjust." The cosmos yawns and takes another spin. There is no cosmic record of our complaint. The cosmos feels no sorrow and has no heart on which to record our complaint. The stars pay us no heed. "Racism is unjust" is a bit of noise tinkling in the midst of "the great cosmic stupidity,"[58] a complaint lodged against an indifferent world, under stars twinkling in a void. The call of unjust suffering, of little, ontic, concrete disasters, falls on deaf ears. It is just part of the whole, of an absolutely innocent game that knows only greater or lesser discharges of energy, only self-accumulating and self-destructive forces, but does not know about the call of justice.

The cosmo-stellar view is always spectacular and lends itself to an aesthetic justification of life, which wipes "ethics" away. But if ethics, what then of obligation? Can obligation continue on after the demise of ethics, without the protection that ethics affords? Can obligation survive, does obligation happen, in so merciless a world as this? That is my question, for which I beg the reader's time and patience.

Obligation is what is important about ethics, what ethics contains without being able to contain. I am prepared to make my way without ethics, without the safety net it affords, even to take a stand against ethics. But it is one thing to raise one's voice against ethics, and quite another to speak against obligation. Am I prepared for life without obligation? Even so, what if I am not? What, then?

Obligation happens. There is/it gives obligation.

It gives: without referring to something entitative, the "it" points to a deep anonymity in things, in the world, in the stars as in ourselves. The lifeless body of a once vibrant person is a reduction of that person to an anonymous substratum, to a core of anonymity by which we are all inhabited. The "metaphysical" for Levinas is an attempt to shatter anonymity, to affirm "something" (which is not some *thing* at all but the Other person) that transcends anonymity, that infinitely surpasses it. I see this metaphysicality as prophetic hyperbole, as a great "as if": act *as if*[59] the Other were an Infinity that surpasses the totality, an infinity "as it were."

But it is also part of my impiety that I do not accept the words of prophets literally, as if the prophets subscribed to a theory of truth as *adequatio*, but hyperbolically, as an excessive expression meant to summon up what is best in us and to effect justice.[60] Levinas's "infinity" is impossible for me, but it must be recalled that I do not drop things just because they are impossible; some of the most interesting and important things are impossible.

That is the lesson I learn from father Abraham and from the famous gloss that Johannes de Silentio has given this story. Abraham is great in virtue of the fact that he expected not the possible or the eternal but the impossible.[61] In Johannes de Silentio this is coded language: the possible refers to the imaginative or the aesthetic; the eternal means the universal and rational, which is philosophy, which includes ethics. But the impossible is the religious, the *re-ligare*, which means the one-on-one bond of the existing individual with the Absolute, the absolute relation to the Absolute. The *re-ligare* is the *ob-ligare*, the absolute bond, the obligation, but without the shelter afforded by the universal, the rational, the eternal. In short, Johannes de Silentio writes a eulogy to obligation without ethics.

I have taken the paradox of Abraham as my paradigm. He it is, the father of us all, who clears the path of obligation without ethics, of the *re-ligare/ ob-ligare* which makes its way without protection of the universal. That is why Hegel thought him an ugly man, because Abraham ventured into an abyss upon which philosophy does not dare, into a land of un-philosophy, unillumined by philosophical lights. If that is so, I follow the lead of an ugly man; I have chosen ugliness as my paradigm. That is not very Greek; it is a little Jewish, or jewgreek, since the Greeks are *also* the fathers of us all. We are all always already Greek, but Abraham is also our father.

In the best prophetic tradition, in a gesture worthy of Abraham, Levinas's works constitute a memorable contemporary eulogy to Abraham, a great and learned midrash on Abraham's *me voici*. Levinas is also great in virtue of hoping for something impossible, viz., to expunge the anonymity of things, to triumph over the anonymous, to exceed and surpass it infinitely. He wants to say that "flesh" is not merely one of the "elements" of the *il y a*, but the surface of the infinite—not of an abstract infinity but of a concrete infinite, something infinite (*infini*).

There is, I fear, no way to annul the merciless view that a colder look reveals, that the Other is a part of an indifferent, anonymous whole, dissipated in a solar disaster. The Other who claims us "ethically" (in obligation) is not an infinity surpassing totality but a part that defies the totality, that resists totalization, that asserts itself, hyperbolically, in the face of a faceless cosmos. The Other is not infinity but a partiality to which we are unapologetically partial. Were I to rewrite Levinas's book, which so far no one has invited me to do, I would start by renaming it *Totality and Partiality*. In the place of Levinas's infinite excess, I would put infinite partiality—and defiance. The "ethical" for me, if we are to keep this word in virtue of a double writing, which for me would amount to nothing more than retaining the classical way to name obligation, does not name the "metaphysical" but the hyperbolical. It names an act of hyperbolic partiality and defiance.

Obligation is a fact (as it were). *As it were*. As if it were a fact, an uninterpreted fact of the matter. As if it were a pure fact, of pure reason, or of the whisper of the will of God in our ear, or the traces of the Form of the Good vaguely stirring in us. As if it were like that.

For Johannes de Silentio, the foolishness of the children of God was in the end a good investment that would be returned a hundredfold. The rich young man would get every penny back.[62] As Johannes said, "Only those who work get bread" is a maxim that does not hold in the world of economics for which it is intended, where it is proved false again and again, but only in the world of the spirit. For although the price of faith is (absurdly) high, one can expect an infinite payback, which is the repetition (which, if you desire further reading, is the name of a work by one Constantin Constantius, who bears an interesting similarity to Johannes de Silentio).[63]

But in this postmodern time of need (and maybe in a possible postmodern Christianity as opposed to Christendom, which is power pure and simple, or a postmodern religion generally), the stakes of foolishness have been raised still higher. It is no longer a matter of being fools for the kingdom of God in which one could eventually expect a good return on one's investment. It is a matter of being fools in a much more distressing sense.

TWO

Between Good and Evil

OBLIGATION'S POET

I who had been promising for some time to write an *Ethics* have been forced to make a series of damaging disclosures. I run the risk of appearing like a man who, having shouted loudly to be given the microphone, having succeeded in quieting the crowd so that all eyes are now fixed intently upon himself, finds that he does not know what to say. It will do no good to tell the man to start at the beginning, because his difficulty is that he does not know where the beginning is. Everything seems to him to go around and around so that he cannot tell where it all starts. In the meantime, his audience grows increasingly impatient. The situation in which I found myself with respect to my *Ethics* was well described by Johannes de Silentio, who was speaking of the *System*:

> The present author is by no means a philosopher. He has not understood the system, whether there is one, whether it is completed; it is already enough for his weak head to ponder what a prodigious head everyone must have these days when everyone has such a prodigious idea.

Still, to my great fortune, I happened upon a saving word in de Silentio's saying:

> The present author is by no means a philosopher. He is *poetice et eleganter* [in a poetic and refined way] a supplementary clerk [*Extra-Skriver*] who neither writes the system nor gives promises of the system, who neither exhausts himself on the system nor binds himself to the system. He writes because to him it is a luxury that is all the more pleasant and apparent the fewer there are who buy and read what he writes.[1]

At last, I had found a task and a vocation. An *Extra-Skriver*! The scales fell from my eyes. I had chanced upon a model, a paradigm, a special calling, to which I was summoned by neither Being nor the Spirit, but by a pseudonym. My task is not to prepare the place where the eagle of *savoir absolue* makes its nest, nor to serve as Being's shepherd, nor to clear a place for Being's new Beginning, but to be an *Extra-Skriver*. This splendid Danish word, which Johannes de Silentio has invented for this occasion, suggests an amateur writer, a freelancer, an author of occasional pieces from which one has little hope of earning a decent living, pieces composed for the sheer luxury of writing.[2] So I need not write an *Ethics*, which would be expecting too much, nor an *Origi-*

nary Ethics (*Ursprüngliche Ethik*), which would be expecting even more. I need only offer certain fragments about obligation, make certain contributions toward a poetics of obligation, which would neither form a *System* nor meet the rigorous demands of *Denken*. I need only collect such bits and fragments of obligation as I find strewn about, like an amateur collector, and present my findings *poetice et eleganter*. Like a tedious old bookkeeper, I will look about for the scraps of obligation that have fallen to philosophy's floor.

Moreover, I will not only be obligation's clerk but also one of its poets, for a poet need not be a hero, as Johannes points out, but rather one who writes *poetice* about heroic feats, like those of Abraham.[3] I hasten to add that I need not be a Great Greco-Germanic Poet, a kin of Hölderlin, who answers the call of Being, who names the Holy, who announces the arrivals and departures of the gods—that again would be too much. I need only be a poet of the sort described by Johannes, one who writes little contributions, supplementary notes, an odd column here or there, essays, parables, and occasional pieces, in sum, a bit of a versifier and a scribbler. Of that I feel myself capable. My task will be to write small, inconclusive, fragmentary contributions—this will be my long withheld *Beiträge*, however out of touch with the Great Beginning—to a poetics of obligation. I will make such unscientific, fragmentary contributions as I am able to the idea of obligation (and to the disaster that threatens to engulf us), with the full understanding that this is no way to earn a living.

That I can do.

That is why I have taken the advice of Derrida—a supplementary clerk *par excellence*, indeed a great clerk of the supplement, one of the greatest collectors of bits and fragments of recent times, one of our greatest scribblers, scriveners, scribes, and ragpickers[4] (I say this respectfully, I am not criticizing him). Derrida advises us to begin *wherever* we are, in the middle of the fix we find ourselves in, in the middle of a text, a phrase, a word, a syllable, with the smallest bit or piece. That at least will enable me to get started, not at the beginning, which is to ask too much, but wherever I am:

> We must begin *wherever* we are and the thought of the trace . . . has already taught us that it was impossible to justify a point of departure absolutely. *Wherever we are*: in a text where we already believe ourselves to be.[5]

Wherever: here, now; here I am; *me voici*. In the middle of a text, on the receiving end of a command, in the midst of multiple obligations. I begin from below, having lost all communication from on high. Under obligation, under a host of obligations, aswarm with them.

GETTING STARTED: UNDER OBLIGATION

I begin with the fact that I find myself obliged, under many obligations. The quasi principle of being under obligation is formulated by Lyotard, who writes, "A phrase is obligatory if its addressee is obliged."[6] But is that not precisely to get everything backwards? Lyotard claims that phrases oblige and, by implication, that the addressor is "authorized" to issue obligatory phrases, only because the addressee is obliged. Yet if obligation is to make any sense, if it has a *logos* (a cognitive basis), is not the addressee obliged only because the phrase is obligatory and the addressor is an authorized authority? Does that not make perfect sense? In ethics, which tries to start at the beginning, one would show that the obligatory phrase comes down to us from an intelligible source, a *mundus intelligibilis*, to which the ethical agent somehow always already belongs. I do not deny this makes perfect sense. But I have begged off from writing an *Ethics* with the excuse that its perfection is too much for me, that its perfection must always be abridged in the name of accommodating imperfection and the pressing difficulties of factical life. As obligation's poet and supplementary clerk, I am relieved of the obligation of making perfect sense; it is all I can do to cope with imperfection and a certain lack of sense (a certain disaster). I am just trying to get started.

For how, after all, would one *know* that the "addressor" is authorized? Such a question would set off an endless search for origins and original authorities, a *regressus ad infinitum*, until one finally chooses to stop the regress at a certain point, to put a halt to the regression, with an authority that one announces one "accepts." That in turn, if it is anything more than an appeal to force, comes down to an appeal to the fact that the addressees feel themselves (take themselves to be) obliged.[7]

Again, how would one *know* the "phrase" is obligatory? How could such a thing be established? One would go around and around with such a question, endlessly supporting p with q and q with p, so long as the interval between p and q is great enough as to allow a certain forgetfulness. That would amount to another interminable regression toward an *arche* or *principium*, toward some fixed point on the slippery slopes of discourse, ceaselessly searching for some element of *différance* that would be immune from the drift and slippage of signifiers. It would, in short, send one sliding down a slope, in a regress without end.[8]

Furthermore—and this is a pragmatic point—does it matter? Does anyone really wait for cognitive reports to come in before concluding that one is obliged? Does one really "conclude" that one is obliged, or does one not just find oneself (*sich befinden*) obliged, without so much as having been consulted or asked for one's consent? Is obligation not a matter of finding oneself from the start, always and already, on the receiving end of commands? Is that not where we are from the start, and hence where we must begin? Is that not just a fact? Here we are, always already obliged, in a bind, in a double bind, in any number of binds.

Here I am (*me voici*, Levinas), faced with a fact, as it were (Kant), in a pregiven factical situation (Heidegger).

Descartes provides a clear and distinct case. Having set out to find everything that is to be doubted (*de omnibus dubitandum est*), having let the entire theoretical edifice waver, having rendered groundless every self-evident ground, he then added a little postscript to the effect that he needed a comfortable place to live during all this fear and trembling, agreeable accommodations while the theoretical ground opened up before him. So he added a note about obligations, a tiny little fragment, viz., that the conduct of life is exempt from the project of universal doubt. That is because the conduct of life presses hard upon us and demands decisions, which is to say that life consists of situations in which the addressee is obliged, with or without the methodic doubt. So Descartes proposes that obligations are provisionally to be maintained as a kind of interim ethics while we await the coming of the *fundamentum inconcussum*.[9] So the correct title of the First Meditation, fully amended, should be: "Of Everything That Is to Be Doubted—Except Obligations." For the time being, of course. He will keep in place the prevailing code of morality and the prevailing religion, even though he doubts everything.

He said this, I presume, without a smile. There are no marginalia in Adam-Tannery indicating to the Jesuits at the Sorbonne that laughter is here permitted, even though it is what is called for and should certainly have been included among the objections sent to him by Mersenne. Descartes did not even take the precaution of having a pseudonym say one thing while he himself remained behind, free to believe something else which happened to be entirely different. Perhaps that is because it does not matter what Descartes said, what he said he doubted or did not doubt. He was obliged; he felt obliged; he kept receiving obligatory phrases whether he doubted it or not, whether he liked it or not, whether he included these little shards and fragments of obligation in his philosophy or not.[10]

Even Thomas Aquinas made a comparable little proviso. Thomas bases everything on the existence of God, ethics included, which he does not treat until the second part of the *Summa*, after he has laid out the basics about God, angels, and the human soul. He begins with God, with the famous *quinque viae*, which is certainly to begin at the beginning. That for him is the very definition of theology: to begin at the beginning, with God, while the definition of philosophy is to begin at the end, with the world. But then Thomas inserted a little *respondeo*, right at the beginning, a tiny little fragment, to the effect that if you cannot follow these proofs, which would also mean that you cannot follow everything that follows, which is certainly the problem faced by many of us then and now, then having faith will produce all the same results.[11]

Even Nietzsche, ferocious as a lion when you gave him a pen, embraced a horse being flogged as he (Nietzsche—we do not know what happened to the horse) collapsed in Turin, if we are to believe a famous story. Nietzsche's tender heart went out to the poor thing.[12]

In our own day, Lacoue-Labarthe, who thinks that after Heidegger's delimitation of ethics there is, philosophically speaking, nothing more to say, has one more thing to say (which is then perhaps not philosophical), viz., that we must of course continue to abide by ethical precepts.[13]

It seems that everyone is agreed, both classical and postclassical thinkers alike, that a phrase is obligatory if one is obliged, that it is not necessary to wait for the cognitive credentials of a phrase to arrive in order to be obliged. Even those who do not agree seem also to agree, so long as, like a good supplementary clerk, a good collector of scraps and pieces, we read their little addenda, every little bit lying around the floor or swept under the metaphysical rug.

If this is true, it poses an ironic and unprecedented challenge to Lyotard, an unanticipated case of universal *consensus*, an unexpected *homologia*, which would be a disaster for him. Lyotard would then have to offer some dissent himself, in the name of saving his heterology.

As for myself, I have not as yet touched bottom on the *fundamentum inconcussum*. I cannot follow the *quinque viae*, and I cannot sit through an entire *grand récit* without a yawn. So I have no choice but to proceed "from below," which is what *beginning* means, in its most radical sense.[14] Having lost communication with Being and the Good, I have no alternative but to begin with being obliged, which is the poetic beginning, not the purely philosophical one. Such a beginning also belongs to what the young Heidegger called the "hermeneutics of facticity." Beginning thus is part of my cold faith or, better, of my radical hermeneutical incredulity. We have no star to guide us, no messages from on high. Life is a dis-aster; the earth is adrift. Obligation is on its own and will have to fend for itself. That is the faith of an incredulous infidel about salvific metanarratives. I begin where I am, from below, on the receiving end of a message from I know not where. Obligation happens.

This is not meant as a cunning move on my part. I have no such prodigious head for clever strategies or deft decisions. It arises, *faute de mieux*, from the lack of an alternative. I begin from below, with the addressee, with the one who is obliged, without knowing how or why or even by what I am obliged, with the one who finds herself obliged, on the receiving end of commands that keep coming in without surcease.

Il arrive: phrases happen—they fly up like sparks—always and everywhere, wherever you are. *Es gibt*: it is a given. Obligation happens.

OBLIGATIONS, PRESCRIPTIONS, FEELINGS

Obligation is a certain communication, a very earthbound signal that is transmitted without the help of heavenly satellites. This does not represent an overarching "theory" of obligation but only an attempt at a good description, an impoverished, somewhat mute pointing of my finger (*indicare*) to indicate what is happening (*arrive*), since according to my theory I am deprived of a theoretical standpoint. I cannot penetrate this fact—

which is a very jarring, phallocentric way to express one's impotence — this most factical fact, of being obligated. I cannot found or ground my obligations. I do not issue obligatory phrases; I receive them. I find myself under their spell; it is part of my *Befindlichkeit*, the fix I find myself in. Obligation puts me in my place and I am at a loss as to how to clear the matter up.

Obligation is a fact as it were, not of pure practical reason, as in Kant, but of our factical life, and as much a fact, in fact, as any other fact, e.g., so-called empirical facts.

Obligation is a linguistic fact: the happening of prescriptives is an irreducible part of any language. That means not only that prescriptives are found in every language but also that they do not succumb to reduction, that no one, Descartes included, is able to put them out of action, to bracket or suspend them. You may "redescribe"[15] them however you wish, but they still keep coming in, still keep arriving. They bob up after every *epochē* because they belong to the irreducible realm of that facticity which Heidegger showed, against pure phenomenology, does not submit to neutralization. You can try to submit obligation to the *epochē* but you will find that it does not take. You cannot leave judgment behind, Derrida and Lyotard tell us; it will give you no peace.[16] Obligations rebound after every philosophical debate, after every academic conference, just shortly after the invited plenary speaker has collected his check and is headed for the airport. Prescriptives are a fact of factical life, of linguistic, social, political, institutional, personal, family life, of any sphere of life.

Obligations are a rhetoricopragmatic fact, a pragrammatological fact, Derrida might say,[17] a part of the Lyotardian flow of phrases, and we are caught up in that flow, swept along in its sweep or train. Phrases happen all around us, left and right, all along, long before we arrive, long after we depart. We find ourselves in the flux of phrases, born into and bathed by phrases, including obligatory phrases, by whose rhythms and intonations, uses and mentionings, we are formed and shaped.

Obligations constitute a "language game" of their own, a language game that is not, however, a game that we play but rather, as Gadamer shows, a game that plays us, that picks us up and carries us along by its momentum.[18] The language game of obligations is not a game I invent or have to justify. The game does not ask me to justify it. The game precedes and antedates philosophers and their philosophies, is much older than me or than philosophy itself. We are unable to call it to a halt or suspend it because of impropitious weather. The game plays on and on.

It plays. It plays because it plays. It plays without why, without any founding grounds or great grounding founders, Greek or non-Greek.

I do not authorize or legitimate the prescriptives that fly up all around me, nor do they wait upon my authorization in order to arrive. I receive them and am assimilated to them. I am amalgamated into the game that plays me. I remain withal always on the receiving end. In principle. It goes to the heart of the prescriptive game, in whose stakes I am caught up, that

I cannot switch places, cannot put myself in the place of the sender. I cannot send myself an obligation. I find myself obliged but I cannot oblige myself, no more than I can tell myself something I do not know.[19] I stand vis-à-vis obligation in the position of the disciple vis-à-vis the Teacher of whom Johannes Climacus speaks; the teacher of obligation is transcendent. Hence the poetics of obligation would be a poetics of transcendence, and the story of Abraham is one of the paradigmatic stories in this poetics.

A prescriptive is a grammatical category, a regime of phrasing, Lyotard says, and as such it is always already in place, as soon as there is language. "There always are prescriptives; one cannot live without prescriptives."[20] We can no more overcome prescriptives than we can wipe away the ocean. But not every prescriptive is an obligation. An obligation is a call we receive to which we must respond, a prescriptive to which we must keep an open line. It is of the utmost importance to be able to sort out among prescriptives, to tell the difference between prescriptives to follow and prescriptives to resist, to differentiate among prescriptives, which often conflict, e.g., or which often oblige us precisely to disobey them.

That is why we have always required ethics, and that is the disadvantage of speaking against ethics.

I am obliged therefore to make a start on coming to grips with the complications of the story of Abraham, which is that, structurally, Abraham's obligation is of the same form as unintelligible commands, like unconscious compulsions or like demands for fanatical blind obedience. Structurally speaking, "that Isaac die" and "that the Jews die" are the same. On the accounting I am giving, we cannot get on top of these commands and adjudicate them from above. We cannot tell when we are dealing with the word of God and when we are not, which would resolve the issue, since no one has seen God or given us a reliable report of what words are God's and of what language game God prefers.[21] We cannot get at it "ethically," from the beginning, as if we inhabited the *principium*, but only *poetice*, by imagining its effect on the receiving end, from the standpoint of the one who is obligated.

In fact, the philosophical (archical) approach can be very dangerous. It is just when people are convinced that they speak in the name of God (or Reason or History—or any other famous European capital)[22] that they will stop at nothing, and that is what puts the rest of us at considerable risk. And who can deny that beloved father Abraham was a little touched by that madness? Even Johannes de Silentio is ready to admit he was a little mad. That is why I would like to hear this story one more time, which is, *poetice*, my right.[23] Perhaps the way to adjudicate, poetically, among conflicting obligations is to tell as many competing stories as possible in order to see which, under the circumstances, is the most obliging, or which obligation produces the lesser evil,[24] that is to say, is less disastrous.

One is fixed in place by an obligation. You cannot mount it or surmount it, get a distance on it, get beyond (*jenseits*) it, overcome (*überwinden*) it, or lift it up (*aufheben*).[25] It is older than we are, at least as old as Being or Truth or the Spirit or the Will to Power. We cannot transcend it, because it is transcendence itself. We are the ones transcended, overcome, lifted up or put down, overtaken, thrown. Obligation is the sphere of what I did not constitute. Obligation is a kind of Abrahamic *Befindlichkeit*. The decision to obey it or disobey it is a choice about the effects of obedience or disobedience, not an adjudication of the *arche* from which it proceeds, which is out of sight. The effects are always in the sphere of facticity and feeling, of life and death, of flourishing and diminution. The effects are measured by the flourishing or disasters we bring about.

Lyotard thinks that an obligation is a feeling. The bond that binds (*ligare*) us in an obligation is a bond of feeling (*pathos*). Obligation is a communication from feeling to feeling:

> The quasi-fact of obligation, though, is like a sign marked upon the addressed entity in the form of a feeling. The obligated one sentimentally infers that there is some authority which obligates him or her by addressing itself to him or her.[26]

On this account—you see the scandal this involves for metaphysics and its ethics—obligation is not a rational utterance (*logos*) received on the other end as wholly intelligible and hence as worthy of being obeyed. That would make it mine, me, a case of auto-nomy and auto-dictation. Obligation is not like a man talking to himself and offering himself counsel, which he judges to be the best advice he can get; it is instead a shock to the I, to my freedom and autonomy. Obligation is not an exchange transacted in the *mundus intelligibilis* but a bell sounding in the *mundus sensibilis*. It is not the outcome of a dialogue, an exchange of *logoi* occurring on a level surface.[27] It is more like a *pathos* that I feel, like a felt shock or a blow that strikes me down. It comes to me from without, in a curved space which lays me low, producing a kind of disequilibrium in me. It is a "materialist" operation.[28]

Obligations ring out like bells, sounding a general alarm, crying out for an idiom, a response, a redress[29]—or for a supplementary clerk, a freelancer, who will tell their story, *poetice et eleganter*. The *glas* of obligation—in *Glas* this would be written: obLiGation—is a bell sounding, the *Klang* of an alarm that summons us to the scene of a disaster. As against Heidegger's *Klang* and *Anklang*, which resonate with Being's history, or the little cowbells that sound the silent peal of Being, you can actually feel the ground shake from these Lyotardian bells; they are more like Poe's bells than Heidegger's cowbells.[30]

DISASTERS

Obligations come over us from the other whose transcendence shocks our freedom and autonomy. But they lay seige to us with a particular forcefulness in the case of what I will call disasters. A disaster, as we saw above, is a matter of being cut off from the star that protects us from misfortune (*dis-astrum,*) a matter of running out of luck. I am borrowing this term from

Blanchot—it is one of the scraps I am sweeping up into a pile—who always uses it in the singular: "The disaster is not our affair and has no regard for us; it is the heedless unlimited." That is true, I think; that is the kind of thought that keeps one up at night. But then Blanchot adds: "it [the disaster] cannot be measured in terms of failure or as pure and simple loss."[31] Now on that point I offer a humble dissent. It is risky to leave "the" disaster at so deep and singular a level, as if there were only one disaster, and as if it ran very deep. That would make it quite profound and require deep thinking, a deep Greco-Germanic language for giving it an idiom. It would in general lodge the disastrous at so deep a level as to require again a quite prodigious head to think it. That would put it out of reach, whereas what I mean by a disaster is something that reaches us, that is visited upon us, with unhappy frequency, something superficial, being written all over the surface of damaged lives. Putting it at so deep a level also invites depoliticization; it runs the risk of believing in a distinction between the "essential" disaster and the little ontic disasters, with specifiable dates and locations, in which people actually die or are laid low. That is why I keep the word in the plural and the lowercase: I have in mind concrete and actual disasters, the sort that *can* be measured in terms of failure, loss, and catastrophic destruction. I favor Lyotard's practice of attaching dates to disasters, so that "disasters" means singularities like Budapest, 1956; Nagasaki and Hiroshima, 1945; Cambodia, 1980s, Sarajevo, 1992 (1914?), contemporary South Africa, Northern Ireland, Salvador, the West Bank—not the Withdrawal of Being. With Lyotard, I prefer beings to Being.[32]

Obligation consorts with disasters, with what Levinas likes to call "the widow, the orphan, the stranger" (Exodus 22:21), which is of course an emblematic expression for a much longer list. "Auschwitz" is another such emblematic expression, one that Lyotard among many others favors, but it needs to be generalized because there were other camps and other times and other victims than the Jews. That is why Lyotard himself finally settled on "*les juifs*," which is Auschwitz generalized. *Les juifs* are not a particular nation or religion, not (only) the historical children of Abraham, but everyone nomadic or homeless or uprooted, everyone whose mind or body, dignity or identity has been damaged or even shattered. *Les juifs* are disasters, in the lowercase and in the plural.

Again, I do not wish to be mistaken for a deep thinker. I insist that I do not mean anything profound or Being-historical by a disaster. I have not touched bottom on anything but on the contrary I have been exposed to another abyss. *What is* a disaster? What is happening there? (That is the Greek thing to ask.) "Is it the world? Is it the soul? Is it God?" Heidegger asks, following Nietzsche.[33] Is it the voice of God sounding through the little ones of the earth? Or is it nothing more than the rumble of cosmic forces, the noise made by the wheel of becoming as it spins out one new configuration after another, signifying nothing?

I do not know. It is beyond me. I have no concept with which to seize

hold of it. On the contrary, it has seized hold of me and carried me off into
its darkness. For this I have no concept, no principle, no *logos* or *ratio*, in
short, no prodigious head. Nor any prodigious will with which to confront
or subdue it. I am not calling for another round of macho heroics, of masculine heroes hurling themselves into an abyss or shattering against the
Overwhelming in order to become great.[34]

A disaster is an economic notion. It refers to an unrecoverable loss. Disasters are events of surpassing or irretrievable loss. By irretrievable loss I
mean a wasting of life, something that cannot be repaired, recompensed,
redeemed. A disaster is a loss that cannot be incorporated into a "result,"[35]
that cannot be led back into a gain. You cannot grow another body; you
cannot regain wasted years. Antigone is a spokeswoman of irretrievable
loss, the loss of what is utterly irreplaceable, of what is gone forever. She
cannot grow another brother; that is a law of the flesh, of the disaster that
besets the flesh. You cannot compensate someone who has spent the best
years of his life in unjust imprisonment,[36] or whose health has been irrep-
arably destroyed, whose family has been killed. You cannot grow new
flesh, new time.

That is why a disaster is not the same as pain or suffering. Very few
things of worth can be accomplished without taking on and enduring a
sometimes considerable amount of pain or hardship. Pain and suffering belong to our pact with life. They are our unavoidable if ominous companions
and they cannot be written out of the script of life.[37] Disasters are constituted by suffering, but not all suffering is a disaster. My suffering, the suffering of the I, is something for me to work through, to get beyond. Disasters always befall the other. Even then, there is suffering and there is
suffering. Short-term suffering may easily belong to long-term flourishing,
to a larger economy of pain and suffering which is understood by anyone
who understands the economy of life itself. To spare others pain and hard
work and suffering may easily mean to spare them everything that gives
their life worth and a greater long-term felicity.

The disaster belongs to an economy of excessive cost, for which there is
no compensating return. The disaster is an utter wasting, a sheer loss.
There is no larger perspective, no larger whole, no totality in terms of
which the loss can be reckoned part of an acceptable expenditure, an acceptable cost that one is willing to pay.[38] Disasters throw all reckoning and
cost-accounting, every *logos* and *ratio*, into chaos. To be surrounded by disaster, to be the victim of a disaster, is to look around at a destruction for
which there is no recompense. That is why disasters are an abyss, an
a-logos, an *a-nomos*. Disasters are events that "ethics"—which turns on
logos/ratio/nomos—cannot contain, that ethics cannot bring under the rule of
its *principium* or *arche*, under any of its favorite master names, that ethics
cannot master. Disasters constitute a loss for which there is no *ratio red-
denda*, a loss which is without why, groundless.[39]

However much a critic of Marxist metanarratives Lyotard became, Marxism has not ended for him in the sense that the disasters of capital are always with us.[40] To this it should be added that disasters of all sorts are always with us—the disasters of capital and the disasters of Stalinism, the disasters of Auschwitz and the disasters of Hiroshima and Nagasaki, of northern Ireland and the West Bank, of South Africa, the south Bronx, and Sarajevo. The killing fields are everywhere and everywhere they are fields of disasters.[41]

The fields of disasters are marked with dates and proper names, which are so many alarms sounding, so many sounds of warning and calls for help. Proper names are so many points on the map of disasters. They are the stuff on which ethics comes to grief and which launches the search for another idiom for disasters.

The suffering of a child is not a part of the progress of the Spirit or the History of Being. It cannot be led to a "result."

Disasters do not produce a result. That is what is meant by a disaster. An obligation is a matter of being bound (*ligare*) to a disaster.[42] That prevents you from looking for a result. It makes the search for a result an obscenity, which means an utter breakdown of the attempt to write *poetice et eleganter*.

BETWEEN GOOD AND EVIL

Having given up on the Good and other Saving Events, I have no recourse but to turn to the life of evil.

Evil, according to the most classical axiomatics, is the lack of the Good (*privatio boni*). That has been the constant teaching handed down to us from Plato and Plotinus, Augustine and Aquinas.[43] Evil is a kind of fall from the Good, a fall into nonbeing, finitude, limitation, privation, imperfection.[44] But it is part of the perversity of this thinking from below, which manages to get things backwards and systematically to reverse them, to prefer evil to Good, to prefer to begin with evil rather than with the Good, a strategy which is invoked *faute de mieux* (*faute du bien!*).

Having been unable to get as far as the Good and thus having to begin where I am, I begin in the midst (*inter-esse*) of life's multiple evils, beset on every side by the perils of daily life. I confess to being neither a friend nor an acquaintance of the Good. I do not know what the Good is. Were I of a more apocalyptic frame of mind, I would say that the time of the Good is over.[45] But my assignment is to be a clerk and a part-time poet; I have been given no epochal mission or commission and I can offer the reader no special information about what is going on in the History of Being, or the History of the Spirit, or History itself (if it has an "itself"). I have no credentials whatsoever to proclaim that the present time is the end of anything. That would be just one more metanarrative, the peculiar "great narrative of the end of great narratives," one more thinking in terms of "the end of some history.''[46] For all I know, the Good may come back with a vengeance, if indeed it has taken its leave.

I can only confess to my own limits, that the Good, in the uppercase, has become a tall tale (*fabula*) to me, along with Being and the Real World.[47] The Good, the *arche* and *principium*, along with any overarching principle that assigns all things their place and holds them mightily in its sway, has become unbelievable to me and has earned my incredulity.[48]

For Heidegger and MacIntyre and Allan Bloom (the list sounds like a category mistake), such incredulity is a symptom of a deep rot, of a decline in Being or the Good or Virtue. We who live in this "time of need" or "after virtue," we who have not been educated in a *Gymnasium* or in a Great Books program, we can do no more now than wait for a new god or a new St. Benedict or a new core curriculum to save us. We who are bereft of the Good are left only with pale, paper-thin "values," insubstantial fabrications of the human will. There are as many values as there are valuators, which means too many, while there is or should be only One Good, which comes to us from On High, which overpowers us with its power and commands our respect. MacIntyre regrets the decline of the Good into values. Heidegger regrets the decline of Being itself (if it has an itself) and the separation of the Good from Being, as if the Good were somehow beyond Being, as if Being were not itself sufficiently commanding to lay down the *nomos*. Allan Bloom can be somewhat more specific; he regrets Cornell, 1969.[49]

The End of the Good is the Beginning of Subjectivity. That is what Being would say were it given a tongue.

Truth to tell, I do not know if now is the end-time of the Good or not, or whether these epochal pronouncements issue from a bit of indigestion.[50] Whether the gods and the Good have definitively taken their flight, or whether the Good will make a stunning comeback tomorrow morning, in plenty of time for the evening news, I have no way of determining. I have nothing reliable to report on their arrivals or departures, on their epochal itinerary. I can only report that I myself have become incredulous, an infidel. I have lost my faith in the Good, which must needs be One and Overarching, which must inspire Piety and command universal Consent (all in the uppercase), which leaves a trail of bowed heads wherever it passes.

But, contrary to the expectations of Heidegger, MacIntyre, and Bloom, I do not hold "value theory" in high regard either, which is for me just more "ethics," i.e., more metaphysics. I accept all of Heidegger's and MacIntyre's declamations and denunciations of the subjectivism of value theory. I am not prepared to turn over the question of "obligation" to value theory. I do not regard the bond that binds obligation to the disaster to be a matter of a "value" we should "hold," or of a "claim" we "make." Obligation is rather—this is what a poetics of obligations brings out and where it starts—a matter of being claimed, in which something has a hold on us, something that is older than us, that has us before we have it. There is nothing subjectivistic about obligation. It is not an effect produced by a subject, not the work of a subject,[51] but rather something produced in me, as in a patient, something that happens to me. I would be the first to say that there is something "out there" — viz., over there, in the place of the other, in the place of the disaster that befalls the other—which turns our head and draws us up short, that places us under its claim. It is my unflagging supposition that there is something about suffering that stops us in our tracks. The whole idea of a poetics of obligations is to find an idiom for the fact (as it were) that we are laid hold of by others, seized and laid claim to, that the fullness of freedom is hollowed out by the hollow eyes of those who suffer. The whole idea of the "subject," the field of my subjective freedom and autonomy, is shocked and disrupted by the one who comes to me from on high. I stand thus far with the philosophers of the Good, among whom Levinas himself is to be numbered:[52] the sphere of obligation is constituted by a power that overpowers me, that forcibly seizes me round about and constrains me to take notice, that sends a shudder through my flesh.

Still, I agree with Lyotard, that big stories like the Good lack credibility and that Levinas is too pious. Furthermore, I do not have the time to wait for the arrival of the last god or a new wave of the Good to sweep over us and save us all. The demands of factical life are pressing hard upon my heels. That is why I have turned to the life of evil(s).

I do agree, and I have never doubted it—I have been extensively prepared in classical axiomatics—that Evil is the lack of Good. Evil is a lack, something missing, a *privatio boni* (*steresis agathou*). Clearly, if you have an *arche*, then evil is to be defined as the lack of the *arche*, the failure to meet the *arche*. But suppose the times are an-archical? Suppose the times have been anarchized by a powerfully pluralizing, disseminating, dissenting plurivocity that makes it impossible to agree on the *arche*? Suppose the Good has become not just diffusive of itself, which is the classical thesis, but just plain diffuse, disseminated, splintered, fragmented? Suppose we lack the *logos*, suppose we cannot start from above, suppose we do not have a *principium*, a principle, and cannot begin at the beginning? Then where do we begin?

Wherever we are, *in medias res*, in the midst of factical life, *inter-esse*. For here we are, buffeted and beset on every side by multiple ills and compounded evils. What comes at us first, *zunächst und zumeist*, what is first in the *ordo cognoscendi*, hermeneutically, in the order in which we meet up with it, are the powers of evil, the angels of darkness, of destruction and destructiveness, which invade our days and destroy our works and damage our lives. Disasters, all. But we do not have an overarching theory for the destructiveness of destruction. We do not have a *logos* to crown our accounts of it. We seem to have been forsaken by both Being and the Good and we toss back and forth between incommensurable discourses and interminable disputes about the Good.[53] That is why I want to start from below, with the multiple disasters (evils) by which we are daily visited, with broken bodies and damaged lives, with the sort of things that are more manifest to our batlike eyes.[54] Whether or not there is some supreme Good up the deep ascent, one that would give us the *logos* to define Evil as its privative lack, whether there is some transcendental high ground from which we could survey the multiple evils that everywhere beset us, from which we could point our accusatory, transcendental fingers—those are questions for which I have neither the time nor the patience. It is like waiting for the master plan of the city to come in while freezing to death in the meantime.

It is Necessarily True, I would swear to this, it is central to the classical *tractatus de malo*, that Evil is the lack of Good. I am sure that this is True in the land of Eternal Truth. But we for whom the clay of factical life is still sticking to our heels have never made it that far. We are not "beyond" (*jenseits*) Good and Evil, but stuck between (*zwischen*) them, being unable to get as far as either one. Instead of an *Ethica* we can only offer some supplementary fragments gathered together under the title *Zwischen Güte und Böse*, being-in-between, *inter-esse*, in the midst of factical life and its daily pleasures and perils. We are just trying to get through the day and maybe make it to next week, dodging the bullets of factical life, trying to stop the shooting, and trying to give one another a certain amount of space and a helping hand. About what comes next, when the last god arrives,[55] or even when time is washed away by what is Necessarily True, in the land where there are all and only Capitals, in the world where German nouns come true, I have no reliable information.

That is why I want to leave the space of the Good open and undetermined, to treat it as a purely negative space, as in a classical negative theology. I would say of the Good in ethics and in politics what Meister Eckhart said about God, that whatever you say God is, that is not true; but whatever you do not say God is, that is true.[56] I prefer to keep the Good in the lowercase and in the plural, to speak of "goods," of which there are always too many and more to come. Come! *Viens!*[57] Let many goods come! That is the radically pluralist, disseminating maxim I favor. The Good is said in multiple ways and there is no closing that space down. Not only am I not waiting for the last god or a new St. Benedict to save us, I am hoping they never show up. I do not even *want* a god to save us. If we must be visited by any more gods or saints, I would prefer that a whole contingent of them arrive, trainloads of them, multiple gods and a whole host of saints, enough to go around. When it comes to gods and the Good, I am a pluralist. This is the Lyotardian sense of paganism that I prefer, an impious, polytheistic pluralism of competing gods and multiple goods.[58] There are many ways to be excellent, many kinds of excellence, and many other things to desire than excellence, too many to contain. There are many ways to love, homosexually and heterosexually, in religious chastity and in marriage. But the ravages of hatred have an ominous sameness. I recommend imagination, variation, and experimentation in the pursuit of Good, in the invention of many goods. In this respect, I think Evil is highly unimaginative and uninventive: it keeps producing the same sort of bloodied, emaciated, or lifeless bodies, ruined, hopeless, desperate, damaged lives; with or without technology (*pace* Heidegger), with or without religion (*pace* academic secularism).

I leave the hermeneutics of excellence to Greeks and other connoisseurs. But I think the claim of victims, who are usually victims of somebody's Good, is singular, compelling, claiming.

Lacoue-Labarthe said we lack the "names," above all the "sacred names," that govern the ethical field.[59] Although I have not done a survey, I think that that may be half true: we cannot agree on sacred names. We have no overarching *arche*, no *hier-arche*, no sacred order. We have too many competing and incommensurable sacred names — the right to life vs. the right to choose; public morality vs. freedom of expression; my freedom vs. the good of all — so many candidates for the sacred honors, that no one can agree. But we see daily the faces of Evil, and we often know their names, the proper names of the victims of unholy forces. That is the only simulacrum of the sacred we have left, the one *mysterium tremendum* in this world where we have not only disenchanted the forest but deforested it too. For us, at least for me, *me voici*, the sacred is not organized around a Good and thereby installed in some hierarchic order but is rather a matter of disasters and proper names. If there is something sacred still to be found, it lies with the disasters and prompts the insurrection of a sacred an-archy. The only sacred names we require are proper names.

Another way to put this is to say that I think the time has come (I have nothing apocalyptical in mind with such an expression; I only mean it's about time) to de-Hellenize ethics, which is another way to characterize the poetics of obligation I recommend. That is an idea that is as old as Luther and that today has caught on among all those philosophers who are out to put the torch to "onto-theo-logic" and the "metaphysics of presence." In Greek ethics everything turns upon beauty and excellence. Foucault captured no small part of the spirit of Greek ethics when he spoke of ethics as the task of making oneself into a work of art (although his interest in disasters — in the insane, the imprisoned, and the ill — was very Jewish).[60] Aristotle was certainly right to say that the prudent man (*sic*) ought not to seek honor but that on account of which one ought to be honored, viz., excellence (*arete*). Aristotle was an aristocratic aretologist. Now I do not want to call the police on Aristotle. There is something to this Greek scheme, to a hermeneutics of *arete*. I do not favor unrelieved gloom. But I am interested in displacing this Greek schema — which moves between honor and that on account of which one is to be honored — with another, let us say a more Abrahamic schema, where the interest turns on those who suffer dishonor. Greek philosophical ethics is an ethics of the "best," of the excellence of *arete*, of making oneself, or one's works, or one's polis, shine with beauty. That was its fatal attraction to Nietzsche and Heidegger and goes to the heart of their intractable aristocratism and elitism, the German's fatal love of the Greek. However much he was a critic of things German, Nietzsche was never more German than in his love of the Greeks.

That is why, in a perverse twitting of Nietzsche's aristocratic nose, which was very easily offended, I would speak of a poetics not of the best but of the worst, not of the noble but of the ignoble, not of good but of evil, not of honor but of the dishonored. I am in pursuit neither of an ethics of virtue nor of an ethics of rules but of a poetics of obligations, a poetics that is focused not on the great creative artists and statesmen and state-founders, but on the outcast, the oppressed who are without a city or a home. I want to run an experiment in which the tide of philosophical discourse is turned away from the notions of agency and autonomy and toward the notions of the patient and heteronomy. Aristocratic ethics, being very eudaemonistic, is focused on making oneself or one's people or one's *polis* beautiful, honorable, virtuous, on personal or civic pride and magnanimity. It turns on the excellence of action, of personal or collective agency. It is focused thus on the exercise of freedom and the conditions of individual agency. Kant, Mill, and modern analytic ethics, even though they have switched from virtue to rules and have put the ethics of values on the map, move largely within the same classical horizons. The Good has been relativized from its Platonic heights to English multiplicity, to the greatest good for the greatest number, which, as far as it goes, is an improvement, a good pagan twist, in Lyotard's sense. But in such ethics one is still thinking in terms of the Good, with or without its Greco-German capitalization. My idea is not eudaemonistic but to worry over those who are beset by evil demons on every side, to start with the disasters who are as often as not, maybe more often (I have not taken a survey), the victims of the Good (somebody's Good).

It is of course a very Greek thing for me to philosophize about disasters, instead of just telling a story that would hold everyone's attention for a while and make a point in the bargain, which is the more Jewish (narratival) way to do it. But we cannot forget that there were many Greeks—too many to speak of "the" Greek—not just Plato and Aristotle, but also Sophocles and the great tragedians, who knew a thing or two about disasters and torn flesh. Greek tragedy is a narratival treatment of disasters, about losing one's lucky star; it is one of the paradigms of it, a discourse on disasters *par excellence*. What interests me is not only disrupting Greeks with Jews, which is very useful, but also disrupting philosophical Greeks with other Greeks and disrupting Jews with other Jews (jews). The idea is to be as jewgreek and greekjew as possible,[61] as miscegenated and disseminated as the police and public tolerance will permit, so as to upset the hegemony of the Good and to disrupt the "apostles of purity"[62] who produce victims wherever there is dissent.

To undertake to write a poetics of obligations, to serve an internship as obligation's clerk and poet, is already a very Greek idea. We who philoso-

phize, including we who problematize "we" and "philosophy," are ines-
capably Greek. But it is also a little jewish, in the sense of "*les juifs*," with a
lowercase "j," because it keeps an eye out for everyone who has been
treated like a Jew, *stricto sensu*. There are many such "jews," all around the
world, including the West Bank and the vast black "ghettoes" (a Jewish
word) in the United States. Wherever there are ghettoes, there are "jews,"
i.e., disasters, in the plural and in the lowercase, people bent and bleeding
from somebody else's freedom and autonomy.

This bit of fragmentary, supplementary writing on obligations should
turn out to be jewgreek/greekjew, miscegenated, contaminated, a half-
breed—i.e., de-Hellenized. That would not be half bad. Were we able to
pull it off, such a clustering of quasi-philosophical discourses would have
allowed what is Greek to be inwardly disturbed by its other and what is
other than Greek to find something of a philosophical idiom. That might
amount to a kind of jump-starting of philosophy, shocking it into place by
exposing it to its prephilosophical or nonphilosophical sources, which was
the excellent idea that the young Heidegger had in mind in the early
1920s—but which he unfortunately abandoned under the Call to march in
step with the Pure, Primordial Greek Beginning.

A LITTLE SUPPLEMENT TO GOOD AND EVIL

Still, it belongs to the most classical axiomatics, to the hoariest metaphysics of morals, that what I have sketched above is impossible (whereas for
me, even if it is impossible, it is the only possibility left). It is impossible to
begin with evil(s) because, lacking a standard for what is Good, we are unable to identify any evil in the first place, and hence unable even to know
that we are beset on every side by evil. Were we indeed bereft of an account
of the Good (so the argument goes), we would be unable to begin with evil
or evils, and hence unable to begin at all. *Ergo, omnis licet*: anything goes.
Or worse yet: nothing gets started. Either way, it would be a disaster for
my tenure as obligation's clerk and poet.

Such an objection proceeds from the forward-moving good sense of
metaphysical ethics, which looks severely on my poetic attempt to proceed
from below (and in reverse). So I must supplement my little supplementary
jottings on Good and Evil, which is not so much an argument (*logos*) as an
apologia, a confession that, having failed to get as far as either one, I do not
know where else to begin.

Let us take the case—let us "begin with" the case—of a disaster, of a
damaged life, of an irretrievable loss, of innocent, avoidable suffering, a
case where we cannot easily blame the victim for his or her destitute condition, say, of a child born with AIDS. Such a child, on my accounting,
"lays claim" to us, "seizes" us, without needing (and without having) a
prior theory of the Good in virtue of which we can adjudicate this to be (an)

evil. To begin "from below," to be the tedious clerk of obligation, means to gather the factical scraps and pieces of disasters that are scattered all around, in a kind of patho-poetico-hermeneutical *epagoge*. The notion that such an experience depends upon establishing a claim like "Health is (part of) the Good for human beings" is quite fatuous and hardly worth the cost of the book. The principle tells the readers nothing they do not already know; it adds nothing to their stock of knowledge except an air of pomposity and philosophical inflation of the sort we get from German philosophy professors—like Habermas.[63]

The being-obliged does not depend on the principle. The principle is a distillation, after the fact, of the being obliged. We do not judge the singular in virtue of the principle, but we draft the principle after the fact by excavating the singularity and erecting a relatively hollow schema—or "principle"—whose cash value is solely the singularities upon which it is drawn. The principles we write are like the checks we write; their whole value depends upon what they have in their account. We do not really apply principles to individual "cases." This needs to be reversed in keeping with my poetic perversity: we apply individuals to principles.[64]

But does not such a generalized, if not terribly informative, claim represent in fact the "implicit" principle, the implicit *arche* or *principium*, that is at work, *in actu exercitu*, in any explicit confrontation with suffering or evil? Not so, not because there is nothing "implicit" that is being explicated by the principle, but because what is being explicated is not a "principle" in any strong sense. I deny that there really is an implicit principle, *stricto sensu*, any grounded, founded *principium*, lying in wait in this experience that reflective thought can then explicate and establish.

The commanding thing about this encounter with this child, with any number of equally terrible situations, remains wholly on the level of an imperative coming to us from the singular experience and on my telling it lacks any *deeper* grounding. I do not think the event has a cognitive back-up, one that simply needs to be brought out explicitly into the open. For it cannot really be established, grounded, founded, or turned into a *principium* or *arche*, as a claim about the Good, even though it is recognized as obvious, in a biological sense, that human beings need to be relatively free from disease in order to live. It is not possible to cut through to some supersensible, universal, philosophical sphere, to some *mundus intelligibilis*, in which laws like this reside, waiting to be applied to mortal men and women (and children).

The sense in which this is so is as follows. Suppose someone claims to be indifferent to suffering, or, claiming nothing at all, simply chooses to walk away from suffering. What then? Suppose someone says: "Life is a cruel game in which we are all out to survive, and this child is one of the losers, just as in nature the weaker falls to the stronger, and the unfortunate to the more fortunate. In 4.5 billion years, this child and her suffering, you and I, our species and all the other species, life itself, and even this planet, our little star, will have vanished and will matter not a whit." What then? How is one to respond to *that* (*es, Ça*)? But being able to answer that is what it takes to be an ethical principle or an *arche* in the strong sense and to earn the right to write the Good in the uppercase.

My view turns on a cold truth.[65] That this child deserves to live a normal healthy life is not a law written in the stars, because the stars are indifferent to the child. The child's life thus is a dis-aster. She has no star to watch over her, no heavenly support. She is out of luck. But the upshot of this non-foundationalist line of reasoning is not that anything goes, but only that the things we favor and endorse—like this child's right to a healthy life—only go so far. If you try to push too hard the claim the child makes upon us, it will not hold up. It is not written in the stars; it has not dropped from the sky. The claim of the child is finite and fragile. It is not absolutely commanding—not a Categorical Imperative that breaks through the world of appearances, nor the Form of the Good gradually being recalled, nor the traces of the Face of God showing up in the child's face. Were any of these very beautiful hypotheses true, we would, perhaps, not let the conditions flourish under which such disasters occur with such savage regularity as we do. What law there is to come to the relief of the child is inscribed only on the face of the child, which is the face of suffering, and it does not extend beyond the singularity of the child. The child herself is the only law. In terms of metaphysico-ethical back-ups, the child is on her own. The call that is issued on *behalf* of the child is also issued *from* the child, not from above. The child is not an instance of the Law, let us say of the Categorical Imperative, which charges us to treat the child as an end in itself. The Categorical Imperative is an inflationary version of the face of the child, of meeting up with a hungry child. It is not "a fact as it were of pure reason." It is a fact as it were (and as much of a fact as any other fact, which is always a function of its presuppositions) of factical life, a fact of flesh, of the power that flesh exerts over flesh, which is highly finite.

No more.

But no less.

That is the point of beginning where we are, of proceeding in reverse, like a clerk on all fours picking up scattered fragments, as opposed to ethics' more dignified posture of offering a *tractatus de malo* that wants to proceed from the top down. The questions of suffering and evil turn on a *hermeneia*, a certain reading of the human condition, and on a certain responsiveness and sensitivity. The best anyone can do is to make the claim of the child look as strong as possible, to let its appeal (*Ruf, Beruf, Anklang*)—this little burst of German is meant for Heidegger, to point to another kind of call beyond the call of Being—ring out as loudly as possible, to sound the alarm of disasters as loud as we can, and to make indifference look as bad as possible, as bad as it is.[66]

If someone really demands a principle or a foundation, if they want a cognitive basis, a theory, or a principle, before proceeding, they will, I fear, never get underway. If they say that, failing such a principle, they will not act or will not act well, then I fear the worst. The sphere of obligation is its own form of life, its own genre, its own justification. That does not mean it is self-evident (*per se nota*), written in the stars, but rather that it is on its own to make the best case it can for itself. It does not derive from anything else, originate anywhere else. It has its own credentials, but it is without ultimate authorization, since who would have the authority to authorize it? And where would that authority originate? *Ad infinitum.* What validity it has is self-validating. You cannot press the claims made by the child back to some *mundus intelligibilis*, cut through to some *logos* that lays the law down. We know our obligations because we meet up with them, face to face.[67] Our obligations are neither as hollow as subjective values nor as solid as the Good. They are not as Deep as Evil but only flesh deep, but flesh is not to be taken lightly. My unflagging presupposition is that we pass our days, *zunächst und zumeist*, between Good and Evil.

Ergo, there is no *principium* or standard of Good behind the child or beyond the child, watching over the child and making the child safe. The child is not safe. The child is a disaster. There is no sure principle that is implicitly at work that renders possible the recognition of the disaster that besets the child. We cannot begin at the beginning, with a *principium*, but only where we are, with the child. We can only begin by responding to the child, who is a disaster, by coming under the singularity of the claim she makes upon us, and by making damaged lives our business. That is where we are. *Me voici.*

EXSULTAT

Furthermore—and this is the second little supplement I will add to my supplementary discourse on Good and Evil—despite the primacy that I assign to evils over the Good, there is nonetheless something to be said, if not about the Good, about which I am speechless, then about "goods"—in the sense of plural, lowercase goods. I am interested in allowing jewgreek paradigms to infiltrate and disrupt the Greek paradigms by which philosophy is typically guided (as well as in multiplying Greek paradigms). Like Levinas, I am no Parmenidean.[68] I prefer to let many flowers bloom, to give diversity a chance. Like Lyotard, I advocate pluralization and novelty, experimentation and innovation. I do not want Being and Thought to be the same, even if that saying is lifted up out of the dreary science of logic and made to mean that they "belong together." I prefer to keep them apart, to let them spin off in indefinitely many different directions.[69]

The goal for me, my Idea in the Kantian sense, is utter nonsense to the Eleatics: to bring Being out of Non-Being. As one of obligation's poets, I advocate creation (*poiesis*), which means doing something new, something different. I throw my support behind real change, *kinesis* with a punch to it.

To pass from ignorance to knowledge, really: not with a Pythagorean gloss, with a theory of *anamnesis*, which takes all the teeth out of learning, but really to learn something new.[70] Or to invent something new,[71] to multiply, to diversify, although I understand that creation will always mean to repeat differently.

Given this paradigm of novelty, creation, innovation, and experimentation, I say let there be as many goods as possible, let many flowers bloom, let many goods come.[72] For I do not know what the Good is and I do not want to cut off in advance any new possibilities. I want to let goods multiply indefinitely into the future, producing new configurations hitherto undreamt of in our philosophies. Let the sea, which is filled with the most exotic specimens, be our paradigm. It would be a loss were the deep to reach a consensus about how the fish should look. There are many ways to make yourself beautiful. Let beauty reign and find its place here. Let beauty multiply itself. *Bonum et pulchrum convertuntur*. If we all reached consensus, we would soon be led, after having found that we are all saying the same thing, simply to shut up. That would on occasion certainly have its advantages, but is on the whole an odd thing for a theory of communication to aim at. If what we seek is universal agreement, if we were all to speak with universal reason, we would be reduced first to sameness and then to silence. Dissent breaks new ground, invents new forms, discovers new stars, stirs up the waters, in an ongoing reconfiguration.

I put the Good on the side of novelty and innovation and so I cannot in principle say what it is, because a good many forms of good have not happened yet. Of the Good I can only say: come. I cannot say what it is, but what it is not. Let it happen.

I hope that it comes.

The jewgreek paradigm of creation turns not on *techne*, on giving defining form to preexisting matter, but on creation, on bringing forth *ex nihilo*, on the commencement of something new. It breaks with the Greek paradigms of circularity and retrieval, or of recollection and emanation, and also of *Aufhebung*, in favor of a more creationist motif of innovation and the production of novelty. I am aiming not at a *Resultat* (leaping back) but an *Exsultat*, an *exsultatio*, at leaping up and leaping out into something new. Along with a moving *Requiem* a good poetics of obligation would also include a stirring *Exsultatio* in its repertoire. The discourse on disasters is the other side of the coin of the poetics of exultation, of shooting stars and of felicity. The joy of events is the joy of new life, of joyous springing up, of birth and rebirth from moment to moment, of savoring what there is, of a leaping forth from moment to moment.[73]

We see the same creationist idea in Ockham and Scotus, from whom it made its way down into Descartes: that the world lurches from moment to moment, that each new moment is a new start, a leap (*saltare*), a gratuitous, exultant event, a gift of a sustaining, conserving God. The world is through and through contingent.

The world happens. From moment to moment. *Il arrive.*

The same idea is found in Constantin Constantius, in his theory of freedom as a "leap," in his notion of "repetition" as moving forward from moment to moment.[74] The future is not guaranteed but contingent and uncertain and so the present resolve needs to be sustained, repeated. The future does not simply hang on by the momentum of the present. That is the basis of Kierkegaard's critique of *hexis* (habit). Such a totally transforming *renovatio* is to be found in Johannes Climacus's account of *metanoia*, the complete transformation of one's life and heart in which one puts on a new mind.[75]

The Good belongs on the side of novelty, of producing new ways to be (*renovatio*), putting on a new life, in indefinitely many ways. This is tied in with dissent, with the right of the individual to produce a new and different and even discordant discourse, rather than of melting into the One or being amalgamated into the Whole. This does not prevent the formation of a "community," in my view, but it does see to it that the capacity of the community to "normalize," to reduce its members to certain common denominators, is kept at a minimum. It gives rise to a certain "weak" community, one in which obligation is recognized, but in which the space of difference is also recognized. Strong communities are dangerous—to everyone else, everyone outside the community, to everyone who chooses to dissent from community standards.

I have a maximally weak and nonconstraining notion of the Good, one which reminds me of one of the most beautiful maxims of the medieval masters: *dilige, et vis quod fac*: Love, and do what you will.[76] Love—that is, answer the call wherever you are needed—and do what you will.

If we must have a philosophy of the Good, let it be a *philosophia negativa* that says that factical life cannot be contracted into some more or less homologous standard of goodness, because goodness keeps disseminating itself, keeps inventing new forms and creating new standards for itself. *Bonum disseminativum sui.*[77] Disasters, on the other hand, have an ominous sameness, which invariably involves spilled blood, limp bodies, broken minds, damaged lives. The Good is disseminative of itself, even as evil contracts into an ominous identity.

THREE

Dionysus vs. the Rabbi

A GIFT

Some time ago I received a gift in the mail that I took at first to be an excellent joke. The package contained a most extraordinary painting. Signed by some prankster who called himself "Abraham of Paris," it depicted an unbelievable scene—of Dionysus with a long beard and a tallith about his shoulders, unfurling a sacred scroll; here before my eyes was the Torah being commented upon by Dionysus. I do not know whether this scene would have made Nietzsche ill or brought a smile to his face, whether he would have been visited with one of his ferocious migraines or would have exploded in laughter. But if Nietzsche himself could imagine a Caesar with the soul of Christ, or Dionysus on the throne at Rome, why not Dionysus with the soul of a rabbi?[1] However Nietzsche may have judged my painting, this Dionysian rabbi represented just the sort of productive tension and salutary miscegenation, the jewgreek polyvalence, for which I myself strive.

I have ever since kept this wonderful painting hanging above my mantel as a daily reminder of my Ideal. For this sublime figure—I do not know if it is sublime or farcical—at any rate, this unrepresentable image, is, I must confess, what I aim at, and I have passed many fruitful and enjoyable hours meditating upon the significance of this image. To this day I am in the debt of my anonymous benefactor whom I am unable to thank. For prank or no prank, the picture is a portrait of my mind, a perfect exemplification of what happens to someone who has allowed the thought, if it is a thought, of undecidability to have its way with his reflections.

Mad as it seems, the image makes a certain sense to me. It reminds me of Lyotard's farcical version of the categorical imperative: act in such a way that your maxim *cannot* be universalized (almost).[2] The Law my Dionysian rabbi was reading must surely be something like that. This impish figure suggested Lyotard's very impious idea of justice, the idea of justice as a kind of impiety. This itself bears an interesting similarity to what Derrida has been saying in recent years about justice and singularity.

The print bore the title "The Heterologist." As it happened I was at that time engaged in a study of the various heterological theories, i.e., dffferent accounts of difference (*heteros*), of the *logos* of *heteros*, if it has a *logos*. Now what I came to see in this figure was the tension between two different heterologies, two clearly different ideas of "difference," which I shall call "heteromorphism" and "heteronomism." The Dionysiac is a prankster, full of gaiety and wild abandon, a lover of diversity and different forms, in short, a "heteromorphist." But the man is reading the Torah and so is clearly a man of the Law, of the heteronomy of the Law, of the Law of Heteronomy. He is in short a kind of Levinasian Dionysus—an Abraham in Paris—if you can imagine such an unrepresentable, impossible thing. This suggests another form of *heteros*, a heteronomic as opposed to a heteromorphic difference. As time went on, however, I became somewhat less sure of this distinction. The lines between the two heterologies began to blur and the two heterologies began to pass back and forth into each other in a swirl of undecidability, persuading me all the more that this farcical gift was no joke but posed a most serious philosophical problem. Or, it was both a joke and a serious problem.

In what follows I offer the fruit of my meditations upon the wondrous image I received in the mail which hangs still above my mantel. The painting provoked in me a series of reflections upon the idea of difference (*heteros*) (if it is an idea), in which I try to sort out in a quasi-philosophical way two different ideas of difference.

HETEROMORPHISM

These heterologists, these philosophers of heteronomy and heteromorphic plurality who interested me—people like Lyotard, Levinas, and Derrida, not to mention Johannes de Silentio—have a common fear. They all keep a watchful eye for the Hegelian eagle that hovers above them, a bird of prey just waiting for a false move on their part. They share the "terrible foreboding" that Johannes de Silentio feels, that some great Systematizer will come along and gobble them up:

> . . . that some enterprising abstracter, a gobbler of paragraphs . . . will cut him up into paragraphs and do so with the same inflexibility as the man who, in order to serve the science of punctuation, divided his discourse by counting out the words, fifty words to a period and thirty-five to a semicolon. . . .[3]

One false move and the Hegelian eagle will have them all, down they will go in one swallow. Everything they have to say about difference will be digested by the System, every bit of *glas* gobbled up and gulped down, ingested, digested, assimilated by *Sa*.[4] With Johannes they all protest this fate:

> This is not the system; it has not the least to do with the system.[5]

But it is just at this point that the greatest care is required. For if we say this is *not* the System, that it has *not* the least to do with it, that will only bring a large smile to the face of *Sa*[6]—if it has a face—like the smile worn by the cat who knows that at last his prey is his. For the System feeds upon ne-

gation. This great fat *Sa* is fed on "nots." It grows larger and larger, is
driven on and on, higher and higher, precisely in virtue of these little
"nots." With every "not" the noose of the System is drawn tighter still
around the neck of difference.

The greatness of these heterologists is to have proceeded with their eyes
open to this danger. They have attempted the most delicate operations of
eluding the Hegelian menace without setting foot in the dialectical trap,
without springing the door of "opposition" which would set off instantly a
giant and irreversible mechanism that would suck up their "difference" in
a flash, leaving no trace of difference behind (only a smiling *Sa*).

One of the earliest, most powerful and seminal presentations of
heteromorphism—by which I mean the love of different forms, a Dionysian affirmation of plurality and multiplicity—of the heteromorphic attempt to elude the Hegelian eagle, is Deleuze's famous *Nietzsche and Philosophy* (1962), published in the same year as *Edmund Husserl's "Origin of
Geometry": An Introduction*, Derrida's first work.[7]

In this work, Deleuze portrays difference as an affirmative, overflowing,
differential energy—he is commenting on the "will to power"—or rather
as a plurality of such energies or "differences," which do not settle into
place as oppositional relationships. The play of forces is through and
through "differential," not oppositional. A force is not a positive or "posi-
tional" structure and it does not, accordingly, stand in opposition with
other forces which it must negate or by which it is itself negated—which
would spring the lever of dialectical movement into action. Deleuzian difference is free play, not the strife of opposition. Deleuze's argument,
which—along with Derrida's more semiological arguments—broke the
grip of the structuralist appropriation of Saussurean difference, is in my
view the opening and perhaps even defining gesture of poststructuralism.[8]
It has found a place in every poststructuralist philosophy since then, each
of which has in one way or another taken over the sometimes notorious
idea of the "free play of differences," which has also acquired a very bad
name.[9]

Deleuze defends a philosophy of pure affirmation, the affirmation of affirmation, a pure and undiluted affirmation of affirmation itself rather than
of something else. This unencumbered willing and affirming means the
free creation and the invention of new values. The essence of willing and of
the free spirit is to steer clear of dead weights and heavy burdens. The free
spirit is no beast of burden, no ass braying "yes, yes" when confronted
with something onerous. Beware the spirit of bearing, which is the spirit of
gravity and taking on heavy weights. Beware the unbearable heaviness of
Being.[10]

The will of the free spirit guards against all "responsibility," which is
nothing but the weight of Being, an ontological weight brought to bear
upon a will made for serving. The heaviness of Being is the center of gravity in classical metaphysics, the basis of the philosophy of the camel and

the ass, of "Being in itself," of Being which is outside the will. In such a metaphysics, affirmation means "acceptance" (of weighty responsibilities). True affirmation can never be a "function" of Being, i.e., of something other than itself, which would reduce the will to a "functionary" — not only of the party, the church, or the state but of Being or truth, of anything that in any way impinges on the will, anything that would bind the will or tie it up. Being, truth, and reality: those are the "avatars of nihilism"[11] that bring being and responsibility to bear upon the will and its willing instead of turning upon such dead weights and tearing them to shreds, like a roaring lion.[12] The destructiveness of the lion is negation, not affirmation, but it is an active negative force, an active negating which labors — nay, dances — in the service of affirmation. The acceptance of burden, however, is the mark of a "reactive" will, a will whose willing has been blocked and which acts, not from its own spontaneous forces but only by reacting to the superior forces that encumber it and which fill it with resentment.[13] The yes that does not know how to say no is but the braying of the ass. The yes that includes the lion's no, that negates everything that weighs the will down, is on the way beyond the human-all-too-human to *übermenschlich* affirmation.

When Heidegger says that the Overman is the one who answers the call of the "Being of beings" as eternal recurrence, when he says that the Being of beings is a weighty matter (*wichtige Sache*), when he says that Nietzsche is one of the weightiest figures of metaphysics, in the same class as Aristotle, not a merely religious writer like Kierkegaard,[14] then Heidegger makes the Overman into a responsible man, placing him at the very height (*über*) of responsibility. When Heidegger says all that, when he makes Nietzsche into a philosopher of Being, "[t]his interpretation neglects all that Nietzsche fought against."[15]

In the philosophy of affirmation Being, truth, and reality are nothing more than inventions of the will, nothing more than fictions devised by life as a show of life's strength. The active will can never suffer the pain of opposition; it never groans under the weight of Being. "To affirm is not to take responsibility for, to take on the burden of what is, but to release, to set free what lives."[16] To affirm is to disburden (*ent-laden*), unleash (*ent-fesseln*), to set willing free in unencumbered affirmation, in the creation of new values, which are themselves the issue and invention of willing itself. To affirm is to loosen and disentangle willing from whatever would tie willing up, whatever would put it in a bind.

True affirmation does not affirm anything in-itself, anything other-than-itself, i.e., anything *other*. What is *other* will weigh the will down. If one insists on retaining the idea of "Being," then Being must not be understood to mean the *object* of affirmation, as if it were something *other* than affirmation toward which affirmation must extend itself or direct itself or subordinate itself.[17] Instead, Being must be taken to mean affirmation itself, the power of affirmation, which is the Being of the will, its own willing. So if affirmation affirms itself, then that is Being affirming itself, which is why, if affirmation affirmed something *other* than itself, that would be nihilism: Being denying itself, the nihilistic acceptance of something other.

Affirming means the creation of value, the creation of something new, in short: becoming. But the affirmation of affirmation is the act that seals and perfects affirmation, that allows it to circle back upon itself and catch itself up in itself, that shields it definitively from the spirit of gravity and dead weights. The affirmation of affirmation is the being of affirmation, the being of becoming.

The affirmation of affirmation completes the ring of willing. The affirmation of affirmation is the eagle completing a vast circle in the sky over Zarathustra's head, the serpent encircling the neck of Zarathustra. (More Greek circles.) It is the will's embrace of itself as its own proper element, its definitive shielding of itself from everything alien, reactive, onerous, slavish, Jewish, Abrahamic, everything *unheimlich*, other. The will does not will something other than itself, some foreign object. That would draw it outside of itself, seduce it into a foreign element, reduce it to something craving and craven, something slavish and desirous of the other. The will wills only what is worthy of itself, which is itself.

Indeed, Deleuze's will is so thoroughly affirmative, so thoroughly active and actual, that it sounds rather like Aristotle's perfect *nous* or perfect act, which knows only itself (*noesis noeseos*) and loves only itself lest its perfect actuality be compromised. Would it not be an odd result for a philosophy of difference to coincide with a philosophy of pure act or perfect presence, with a philosophy of *parousia par excellence?*[18]

The will is the will to will, the will to greater and higher expenditures of willing and creating. It is not what the will creates that matters—for its products are effervescent constellations that come and go—but the willing itself, the perfecting of the will's willing, which wants itself, which wants recurrence and eternity, which wants the highest joy.[19]

The will that wills willing, the affirmation that affirms only itself, loosened from alien being and shielded from otherness,[20] is the freedom of woman released from man, an emancipated woman, Ariadne abandoned by and so emancipated from Theseus. Dionysian affirmation, the creative affirmation of values, is the first affirmation. But that pristine affirmation is in danger of falling down before what it creates, of an idolatry that idolizes its own creations. Ariadne, on the other hand, is the affirmation of affirmation itself, and hence the ultimate shield and aegis of willing, its protectress, the circle of affirmation completed and made perfect. As Ariadne returns to her own element, her feminine power, and shields herself from all opposition, so affirmation is secured in a purely affirmative element.

When affirmation is complete, then affirmation is loosened from dialectical entrapment. For in the dialectical course affirmation stands in opposition to negation, still tied to negation. Dialectics is the very opposition of affirmation and negation, an opposition in which affirmation is inhabited by negation, caught up in dialectical labor and strife, forced to wail and strain as it labors against the weight of negation. Dialectics is war, the battle of master and slave, the battle for mastery in which the master is ultimately enslaved, whereas perfect affirmation is joy without conflict. When affirmation is complete, when it completes the circle, then affirmation is opposed by nothing (other), does not strain against anything, does not do battle, but has become wholly affirmative, consisting entirely in "the enjoyment and play of its own difference."[21] "[D]ifference is happy."[22]

The play of difference is the end of opposition and hence the end of dialectics and of the Hegelian eagle. The play of difference is not oppositional difference but, let us say, differential difference, the pure play of multiplicity, becoming, and chance. So the affirmation of affirmation is "difference raised to its highest power."[23] Pure affirmation affirms itself in a differential play. Affirmation is not fed by the fire of opposition, driven by the power of negation, but affirms itself freely in the free play of itself, of its own excess and joy, exuberantly, excessively, full of dance and overflow. Difference is the self-disseminating play of affirmation, which multiplies and differentiates itself. Difference thus is not negation but self-disseminating affirmation.

Affirmation returns; it deserves to return. If you affirm the one fateful number you roll, then you get the dice back, and you get to throw that number again and again.[24] It is not what you roll but how you roll. The pale, sickly moralist, on the other hand, wants to keep throwing the dice until he rolls a good number. His sunken eyes and joyless face tell you he is not playing. As he rolls the dice again and again, compulsively rejecting one number after another, you know he is deadly serious and does not get the idea behind the game. The affirmation of affirmation effects the return of affirmation. Affirmation returns. Affirmation breeds affirmation. Affirmation is a good breeder, which breeds higher types by selecting out (*züchten*) sickly, reactive forces. So there is something irresistible, something fateful, about affirmation that will eventually breed out and boil away the dark, snarling, reactive forces of the Judaic priest—"you're guilty"—and bad conscience—"I'm guilty"—that will disburden us of the dead weights of church-dark gloom and the eerie smell of burning incense.

All reactive forces are denied; all forces become active. "There is no *other* power but affirmation, no *other* quality, no *other* element; the *whole* of negation is converted. . . . This is the conversion of heavy into light, of low into high, of pain into joy."[25] "[O]nly joy returns."[26] The negative and reactive draw their last breath at the gate of Being (affirmation). "Opposition ceases its labor and difference begins its play."[27] "Man"—sick, reactive, Abrahamic, Judaic, Christian man—inhabits the dark side of the earth.

(He must be very ugly.)

But on the day when every reactive force is transmuted, when everything has been revaluated, when affirmation and being active are the sole qualities,[28] on that day—have I not read this somewhere in Deleuze? I cannot find the page—you will see the Son of Man, the Overman, coming on a cloud, surrounded by a heavenly host singing glory and honor and power to the Child.

ALL THAT NIETZSCHE FOUGHT AGAINST

This Nietzsche, Deleuze's Nietzsche, is very beautiful and I love him very much. I have learned a great deal from him. He explains why it is that the rabbi in my mysterious painting does not wear a long black coat underneath his tallith but instead a coat of many colors. I see why his face is crossed with laughter, why there is a great exuberance, a most affirmative spirit, in his bearing. My rabbi, the one hanging over my mantel, is a happy man.

Still, I am troubled by this Deleuzian Nietzsche. The question he provokes in me is whether Deleuze's Dionysiac has not lost his nerve. Is this what "difference" really means, or all that it means, for Nietzsche? I fear there is not enough of Nietzsche in this *Nietzsche.*[29] For Nietzsche, my Nietzsche, ventures on most dangerous seas, on waters tossed by fierce winds, on a deep inhabited by the darkest monsters. Nietzsche is a bold searcher and researcher who "embarks with cunning sails on terrible seas."[30]

"Nietzsche": the name of the thinker is the name of a disaster.

That is the Nietzsche who keeps me up at night, who disturbs my sleep, who has me pacing my floors at all hours. I cannot get over the feeling that Deleuze has picked my pocket, quietly slipped a pocket edition of Nietzsche's *Werke* out of my inside pocket just when I least suspected anything was going on. He has robbed me of *my* Nietzsche,[31] the most dangerous, the most disastrous, the most disastronomical of the great philosophers of recent times, the most extreme Nietzsche:

> The spell that fights on our behalf, the eye of Venus that charms and blinds even our opponents, is *the magic of the extreme*, the seduction that everything extreme exercises: we immoralists—we are the most extreme.[32]

For the Nietzsche that most interests me, a mere clerk assigned the job of picking up the pieces of obligation I find scattered here and there, is a tremendous wind, a cataclysmic, disastrous storm that sweeps over us, a merciless burst of what Nietzsche calls his "truthfulness" (*Wahrhaftigkeit*),[33] which frightens me—I speak for myself—half to death. The only argument I know against my Nietzsche is Johannes de Silentio's, that it would be too extreme, too terrible, a disaster, really, were it true (were Nietzsche really being truthful). To which Nietzsche responds that a good philosopher (citing Stendhal) must be like a good banker: he cannot afford to get sentimental, because that could cost him a lot of money.[34]

Nietzsche for me is the great philosopher of the disaster, of the loss of a heavenly guide, of being set adrift in a cold, merciless cosmos that cares not a whit for our well-being. He is the one thinker to have followed this thought through, down to its most merciless, most extreme conclusion, not to have backed off from it. (Then he proposed, in the most coldblooded manner, an "aesthetic justification"[35] or affirmation of the disaster.) For Nietzsche, "ethics" (he usually said "morals") and "metaphysics" represent a collective loss of nerve in the face (or facelessness) of the disaster, a will not to see, an inability to look upon the world with unvarnished "honesty," to come to grips with the cold truth—which would be enough to kill you.

Nietzsche's "magic" is the spell cast by a merciless lucidity in virtue of which truth—"'Truth'? Who has forced this word on me? But I repudiate it; but I disdain this proud word: no, we do not need even this; we shall conquer and come to power even without truth"[36]—is not something to discover but to "endure" and a source of great suffering.[37] The world is a "monster of energy," a "play of forces" without disgust, a Dionysian world of endless restlessness that destroys whatever it creates, and you and I are bits of energy—"and nothing more." *Und nichts außerdem!*[38] What "justifies" such a "monster" (*Ungeheuer*)—such a disaster—are the sublimely beautiful moments that it brings forth, the passing, transient instances of higher types, the fragile, fleeting flowers which are too soon trampled under by a cosmic play that cares not for them or their works or anything else. His merciless "truthfulness" (*Wahrhaftigkeit*) is all that is left to us after we have lost our grip on *Wahrheit*, when we disdain that proud word and find ourselves in the midst of the disaster, when we see that he sees through every attempt to sweeten, veil, attenuate, or blunt the distress of our condition.

Nietzsche is the disaster's poet, the author of the greatest poetics of the disaster we have seen in our times; he is our own Greek tragedian. As for me, I who mean to be a part-time poet of obligation, who cannot even expect to earn a living by my occasional pieces, I am frightened half to death by this poetics, and I have no wish to hurl myself into this abyss.

For what is the child on this cold vision? Or Auschwitz or Salvador or Sarajevo, or killing fields anywhere? What is there left to say once we have declared the innocence of becoming? What else can such violence be— when you attach proper names and dates to it, when you give it flesh— except a bit of ill will, of needless cruelty by which the higher types should not be sullied? *Und nichts außerdem!*

What Deleuze leaves out, the Nietzsche that Deleuze tries to sweeten, veil, attenuate, or blunt, is this merciless, disastronomical Nietzsche, the one for whom "difference" does not mean the gay play of egalitarian forces tripping the light fantastic but what Nietzsche calls again and again the "pathos of distance." Nietzsche does not try to *elude* opposition "differentially" (and thereby confound dialectics), as Deleuze argues. Rather he *embraces* opposition "tragically," to an "extreme" that makes dialectical progress absurd. Deleuze has no heart for the conflictual character of the will to power, for the heartlessness of Nietzschean difference. For Nietzsche, difference means distance, *feeling different*, being full of the feeling of distance, without feeling bad about one's superior distance, one's superiority. That is what Nietzsche calls the order of rank, which separates the highest from the lowest. Difference is the *pathos* of distance, feeling apart, and it is threatened by the opposite *pathos*, the Christian-moral-socialist *pathos*, feeling the same, feeling-with (*sym-pathos*), the *pathos* of "proximity."[39]

Unlike Deleuze, Nietzsche was no lover of Scotus on the univocity of being.[40] Nietzsche did not want everything to be univocally different, but differently different; he did not advocate a differential difference but an ordered difference, rank ordered. He did not think that each thing had its own precious *haecceitas*—Scotus was a Franciscan with a Christian conception of the immortality of the individual soul—but rather that most things were extremely coarse and only a rare few were exceptionally fine. Rare and difficult are the best. And he used his nose as a guide: the worst smell the worst.[41] Or his stomach: the worst fill him with nausea; or his palate: the worst fill him with disgust and make him want to vomit (*Ekel*).[42] The order of rank is—shall we admit it?—also an odor of rank. Rank and order are not merely a matter of bells tolling (*glas, classicus*) but of noses smelling; not only a matter of the ear of the other but of the nose and the palate:

> I was the first to *discover* the truth, in that I was the first to sense—*smell*—the lie as lie. . . . My genius is in my nostrils.[43]

Deleuze backs off from Nietzsche's extreme, Nietzsche's scandal:

> One cannot overemphasize *the extent to which the notions of struggle, war, rivalry or even comparison are foreign to Nietzsche and to his conception of the will to power.*[44]

That, for me, is an unfortunate, even an amusing "moralizing" of Nietzsche, an attempt to make him a pacificist, a radical egalitarian democrat (which, for Nietzsche, means a Christian),[45] in short, to turn Nietzsche over to "all that Nietzsche fought against"; in short again, to identify him with everything that smells bad and induces nausea, with *adiaphoria* and leveling. It swings Nietzsche to the left and is the core of "*Nietzsche Aujourd'hui*,"[46] or what Bloom calls, with a sneer, the "Nietzscheanized left."[47] Now far be it from me to call the police on Deleuze or to speak against the left, which I certainly love very much. Let many flowers bloom. I do not want to say that Deleuze's Nietzsche is illegal or of no use. On the contrary. I just want to say it is not dangerous enough, not disastrous enough, and so it leaves out something essential about the heteromorphic possibility he embraces.

Let us come back to the Hegelian eagle, for that is what concerns Deleuze, Lyotard, Derrida, Levinas—and Johannes de Silentio. It is certainly true that Nietzsche is an enemy of dialectics, but not for the reason

Deleuze gives. What Nietzsche *approved* of in Hegel was precisely Hegel's introduction of opposition and negation into philosophy. The significance of Hegel, he says, is that "evil, error, and suffering are not felt as arguments against divinity."[48] Nietzsche's objection to Hegel is not that Hegel conceived of difference as opposition, as Deleuze claims, but that Hegel undertakes a "rational" justification of struggle and opposition instead of justifying it "aesthetically"—that is, by way of a poetics of the disaster. Hegel puts the hard work of opposition in the service of a higher composition, a more long-range production, instead of seeing the disaster in which things are swept up. In Hegel opposition is a detour on the way to a higher production; in Nietzsche, opposition is the merciless destruction of whatever is produced. In Hegel what is real is rational; in Nietzsche what is real is merciless and self-destructive, but we should love it anyway. That is Nietzsche's own Jobian ordeal, his own great ascetic/aesthetic ideal:

> Yea, even though the will destroyeth everything that it buildeth up, even though it shall slay me, even then shall I love it. The Will giveth and the Will taketh away. Blessed be the name of the Will. Thus spoke Zarathustra.[49]

Nietzsche advocates a kind of reverse Hegelianism, a perverse totalization, an affirmation of the *whole* of life, of the position and the opposition, of creation and destruction, of joy and suffering, of pleasure and pain, precisely in the face of the cold fact that becoming makes no dialectical progress, that it does not recoup its losses, that the flux is the endless destruction of whatever it produces, that the whole has no *telos* and makes no sense, that the whole is a sheer a-telic becoming. Nietzsche is not opposed to a certain totalizing thought—everything is interwoven, a circle, and everything is to be affirmed—but his totality is a negative one, a totality without goal or origin, without a finger of God, without unity or a divine sensorium, without a guiding star.[50] It is the totality of the disaster, of the *nichts außerdem*. Life is justified "aesthetically," by the appreciation that one golden moment redeems immeasurable misery, meanness, and destitution, that one high noon redeems the darkest midnight, that a single moment redeems the whole. Nietzsche did not see the flux in terms of the dialectical spiral of the Spirit, moving progressively higher and higher as it recapitulated lesser, earlier forms within it. He saw it as a wheel that passes through certain high noons whose splendor justifies the inevitable destruction. The best justifies the worst, although the best is itself always destroyed and never *aufgehoben*. But the importance of Hegel and of German philosophy generally is the discovery of opposition, which is the true test of affirmation, the ordeal through which life must pass, the test of whether it is an angel or a demon that whispers in our ears and tells us that life goes on and on, without remission.[51]

Nietzsche does not elude opposition; he confronts it in a more merciless and ruthless way than does Hegel, who wants to tame and rationalize it.

Nietzsche does not evade opposition by turning affirmation into a differential play[52] but he embraces opposition as the self-destructiveness of everything positive. His play is not an egalitarian play of forces but struggle, war, and violence, a matter of hardness, which sets the measure for the *pathos* of distance between the best and the worst.

The world for Nietzsche is a "monster of energy, without beginning, without end,"[53] a sea of forces boiling up and overflowing. It would be a great indignity to the forces, a moralizing of them, to make them "effects" of something, to submit them to the force of something else that would determine their action and deprive them of their own inner force, to separate them from themselves. There is no external cause, no divine hand directing their course from without (*ab extra*). The system as a whole is constant but within its borders it is eternally restless; it abhors equilibrium and equality. There are "high points of becoming," points of "divinization" (*Vergötterung*), when the highest forces dominate the lowest, when all is well in the order of rank. "God" is not the prime mover of the system, external to the system, but a name for an internal state of the system, viz., its point of optimal organization. But at the point where there is nothing left for the forces to dominate and organize, the point of divinization in which the highest forces discharge their power and the lowest forces stay in check, the forces have no other recourse but to turn upon themselves and break themselves up. That leads to extreme de-divinization (*Entgötterung*), an ignoble organization, which consists in equalization, even distribution, democracy, in short, the destruction of the order of rank and the undermining of the *pathos* of distance. That *adiaphoria*, that extreme egalitarian de-divinization is precisely the result to which Nietzsche is led by Deleuze. To divinize is to hierarchize, to set out a sacred order of rank; to de-divinize is to equalize, to fall into an unholy anarchy where the worst and smelliest and most mediocre are set loose.[54]

It is a moralizing illusion, contrary to the essence of the forces, to imagine that the regularities within this incessant fluctuation are the product of law. That is a Christianizing fallacy, the invention of Jesuitical physicists who want to imagine obedient, God-fearing forces.[55] The forces are themselves too divine, too noble, too proud to obey any God but themselves, to obey any lawgiver, to "obey" at all. Whatever regularity there is results from the fact that the forces are what they are, that they are constituted as they are, that they discharge their energies in accordance with the necessity which they themselves are.[56] The regularity of the forces means nothing more than that they are unable to be otherwise than they are. Such regularities as are observed are simply tautologies, the laws which the forces themselves are, their own autonomic systems.[57] Everything among the forces happens *ab intra*, from within the forces themselves, from their own autonomic systems, from within the center which organizes the perspective which they themselves are.

Nietzsche knows of course that he is fighting a losing cause. Ultimately, ironically, Nietzsche knows, Nietzsche *wants* — I would say that this is *what wills* in Nietzsche (*qui veut*) — these most excessively beautiful and powerful productions, the issue of the best and highest struggles, to be losing efforts. Like a great actor who knows how to hold his audience spellbound with the death scene, Nietzsche has the best forces succumb to the opposition. Ever the thespian, ever the lover of the spirit of tragedy and the tragic touch that moves the audience, this is Nietzsche's most poetic and sublime moment, his heroic side — and also an expression of his most extreme elitism. This is his own sublime *ressentiment* against modernity. His valiant, Greek forces go down (*untergehen*), too beautiful for this crude world. They accumulate into exotic, magnificent, and unique beings, become rare beauties and beautiful rarities, brilliant solitary flowers, only to be suffocated by coarse hardy weeds. The most powerful forces are woven into the most exquisitely beautiful patterns, but being of a delicate constitution they cannot survive. They are trampled under by the crude masses whom modernity has set loose. What is coarse is hardy. The best forces die a beautiful death, a death worthy of a Greek hero — or a good actor.

That is Nietzsche's revenge, his ill will toward modernity and the French Revolution, his attempt to give it a bad conscience, his *ressentiment*. Modernity is a matter of coarse hands fingering antiquity's finest linens. He wants to make democratic instincts sick, guilty. He knows he fights for a losing cause but he wants the victors to feel bad about winning and he wants the losers to feel superior. The first philosopher to argue with his nose,[58] he will have modernity know that it smells bad, that it induces nausea, that even though it tramples down his most exquisite flowers it does so with filthy feet.[59]

That is why I suspect pure laughter, pure Dionysianism, as I suspect purity generally. For the serpent of resentment is no less capable of hiding under the rock of laughter; the ill will of the tarantula can mask itself in gaiety and dancing. Resentment does not always inhabit church-dark gloom or reek of incense. Cannot the sneer of resentment also take the form of laughter?

My question then must be, why is my Dionysiac rabbi laughing, the one hanging over my mantel? Is he reading something funny on his scroll?

HETEROMORPHISM VS. HETERONOMISM

I am not embarrassed, or only slightly embarrassed, to say that the *Übermensch* — either Nietzsche's or Deleuze's — is too much for me. I find it too exhausting, all this outpouring and overflowing, all this firing away of forces night and day. The man must never sleep.[60] Having begun where I am, in the midst of factical life, I find myself everywhere surrounded by obligations from without, *ab extra*, put upon incessantly by numerous heteronomous demands. I do not at all feel so purely, wholly active, so autonomic and *unabhängig*. I am constantly called upon to react and to respond. I do not know about Nietzsche or Deleuze, but speaking for myself, obligation happens to me all the time. I will even go so far as to admit that a good deal of what Nietzsche calls slavish, socialist, egalitarian, democratic, Jewish, Christian, feminine, and anarchical is quite appealing to me. A good deal of my service as a part-time poet and clerk of obligation consists in making these things look good, and certainly much better than Nietzsche makes them out to be, in providing them with an idiom, as Lyotard would say.

Make no mistake. I am not calling the police on Nietzsche. I am transfixed by Nietzsche's tragic vision, kept up at night by his account of the disaster, but I have an almost exactly opposite response to it, not a *pathos* of distance but a *pathos* of proximity.[61] I have no heart for a battle with the abyss, for testing the mettle of my will, for firing my *pathos* of distance. On the contrary, I feel drawn together with the other mortal victims of this disaster. We are disasters all, some of us more than others, but this for me has the effect of binding us together. We are all siblings of the same dark night, tossed by the waves of the same dark sea, huddled together for companionship and mutual support, held in a fragile link by a *pathos* of proximity and *consolatio*.

I do not at all think, and I am not saying, that Nietzsche favored inflicting suffering. He clearly regarded that as ignoble, as "beneath" his higher types. But even that is said from the point of view of the self-respect and autonomy of the agent, its obligation to *itself*, a sense of Greek magnanimity, not of the jewgreek, heteronomous demands placed upon the agent by the patient. Nietzsche was, however, moved by the disaster to look with disdain upon the joys and sorrows of ordinary, unmemorable, modern, "mediocre" people, people who were not going to make their life a work of art, at least not one that could command attention for more than fifteen minutes. He regarded the attempt to lift the meanness of their lives as having a leveling effect on the rest of the system of forces, one which was not worth the cost to the best. So he was willing to tolerate a maximum of misery and a minimum of flourishing among those whom he regarded as mediocre.

I, on the other hand, regard the multiplication of the flourishing of the "mediocre"—of the "many," of the "masses," of the folks who tend to fare poorly in the several orders of rank—and the relief of misery wherever it is found, to be a very happy science, the happy science *par excellence*, an important part of what I would call my quest not for a *Resultat* but for an *Exsultat*, a generalized exultation in which all can share. I am not interested in the great and heroic, in the History of Being or the History of Spirit, or in explosive macho-moments of divinization in which the Will to Power hits a peak and flows over. That is just more Greco-German bombast, which makes me nervous. As facticity's clerk, my interests turn toward the small and everyday, the bits and pieces, the lost fragments, the *minima moralia* of everyday lives, toward what Greco-Germans regard as the *me onta* (I Cor. 1:28). As for great and sustaining works of art, let them happen. They will happen anyway. They do not "justify" the suffering of the child. Indeed, they are at their best when they are *about* the child, about the bonds that tie us to the child; when they rise up like the lament of the child, a lament for the child, when they remind us, in a way that hardly anything else can, that we are all siblings on the same dark seas.

That is why I am a lover of Abraham and why, no doubt, this odd painting that disturbs my peace and quiet is of a Dionysiac who—if you can believe it—is reading the Torah. This highly jewgreek image is also an image of a heteronomist, i.e., a lover of the *other* and of a certain *law* of the other. That introduces another kind of heterology, another *heteros*, another, a different sense of "difference." This difference comes down to us from Abraham and has oddly infiltrated a very Dionysian, Parisian scene, creating an amazing, an almost impossible image of Abraham, or of something Abrahamic, among the postmoderns. How is that possible? Can that be represented? Could anyone paint a picture of it? The ideal in my poetics, what I dream of day and night in my poetics, but for which I lack the concept, is of Abraham on the stage of Dionysus, starring in one of his festivals, in a great jewgreek tragedy. That would be very beautiful, but with a beauty that is otherwise than Hegelian, a sort of beauty which is at present an Idea without a concept.

To sort all this out, I will return to my clerical duties and introduce certain distinctions, certain matters of bookkeeping, in the hope of putting some order in this house.

Deleuze defends difference in the sense of *diversitas*—diversity, variety, and variegation. Difference is always taken in the plural; there is always a plurality of differences, a play of differences, in which differences arise from a certain differentiality, a playing or spacing between one element and the next. Difference in this sense is polyvalent and polymorphic. The play plays on, spacing and outspacing itself, disseminating itself, taking ever new turns, inventing ever new moves, in a kind of intoxicating dance, a whirl of new forms, making it impossible for the circle to close and so making dialectical enclosure impossible. Instead of circling back upon itself the play invents endless loops and spirals, tangents and ellipses, amazing mazes and wild scribblings that cannot be ordered, dominated, or untangled. Difference in this sense is exceedingly experimental, endlessly innovative. It loves to multiply itself, to spread wildly, rhizomatically, across multiple surfaces. That is what I have been calling *heteromorphic* difference, which I defined as the love of different forms.

But Nietzsche himself regards this pure, unordered heteromorphism, this heteromorphism without the order of rank, as a kind of rank anarchy. It makes Nietzsche's nostrils twitch. This heteromorphism unleashes just what should be held in check and held at a distance, just what destroys the feeling, the *pathos*, of distance. It is a soft, effete version of a real philoso-

phy of affirmation, a womanizing of a more manly version of the philosophy of forces, a dilution of a more robust, macho affirmation, which requires ice water in one's veins. Nietzsche does not deny the other or want
to evade opposition; he wants to take on the other because the tensions
between the forces are the best test of the will, the stuff on which the forces
feed, growing stronger and more dominant.

But by correcting Deleuze's "philology"[62] and giving a more rigorous,
merciless rendering of Nietzsche, by respecting the extreme which Nietzsche represents, we bring into view all the more clearly what is missing
from both views, from both of these Nietzsches. For with all its talk about
difference (qua diversitas), heteromorphic pluralism is in fact quietly stealing
away from the other, the other one, alter, the one who lays claim to me. If
Deleuze wants difference without the opposition of the other, Nietzsche
loves the battle with the other. But what both resist, what they do not
want—this is what is willing there, qui veut—is the other as the law, the
other who gives the will the law. They resist, they do not want (qui ne veut
pas), the notion of heteronomy, of difference qua alter, and hence of what I
am calling heteronomic difference. That is a second kind of difference, a different difference—to which I will return shortly—and it is a difference that
makes a difference. It helps sort out for us (at least) two kinds of poststructuralist theories, say of the heteromorphic sort represented by Deleuze,
Guattari, and Baudrillard, on the one hand, and that of Derrida and Lyotard, who have been influenced by the heteronomism of Levinas, on the
other hand.[63]

What then is heteromorphism? Heteromorphic difference, the difference
common to both Deleuze and Nietzsche, is organized around a paradigm
of discharge and dehiscence, of the overflow of an all too great fullness. In
this case, difference differs and defers by way of parting and parturition. A
gathering of forces, full and overflowing, pregnant with multiple offspring
and seeds, collects itself together, gathers itself into uncontainable fullness,
becomes overrich and brimming over, and then erupts. The forces differentiate themselves, break up from within, by reason of their own internal
instability, their inability to hold themselves in, to keep themselves intact,
by reason of their own uncontainable plenitude. The forces break apart,
break open, multiplying themselves in a kind of joyful self-destruction and
dissipation, in a work of profligacy and dissemination.

Here the action is ex-plosive—a powerful thrust outwards (ex), which
prevents closure and occlusion—and volcanic, tremendous forces building
up from within and then spilling over; inner perturbation and rumbling,
restless and seething turmoil, seeking an outlet, an overflow, discharge.

The forces are set on a course of jubilant but impossible self-accumula-
tion, aggressive self-aggrandizement that is doomed to fail, like a doomed
monadology, with no master monad to oversee the strife, with no essences
to see each monad to a happy end (entelecheia), the strife of monad with
monad, of conglomerates of monads achieving fleeting domination. The

forces aggregate, accumulate, here, for a while, in one place, and then come undone, dissipating in happy abandon, only to recommence the same process, again and again.

Here all action is *ab intra*, from within. Nothing foreign invades, dominates, subdues the strongest, best, and noblest forces, which would only be to humiliate and degrade them, making them into slaves. The only defeat and impotence of the forces is their inability to retain their spoils, to keep everything they have conquered, and so they disrupt themselves, break themselves up, discharge themselves in a mighty expenditure, a final glorious death which sets in motion new accumulations of energies, new centers, new unities that will repeat again and again the process of accumulation and discharge, in endless, joyful cycles.

Here difference is the issue not only of power but of the impotence of power,[64] i.e., the inability of the pulsing tension of the same to hold itself back, to contain all that it has accumulated, the impossibility of reaching *entelecheia* without bursting, the incapacity for totalization. There is a law inscribed in the forces in virtue of which they must discharge and self-destruct, and this precisely at some strategic or optimal point, the point at which they have become as powerful and as beautiful, as noble and full of splendor, as they are permitted to be.

What law there is is their own law (*auto-nomy*), the law of their own inner constitution. To say the forces obey any law at all is but a moralistic way of saying that they are what they are, that they do what they do, for such is the force of which they consist.[65] The forces do not obey anything, do not re-act, do not act *ab extra*. What they do is their own doing, their own being, their own willing, their own fate.

To this model of difference there corresponds a certain "giving" and generosity. Here to give means to give of one's overflow, of one's fullness. This giving is like the giving of the sun, which cannot hold back its heat and light, which would be nothing if it did not have us to spill all over.[66] Giving is the radiating of what cannot contain itself, of what, having worked itself up into a considerable heat, cannot hold itself back. It must flow out and flow over everything around it. This is its fate and its necessity, which it wills and dearly loves.

Giving is giving what one has too much of, what one cannot keep or contain, what one must in any case part with. Giving is spilling over, the generous expenditure of oneself at the point of optimal life, at the peak of life, when it has reached the fullness that is allotted to it, become what it is, become full and pregnant with new life in a wondrous self-impregnation. This rich, ripe, full, pulsating life donates everything to the cause of new life in a final act of death and donation and parturition, of going under in the very act of going over.

Giving does not respond to anything outside itself, to *other* forces, for that would be slavish, reactive, re-sponsive. Giving does not arise in answer to anything outside, anything that puts a demand upon the giver, anything that has power over the giver and makes a demand upon it. That would lower the energy of the giver, demean and degrade it, separate it from its force. Generosity must be wholly *ab intra*, from within its own immanent energies. It cannot be an answer, a response, a reaction, or any form of passivity. It does not pass under a demand, submit to something from without which lays claim to it. Giving is not laid claim to, does not repay a debt, does not owe anything. The purity of its giving is that it does this on its own, without external prompting, without owing—*schulden*, *schuldig*—anything to anything. Otherwise it would be slavish, ignoble, unfree, guilty.

This produces an odd result. For this philosophy of force and *energeia* reproduces with surprising exactness an old medieval quandary about God, about how a being that is *actus purus* could ever respond to our needs or answer our prayers or be in any way responsive or responsible while yet not falling into a kind of passivity and thereby compromising its character as pure act. The action of God must always be *ab intra*; it can never be *ab extra*. The solution the medievals found was to invoke a Neoplatonic model of generosity as overflow of the sort one sees defended here.[67] So for Deleuze the old God, the theology of God as pure act, is not quite dead. What would be interesting, what might astonish Deleuze, would be a new theology, one where God *suffers*. Another possibility: just stop trying to be like God (pure act, purely active) and be more like Abraham.

This generosity is not in response to a request arising from something else, for its only responsibility is to itself, to become what it is.[68] It does not have debts or promises to fulfill. It makes promises only to itself. That is the one and only responsibility it tolerates. That is the nobility of this giving: giving proceeds from a being capable of making promises only to itself, of being endebted only to itself, and it promises itself it will be generous to everything else, everything that is less than it, everything upon which it should shine, whatever is lower and needs the warmth and light that it radiates. What is lower than the will cannot lay claim to it, but the will promises itself to be generous. Its generosity is not slavish, it does not answer a demand. Giving is its own doing, its own being, its own radiance, in virtue of which it gives to what is lesser, lower, colder, and darker. It does not hate, which is reactive, or pity, which is slavish. It just gives; it gives of its overflow because that is the very nobility of its being, the very being of its nobility.

It gives like a great, kind, generous benefactor, like a wealthy but generous lord, not because the common folk around him have any claim upon his wealth. That would be a tasteless, unpleasant thought, a very vulgar conception, a completely plebeian way to conceive a gift. That would be a Jewish, Christian, womanly, socialist, Chandala way to think. The recipients of this giver's gift do not deserve what is given to them. There is no question here of deserts, or of just deserts. That would not be a gift but an obligation. It is testimony to the greatness, the nobility, of this giving that it gives because it gives, that it does not respond to anything, but gives by its own inner generosity and immanent will to spill over.

If one were to speak of "justice" here, then justice is the sheer overflowing richness of expenditure. When the will spends and expends itself it does not pay back a debt. That would be demeaning, ignoble—and unjust. More *Schuldigkeit*. Justice for it is the justness by which it spends itself, of itself, without exterior determination and enslavement. Justice is the order of rank, that the higher gives to the lower, that the lower receives and the higher expends; that is just the way it should be. It would be rank injustice, an injustice of rank, were the fuller, richer, overfull, overrich one somehow to come under the influence of what is poorer, needy, weak, indigent. Heaven would cry out against such an inversion, such an overturning, such a revolutionary perversion of the order of giving, the order of justice, the order of rank.

Heteromorphism is, I would say—I am trying to be delicate—somewhat phallic and orgasmic, with all this self-dissemination and giving of one's overflow. Even pregnancy itself here is the issue of self-impregnation, self-insemination followed by self-dissemination. Now let there be no mistake about it, I am not against orgasms or other forms of joyful wisdom. Far from it. *Cuique suum placitum.*[69] I have no mission.[70] I am a simple clerk, trying to make an academic distinction about two different kinds of difference.

In the first sort of difference, *heteromorphic* difference, *heteros* means multiplicity (*diversitas*). But in the second form of difference, *heteronomic* difference, *heteros* is not multiplicity but alterity—which is different, a different kind of difference (*alter*).

Here, in this second kind of difference, everything is precisely *ab extra*, from without, so that heteronomic difference is the almost perfect opposite of heteromorphic difference. At least it moves in the opposite direction. Totalization is not destroyed from within, by an uncontrollable dispersion which the system is helpless to contain, but from without, by an unencompassable other which throws the same into confusion, so that the same and the other cannot fold into a unity. Difference is not a matter of an eruption from within (*ab intra*) but of disruption from without. In each case rupture and the blocking of totalization, but in the first case eruptive rupture and in the second case disruptive rupture. Not a volcanic action, from within, but more like a meteor—something very exorbitant—from out of nowhere, shocking us out of orbit. In each case there is a de-centering, in the one case from within and in the other case from without. Something foreign, strange, other, *alter*, invades, overcomes, overtakes the same and holds it in its power.

In heteronomism there is no squeamishness about re-sponsiveness, no fear of looking like a slave, a lower type, doglike, reactive. Here everything turns on openness and responsiveness to what comes to us from without (*ab extra*), from on high, in short from the other. Here everything turns on a respect for difference, for the other one. In heteronomism, one is not trying to be like God (*actus purus*), but like Abraham, under the law, before the law, and one lets the other occupy the position of the Most High. There is no squinting here over obligation, no anxiety about gravity and heavy weights, no hand-wringing about being tied down. Here the love of difference is the love of the *other* and being held hostage by the other is not considered demeaning, degrading, ignoble but rather uplifting and challenging work. The other is not rival, competitor, something to be appropriated, but the law and the measure by which freedom measures itself. Freedom is frightened not by the weight of responsibility but by the murderousness of its own aggressive forces, which love to dominate others. Freedom is concerned not with its own free discharge, but rather with letting the other be free. The weight of the other, the ponderousness of what comes *ab extra* is precisely what swings against the same, shattering freedom and decentering the subject. In heteromorphism, the aim is freedom from inhibition and blockage, freedom from the weight of being, from the weight of values thousands of years old, from the old God, from Being and Truth, from everything that weighs the will down and makes it heavy, grave, from everything that holds it in check and makes it obey, everything that prevents it from dancing. But in heteronomic difference, freedom is suspect, suspended, held in question, because it is aggressive, self-accumulative, and eventually, finally, murderous. Heteronomism wants to let the other be free while one is oneself held hostage. It defers to the differend, is held in the spell of the differend, of what differs from the same and puts the same into question.

In heteromorphic difference, the forces are bent on *self*-accumulation, on aggressively gathering themselves together, so that heteromorphism is an autonomism, an auto-nomic, endo-thermic economy, an auto-economics. To be sure, and this merits emphasis, *autos* here does not mean the interiority of a subject, the "inwardness" of "consciousness," of an *ego cogito* or an *ego volo*.[71] *Autos* here means rather a gathering of forces in a single place, in this place, here. *Autos* means a plurality of forces dominated by one dominant force, which forges a temporary constellation that is held together only for so long, and only very precariously. *Autos* means an alliance which is doomed to fail precisely because of the delicacy of its network, the intricacy of its constellating system, the rarity of its breed (*Zucht*). But always *its* intricacy, *its* splendid configuration, *its* breeding, not the other's.

The difference between these differences, between heteromorphism and heteronomy, is the difference between *alius* and *alter*. *Alius* means different in the sense of *diversitas, discrepans, dissensio*. Different people do different things (*alii alia faciunt*), and they do them differently (*aliter*). *Alius* is very heteromorphic. *Alter*, on the other hand, means the other one of two, *the* other one, with a force of singularity, not multiplicity, not one more among many others, but just one, just that other one, over there. Alterity means being one-on-one with the other (*der Andere*).[72]

But *alter* also has a dangerous, wondrous, even fatal ambiguity. For it can mean one more just like the first, *noch einmal,* a second one of the same type, as in *alter ego,* and so it can land you back in autonomy and egology, which is the famous lesson of Husserl's *Fifth Meditation* and the very nemesis Levinas is always combating under the names of violence and ontology.[73] *Alter* can take on either of these meanings, and it makes a difference which one is at play. Heteronomic difference wants to center on *alter simpliciter,* that is its desire. It desires the one who is simply different, not a second of the same, but the other, simply, and, as Levinas likes to say, the Other which is infinitely, absolutely other—which is, I will also argue, too pious and problematic an expression.

Heteromorphic difference loves the theatre, the show, a plethora of masks, plays within plays, disguises, masquerades, pseudonyms, assumed forms, temporary roles. It makes a fantastic, carnivalesque display of differences, variety, and variegation. Heteromorphism is the love of different forms. Heteronomic difference is self-effacing and makes itself invisible. It loves invisibility, infinite recesses, recessed infinity, and it stays away from theatres. It loves what cannot make a show at all, what is embarrassed at its impoverished appearance. It is taciturn, sincere, with a bowed head, without dissemblance, *honnête.* Heteronomism is the love of the rule of the other, in the singular.

Heteromorphism is gay, happy, *fröhlich,* impious, insouciant, a lover of carnivals and gaiety. It shows up wherever there is a show, wherever multiplicity is celebrated, wherever there is a celebration at all. It loves intoxicating novelty, ever new forms, brilliant colors, splendor, whatever is splendid. It is experimental, iconoclastic and ever in search of new icons. Heteronomy on the other hand is very pious, grave, and serious and it steers clear of graven images. It respects the law and bows ceremoniously before the other, with oriental courtesy. The other one who calls to us, who calls upon us, fills it with respect.

One might say that heteromorphism is very Dionysiac, exuberant and intoxicated, whereas heteronomism is very rabbinic, sober as a judge or a rabbi. Heteromorphism wears gay colors and strange hats, whereas heteronomism has a long beard and a black hat and coat.

Heteronomism is respectful, responsive, and responsible, even religious. It is a lover of one family of "re-" words, which emblematize the look it re-turns, sends back (re-) to the other, the re-gard it has for the other, and the mark of its heteronomic posture and immeasurable courtesy, its re-spect and re-sponsiveness. Heteromorphism loves only a few re- words, like "re-lease" (*ent-laden*), which means disburden, discharge, and spill over, and "re-petition" (*Wiederholen*) and "re-turn" (*Wiederkehr*), which means to love the circle, the cycle, the infinite affirmation. But even re-turn and re-petition fill it with dread, nausea, and despair, for return smacks of the breakdown of difference, of *taedium vitae,* of no more difference and novelty, of homomorphism.

Heteromorphism cannot oblige the *alter;* it cannot accommodate an obligation to the other, to whatever comes to it *ab extra*. Response, religion, regard for the other are all reactive, slavish, doglike, Königsbergian, a lowering of its vitality, ascetic impulses killing off its affirmative instincts, its self-affirmative drives. Although heteromorphism exposes the fiction of the conscious subject, it always wants to occupy the position of the sender, never of the addressee, to put it in Lyotardian terms. Its only obligations and responsibilities are to itself (*autos*), to shine with glory and to make itself as noble, as beautiful, as unique, as different (*alius*) as possible, to fill itself with itself, to accumulate forces, until it reaches the optimum, the point of fullness, dehiscence, profusion.[74]

Heteronomism on the other hand is very obliging, always very much obliged to the other; it is ever the receiver of what the other (*alter*) sends its way and is devoted to its obligations. The only thing it discharges is its obligations and the only obligations it has are to the other.

BETWEEN PIETY AND IMPIETY

The more I considered the terms of this distinction the clearer it became to me that it cannot be a matter of choosing between them, of resolutely and decisively deciding for one and making a clean cut from the other.[75] I found myself adrift in undecidability, the ground shifting beneath my feet. You see then why I have been given such an odd image to meditate upon, why this prankster signed his name "Abraham of Paris." Dionysus and the rabbi constantly pass back and forth into each other and form a single, if polyvalent, figure. I am enamored of *both* the Dionysian festival and rabbinic solemnity, of carnivals and medieval monasteries, of celebrations and solemn rites, of gay laughter and the soft hush of monastic matins. I could never live in a place where there is no change of climate. There is more than one day in the week and I do not want always to wear my Sunday best or always to knock around looking unemployed.

I endorse jewgreek difference and diversity. But that is to admit that instead of a single *Grundbestimmung* moods can change in a flash, go from day to night, that beneath laughter and good cheer there lurks a most sober, meditative, even melancholy frame of mind. I favor the idea of having many moods, of being tuned in many ways. I love the first book of the *Poetics* and I weep over the loss of the second. The very idea of heteromorphism, after all, so embraces the idea of many forms that one can be inclined—*inter alia*—also to be very grave; a person of deadly seriousness, of church-dark brooding, no stranger to altarity and tears.[76] I understand why Johannes Climacus could spend his Sunday afternoons lingering around cemeteries.[77] *Dies irae* is one of my favorite tunes and I keep a collection of *Requiems* from Mozart to Andrew Lloyd Webber, to which I have occasionally been discovered tapping my feet. In short, as a heteromorphicist, one can be—*inter alia*—also a man of the most serious solemnities.

On this point—of miscegenation—I am influenced by Lyotard and Derrida. They are both heteromorphic lovers of many genres and disseminative plurality, yet dedicated, *inter alia*, to the Law. They share an impious belief in the Law and a belief in justice as impiety, which is exactly how I would organize my treatise on justice. Lyotard has put it best:[78]

> The law should always be respected with humor because it cannot be completely respected, except at the price of giving credence to the idea that it is the very mode of linking heterogeneities together, that it has the necessity of total Being. This humor aims at the heterogeneity which persists beneath and despite the legitimation. . . . The respecting of the event which comic laughter is should be granted its ontological dignity, and the tragic tear should be put back in its place, which is merely the highest one (Book II of the *Poetics* did this, only for that book then to be lost).

All this ought not to be mistaken for a merely philistine interest in church music or in medieval architecture and still less as a mark of indecision. Undecidability is not the opposite of decision but a condition of its possibility, a way of underlining the difficulty of decision. Undecidability recognizes the wavering between the disjuncta in any either/or and the lack of a clean break (*de-cidere*) between them. To be capable of choice, of making the cut, ought not to mean masking the confusion and the ambiguity which beset our choices (before, during, and after) and the impossibility of decontaminating one disjunct or the other.[79]

My painting, a figure of undecidability, is meant to keep me straight, i.e., not straight, off-balance, on the fence, straddling the slash between Greek and Jew. It is very useful to distinguish heteromorphism and heteronomism, but we must beware of instituting still another tiresome binarity which will eventually come unstrung. Factical life is a messy affair and the source of the most troublesome difficulties. Binary terms are inevitably contaminated by each other, each inwardly disturbed by the other.

Abraham of Paris is a tricky hermeneutic messenger (and the closest I will get to a god sent to save me), who has been sent my way to break the spell of "infinity" and keep me in tune with factical life. I distrust philosophies of infinity—I who find my factical feet fixed firmly in the *terra firma* of the finite—whether they take the form of infinite affirmation, of affirmation *ad infinitum*, or of infinite alterity, of the infinite excess of the other. I cannot accept the unbounded infinite affirmation of Deleuzian apocalypticism, or the infinite alterity of Levinas's propheticism. Both of these views proceed for me from the dream of being without *différance*, from a kind of neo-Neoplatonism of being-to-excess which lacks the restraint of *différance*. I find myself, factically speaking, moving in the limited space between these two infinities.[80] That space of finitude is the field in which my odd "Heterologist" roams about.

I myself am of both a Dionysiac and a rabbinic disposition but I hasten to assure the reader that I do not have in mind anything like an *Aufhebung* of the two positions, some sort of peaceful lifting up and reconciliation of the two into a higher unity. I have the sense to keep watch for that ominous Greco-German eagle. I advocate a continual mutual disruption that refuses to let either position get securely in place and thus set in motion the dialectic operation. I do not think there really *is* any such thing as heteromorphism or heteronomism, that any such "identities" as these ever get established. Hence it is impossible for the gears of the dialectic ever to engage and weave them into a synthetic mesh. I see only the continual mutual disturbance of each side by the other, which makes it impossible for the dialectical progress of the spirit to make a single step forward. The strategy behind *différance* is to see to it that no thesis or *positio* ever gets firmly enough into position to begin its course of opposition and composition. No dialectical relief is ever attained. The dialectical machine is jammed from the start, because heteromorphism and heteronomism never really are what they are, and hence never even get to the starting gate of the dialectical course. They are not identities but differences, and so each is invaded and disrupted by the other.

For heteromorphism is too pluralistic to exclude grave and solemn keepers of the law from its premises, and heteronomism is too obliging to the other to exclude these multicolor polymorphs from attending synogogue if they wish.

Dionysus and the rabbi are never far apart.[81] Dionysus always manages to get into the rabbinic beard, to break him up, to cause him to erupt in laughter, just when he was trying to be deadly serious, by telling him a few kabbalistic jokes, tickling his very considerable Hassidic sense of humor,[82] endlessly inventing new midrash until the heartiest heteromorph begs for relief. Even so, any rabbi worthy of his name is capable of stopping Dionysus in his tracks. In the midst of the most intoxicating exuberance, a rabbi could sober Dionysus up on the spot with his rabbinic appreciation of tragic suffering.

Dionysus and the rabbi are each tragic-comic figures, equally jewgreek, each full of tears and laughter, tears of laughter, trying to convert tears into laughter. Two hermeneuts with a taste for tricks; two tricksters with a taste for hermeneutics. Tears/cheers.[83] They are each lovers of plurality and novelty and not in the least loyal to Eleatic boredom, which is why I love both figures. They spend their lives trying to meditate not on why Being and Thought belong together but on how they pull apart. Rabbis love multiple interpretations over which to argue and all forms of novelty and creationist innovation (*ex nihilo*); they hide a wide heteromorphic smile beneath their beards.

So it is imperative, in my view, a serious obligation that weighs heavily upon us, to break up rabbis or anyone else who think they are (or have) "the ear of the unpresentable."[84] This is above all true of Levinas, who loves to burden us with infinite weights and unlimited obligations and who is against pagan impiousness. The same thing is true, *mutatis mutandis*, of Heidegger, who, as Lyotard says, thinks that Being

> wants to phrase itself through you as its go-between, that it wants something
> from you because it would like to be itself. . . . [But] It wasn't waiting for you.
> You come when it arrives. The occurrence is not the Lord. The pagans know
> this and laugh over this edifying confusion.[85]

The only way to greet the thought that the Spirit has taken up residence in Prussia, or that Being needs you or me, or that it needs Greek and German in particular, or that the Lord has chosen one people, or one gender, with whom to cut a special deal (a "covenant"), is with pagan laughter. I would myself say that Being needs every warm body and sharp tongue it can appropriate and that the Lord cuts a bargain with everybody who is willing to deal.

My impiousness demands that I celebrate piety as one more form of life and my piety demands *pietas*[86] in the face of everything different. I stand decisively, resolutely, right on the slash of im/piety, in a kind of archi-impiety.

Piety unbroken by laughter spills blood. Excommunication, extermination, execution, exile, exclusion, *extra ecclesia nulla salus est*:[87] that is the issue and outcome of pure piety and of a preoccupation with saving powers. I do not want to be "saved." I just want to make it through the day and hopefully to help someone else make it too. If someone insists on saving me, I insist it be with laughter. When I retire I intend to write a treatise entitled "critique of pure piety" which I hope to fill with a collection of excellent humor.

But if heteronomic piety without laughter makes me uneasy, heteromorphic gaiety without obligation is no less disturbing. In my retirement I will owe the reader a "critique of pure piety," followed by a "critique of pure heteromorphism." Perhaps it will turn out to be a trilogy, capped off by a "critique of pure purity," *Kritik der reinen Reinheit*, of any sort of purity, racial, spiritual, intellectual, political, ideological, etc. I am not against a certain amount of purity. I favor just a bit of purity, a dash of purity here and there, so long as it is tempered and blended with other things.

I have said that heteromorphism of itself (if it has an itself) is—I am trying to be delicate—phallocentric. When this swollen constellation of forces bursts open, flowing out and spilling over, releasing itself in the most explosive and pleasurable discharge—when that is described as a woman, as Ariadne, one cannot contain a smile. She must be a hermaphrodite.

Again, when this force, which refuses all action *ab extra*, which never responds or is responsible except to itself, to its own noble nature, which always initiates action from within, which is very auto-erotic, I think—I am still trying to be delicate—when this force, this constellation of forces, is said to be generous because it gives of its overflow, then I am inclined to remark that this is only one kind of giving and generosity.[88] I suppose it is somewhat generous to give of one's overflow, to give what it gives great joy (*jouissement*) to release, to give what one cannot in any case keep for oneself anymore. I suppose that such a man deserves a modest round of applause. But I would be loath to give this fellow much of a tax break for charitable contributions.

I have to say that the old jewgreek narrative of the widow who gives two copper coins, even though she does not have enough for herself, elicits a more profound bow from me and much deeper admiration. The widow—a very Levinasian figure—does not give out of her overflow and abundance (*ek tou perisseuontos*) but out of her poverty and privation (*ek tes hystereseos autes*), and she gives everything she needs for herself.[89] She does not first take the precaution to build herself up to the point of breaking open and breaking asunder with her overripe, overrich plenitude. She is actually a little on the thin side, a bit drawn and not very well attired. According to the story she is very needy and indigent herself, yet she gives what little she has, all of which she really needs to live on (*olon ton bion autes*). She is a fool, no doubt, a fool for giving and forgiving, for mercy and for justice. She gives not of her excess but of her very substance.[90] I do not wish any ill to this overrich fellow (whom I do not imagine to be very trim and lean), but in the category of gift-giving my hat is off to the widow.

The widow is a rabbinic *persona*, one of Levinas's favorite paradigms, not only as a giver of what she needs for herself, but also as the figure of the one in need, part of the famous triad from Exodus, "the widow, the orphan, the stranger," around which Levinas has organized all his work. The widow is a figure of responsiveness and responsibility, of answering calls and of calls to be answered, of responding to the other (*alter*), of a radical alterity and a "radical altruism," which is Wyschogrod's definition of a "saint" and of the postmodern streak in saintliness.[91] The notion of a "postmodern saint" or a saintly postmodern—a hero of alterity who gets altar rites[92]—is sufficiently ridiculous, sufficiently bizarre, sufficiently miscegenated and unpresentable as to elicit my deepest admiration. That is the sort of thing that belongs to the hermaphroditic, Dionysio-rabbinic, twelvetone disposition (*Stimmung*) of the *Befindlichkeit* I wish to cultivate. It is a little like the uncanny creatures in (Saint) Genet's novels, reproduced in the right-hand column of *Glas*, transvestites with names like nuns, who gum up the gears of the dialectic, and whom Wyschogrod calls "saints of depravity."

Now of course you could always say that the widow is consumed by her ascetic ideals. That no doubt is why she is so thin and looks a little consumptive. You could say she has a bent, distorted, serpentine will to power, which has found a way to make the strong and the powerful ill, to make them feel their health as sickness. She is a resentful, dishonest creature, a tarantula, who wants to make her weakness into a twisted form of strength. The advantage of that explanation is that you get yourself out from under the story and you do not feel compelled to give what you need for yourself, although you might later on, when things are not so tight, give of your overflow. In general, I would say that the problem that besets this time of greed, this epoch of protecting the rich against the poor, this age of defending the strong against the weak, is not the secret, serpentine motives of giving to the poor or helping the needy. The problem lies in the indifference with which obligation is treated, the silence, invisibility, and lack of idiom with which the neediest and most destitute people are cloaked.

The heteromorphic critique of responsibility, of responding and responsiveness, is—I am groping for the right word—irresponsible, in a literal sense. It is unresponsive, unmoved by the call of the other (*alter*), the response to which it says is essentially reactive. The sense of generosity it favors is that of overflow, of reaching a point where the richest and most well endowed will eventually overflow—and trickle down—on to the rest.[93] Now, for one thing, it would be quite exhausting, and a little unrealistic too, as we said above, to expect always to be active, to be essentially or exclusively active, never to be reactive and never to catch up on one's sleep. But the essential point is, if I may say so, that being "active" or "reactive" is not an essence, not essentially good or bad, higher or lower, not in itself (*quoad se, an sich*). "Active" and "reactive" are economies and so they have many meanings, depending on how and when and where they are deployed. As an advocate of factical life, and a lover of polymorphic, polyvalent pluralism, I do not subscribe to the notion of essence at all, whether essence is taken as a thoughtless nominative Latin *essentia* or as a deep and profound German verbal *Wesen*. I subscribe instead to pragmatic situations, diverse contextual deployments, universes of phrasing, meaning as use. Active and reactive mean many things for me, as many as we need, too many to nail down or set forth in some order of rank, to categorize, systematize, and tabularize as higher/lower, healthy/sick, noble/detestable, etc. Active and reactive mean what they mean in the singularity of the situation in which one finds them.

In certain situations activeness and agency should be made to tremble. When agents produce patients, people who suffer, I want to let agency waver in insecurity, to let autonomy and spontaneity and creativity and freedom feel their own murderousness—instead of singing hymns to them. Reactiveness, on the other hand, is not a bad thing at all, not in itself, if it has an itself (I will need to include a "critique of pure *Ansichsein*" in my trilogy). Knowing how to react, having good reactions—reacting spontaneously, reacting with insight, reacting with generosity—to the demands that are placed on me by the other, answering the call that is sent my way from without, coming under the influence of what is other—all of that seems to me to belong to the facticity of factical life, to the relations of power/obligation that spring up like the crocuses of spring. What draws me out of myself and knocks me off my pins, what comes over me and calls me beyond myself, that is a salutary opening and ecstasy. It is my obligation. Having the wherewithal to respond to what a new or otherwise difficult situation demands of me (a certain *phronesis*) is no mean achievement, nothing to demean. Indeed it is something that all heteromorphs worthy of their name—everybody from Aristotle to Derrida and Lyotard—would want to include in their repertoire.

Having good reactions, I would say, is a sign of someone very noble (*edel*), who deserves a tip of our hat. There are masters of action and masters of reaction, there are slaves of action and slaves of reaction. Indeed there are slaves whom I prefer to masters and masters I prefer to slaves. There are as many crossed lines and blurred distinctions as one has the patience to sort out. If you took enough time, practically everything would blur, and very nearly everything would require scare quotes.[94] Fortunately we do not have the time to cause so much confusion, i.e., to let *différance* do its work.

The point of serving as obligation's poet is to make this sort of unresponsive irresponsibility look as bad as possible and to make responsibility look as good as we possibly can. The story of the widow who gives up her two copper pennies is a paradigmatic piece of the sort of jewgreek poetics I endorse. By giving up what she herself needs to live (*ton bion*) the widow raises her life up a notch over those who give what they do not need, who are content to trickle down. By looking out for others, not only for herself, she acquires a look that commands our respect. I do not recommend calling the police on this overfull fellow who keeps overflowing. But do not ask me to stretch my admiration for him, or to call him a higher type, or a man of the future, or a creator, or a new beginning, or to will his eternal return. When it comes to gift-giving, he is no match for the widow. Nietzsche thinks that one should wear gloves if you touch this widow, or hold your nose. These Chandala stories from the poetics of obligations offend his sensitive nose.[95] I am inclined to think, *pace* Nietzsche, that if you or I or Nietzsche touched her, or if this overrich fellow brushed against her skin and bones, we would feel the power flow from her to us, down to us, for she comes from on high.

The widow puts everyone in his place who wants to go to the head of the table or sit always in the sender position. She puts us on the receiving end, confronts us with infinite recesses, with infinity itself, according to Levinas. That may be an exaggeration, a trifle hyperbolic, but it is a good story, a classic jewgreek narrative, a powerful piece of the poetics of disasters, and it puts pure heteromorphism in its place, situates it and disturbs it from within.

But "[t]his sounds almost like seriousness,"[96] and one must be vigilant about the spirit of seriousness and the power of piety. I follow the advice of Constantin Constantius: on my mantel I keep a coach horn—the emblem of heteromorphic diversity, because it cannot make the same sound twice—just under my painting of the Dionysiac rabbi.[97]

FOUR

In the Names of Justice

MEMORY

Like Johannes Climacus, I too visit cemeteries on my day off,[1] especially old cemeteries. I read the barely legible names of faded lives, saying them out loud or reading them quietly. Dates of birth and death, the last traces of the joys and sorrows that filled distant days, frail vestiges of a long life or of lives cut short at birth, in childhood, in childbirth. Old, worn names etched on listing, storm-beaten stones: magnificent lives and damaged lives, commonplace joys and small sorrows, all marked by death's dark disaster, all on the edge of oblivion.

People who make rubbings of old tombstones in order to restore those old names do more to recall the meaning of Being (if there were such a thing) than all German philosophers combined.

Having been abandoned by Being (*Seinsverlassenheit*), I have attached myself to proper names,[2] to everything that Being quits, to everything Being leaves behind, all its remnants and leftovers, the jewgreek fragments that played no part in the First Beginning; that cannot get a reservation for the Other Beginning.

Having attached myself to proper names, I have (in return) abandoned Being. "Not Being, but one being, one time."[3]

The fields of factical life are marked by proper names.

My attention has turned—this is my *Kehre*—to beings with proper names, with dates and places. Sometimes unbearable names like Auschwitz and Buchenwald, Salvador (which means Saviour) and South Africa—and all other such names "equally abominable,"[4] names that sound alarms in the midst of factical life. Sometimes forgotten names, lost in remote places in distant times—which is what gives oblivion, forgottenness (*Vergessenheit*) a cutting edge.

Oblivion means to suffer in oblivion, to suffer namelessly, helplessly. The oblivion of Being, on the other hand, is a fantastic invention of fantastic thinking, a Greco-German phantasy, which I think is best forgotten. My theory of *Seinsvergessenheit*: Forget Being!

A name gives a victim an idiom, at least the start of an idiom, and a chance to sound an alarm. The best monument to victims is just to write down their names, one by one, to make a long, detailed list of the proper names, all sixty thousand—and to drop the speeches.[5] What more eloquent memorial, what more moving way to remember, than that?

Forget Being, actively cultivate the forgetting, in order to remember, to make room for the memory of proper names, which is the element and the language of obligations.

As a part of my service as obligation's clerk, I will need to write a short grammar of proper names, nothing that would require a prodigious head, just something to enable me to breathe in the element of proper names. This will be a brief *grammatica practiva* (we have had enough of the *grammatica speculativa*). One of the principal paradigms in my grammar will be the following:

Abraham!
Me voici!

Notice that the first phrase is a proper name used as an imperative, and the second phrase employs the accusative (and in French). (As to whether there is an inner spiritual connection between Hebrew and French, or whether the grammar of obligation must take the form of a Franco-Hebrew grammatology, my *Grammatica* will venture no opinion.) It will emerge in my *Grammatica* that, in an obligation, both the addressor and the addressee must ultimately bear proper names. Obligations are communications between proper names and proper names provide the element in which obligations are communicated.

That would mean you cannot have an obligation to Being or the Spirit or the People, nor can Being or the Spirit oblige anything. Being, Spirit, History, Man: the playthings of Greco-German mythophilosophizing, which is my somewhat free translation of *die Sache des Denkens* (which I claim, as a translation, is *wahr* if not *richtig*). Nothing happens in or to Being and Spirit. What happens happens to beings that bear up or bend under what is happening. Being cannot suffer a disaster, or suffer oblivion, because it does not suffer at all. Being and Spirit are mytho-super-Subjects, the upshot of totalizing attempts to describe what is happening, which end up abandoning what is happening, leaving those of us with proper names to face the worst. History and Being, History and Spirit, the History of Being, the History of Spirit: so many tall tales and meta-narratives, gigantic[6] stories that forsake the *minima moralia* of damaged lives,[7] the minute scraps and remnants Being leaves behind.

A disaster is a damaged life, damaged beyond repair.

Being shows no interest in damaged lives; they are none of Being's business (*Sache*).[8] Indeed, many bleeding bodies may well be a sign that Being or the Spirit is on the mend, or on the march, healing itself and making itself Whole or Holy, getting ready for the Other Beginning, while the dead are left to bury the dead.[9] Forget Being. There is nothing to remember. Replace it with a mnemo-technique for remembering proper names.

Being does not have a proper name. It is nobody, neither this one nor that, *ne uter*, neutral.

One of the more interesting experiments in the history of metaphysics was the medieval attempt to say that Being is someone after all, *esse est deus*, that God is both Being (*esse subsistens*) and Someone (*persona*). That very beautiful idea failed as an argument, although it succeeded in providing an idiom for a form of life, which is all that you can ask of an idiom. It was worth trying to think Being beyond neutrality, and the medievals made a fascinating attempt to say "You" to "Being," to bring father Abraham and father Parmenides together in the same room, to get them to speak the same language. That is what Thomas Aquinas tried. Here is Thomas Aquinas's version of the pragmatics of the exchange between Moses and God, in a somewhat free translation (my Hebrew is rusty) of Exodus 3:13-14, one of the most important bits of Hebrew text in medieval metaphysics:

Who shall I say has sent me?
I am Being. So tell them Being has sent you.

Thomas tries to frame this exchange between Being and Moses in terms of *Ich und Du*, so long as Moses understands that that is as much as he is entitled to know, that he is not going to learn God's truly proper name, for that is none of his business.[10]

Near the end of the medieval experiment, when it had just about spun itself out, Duns Scotus recommended that we empty the word *ens* and return to *haecceitas*. *Haecceitas* is what is happening, the sphere of factical life. *Haecceitas* is where we are, that from which we never manage to depart, with which we must always begin. The theory of *haecceitas* is one of the reasons Scotus could count both Gerard Manley Hopkins and the young Heidegger among his admirers.

The medieval experiment, which was much admired by a good Protestant like Kierkegaard and his socius, Johannes Climacus, belongs to the argument of Johannes de Silentio, that it would be too terrible to imagine were Being a *neutrum*; ergo it is not so. My idea is to confess that I know no way beyond the neutrality and indifference of the stars, to acknowledge that obligation is not safe, and, for better or worse, to take up the study of proper names—which means to avoid the highly dangerous business of thinking that Being has called upon us for a service, particularly to give it a Greco-German name.

There is/*es gibt* only (but this is quite a lot) the plurality of particulars. Even *es gibt* itself can lure us into the trap of *das 'Es'*, with a German capital and the mythologizing of the *Geben* of *Es gibt*. *Es geben*, there are, is only slightly better. I am always looking for the loosest, most minimal grammar possible, the least constraining idiom, in order to let things happen, in order to hang loose. The idiom of "events," of the uncontrollable plurality of what is happening, is better, looser, less likely to get in the way. To say there are/it gives events, is just to say that events happen.

That is why I have turned to the study of proper names, which is the element of obligations. They allow us to say when and where obligation is happening, and to whom, and they help us to remember.

A true and accurate account of obligations would be like the old idea of the "book of life," a list of the names of everybody, with every proper name, stretching back to time immemorial and stretching forth to all who are to come, so that no one is forgotten or unanticipated (which would require a large contingent of bookkeepers, all full time).[11]

But such a great *liber obligationum* is what the deconstruction of ethics would come down to, if you could ever finish it. If you let *différance* have its way in ethics, you would never stop writing, because you would have to write down the names of everyone, one by one, and say what is happening with them. That is the element of obligations, by which I mean the space of obligation, where obligations happen—down low, well below the range of philosophical conceptuality. That is why deconstruction must write from below, at the threshold of the utterly idiosyncratic. Deconstruction situates itself on the threshold between the universal and the singular, the common and the proper, in between. (If Hegel is in the left column, and Genet is in the right column, where is Derrida? Nowhere? In the empty space between the columns?) Deconstruction situates itself in the im/possible attempt to write proper names, the im/possible attempt to remember them.

Deconstruction consorts with the irreducible plurality and im/possible heteromorphism of proper names. Deconstruction is excessively heteromorphic, and not a little heteronomic.

EFFANINEFFABLES

Proper names have always been too much—or too little?—for philosophy (which is metaphysics) and ethics (which is philosophy).

A proper name is the name of a singular event, or a singular constellation of events. It may be a personal name, like "Thomas Jefferson" or "Gandhi," or a place, like "Plymouth Rock" or "Alabama," or a thing, like the Berlin Wall, or a date, like August 6, 1945. It is the sort of thing you do not pluralize. You cannot say there are some of them; once you do you rob the proper name of its propriety.

In classical metaphysics the philosophical problematic posed by proper names was most clearly approximated by the enigma posed by "individuals," for which, it openly confessed, it lacked both the logic and the grammar.[12] A proper name is not to be identified with an individual, partly because an individual suggests a classical metaphysics, an individual thing or substance, but chiefly because a proper name may well announce a constellation of individuals—of time, place, people, things—like "Auschwitz," which is a disastrous constellation.[13]

Classical metaphysics foundered on the problem of individuals with almost perfect precision, signaling an opening for deconstruction, a certain trembling within the classical systems of exactly the sort predicted by *différance*. Metaphysics suffers the systematic misfortune of containing what it cannot contain, of harboring what it cannot protect (e.g., obligations, individuals), like a man who has swallowed something he cannot digest.

The individual, according to the most classical axiomatic, is ineffable (*individuum ineffabile est*). That is to announce with admirable rigor a breach in the surface of philosophy. It formulates a principle for what falls outside principles, a covering law for what law cannot cover, for a kind of out-law. It announces with all desirable clarity that the individual is both necessary and impossible.

The individual—who is, after all, very small, no more than a bit or a fragment—is more than metaphysics can handle. Philosophy founders on something quite small; it chokes on a small fragment, a bit of microeconomics. For to understand metaphysics, which takes itself to be the science of what is real, one must understand that the only thing that is real, the individual—*sola individua existunt*—is the one thing of which it cannot speak.

That puts ethics, which is a (certain) metaphysics (of morals), a metaphysics charged with making obligation safe, in a difficult position. For the idea behind ethics is to have something to say about the particular choices and particular situations in which individuals find themselves. When Aristotle, at the beginning of its history, said not to expect too much precision from ethics,[14] he marked off quite precisely the beginning of the end, the delimitability, the deconstructibility of ethics.

Writing a discourse on individuals is very difficult. It is too much for me, and too little for philosophy. Such a discourse is in a double bind, tossing back and forth between two intolerable binds. On the one hand, we cannot speak about the individual, because the individual is ineffable and falls beneath the repeatable, universal terms in which language trades. On the other hand, we must talk about individuals—about people with proper names, e.g.—because the individual is the only thing that exists, and from time to time we desire that our discourse have something to do with what exists. What exists is, after all, among the most pressing concerns of factical life. I cannot speak about the individual, but I must and I do so all the time, since proper names happen. An intolerable constraint (I cannot but I do) coupled with an impossible demand (I must but I am unable). That is what people who read the latest journals in philosophy call a "double bind,"[15] although I do not draw any consolation from having a name for my malady but not a remedy. I would rather have a nameless cure.

Such a difficulty can be called, with a certain shorthand, "im/possible," i.e., what operates under a dual condition of possibility and impossibility. That is what Derrida calls a "quasi-transcendental" condition.[16] "*Différance*" makes it possible (almost) to speak about the individual, even as it makes it impossible (almost). "*Différance*" is a kind of transcendental almost, almost a kind of transcendental. We pass our lives for the most part in the space of this transcendental almost. It seems impossible to get beyond the "as it were" (*gleichsam*).

Let us consider this matter more carefully. The individual is ineffable (*individuum ineffabile est*): that means that the individual is too much—or maybe too little—for words. The only thing that exists is too difficult to express. *Fari*: to speak, to speak out (*ef-fari*), to tell a story (*fabula* from *fari* + *bula*), as in to say something "fabulous," literally. The individual is in-effable, too fabulous for words, too small or too tall a tale.

The ineffable individual is what is *in-divisum*, without division or incision, like a seamless garment, without a stitch or a mark on it, unmarked by any genus or species, any category or class (*glas*). The individual is beyond the reach or beneath the grasp of word or concept, speaking or thinking, *legein* or *noein*. Metaphysics has always dreamt of a land of pure individuals, an unexplored, unmarked, untouched, virginal, pristine terrain upon which no philosophical foot has trod, an arctic or antarctic land of pure polar snow, without marks or traces.[17]

But that is the dream of being without *différance*.

For it is already too late. The land has already been settled. By the time we arrive they have already built a shopping mall there. If we cannot say a thing about the individual, we have already said that much, which is too much, which means it is already too late. We have already been speaking, long been using proper names, left and right. We have already said too much, already marked off Arctic or Antarctic parameters, already marked it on our map, situated such a remote land or unexplored sea-bottom squarely within known horizons. "The individual is ineffable": that is already to get a fix on the individual, to situate the individual thus far and to that extent within our view and within our grasp, in advance. This is already to set our sights on the concrete particular as a kind of gap or caesura within the grids of words and concepts, to fix it within the cross hairs of language. We thereby bring the individual—this is Levinas's nemesis, what he is always trying to ward off—within our fore-having, fore-seeing, and fore-grasping.[18] To just this extent, to the extent that we have marked off the singular as unmarked, as pristine and virginal, we have already anticipated it, made ready its arrival, so that it does not arrive absolutely unannounced, without a proper invitation, as an absolute singularity, an absolute novelty, an absolute surprise.

We cannot be *absolutely* surprised—that is the perhaps not wholly melancholy implication of *différance*. Were a surprise absolute, were we confronted with something absolutely novel, that would make it impossible to recognize the surprise *as* a surprise. We would not know that we were being surprised or indeed that anything was happening at all. A surprise means that something else happens relative to a horizon of expectations; conceding this "horizonality" and "relativity" means that the surprise is not absolute.

The ineffability of the individual is, I submit, a *hyperbolic* matter, a matter of excessive eloquence about the fascination of distant lands. "Ineffability" conjures up images of dark sea bottoms and unexplored lands, of a world that is there without us. "Ineffability" is a high-powered discursive resource, the product of a language that has been refined and defined until it is sharp enough and nuanced enough to announce all this ineffability. "Unsayability" is a modification of what is sayable.

That is why mystics (*mystein*: quiet; keep it a secret) and negative theologians (I cannot say a thing) are among our greatest poets, spokespersons, dialecticians, and rhetoricians. My favorite mystic, the one I love the most, is Meister Eckhart, O.P. — *Ordo Praedicatorum*, order of preachers, order of praisers, order of predicates, predications, predicables, and praises.[19] Meister Eckhart, who was a very great negative theologian, said that the name of God is a *nomen innominabile*, that God is a nameless unity without any properties or proper names, that God is neither this nor that, etc. He said these sorts of things again and again; he said them repeatedly.[20] Meister Eckhart was the greatest preacher of his day and the author of voluminous *Deutsche Werke* and *Lateinische Werke*. He was a linguistic genius who helped forge modern German by translating the language of the schools into the vernacular for the women and laity who did not know Latin. Meister Eckhart said: Keep quiet! Hush! I (you, we) cannot say a thing. That was Meister Eckhart's solemn word.

But, then, were Meister Eckhart's *Werke* a forgery? Or a fraud? Was he not sincere? With all this preaching and writing, did he never say a thing about God? Was he talking about something else? Perhaps that is why he got in trouble with the Curia, which then silenced him. Still, silence is what Meister Eckhart wanted for himself anyway; silence is what he always said we should strive for, which shows that having a Pope does perhaps, on occasion, serve a purpose.

The case of Meister Eckhart shows that it is very difficult to succeed in such matters, i.e., actually to avoid speaking about something, e.g., God. *Comment ne pas parler?* Derrida asks. How not to speak; how to speak "not"; how to not-speak; how to avoid speaking. It is difficult — practically impossible, I would say — to say that something actually is ineffable, like God, who is too much for words, or the individual, who is also too much, or maybe too little, for words. (God and the individual are, on this point at least, comparable. That is also a Levinasian point, for Levinas treats the infinity of the other person as a trace of a still more absolute and more infinite infinity.)[21] It is difficult because it is already too late. By the time one has said that something is ineffable, or that one cannot say a thing, one has already been speaking for some time and one has already said too much. One has already let the cat out of the bag and begun to tell tales (*fabulae*) about it. One has failed to avoid speaking and things have become more and more effable.

It is as if one were to say *silentium laus*. But *laus* is praise, *praedicatio*, a kind of song, and this is very beautiful, alliterative Latin, a lovely language in which to sing songs to silence. Silence is sometimes quite eloquent phrasing, sometimes the best way to get something across.

A "quasi transcendental" means both that there is nothing (e.g., individuals) outside the text (almost) or that there (almost) is; it depends, strategically, upon what you need to emphasize. This is to cite one of deconstruction's, Derrida's, most famous, most notorious declarations, one that has convinced the keepers of the Truth that deconstruction is bad. To cite this text is to incite the officials of antideconstruction, to fan the flames of antideconstruction. This text has, almost single-handedly (if it has a hand), persuaded everyone that deconstruction is irresponsible, for there is— these are its own words—nothing extratextual to which it can respond.

But, to employ the most classical idiom, Derrida is not denying "reference." He is arguing, however, that it is not quite "consciousness," within the solitude of its intentional life, that does the referring, so much as it is the signifiers themselves, whose levers the subject is constantly pulling. There is certainly something outside the text, something beyond phrases, something that is referred to.[22] There must be, otherwise textuality would be a closed system, an internally coherent system, uninterrupted by anything else, anything *alter*—which would be to embrace everything that deconstruction resists. Derrida does not deny but delimits reference; what he denies is reference-without-difference. Without *différance*. *Différance* does not lock us up inside anything. On the contrary, *différance* is a doorway, a threshold (*limen*), a door through which everything outgoing (reference, messages sent, etc.) and incoming (messages received, perceptions, etc.) must pass. A threshold supposes both an inside and an outside.

Every time I say "this," and thereby make reference—or rather: every time a reference is made or a reference "happens"—to this or that thing, or every time I say "you" or "Maria," and thereby address you or Maria, or every time you say "you," and thereby address me, the closed system is breached, the door flings open and the phrase flies outward toward some individual or another.

On this accounting, proper names refer *in actu exercitu*, in the exercised act, in actual use, in the concrete happening or the factual event, in the act of using proper names or pronouns, or of having them used on me. *Il arrive*: phrases happen and the reference to the individual happens, all the time. It never stops. It is a wonder, a little difficult to account for, but it happens. In the concrete factical situation "signifiers" hit the mark of something singular. This happens in virtue of what might be called a certain "principle of factical life," except that factical life is a fact, not a principle, something that philosophy is forced to swallow while being unable to digest. It is a fact (as it were); it happens.[23]

But it seems to happen by a kind of magic, because I cannot find a proper name or a singular term that—of itself, by itself, outside of its actual, factical deployment—hits the mark of the individual, that picks out one and only one individual. No matter how specifically I determine a proper name, by adding the time and the place of the person who bears the name—so and so, at such and such a place, in such and such a time—there is nothing that prevents me from citing it, or from repeating and recontextualing that name so that the proper name and place and time become elements in a novel or a film, say. Thus the initials "JFK" and the date November 22, 1963, can also be repeated fictionally, in a film. Then the signifier does not pick out a real individual at all but a more or less imaginary one. A proper name acquires referential specificity only while you use it in the presence of the referent or by a kind of contextual-pragmatic magic which holds it in place just long enough to let it work. But it is always *structurally* capable of detaching itself from you or from that context or from that referent and hence of functioning in the absence of you, the context, or the referent. That is because it is a name, which means it is structurally able to be repeated otherwise. Otherwise it would be unrepeatable, i.e., absolutely illegible.[24]

That is the point of the famous "this" described by Hegel, seemingly the most singular of all terms. "This" sets out to name something singular and particular. Yet what is there that is not some "this" or another? "This" succeeds in getting specific reference and determinate direction only locally and temporarily, here and now, for just a moment, precariously, here, in factical life, while you are using it or, better, while it happens. You have to be there. You cannot leave the scene of the event where it is happening. If you leave, if you cease to use "this" *in concreto*, and merely mention "this" *in abstracto*, then "this" comes unstuck and spins off into the element that metaphysics loves, the element of repeatability and universality, which is the element of language, and which, while clear and serene, has the disadvantage that it does not exist.

That is why it is also true that there is nothing outside the text, nothing outside the universe of phrases. But that only means—which is really quite a lot—that there cannot be an object of reference without a phrase-event. How could there be talk about something we do not talk about? How could one speak of leaving language behind? How would you phrase it? "This" is good talk and we need it. Without "this" we would be in quite a bind. It helps us out. "This" is a bit of phrasing that marks off one thing from another, helps us sort things out, to keep them separate.

Ergo, there is and is not something outside the text, as is demonstrated by "this" and the case of proper names. What that means is that while there is nothing outside the text there really is nothing inside it either. Textuality is the border between inside and outside, the threshold between inside and outside, the inside/outside itself, if it has an itself. Textuality makes it possible for us to address extratextual entities (and even to speak of something being "extratextual" in the first place). Referring is a textual operation, an operation of textuality, that aims at certain objects. But this also makes it clear that it is impossible to carry this operation out without the aid of textuality itself. Derrida delimits reference by denying reference-without-difference. He denies that there is some word that is the word of just this thing, that just melts away in favor of the thing itself, the word this thing would speak if it could, the thing that would just rise up into presence and be its own word. Whenever reference happens, it happens within a differential context. There is nothing (= no reference) outside the text (= without the differential operation of textuality). There is no pure, naked reference that can, as it were, leave the chain of signifiers behind and embed itself in an object, *an sich*.

Textuality is a quasi-transcendental condition, the impossible condition, the condition of possibility and impossibility of referential operations, the condition that makes it possible for reference to be effected and the condition that makes it impossible to do so without a differential-textual event. The existing individual, the referent, is in this sense "im/possible," "in/effable," effable and ineffable, or, to cite the admirably precise language of a great poet, who thinks poetically and poetizes thoughtfully (not about Being or the Holy, but about cats), "effanineffable."[25] We are always inside/outside textuality, for textuality makes it possible to say everything we have to say about the individual, including that the individual is ineffable, which is the most striking thing we say about individuals. But textuality makes it impossible that we would ever reach a pure, unmediated, naked, pre-textual, un-textual, de-contextualized fact of the matter. Textuality is the condition of im/possibility, the condition that makes it possible to address the individual or to be addressed by individuals, and the condition that also makes it impossible that we would have to do with some sort of pure, naked, virginal individual. Textuality marks the individual up, leaves marks and traces all over it, leaves tracks in its polar snow, sends a camera crew down into the bottomless depths. All this eloquence about ineffability, these striking images about polar regions and virginal lands and untouched *Ansichsein*; in general, all these striking representations of the unpresentable, bring home to us hyperbolically the individuality of the individual. Textuality makes it possible to say that it is not possible to say anything about what is absolutely individual. Unsayability is a modification of sayability.

The proper name is a name for what is im/possible. Were a name truly proper, were there, properly speaking, truly a proper name, no one would understand it. Were it unique, were we utterly and totally unfamiliar with it, were we completely unprepared for it, wholly unable to anticipate it, then we would not know it is a name, we would not use it or understand its use, and it would not get known because it could never be repeated. Were it not to come as the coded answer to a coded question like *Wie heissen-Sie?* or some other such code, we would not know it is a name, or that someone was speaking, or that this is a bit of language at all, and not just a squeak or a scribble, a grunt or a purr. A proper name belongs within a common code of recognizable and repeatable signifiers. A proper name, like a good experiment, must be able to be repeated, must have common, generic, im-proper features. A pure proper name would be an absolute secret and hence quite unknown. The condition of possibility of proper names is their impurity and impropriety, viz., that there be no absolutely pure proper names. Proper names are im/possible, im/proper, im/pure.

HYPERBOLIC NAMES

The "absolutely Other" of which Levinas speaks is a fabulous story. I am speaking sincerely, literally. The "absolutely Other" is a gripping tale, very moving and very powerful, a tremendous and salutary shock that Levinas delivers to contemporary philosophy. It is as if Abraham himself has descended upon Paris and let us all have it.

We are from the start, this Abrahamic story goes, before we are even asked for our consent, always already laid claim to by the Other, always already addressed, overtaken, held hostage by the Other, who comes over us from on high. This talk of what comes over us from "on high" is a powerful discourse. It soars like a dove, not the Hegel/*aigle*, which wants to lift up every particular into the universal, but with the gentle lift of the singular itself, of the Other One—I believe that the upper case is irresistible here—who comes from on high while remaining one-on-one (One-on-one).

Levinas has straightened us all out. I am speaking sincerely. Everybody needs to have a rabbi and the so-called "postmodern" philosophers, who are very heteromorphic, are fortunate to have their own teacher of heteronomy. Levinas has made sober men and women of us all, we who are wont to sip to excess of the fruit of the Dionysian vine. Levinas is our Other. He lifts over us on the wings of a dove, overtakes us with a strange and magical discourse, like a voice from across the centuries, like a biblical prophet,[26] like Abraham and Amos letting us all have it because we are too much in love with dehiscence and overflow and discharge. He shocks us with this utterly strange talk about "the widow, the orphan, and the stranger," we who were trained to talk about noesis and noema or to master the transcendental deduction. He scandalizes us with his absolutely demanding imperative and with his commanding voice. He shocks us with his absolutely impossible, Abrahamic demands. Where does he (*il*) get his authority, him (E.L.)?[27]

The absolutely Other is a fabulous story, a *fabula*, a powerful, (effan)ineffable tale, a piece of the most powerful poetics of obligation contemporary philosophy has yet produced, more powerful, if such a thing were possible, than the poetics of the jug.[28]

I believe it. Almost. Which means that I do not quite believe it. That is my impiety. For that I am prepared to head to Holland, into exile and excommunication, like Spinoza, to consort with heretics and other heterologists who have dared raise their voice against their rabbi. (Still, am I not free to dissent from my rabbi? Is that not my business? Is not dissent an unbroken rabbinical tradition and one of the main advantages of having a rabbi instead of a Pope?)

Levinas is a great prophetic voice and I love him, as I love father Abraham and all the prophets. But I have always allowed myself to think that it is not necessary to believe the stories the prophets tell, not literally. That would be a great disservice to them in the long run, because they tell very tall tales and if you try to make prophetic stories come out as true, you succeed only in making the prophets look bad. These tall tales belong to a powerful poetics; they are the work of very great poets of obligation. The point behind prophetic poetics is not to hold it to a correspondence theory of truth, to measure whether it is getting things right or correct, to hold it up to the test of *adequatio* or of *ad literam*, but rather to let it seize hold of us. The point is, I believe, that one is always in-adequate to the sayings of the prophets, that we are no match for their stories, that we cannot keep up with them, that they exceed us, infinitely (as it were). Nothing ever is up to what they demand. There never is any *adequatio* with their demands. Prophetic talk of what is absolutely Other and otherwise than Being is to be understood as otherwise than *adequatio* and otherwise than literally. Levinas tells an un-likely story, a story of what is indeed absolutely un-like(ly). The words of the prophets soar over us, like a dove, beyond our reach, our grasp, our ken. Prophets are not reporters, sending back eyewitness accounts of what exists. They are poets and storytellers, who throw us into confusion with soaring, searing tales, with powerful poetic productions that soar far beyond what eye has seen or ear has heard, telling us all how to shape up.

Levinas weaves a fabulous, poetic story about absolute alterity, the infinitely, ab-solutely Other which is not being-otherwise but otherwise than being. I love him and I believe him (almost). That is not at all a frivolous attitude to take toward one's rabbi or anyone else, not a sign of bad faith, because cognitive phrases and poetic phrases belong to different regimes, to invoke a move of Lyotard's. Levinas posits the absolutely Other on one side and he posits the same on the other side, but not as opposites, not oppositionally, for then the dialectical machine would be set off. Still, they are related, and this relation, which is the ethical relation, is what matters most to him. Levinas puts absolute alterity on the one side, the side of the Other, while on this side, our side, the side of the same, he puts absolute altruism. Alterity and altruism—both very hard sayings—then must be "correlates." But how can you have an absolute relation to an absolute? Would not the very relation and correlation dissolve the absoluteness? How could anything be cor-related to what is ab-solutely Other, since the absolute absolves itself of all relation and correlation? If something were, properly speaking, absolutely Other, then it would not be a matter of concern for us and we would simply ignore it, being quite oblivious of it.[29] Now ignoring the Other would greatly distress Levinas, since the Other lays unconditional claim upon us. But that means that the Other is related to us after all, viz., in a very powerful, unconditionally commanding way. We in turn should acknowledge this relationship by responding to it, by answering it and taking it up, decisively and unequivocally.[30] So in fact the absolutely Other is only relatively absolute, almost absolute, not quite absolute. By the absolutely Other, I would mean what is transcendent, quite transcendent, indeed quite a lot, *ad infinitum*, but not absolutely. "Absolute alterity" *ad literam* would be a poetic way of saying *ad infinitum*, which is of course something we never reach.

There is another way to put this little disagreement with Levinas. I would say, *pace* Levinas, what is otherwise-than-being cannot help ending up as being-otherwise. I believe that Levinas's gesture is very classical, even a little Greek and perhaps even—he will hate this—a little ontological. What comes to me from on high, across the curved space of ethics (that is a very powerful image), is a face, a phenomenal face, the appearance of the Other, visible and full of flesh. But this face is not a face, is more than a face, is not a matter of flesh and blood, is nothing finite, phenomenal, visible, graspable, perceptually constituted. That is because there is an excess, an infinity, an invisibility. Ergo, what comes to me from on high is more than a face, otherwise than a phenomenal face, a certain *hyperousia*, a superessential face, supereminent and transcendent.

But if I am not mistaken, I recognize this gesture: what comes from on high is a face (*via affirmationis*); but this face is not a face (*via negationis*), but more than a face, a supereminent face (*via emientiorae*), a fabulous face (effanineffable).

I have heard this before, from the same Meister Eckhart: "When I said that God was not a Being and was above Being, I did not thereby contest his Being, but on the contrary attributed to him a more elevated Being."[31] So this is a kind of Neoplatonic face, a little like the face I had before God created me.[32] What is otherwise than being is a phenomenal face *eminentiore modo*, in a more eminent mode, the most fabulous possible version of a phenomenal face. It is phenomenal being raised up and elevated, made to soar from on high, allowed to be otherwise than other members of the phenomenal world. It is the being of the other person raised up to infinite worth, given an infinite charge or coefficient, infinitely valorized. Here is a face whose eminence just goes on and on, *ad infinitum*, with a kind of infinity, as it were (*gleichsam*). Such a face has been raised up to what Eckhart called the *puritas essendi*.[33] This is a double genitive: purity or freedom *from* being (otherwise than being), which cannot help also meaning the purity or plenitude *of* being, being in its purest state (being otherwise).

So we are, after all, somewhat ready for the Other; we are not wholly unprepared; we know a little bit about how to anticipate the Other, how to situate the Other within a horizon of some sort of being, within a framework that is not wholly unprepared for a fabulous phenomenon, something really phenomenal. Up to a point. It is a kind of face, albeit a supereminent one—as opposed to a rock or an animal (a cat, e.g.) or a subatomic particle, which would be violence vis-à-vis a face. We have set our sights on it, set our own face toward it, set up our quasi-hermeneutic forestructures. It will always surprise us with its novelty, always overtake us with its unanticipated moves, always seem to us like a past that was never present. (I have also heard that before.[34]) But not absolutely. It will not surprise us—as Levinas would himself insist—by turning out to be a bit of indigestion, which is the coldhearted suggestion of my more merciless Nietzsche. That is something we may be confident about "in advance."

That is why I do not quite believe my own rabbi. For this absolutely Other, this infinite alterity, is, as it stands in Levinas, the dream of virgin lands and arctic snows, of absolute nonviolence, of full presence utterly unmarked, unmediated, unmodified. It is the dream of absolute presence in the mode of absolute absence, the dream of a world without *différance*, without textuality, without phrases, without horizons, contexts, settings, frameworks, or any form of mediation—and all this delivered up in *le dire*, not in *le dit*, that is, in phrasing. So it is an impossible dream, even a dangerous dream, inasmuch as promises of what is absolutely unmediated are usually followed by the most massive mediations.[35] That is also why Abraham's voices are dangerous (although, as Johannes de Silentio astutely points out, the danger is greatly diminished by the drowsiness that overtakes the congregation during most sermons; still one has to be on the lookout for the occasional insomniac who would actually hear the sermon).[36]

Levinas goes to excess. That is exactly what I believe this is: an excess, an excessive statement, a bit of hyperbole, which is an operation of *différance*, a story—but a fabulous and important story that I love, a piece of powerful, impressive poetics. The absolutely Other is not, *stricto sensu*, an ineffable alterity but a fabulous tale. The notion of an absolutely Other lays me low, looking back up at it in awe and respect. It strikes down my self-love and fills me with respect. This is a fabulous story. I have read something like it in Kant, who Hegel said was a Jew, and in Eckhart, who was a reader of Rabbi Moses.[37] This is a fable that borders on ineffability (almost) and bears repeated telling. I never tire of hearing it retold. You can tell it again and again, *ad infinitum*, and I will not tire of it.

What Levinas says is impossible, but that is why I love it. Thinking the impossible, trying to think the impossible, is among the most important tasks of philosophy, which leaves what is possible to the other disciplines. The impossible is what pulls us out of our most sedimented thoughts and opens up for us new possibilities. So it is not a final objection to Levinas to say this is all impossible. It is just a way to sharpen our appreciation for his poetics.[38] All this talk of the "absolutely Other" is like the secret name of the cat.[39] If you ask the great (but not German) thinking poet how he *knows* that the cat has an absolutely secret name, given that it is absolutely secret, if you want cognitive legitimation, you ruin everything about the poem and in the process you make yourself look bad. You show that you do not know much about poetics. The point is that this is a fabulous story, or very good poetry, not at all ineffable, properly speaking. Except that "ineffable" is one of our best words, one of the best ways we have of saying that something is not only such-and-such, but very much so, indeed quite excessively, hyperbolically so.[40] The "absolutely Other" is a very nicely turned phrase, a quasi-philosophical notion that says quite a lot. It has taken philosophy by storm, a rabbinic-Semitic storm, and it has stirred up a lot of philosophical discourse among the philosophies of difference. For that I am grateful—endlessly, infinitely, as it were. But for that reason it is, I would say, neither purely Semitic and not quite Greek, but a certain wonderful jewgreek mix.

The absolutely Other is a poetic name, a hyperbolic name, the name to which we have recourse when we want to say: here is something striking, something shocking, to which we should pay attention, especially we philosophers, who have been taken in by the Greeks—since philosophy *is* Greek—who, as beautiful as they are, were too much in love with autonomy and immanence and beauty. This is a way of saying: here is something that overtakes us, that comes over us and seizes us by the collar. Here is something that we do not (only) lay claim to but that lays claim to us, that we do not (only) constitute but that is always already constituting us, that comes to us from above, on high, across curved space, commanding and demanding our respect, our response. Here is something older than us that requires something of us.[41] That is fabulous.

The absolutely other is a poetic and hyperbolic name for the fact, as it were, of obligation, of heteronomy, that we do not belong to ourselves, that we are always already held fast in the grips of something I know not what, *je ne sais quoi*, something *heteros*, something absolutely *heteros*—almost. It is a way of saying: obligation happens, *emphatice!*

When it comes to the absolutely Other and absolute heteronomy (altruism) I remain, as always, forcefully and decisively, to an almost excessive degree, inside/outside. I subscribe to the absolutely Other—almost, so long as we all understand that this is a hyperbolic expression for something that is very important *quoad me* (for me). I subscribe to absolute altruism, so long as we all understand that altruism is a good (for me). If I do something very altruistic, for the Other, that is because I want to and it is a good (for me). Whenever I do something I do it, as the masters say, *sub ratione boni*, because it is a good (for me).[42] I cannot get absolutely outside, to an absolute *alter*. I cannot shake off this little tag end, rag-tail ("for me") and make a clean cut.[43] I do want to be absolutely altruistic—*inter alia*. I want to. But if that is what I want, then if I am altruistic I end up doing what I want.

On the issue of absolute alterity and absolute altruism I am resolutely and decisively a heteromorph. It is one of the things I believe in. I think it is fabulous, hyperbolically speaking. But I also think that Levinas—if you insist on taking him straight, without a twist of deconstruction—is too pious, that his poetics are too grave. I tire easily of always wearing black, whereas my Rabbi Dionysus wears a coat of many colors. Such a Levinas—outside of a poetics of hyperbole—thinks he touches bottom on an infinite abyss, or has achieved an absolute relationship with the absolute. Absolute alterity and absolute piety are of a piece. That undeconstructed Levinas has a center, a transcendental signified that organizes and centers things for him, not around the same, to be sure, but around the Other. For all his resistance to totalization, and all his talk of decentering the same, the fact is that things are radically recentered for him around the Other, which is an infinite and absolute ec-center, a kind of transcendental eccentricity.

It is a part of my infidel nature that I attribute to this undeconstructed Levinas a transcendental move. In the way that Kant says that the Ideas of reason are the result of carrying categories of the understanding to completion, beyond the limits of their legitimate employment, Levinas maximizes the phenomenal face and the finitude of obligation, pushing them to a transcendental completion, to an extreme — *ad infinitum* — and beyond any limits. You might even say that he engages in a kind of totalizing — in the sense of maximizing — of otherness.

Let us come back to this question of indigestion. One of Nietzsche's greatest and most profound taunts against morality is that moralists have not taken into account the role of digestion in the formation of moral views. In addition to Levinas, I also love Nietzsche, although I am always scandalized by him; or rather I love Nietzsche precisely because I am always scandalized by him. I love him the most when he is the most scandalous, not when he is made out to look like a Parisian leftist (even though I agree you can do that). So the backup for the curved space of ethics, the genealogy of the ethics of the Other that Nietzsche would offer, is not metaphysical infinity and absolute alterity, but rather a weak digestive tract, one with little or no stomach. Nietzsche would say that Levinas carries out a maximization not *ad infinitum* but *ad nauseam* and this nauseating poetry upsets Zarathustra's stomach. While others look up to the sun for a source, Nietzsche is a subterranean excavator who tunnels into dark recesses.[44] The Germans, e.g., have very poor diets and that explains the poverty of their philosophy, the pale, northerly Köngisbergian spectres that haunt them and disturb their sleep. Nietzsche much preferred French cuisine and French *philosophes*,[45] although I am sure he must have thought both the cuisine and the philosophy went into sharp decline after the fall of the aristocracy.

Now there is, as always, a deadly serious point to all such taunts. This sense of absolute alterity, of the command that comes to us from on high, just what is that? It belongs to its very character as radical alterity that we do not know what it is or whence it (really) comes. Or how it happens. It happens. Obligation happens. Obligation to the Other who comes from on high happens, but we do not know the origin of this coming or happening or height. This is the scandal of the obligation that overtakes Abraham. We must be prepared, precisely in virtue of its cognitive density, to concede that, when it comes to obligation, we do not know what we are talking about. We are always on the receiving end of such obligations; we cannot trade places with the sender and put ourselves in a position to know the source of the message being sent. Otherwise we would be in a position of autonomy, which is a cognitive model, and we would be back in the position of the solitary soldier on the drill field congratulating himself on his ability to take orders. Such powerful messages, coming from without, are, in principle, and by the very nature of the case, vague and opaque as to their provenance.

Levinas locates the place of obligation in the face, above all of one who suffers, in the call that calls forth from the Other, above all from suffering. To be sure. I hear the same thing and feel the same responsibility. But what calls to us from such a place? The Thinker asks, very piously: "Is it the world? Is it the soul? Is it God?"[46] Nietzsche snickers, very impishly, from the back of the auditorium, his hand over his mouth but still quite audibly: "Is it the stomach?" I do not know. I was not around for the First Beginning and I know nothing about the "Origin of Obligation." If you press me for an answer on the matter, I will develop a serious cough and ask to be excused. I know that I am under an obligation, that the call is received, that I am laid claim to. The rest is silence — or coughing. The child is a disaster, cut off from the star of redemption. I answer the call of the child, not knowing whether the call issues from infinite depths, whether the face of the child is a trace of the Infinite or just a little blip of energy in a great cosmic dance of forces. I do not know whether there is anything infinite at all. I answer, perhaps from some obscure unconscious compulsion, perhaps from some blind instinct, perhaps from a bit of undigested beef, perhaps in response to the voice of God who calls out whenever the least of Her children is laid low. In 4.5 billion years, not a trace of the child or of me or of this spaceship earth will remain, and so perhaps none of this matters a whit.

The call that calls to me from the Other, say from the child who suffers needlessly, is finite and fragile, not infinite and absolute. I will call this call an "appeal," but not quite a categorical command.[47] To respond is to answer a call from I know not what. Obligation comes down to a deep or dark or radical hermeneutic, to construing shadows and wrestling with the powers of darkness. We do not know who we are or who the other is, and the solace we show one another is a matter of offering one another short-lived comforts. We huddle together for warmth in the midst of starless nights and polar storms. I answer but I do not know who or what I am answerable to. I cannot make a good argument against the merciless suggestion that it is a bit of indigestion that sends this obligation my way.

Obligation happens. It is a fact, as it were. For there are no facts, only interpretations. Obligation too is an interpretation, a *hermeneia*. The "as it were" is the "quasi," the transcendental almost, almost a transcendental. The Other is not an absolute, not a transcendental fact, not a fact of pure reason, but a factical fact that I have construed in a hermeneutics of facticity that includes a section on the poetics of obligation and that has made its mind up to have a heart.

THE NAMES OF JUSTICE

Derrida too speaks of something fabulous, something excessive, and — he has gone so far as to say — something "undeconstructible," something he calls "justice." The law, he says, which is always a construction, something drawn up or handed down, is deconstructible. Whatever has been written can be rewritten. Whatever has been passed, can be amended. Whatever has been said can be altered in the retelling. A law that cannot be deconstructed would be an iron law, inflexible and dangerous. That we expect to hear. But then he said what no one expected to hear (except perhaps in an interview he would leave behind to be published only posthumously in *Le monde*):

> Justice in itself, if such a thing exists, outside or beyond law, is not deconstructible. No more than deconstruction, if such a thing exists. Deconstruction is justice.[48]

This has stunned everyone, not only the officials of antideconstruction, the self-appointed defenders of the Good and the True, but even Derrida's most loyal troops, deconstructors everywhere, with and without tenure, buzzing about in airports on their way to the next conference on postmodernism:

> If I were to say that I know nothing more just than what I today call deconstruction (nothing more just, I'm not saying nothing more legal or more legitimate), I know that I wouldn't fail to surprise or shock not only the determined adversaries of said deconstruction or what they imagine under this name but also the very people who pass for or take themselves to be its partisans or practitioners.[49]

So he says that he will avoid saying it, but of course it is already too late.

"Undeconstructible justice"? What is that if not another tall tale, another *grand récit*, another classic to contend with, more authority, more rabbis and black-robed judges all over the place? What is that if not the return of the transcendental signified, of being-in-itself,[50] of pure presence, of the *fundamentum inconcussum*, of God, or worse, of Plato? What is that if not a transcendental signifier that detaches itself from the chain of signifiers, that claims for itself a special exemption from the quasi law of *différance*, as if the worst injustice, the most bloody and unjustifiable transgressions of justice, are not committed daily in the name of justice, under the protection of the name "justice"; as if "justice" alone succeeded in maintaining its identity and never became injustice; as if the name "justice" were one name and meant some single thing?

Is this any way to reward one's loyal friends? Has Derrida been seeing a rabbi on the side and has he been keeping that from us? Let us keep a cool head and think this out. This may not be the end of deconstruction but the beginning.

Deconstruction takes the side of, or identifies with—he says "is" and the translation is good, I have checked it—justice, not law. The law (*droit*) is exposed to deconstruction—he has not taken that back. But in deconstruction something is deconstructible, or gets itself deconstructed (keep decon-struction in the middle voice and avoid having too many agents and agen-cies on the scene—that's a law) in virtue of what is undeconstructible, which is justice, which must then be somehow outside or beyond law, something ineffably *hors ou au delà du droit*. That is where the scandal is lodged.

Justice, then, must be too great, too gigantic to deconstruct. But, on the contrary, it is actually just the littlest bit. Justice is not deconstructible, not because it is so grand and powerful, so infinite and overwhelming, but rather because it is quite small, so far beneath the law. When he says "out-side or beyond" the law, I say he means "beneath" the law, beneath its consideration, or even "before the law," prior to its jurisdiction, anterior to the law, like father Abraham. That is how I am glossing this. Deconstruc-tion situates itself in the distance between the large, honorable, hoary in-scriptions of the law and little proper names, which are but little bits of things, what Johannes Climacus called a fragment (*Smule*)—ineffable and invisible (almost).

Laws should be general. "That is, it must be possible to formulate them without the use of what would be intuitively recognized as proper names, or rigged definite descriptions."[51] You should draw up laws, Rawls thinks, under a veil of ignorance, that is, in such a way that you do not know what part of that world you yourself will inhabit. The idea behind the law is to veil itself in ignorance about proper names.[52] If you play this game, you will not be allowed to know what name you will be given when you make your entrance into the world, whether you will have a Waspish or an ethnic proper name, for example, or a male or a female one—which is only fair. The law, and the justice that the law wants to have, legal and judicial jus-tice, means fairness, justice under the law (whereas Derrida puts the law under justice). The law is a schema that tries to cover as many cases as it can, as fairly, equitably, and even-handedly as it can. But it never quite can. The law inevitably, structurally, falls short of individuals, because it cannot see what it is aimed at, about which it systematically, structurally, keeps itself in the dark.

Deconstruction, which "is justice," on the other hand, keeps its eye peeled for the little bits and loose fragments easily lost sight of by the law. Deconstruction is on the watch for the exclusion, the victims, the injustice produced by the law, which even the best laid laws inevitably produce. Laws always silence, coerce, squeeze, or level someone, somewhere, how-ever small. Deconstruction's justice does not aim at disinterested impartial-ity but at a preferential option for the disadvantaged, the differends, the losers, leftovers, the little bits and fragments. Far from being blind, justice cultivates a fine, suspicious eye, one might even say a "prophetic" eye, an eye too many as far as the law is concerned.[53]

The effect that deconstruction—which "is" justice—has upon the law is not the simple destruction of the law. The "deconstruction" of something—does this still need to be said?—does not mean leveling it, knocking it down, simple destruction, *destructio simpliciter*. Indeed it is just this *simpliciter*, this simpleminded, one-sided univocity, of which deconstruction is systematically suspicious. On such a simpleminded interpretation, deconstructing the law would let the winds of lawlessness sweep over the land and somehow, simplemindedly, put an end to the construction of law. But the deconstruction of the law presupposes, depends upon, and indeed affirms the ongoing, incessant and continual construction of the law, of the best laws one can write. Deconstruction is a kind of memory, a small and modest reminder, a little bit of recall, that laws are deconstructible (and that lawmakers can be recalled)—and this in the name(s) of justice. Deconstruction is memory, the memory of what the law forgets, of proper names. Deconstruction encourages writing with both hands, on the one hand writing laws (the right hand is good at this), and on the other hand (the left, no doubt) keeping watch for everything that the law excludes and forgets, so that one writes laws that keep the law in question, in an ongoing jurisprudence of the almost effable, almost ineffable, and a "politics of the effanineffable."[54]

Laws are always oversized or undersized, too sweeping or too narrow, more or less bad fits. A perfect set of laws would have to be cut to fit; it would have to mention everybody by name, a project which, I will be the first to concede, is too much for me. It would include a biography of everyone—including the strays, the stragglers, the nameless and homeless, the nomadic, the ones the census takers do not count, the ones who do not count. It would give everyone a half a page each, and so would be of an inconvenient size. Only the most affluent, the most overflowing, would be able to afford a subscription to the whole set. A perfect set of laws would be like a map so perfect that it would match in size the region of which it is the map. That would be very inconvenient and would spell the end of law. It would fulfill the purpose (*finis*) of the law, like a kind of *pleroma*, but it would also finish it off (*terminatio*), since generalizing goes to the heart of what law is. A Book of Justice, a book in which the distance between justice and the law would be closed, would be quite a size, larger than the old Chinese project of a universal encyclopedia that was to come to seventy-nine thousand volumes.

But that is not because "justice in itself, if such a thing exists," is something grand and great but, on the contrary, because it is very small, infinitesimally so, and pays infinite attention to details. Justice in itself is a limiting idea that operates at the extreme limits of invisibility, inaudibility, and ineffability. Justice must be dispensed name by name, "case by case." "Justice in itself" demands absolute, perfect casuistry—but without a Jesuit in sight. But perfect casuistry would be the end of casuistry—both its final cause and its finish—because the proper name is not a case of anything, not a fall (*casus*) from anything general.

"Justice in itself, if such a thing exists (*si quelque chose de tel existe*) . . . ":

this little "if" (*si*) is the transcendental almost, the quasi-transcendental "if," a little fissure in justice in itself, a little bit of a split in the seams of a supposedly seamless garment. But that is big enough to assure that justice in itself is just slightly out of reach, that we do not know all the perfectly proper names of justice. That is enough to see to it that justice is not one name, that it breaks up into innumerable pieces, into an infinity of proper names.

Justice is not one thing, not one name, but an uncontrollable plurality of names. *Justitia disseminativa sui.*

The book of justice, whose pages are filled with proper names, is thus another story on our shelf, not just any story, but one of our favorites. This is a fabulous story, better than *The Arabian Nights*, about the (almost) ineffable singular one. It is a powerful story, not because of its comprehensive eagle-sweep, but because of its earthbound attention to detail. Far from transporting us to a mythic land of being itself, or of laying claim to the transcendental signified, justice in itself comes back to a hyperbolic operation of *différance*, to a hypervalorization of everything singular and idiosyncratic, an emphasis, *ad infinitum*, on the least among us. Justice in itself is a hypersensitivity, a hyperresponsiveness and responsibility, to the smallest and most singular—the *idiotes*—a way of speaking sensitively, *emphatice*, of giving singularity a singular emphasis, of giving singularity its due. Justice in itself is a parabolic, very hyperbolic, and even elliptical story about every hair on our head. It mentions everyone by name, which spells the end of the book. That is because justice cannot be dispensed *in absentia*, from a book (but do not dream of getting away from writing). You have to be there, you cannot leave. Justice is like "this." It is in each case different, *jeweilig, jemeinig*, or rather *je-dein-ig*: in each case yours.

The law falls short—inevitably, structurally—of justice, which deals in proper names. That is why I would say that the law is a fall from the individual; the individual is not a fall, a case, *casus*, from the law. Accordingly, you should not apply laws to individuals, but individuals to the law.[55] Justice operates at the point of failure, wherever the law fails, falls short. Justice is there, on the spot, in the individual situation. The individual, who always knows better than the law, always protests "but this case is different." That is because "this" is always different (even as difference always involves a "this"), and justice is a function of the "this."

We pass our days in a double bind, tossing back and forth between two impossibilities, two equally tall tales: good laws and justice in itself, covering laws and perfectly proper names, law books and the book of proper names. The intermediate space in between, the distance between justice and the law, the space between these two mythic spaces, is the real space of factical life—as imperfect, inexact, unfair, in short, as difficult as it is. The mark of factical life, Aristotle (almost) said, is unfailingly found in its difficulty.[56] Good laws try to defend the weak against the strong, to lift up those who are laid low. But the law cannot see what it is doing; it is against the law to use proper names.[57] So the law produces injustice in the very act of promoting justice. The law wants justice but justice is always wanting in the law.

As hard as the law tries, there is always something left over after the application of the law, a remnant, an undigested morsel, a loose fragment, a shard. "What, after all, of the remain(s), today, for us, here, now, of a Hegel" — and in the opposite column — I am citing something here — "shit" ("what remained of a Rembrandt torn into small very regular squares and rammed down the shithole").[58] When the law is too blind, more blind than it has to be, too veiled in ignorance, too inflexible, when the columns of justice will not give at all, then the individual is shit. Again, I must say, I am not trying to be vulgar or scatological; what I say is meant *stricto sensu*. Philosophical fragments are really philosophical excrements: the fragments of philosophy, little bits and pieces that philosophy fragments ("frags"), breaks up, excretes. The Greco-German eagle's droppings in its soaring work of *Aufhebung*. This is another reason why "justice in itself, if such a thing exists," cannot be Platonic, but the almost perfect opponent of Plato, because justice in itself consorts with mud and dirt and shit,[59] with little shards and fragments, for which it would be scandalous to say that there are forms, unless it be the form of difference. Justice in itself consorts with everything that offends Nietzsche's patrician nose and delicate palate — *ad nauseam*.

Justice hovers over the individual like a paraclete — here I use a much more sublime, uplifting simile, in order to restore my good name. This somewhat Parisian paraclete is a helper who enables the individual to speak in tongues, which means to invent a new idiom for herself. It gives individuals a voice whenever they are reduced to silence, whenever the relentless equity of the law grinds them under. This poetic paraclete has nothing to do with bishops or cardinals: it is a postmodern, Lyotardian paraclete, a multilingual, elliptical, heteromorphic, somewhat jewish, parabolical, paralogical paraclete. This paraclete operates in an almost perfectly opposite way to bishops and cardinals, who use their paracletic powers to enforce silence and to still tongues. No eagle she, this is a gentle white dove, which keeps its soft eyes peeled for the black and red of Roman cardinals and of soaring Greco-German eagles, for onto-theo-logical birds of prey.

Justice in itself, if such a thing exists, is — here I will try to be decisive — a quasi-prophetic, quasi-rabbinic, quasi-Semitic imperative that belongs to the poetics of obligations. Such justice is, to be exactly on the mark, precisely hyperbolic. So it cannot possibly be prudent, for prudence (*phronesis*) seeks always to avoid excess (*hyperbole*) and defect (*ellipsis*). Prophetic justice is not Greek justice or Greek moderation, not a matter of hitting the mean mark or of dropping a veil of ignorance over everyone's head in order to keep them disinterested. Poetic-prophetic-rabbinic justice is not the mark of upright and honored men whom all the polis honors for their temperance, good judgment, and fine sons. This is not the rule of Athens' best, not rule at all, but the cry of wild men, crying in the wilderness, unshaven and unkempt, still reeking of the wild, who have not had a chance to bathe, crying for justice from the midst of injustice, quite mad really, mad for justice, and mad about injustice.

The prophets were strange types, dressed in sheepskins and living on locusts and honey, knights of faith who looked like knights of faith, not like tax collectors. Not a little mad, they made mad claims on everyone, not least on themselves. They asked for impossible things—to hold oneself hostage to the Other, to let one's freedom shatter against the good of the Other, to regard oneself as murderous, to alienate and dislocate oneself, to be infinitely sensitive—sensitive *ad infinitum*—to the good of the Other whose good is absolute, to let justice flow like water over the land. The powers that be—the princes, *principia, archai* of this world, wherever they are found, in church or temple, state or university—are inclined to put up with that sort of thing for only so long. So, in the end, it usually costs prophets their lives (or at least tenure) if they persist in being mad.

I am not saying that Derrida is a prophet. Far from it—even though some of our best prophets are very good deconstructors. He does not look like either a tax collector or a knight of faith. This is at most a quasi-prophetic tone that he has recently adopted. "Justice in itself, if such a thing exists": that is a fabulous story, a piece of powerful poetics, a tall, quasi-prophetic tale, Semitic hyperbole, which soars over us like a jewgreek dove and catches us up short, or which alights softly of a summer night and fills us with the gift of tongues.

"Justice in itself, if such a thing exists"—that is the face of the child. But the child is a disaster and Derrida is no prophet. This discourse on unde-constructible justice is at best "not far away" from prophetic discourse.[60] It lives in the same jewish neighborhood. Derrida is not a prophet but "a kind of a philosopher"[61] who does not quite believe his rabbi, or in abso-lute ineffability, or in absolute infinity, or in absolutely proper names, or in justice in itself. His is a certain philosophical type, which, if philosophy is Greek, represents a certain jewgreek philosophy. Let us say that this is a philosophy and a philosophical justice that allows itself to be inwardly dis-rupted by what is not Greek but Semitic, not philosophical but prophetic, not universalistic but singular. Let us say that this is a philosophy that wants to shock philosophy into place by making the singularity of the child—of "the widow, the orphan, and the stranger"—the matter for thought, *die Sache selbst*. It wants to scandalize philosophy by letting wild-eyed prophets and severe rabbis, not to mention convicted thieves, have their say, by giving them an idiom, even if that means inviting them to con-ferences and giving them tenure (then you really would have tenured rad-icals). It wants, as Derrida says, at one and the same time to prove itself according to the most rigorous demands of the university and to press the university to the limits, to see how much the university and its philosophy can bear before it calls the campus security to throw the rabble out and put an end to the idioms this poetics keeps inventing.[62]

This is not prophecy but a certain kind of philosophy, which suits my tastes and my purposes. It is all the philosophy—and all the ethics—I can stand. For it is sufficiently unorthodox, sufficiently a friend of heresy, heterodoxy, heteromorphism, and a general impropriety to say that disasters are a proper subject matter for philosophy. For the question of justice is for me—and on this point I seek a consensus—above all a question of disasters, of unwarranted or innocent suffering, of a loss beyond recompense, of damage beyond repair, and of vigilance about our capacity always to create new suffering, however we twist and turn. After and apart from the minimization of suffering, justice is a question of the maximization of difference and of letting many flowers bloom. The rose is without why.

Justice, come! *Viens!* That is his or my—or whose? Derrida's? Lyotard's? Levinas's? Father Abraham's? Johannes de Silentio's? I do not know; I am getting these voices mixed up—quasi-prophetic call made from the bowels of jewgreek philosophy. I do not know what justice is or in what it will consist, and I will never make a finish if you insist on pressing me about this. In any case (in each and every case), I think justice is less a "what" than a "here, now" or a "this," which means a certain *haecceitas.* I am not proposing a program, although programs are necessary and need to be proposed. When it comes to programs, I ask only that our planners and programmers remember justice, that is, what the program leaves out, that they remember the proper names of the disasters, which is a dangerous memory.[63] Justice is always to come, *à venir, zu-kommen, Zukunft,* the *vita ventura,* in a future that will never be present. Justice is a possibility to be cultivated as a possibility,[64] which means to be kept open. Justice affirms the impossible possibility, the possibility that never exists. Justice is the future of the justice to come. Justice is coming and it will give pleasure when it comes. Justice delayed is justice denied but justice promised is justice coming.

I do not favor the man of the law but the woman of justice. But then again it is not a matter of choosing between them. I love them both in ambidextrous, hermaphroditic, heteromorphic, transvestite confusion. I strive to abide by the law, but only one law, which is not quite a law, but somewhat outside or beyond—or beneath or before—the law, a certain quasi out/law that tries to deal with proper names: *dilige*: respond to suffering; *et quod vis fac*: and multiply differences. A bishop said that, but do not worry about all this ecclesiastical authority, all this red and black. I have glossed this text with *Glas* and other glazes,[65] and I trust I have gotten it just right (*au juste*).

FIVE

The Epoch of Judgment

How am I to judge, I who have come out against ethics? Will that not prove to be a foolish decision, rash and imprudent, altogether a bad judgment? How am I to judge, I who have forsaken the protection of ethics' guiding principles and its supportive criteria? Does not ethics now get its revenge against its detractors? How am I to judge, I who have sat down to table with undecidability? How am I to decide anything? What am I to do, I who have even given up waiting for the last god?

This is no time to panic. I must regain my composure and take one step at a time. I begin, as is my rule, in the situation in which I find myself, that is to say, in the midst of what is happening, for judging is a matter of judging what is happening.

JUDGING EVENTS

What happens (*qui arrive, was geschieht*) is called an event.[1]

To understand this does not require a prodigious head. It is rather an ordinary idea, nothing pretentious or grandiose, not meant to set off another wave of German metaphysics. God forbid! We have had enough of that. Still, it is not possible to be purely nonmetaphysical or to stand entirely outside metaphysics. The double bind in which I find myself is that I cannot wholly escape metaphysics, twist free from it and make a clean break, even as I have no such prodigious head as is required to erect a metaphysics. I have a head neither for metaphysics nor for "overcoming" metaphysics. I find myself in between, inside and outside metaphysics, on the margins between the two.

At best (at worst) I am trying to hold metaphysics to a minimum, the minimum of metaphysics you need to get a discourse moving, while being vigilant about the sorts of metaphysical assumptions that inevitably work their way into our discourse. At most (at the least), I am deploying a minimalist metaphysics. I am mostly providing an inventory of good English words like "event" and "happen," and trying hard not to encumber them with the History of Being, or the History of Spirit, or History itself (if it has an itself). I am trying desperately not to let a good English word like "event" become an Event of Appropriation, fully equipped with capital letters and the onus of Ownness, capable of eventing of itself (*das Ereignis ereignet*). The sense of event I favor comes equipped with dates and places. Events in this sense are no Big Metaphysical Deal (*ein Sache des Denkens*).

Events are not part of any such grand metanarrative. On the contrary, they are its almost perfect opposite. The whole idea behind all this talk of events is to face the consequences of thinking about things without the aid of such overarching ideas and sweeping *grands récits*.

What happens (an event) is unreproducible and idiosyncratic. What happens is a singular configuration of circumstances, an unrepeatable constellation of times and locations, of people, things, and relationships. A date—March 18, 1980—is a perfectly good example of an event. An event is always a particular event. Even if, *per impossibile*—it could never happen—two events were in every other way the same, they would differ in that they occur at different times and hence that one is before or after the other. The very idea that at any given time there is, as a whole, only One Event taking place—everywhere and at the same time (*simul et ubique*)—is a totalizing illusion induced by the idea of an ideal observer, an outsider taking the view from nowhere. At any given time, there are innumerable events.

Events divide infinitely into other events. There are no irreducibly simple events to put an end to the analysis of events, to bring it to a satisfying rest. Because of their complexity, events cannot be fully fathomed or analyzed, but only inhabited, settled into, coped with. An event cannot be saturated by thought; it is too dense for that. Events are the complex settings for action, the impenetrable background in which agents act, in which action happens, in which anything at all happens. An event contains other events but cannot be itself contained or totalized by a master event or a master code. Events are complex conglomerates and constellations of other events, and this without end, *ad infinitum*, without hope of reaching atomic simples. It would always be possible to vary one's perspective and hence to find new ways to think an event. That opens the door to a flood of new events. In this sense, there are no events, only interpretations. Or rather, events are a function of the plurality of interpretations.

An event is not reducible to either a natural or a historical event. I am not going to try to make one the substratum upon which the other is layered. An event is neither *Geschichte* nor *Natur*, but rather the interpenetration of nature by history and history by nature. I would not know how to choose between or cleanly separate the one from the other. Events are geo-historical, bio-spiritual, ideo-material, econo-religious; in short, highly contaminated. They occur in natural time and historical time, in geographic space and social space. What happens is a fusion and confusion of physical forces, social forces, personal intentions—and who knows what else? What happens is whatever happens. You see the non-exclusionary character of this minimalism. Remember that minimalism is no Big Deal.

The complexity of events can be seen as a matter of *différance*, in virtue of which there is no such thing as "one" event, a simple, atomic, decontaminated event. Rather, we always have to do with complex webs of events, multilayered tissues of events interwoven with other events, a textuality of events. That means that events belong to still more complex contexts and that events are always, indefinitely recontextualizable.

Events are concrete and singular. "Singularity" is in the first place the singularity of events, their unrepeatable and unique configurations or concretion of time, place, circumstance.

An "individual" is a subject of a particular event. Events happen to individuals, who bear them, or bear up under them (or fail to). An individual is singular, not because the individual is a deep subjectivity or interiority, but because an individual is always a specific nodule in the web of a singular event, always already embedded at some juncture in a unique constellation of circumstances.

But an individual is itself also a complex configuration of still further events, a multiplicity or constellation unto itself. An individual is anything but an atom or atomic substance. The individual is a perspective, the perspective of the here, now, at this point. As soon as you turn your eye toward the individual embedded within events, the individual breaks up before your eyes, into a multitude of further events. The simplest way to think of an individual is to see that an individual has, or can have, a proper name. You can lose a lot of time debating whether the individual who has the same proper name at age six months and at age sixty-six is the "same person." If you press me for an answer on this tormented subject, I will say, quite decisively, that it depends.

An event is neither a "subject" nor an "object" but rather the point of intersection where subjects and objects meet. "Subjects" and "objects" are ways to simplify events, perspectives we introduce to reduce complex events to manageable proportions. Subject and object are complementary sides of the same event. A subject is the agent which acts, or is acted upon, or reacts, which addresses or is addressed. An object is what the subject acts on or reacts to.

The singularity of the subject is to be embedded in and to belong to a singular event. The subject is never an "agent" through and through. For one thing, the subject is just as often something acted upon, subjected to events. The acting subject is something acted upon even in its very acting, for the acting subject is itself a function of the anonymous, presubjective forces by which it is traversed—by language, the unconscious, by the weight and momentum of its own past, of the collective past to which it belongs, by the biochemistry and neurophysiology of which it is constituted, and by numberless (because anonymous) other forces. When the subject acts, we cannot be sure what acts, i.e., what is happening, because the individual subject is an irreducible complex of other events.

On a certain level, the subject is an "author," a layer of free intentional acts, a more or less simple, authoritative agency. That certainly happens. But in my view this subject/author is best conceived as a kind of delegated ministerial voice in a wild, slightly uncontrollable parliament, a pandemonium of feelings, thoughts, and desires which are simmering beneath the surface of the

subject.[2] The author/subject is like a member of congress who has been delegated to make a statement to the press that summarizes and simplifies the tu-
multuous deliberations of the congress behind closed chamber doors.

The author is only one way to become a subject. Another way, more per-
tinent to the present study and present purposes, is to become the subject
of obligation, the subject to which obligation happens. A subject is organized into subjectivity, galvanized as a responsible subject, by the obligation that descends upon it and organizes the multiplicity of forces by which
it is inhabited into a unity, at least a temporary unity. The force of the obligation summons the energies of the subject, elicits the subject's actions,
subjecting the subject to its influence. The "responsible" subject is like a
congress that has put aside factional differences in order to respond to the
seriousness and urgency of the matter before the house.

Still another way to become a subject is to be subjected to misfortune or
misery. Pain and suffering have a way of recoiling the subject into itself in
a kind of unhappy subjectivity. So in addition to the subject/author and the
responsible subject, there is the subject/patient, the suffering subject, the
disaster.

Individual subjects act in singular situations, responding to the idiosyncratic demands of unrepeatable events, to the *sui generis* character of what
happens. The subject faced with acting is always asking "what is happening?" That is, "what is the event?" Or, "what is *this*?"

Principles, universals, laws are attempts on the part of thought to penetrate
the density of events, to find the secret formula of events, to provide guardrails that safeguard the subject through the most treacherous twists and turns
that events take. Events can be dangerous and principles try to make safe, to
keep us safe in the midst of dangerous events. Principles are to supply the
rule that governs the unfolding or happening of events, or to provide a guide
through the maze of events. Principles are so many attempts to regulate or to
find what regulates the *es gibt*, the sheer giving and coming to pass of events,
the *il y a* or *il arrive*. Principles try to give us a standpoint above what happens
and thus to get beyond events. The difficulty with principles is that principles
are themselves caught up in what happens. The reason for that is that the authors of principles are no less subject to what happens than is anyone else,
although they sometimes try to conceal this fact and to erase the genealogy of
the principles they champion.

Otherwise you would have to say the principles fell straight from the sky
and into our laps. That has been said, and metaphysics often says something rather like that,[3] but the *onus probandi* falls on those who lay claim to
such heavenly gifts, not on us who claim only to have suffered a disaster,
to lead a damaged life, to be bereft of a heavenly guide, to begin where we
are. From the standpoint of this minimalist metaphysics of events, a disaster simply means that we are caught up in the maze of events and are unable to catch sight of a guiding star.

Events yield to other events, but they do not yield to principles. Events follow other events, but they do not follow rules. The transition from one event to the next is neither necessary nor capricious, neither rule-bound nor disconnected. The transition is always something of a leap, a little chancy, perhaps, difficult but not impossible.

The individual is always more or less on its own with this leap, always faced with more or less unique and idiosyncratic circumstances in which to make its way. The subject is forced to wade into the complexity of events, to make a first cut into a relatively dense thicket, a thicket that is (almost) impossible to clear. Clearings hardly happen.

Philosophy, which is metaphysics, has conceived the question of the action that the individual takes in the midst of the singularity of an event as the problem of "judgment." Judgment is a function of the "faculty" of "applying" "principles." On the traditional model, the problem is to judge what happens with the aid of principles. If that is what judgment is, I must take a stand "against judgment." But judgment is in a much more difficult situation than that, much more radically menaced and on its own than traditional philosophy is prepared to admit. Metaphysical ethics wants to make judgment safe, but judgment is not safe, and this for two good reasons.

For how are we ever to get as far as a principle? How are we to get a consensus on the principle? That is the first problem. If judgment is unable to start out from the principle, unable to proceed from on high, then how are we to judge, how are we to ride out and absorb the shocks and jolts of factical life? Suppose we never have the advantage of knowing what universal schema to bring to bear upon the singularity of the event? Suppose we are always already caught up in the thicket of factical life, in the density of events, without a sure guide or firm guardrails, and we are forced to proceed from below? What then?

But even granted that we are able to attain some stable principle, how are we to "apply" the universal to the particular, to close the distance between the universal and the particular? This would come down either to finding the application for the principle or finding the principle for the case. But that always involves a leap and always costs more than metaphysics is prepared to pay. At some point the transition from the generality of principles to the singularity of events must be made, but that can occur only as a leap into an abyss, a plunge into the density and impenetrability of the event, the novelty and the surprise of singularity. Such a leap is never quite safe. The doctrine of judgment reveals a breach in the surface of metaphysics, a fissure in which deconstructive analysis makes its nest. That is the second problem.

Metaphysical ethics founders on judgments as it founders on proper names and obligations. It harbors a doctrine of judgment that it cannot contain. Judgments are one more bit metaphysics has swallowed but cannot digest; more metaphysical indigestion.

Events are what happens, what "is." Heidegger said that the event is the "and" in "Being 'and' Time" or "Time 'and' Being." I have no idea. I will take Heidegger's word for it. He spent his whole life thinking about that. But the word I will not take is *Ereignis*, if *Ereignis*, as Derrida showed, is drawn into the metaphysics of propriety and allowed to grow into a great Greco-Germanic metanarrative.[4] I am trying not to be lured into "appropriation." Heidegger did better, in my view, when he spoke of the anonymous, impersonal, improper "it gives" (*Es gibt*), although "it happens" (*es geschieht*) would have been still better, and when he did not burden "It" with the myth of Being's primordial beginning and next coming. He did better just to say "it gives" but he did the very best of all, on my accounting, when he said "it plays" and that it just plays, playing "without why." Heidegger is at his best when he says it just plays, just gives — without purporting to be Being's ticketmaster, to know Being's schedule of arrivals and departures. That makes judging a matter not of applying principles but of staying in play with the play, knowing how to cope with the play in what happens.

It is always necessary for me to act, to do something, to decide what is happening in the midst of considerable undecidability. What's happening? I am not sure, but I must decide. Even if the way to judgment is blocked, I must still judge. The question is how? How am I to judge?

HOW TO JUDGE (LYOTARD, ARISTOTLE)?

"Comment juger?" "How to judge?" Derrida asks — Lyotard.[5] How to judge? Lyotard asks — Aristotle.

But how are we to judge judgment itself? Should we not first ask, in accordance with the classical Greek axiomatic, *"what is* judgment"? Yet far from being less prejudicial, the latter question would only serve to reintroduce the whole body of presuppositions (*préjugés*) of the traditional problematic of judgment. That would make the question of judgment turn on the essential quiddity of judgment and its predicates, knowing which promises to give us mastery over judgment. The more pragmatic question *"how* to judge?" underlines, on the contrary, our sense of "impotence, anxiety, fright" in the face of the "double bind" or the "undecidable."[6] How to judge when the way is blocked, when we do not have the means or the criteria?

In *Just Gaming*, Lyotard writes, "Absolutely, I judge. But if I am asked by what criteria do I judge, I will have no answer to give." And again, "No, we judge without criteria. We are in the position of Aristotle's prudent individual, who makes judgments about the just and the unjust without the least criterion."[7] It is a mark of prudence, on Lyotard's accounting, to judge without criteria; one might have thought that a mark of imprudence!

When we take up the question "how to judge?" we enter a scene of judgment where the lack of criteria is the "law." Were such criteria at our disposal, Derrida says, then "technique" and "application" would replace the "disquiet of judgment" and the need to ask "how to judge?"[8]

We must judge even if we do not know how to judge. That is where we are. Life does not ask if we are prepared and it does not have the decency to wait until we are ready. Even though we lack a criteriology, a law of laws, we are still not dispensed from judging. We are from the start before the law, forced to act and choose, to judge and respond.

We live in an "epoch of judgment," Derrida says, i.e., in the age of its (attempted) *epochē*, an age which has bent its efforts on delimiting and suspending judgment. We have witnessed three such attempts on the life of judgment: that of Husserl, who wanted to suspend *(epochē)* judgment in order to find its antepredicative source; that of Heidegger, who displaced the truth of judgment in favor of *aletheia;* and that of psychoanalysis, which sharpens our wits about what is really going on in "denials."

The singularity of Lyotard, Derrida says, is to have inhabited this epoch in all three phases—Husserlian, Heideggerian, and Freudian—and to have defied it, even to have laughed at it. "He [Lyotard] tells us: you have not finished with it; we will never make an end of judgment." "It will not leave you in peace so soon."[9] Whether judgment is primary or derivative, founded or founding, it will not leave you alone. So if "modernity" consists in rising above or probing beneath the surface of judgment, whether by science or meditative thinking, then postmodernity consists in confronting the ineluctability of judgment. The epoch of judgment turns out to be the postmodal epoch.

But how are we to judge? It is very difficult. The road ahead appears to be blocked.

Events make requirements on us. They press in upon us and force us to ask "what's happening?" They bring the force of circumstances to bear upon us and put us into double binds. (Why not triple? Who knows the multiple?) Events demand something of us, here and now. But an event is an idiosyncratic situation, a just slightly unprecedented configuration that we have never quite met before, unique and not exactly anticipated. Each event sets its own requirements, its own idiom, demands that we invent a new idiom, not an absolutely new or absolutely idiosyncratic idiom, but new enough, idiosyncratic enough. The capacity to invent such an idiom is what Aristotle—and Lyotard assures us he is trying to be very Aristotelian—called *phronesis. Phronesis* is not without recourse, not completely on its own; it is not lost, not without a guide or a schema. On the contrary, *phronesis* is the ability to bring to bear a general schema upon the particularities of the situation. So the *phronimos* has not entirely lost his bearings. Even as events bear down on him, the *phronimos* brings a schema to bear on events and finds a formula that is good here and now. *Phronesis* is a way of staying loose in a binding situation.

How to judge the difference between a danger that is to be avoided and a danger to be confronted? How to judge when you are being rash and when you are being cowardly, when to charge head-on and when to show your heels?[10] That, young man (Aristotle is speaking to his nephew), requires experience, judgment, *phronesis*. It is not fortuitous that the addressee is young (or a man) and very little seasoned by events. The *phronimos*, on the other hand, is a grown man and he knows what is happening. He has been shaped by experience, matured by events, and has acquired the habit of having an insight into what events demand. A good many things have happened to him, each of which was just different enough from the other as to demand from him a *nous*, an insight into its novelty, a capacity to reinvent, reapply the schematic. He has, over time, cultivated an eye for the idiosyncratic. He knows what is needed at the time, what is too much and not too much, when enough is enough or not enough, neither an excess nor a defect. That is the skill of judging *in concreto*. That is a matter of hanging loose, of having a nice or a delicate sense of what is required, *au juste*, here and now. He knows what is appropriate to the situation, how to appropriate the schema, here and now.

Phronesis always proceeds from and by way of a schema. Still, there is a little difficulty here, and it puts a bit of stress on the *phronimos*, the stress that *phronesis* is built to bear. The difficulty is that the schema is without a schema, that the recourse the *phronimos* has is itself without recourse. The difficulty of factical life, when it comes to putting courage (or any of the other schemata of *arete*) to work, is not that there are no rules — for courage is a kind of rule — but that the rules have no rules.

When Lyotard, telling his ethics to Thébaud, the young man in *Just Gaming* — is this Lyotard's nephew? — says that *phronesis* is judging without a concept and judging without criteria, the older man, in my opinion, is just trying to scare the young man. It is not precisely (*au juste*) that there are no criteria, for, *pace* Lyotard, in Aristotle courage has a conceptual coherence and it does imply certain criteria. There is a rule, Aristotle says, but sometimes it must be like the rules in Lesbos, made of lead so that it can bend with the bent.[11] The problem is that the criteria do not have criteria. Lyotard is making a good point, but he speaks *emphatice*, i.e., he is trying to terrorize Thébaud in a salutary way, just a little, a little justly — this is just gaming — and that is because he is ultimately scared himself, scared of terror itself and of producing victims and *différends*, of putting people in new and deeper binds.

More nicely put, the precise difficulty is that the rules are ruleless. If there were still more rules, if there were more fine-grained microrules for the larger rules, then the microrules would have no rules.[12] In the sphere of rules, you cannot proceed *ad infinitum* (or *ad nauseam*), for rules have their limits (*finita*). Somewhere down the line that leads from the universal schema to the idiosyncratic situation, from the general idea to the singularity of the event, to what is to be done here and now (*agendum*), there is a gap that must be crossed. That is the abyss, the unrule, the unregulated irregularity, the outlaw that infiltrates the law. That is the place in which

Lyotard and, I would add, a deconstructive analysis want to situate themselves, from which point they—Lyotard and Derrida together—try to cause as much trouble as possible, i.e., to keep things loose and in play.[13]

Aristotle's *phronimos* knows how to take the measure of this measurelessness, knows how to cope or deal with it; that is what having *phronesis* means. He abandons the security of the universal in order to cope with the unintelligibility of the singular. For matter and singularity are principles of unintelligibility for the Greeks; the *eidos* shades down into shady singulars; *hyle* is a principle of unintelligibility. Duns Scotus tried to counter the Greeks on this point by making the individual more important—that is a jewgreek point which comes of emphasizing every hair on our head—a principle of intelligibility, a form, which is what the notion of *haecceitas* is all about. Scotus was more interested in protecting the singularity of the event, which is also why he drew the attention of Gerard Manley Hopkins.

At that point, of singularity or unintelligibility, precisely (*au juste*), the *phronimos* has to proceed without a concept or criterion because the point he has reached is the point *between* the concept and the case. The singular is not compounded out of universals. *Individuum ineffabile est.* You can never reach the singularity of the singular by multiplying predicates. You have to take the leap, cross the gap, swing over the abyss, into the *tode ti,* the *hoc aliquid* (this something), the "this," the here and now. If that is not to your taste, if you cannot cope with that kind of flexibility and give, if you have a strong need for more precision than that, if you want things bound up more tightly than that, then Aristotle's advice is to take up geometry. This imprecision, this give in the *es gibt,* is the limit of *phronesis,* but this is felt as a limit only to someone with a predilection for universals, grounds, principles, *archai,* for general classes, for the *glas* of classes, genera, and generalities. To someone with a predilection for factical life, whose feet are planted in the facticity of worldly life, *phronesis* is *nous* at its best, *nous* at full steam, a *nous* which does not miss a step. *Phronesis* is the nimbleness and dexterity of a mind capable of coming to grips with the complexity of factical life itself, with the difficulty of the idiosyncratic and unexpected. *Phronesis* is the capacity to act on the spot, to think on one's feet, to invent what is needed at the time, to innovate, improvise, experiment, a capacity to move with the mobility of events, to let one's *logos* hang loose. The medieval schoolmen said that *phronesis* means having the *recta ratio,* the right touch, a sense of what is just right, *au juste,* for what the situation demands (*agendi*).

Phronesis is a Greek way to love the abyss.

Up to a point. For if the *phronimos* makes a leap, it is a more or less safe one and he has trained extensively for it, like a good Greek athlete. The *phronimos* is adept in crossing abysses, bridging gaps, but ones that have been fairly well narrowed down in advance. He gets a good running start down the path that has been cleared by the schema, so this leap is not too hair-raising. But how are we to judge if things get more difficult than that?

Suppose the runway is blocked? Suppose the times are out of joint, that the gods of *arete* have flown, that we live "after virtue," or after "Being" and the gods have taken flight, or after History, or after Marxism (has—almost—ended), in times still more needy and destitute than even Heideggerian *Denken* will allow? Suppose, in short, that we do not know *what* schemata to apply or appropriate? Suppose that there is no general agreement or consensus about the schemata, and that we cannot agree on who the *phronimos* is? Suppose, on the best heteromorphic grounds, there are in fact many prudent men, and quite a few prudent women too, too many to keep track of, too many to forge (*bilden*) a set of coherent schemata? Suppose there is no consensus? Suppose events present us with a constellation of conflicting and incommensurable schemata, with a certain deconstructed constellation, a kind of de-constellation, or dis-astrous constellation or configuration? Suppose indeed that "events" are a disaster, a string of happenings transpiring without the benefit of a guiding star or *grand récit*, more a deconstellation than a constellation, more star wars than a heavenly sweep? Suppose an "event" is what happens, but without the big story of Being or the Spirit or Freedom to keep it in line?

In short, suppose that events are a disaster even as *phronesis* depends on being shaped (*gebildet*) by events?

Then the *phronimos* is a little lost. He has to find its own way. We cannot count on events to shape, to cultivate, to build up a *phronimos*, to give him *eine gute Bildung*, a commanding, paradigmatic, edifying formation. For events will bring forth too many *phronimoi*, conflicting and incommensurable *phronimoi*, which will throw us into amorphous or, rather, heteromorphic confusion. Then we will require a kind of meta-*phronesis*, which means the ability to cope with, to judge among, competing and incommensurable schemata,[14] a more radical, deconstructed *phronesis*, one that is ready to face the worst, to wade into the difficulty of factical life without the guardrails of metaphysics or ethics. The deconstruction of *phronesis* does not consist in leveling it or brushing it aside, but in keeping it still more loose, leaving it exposed, out in the cold, in the midst of factical life without the protection that metaphysics and ethics want to provide. *Phronesis* is not safe and cannot be kept safe by metaphysics. Metaphysics harbors *phronesis* but it cannot contain it, because *phronesis*, more radically conceived, undergoes a colder, more merciless exposure to events.

Such a more radical *phronesis* would make for a more radical ethics. One advantage of the word "ethics" (or of the Latinate "morals," if it is closely linked, etymologically, with *mores*)[15] is that it suggests the formation of conduct by *ethos* or "custom," that is, by events, by what is happening. In that sense an "ethics of events" is a redundancy, since *ethos* is the shape given to life by events. But if you do not share the optimistic assumption that there is a single *ethike* embedded in *ethos*, one unifying and overarching paradigm, one that will shape a paradigmatic *phronimos*, then you are on the way to a more radical ethics and a postmodern version of Aristotle.

That I think is what Lyotard is reaching for when he cites Aristotle. Then the deconstruction of ethics I am undertaking here, which links Lyotard and Derrida together, could be said, in virtue of the need for double writing, to issue in a more radical, decentered, disseminated ethics, an "ethics of dissemination,"[16] and we would use the word "ethics" *sous rature*. That is how I could make my peace with the word "ethics," the result being a kind of quasi ethics. But I have, rashly and in an unprecedented exercise of bad judgment, chosen instead to make trouble for the word "ethics," to question its prestige, to say with Heidegger that ethics waxes as thinking wanes, in order to make a point about both the groundlessness of obligation and its urgency. I have had the imprudence, the foolishness, to speak against ethics. But never forget, if the police of Truth drag me off never to be heard from again, that what I meant by against ethics also included the sense of having been driven up against ethics, reaching the point at which we all press "up against ethics," where we are pushed close up against the face of ethics. Perhaps that will help protect the memory of my name.

The interesting thing about this more radicalized, perhaps slightly imprudent Aristotelian quasi ethics is that, in keeping with the polyvalent quality of good philosophical texts (like those of Aristotle and Nietzsche), there is a side of Aristotle that recognizes all this and feeds the Lyotardian machine. But there is another side of Aristotle as well, insisted on by the "natural law" tradition, that thinks that an ahistorical "human nature" hovers over and steadies the course of events, and these texts feed another, and in my view more ominous, normalizing machine, at least here and now, "after Being" and "after virtue."[17]

THE APORIAS OF JUDGMENT

How to judge? How to judge judgment? It is difficult and the road ahead appears to be blocked.

Derrida has nicely summarized the difficulties that block judgment in this time of need—the time in which we need judgments, in which judging has become more urgent than ever—and in a way that brings him into a certain proximity with Lyotard (as he himself seemed to hint at Cerisy).[18] I am speaking (again) of "The Force of Law," where Derrida is speaking of the law and lawyers, of judgments made by judges, not exactly of the ordinary choices made by those of us who do not wear long robes (at least not in public).[19] But the points he makes apply to the rest of us, I think, *mutatis mutandis*. He speaks of the three "aporias" that beset judging justly, but he warns us that really there is just one larger aporetic distributing itself in three places, all of which have to do with the distinction between justice (*justice*) and law (*droit*):

. . . between justice (infinite, incalculable, rebellious to rule and foreign to symmetry, heterogeneous and heterotropic) and the exercise of justice as law or right [*droit*], legitimacy or legality, stabilizable and statutory, calculable, a system of regulated and coded prescriptions.[20]

These aporias make their nest in the mutual implication of justice and law, that is, in the fact that this is not a true, strict, rigorous distinction, inasmuch as laws are supposed to be just and justice has to be dispensed in and through the rule of law. So the whole idea of this distinction is to keep the distinction to a minimum—as much as possible.

(a) The first aporia Derrida calls the "aporia of suspension." To judge, it is never enough merely to apply a law, because laws always require interpretation. They demand that we make what Stanley Fish calls a "fresh judgment." A fresh judgment is always both regulated (it looks to a rule and previous experience) and unregulated: we must be able to "suspend" the law just long enough to "reinvent" it in the present situation. "Each case is other, each decision is different and requires an absolutely unique interpretation, which no existing, coded rule can or ought to guarantee absolutely."[21] Otherwise judgment can be turned over to a "calculating machine." Judging is not a mechanical reproduction but an agile production. This aporia, we can see, is an aporia of *phronesis*, which, important as it is, remains within the framework of an Aristotelian, Gadamerian, even a Fishian theory of judgment.

(b) The second aporia, which Derrida calls "the ghost of undecidability," is more distinctively Derridian. Judging is deciding. To judge is to make a cut, to de-cide, which presupposes that it takes place in the element of "undecidability." Judging operates in the "oscillation" between two forms of respect: "respect for equity and universal right but also for the always heterogeneous and unique singularity of the unsubsumable example."[22] Judging must give itself up to "the impossible decision," the "ordeal of the undecidable." Otherwise the decision is not a judgment but a programmable result, the effect of a calculation process that, once again, could be turned over to a machine. Thus, far from undermining decision, as its critics charge, "undecidability" is what assures that judging will be judging, and not merely a mechanical operation. Undecidability is the condition of im/ possibility of decision.

The "ghost" of undecidability hovers over the decision, before, during, and after the decision. It haunts it, lingering like a spectre, even after the decision. We do not dispel the ghost by deciding. We do the best we can to be just, here and now, under the law, but we must live with the consequences:

> The undecidable remains caught, lodged, at least as a ghost—but an essential ghost (*un fantôme essentiel*)—in every decision, in every event of decision. Its ghostliness deconstructs from within any assurance of presence, any certitude or any supposed criteriology that would assure us of the justice of a decision, in truth, of the very event of a decision.[23]

Every decision oscillates between the undecidability of justice and injustice, in the uncertainty of whether it is justice that we are enacting, here and now, or violence. For justice in itself is an "infinite idea"—these are among Derrida's most Levinasian texts—"infinite because it is irreducible, irreducible because it is owed to the other, owed to the other, before any contract, because it has come, the other's coming as the singularity that is always other." Justice demands a "gift without exchange," "without calculation and without rules, without reason and without rationality." "And so we can recognize in it, indeed accuse, identify a madness. . . . And deconstruction is mad about this kind of justice."[24]

In this aporia, justice takes on a quasi-messianic tone. It is almost messianic, but not quite. That is in part at least because Derrida does not want to think of justice in terms of a distant horizon, as an ideal in the distant Kantian sense, but of what is needed here and now, in the time of need of judgments, the epoch of judging. That is what leads to the third aporia.

(c) He calls this the aporia of urgency, which means that justice cannot wait. Justice may be an infinite ideal but justice cannot wait. We may be sure, in virtue of *différance*, that justice in itself is always delayed and deferred, but nonetheless justice cannot wait. We can never get as far as justice in itself, but still justice cannot wait. Justice delayed and deferred is justice denied, but it is no less true that justice cannot wait. Derrida does not take the urgency of justice, the need to act without delay and deferral, as the refutation of *différance* but rather as part of its axiomatic, part of its im/possibility, part of the difficulty imposed on life by *différance*. We do not always have the time to think a decision all the way through, thoroughly and exhaustively, and even if there is time for extensive deliberation, still there comes a time—"a finite moment of urgency and precipitation"—when the leap must be made, the gap crossed, the decision taken:

> Even if time and prudence, the patience of knowledge and the mastery of conditions were hypothetically unlimited, the decision would be structurally finite, however late it came, decision of urgency and precipitation, acting in the night of non-knowledge and non-rule.[25]

That is called the moment of decision.

"The instant of decision is a madness"—that is a very Abrahamic thing to say. That is a citation of Derrida citing Johannes de Silentio, which is the name that leaps to mind as we read the aporias of the leap. If the first aporia is Aristotelian, and second more Levinasian, the third reminds of Johannes de Silentio meditating in fear and trembling over the fate of father Abraham. Has Derrida let a certain Kierkegaardian cat out of the bag of deconstruction? Am I hallucinating? Do I spend too much time hanging around cemeteries? Too much time reading pseudonyms? Or does this discussion of these aporias of judgment not have the ring of *Fear and Trembling*, the very text in which I found my own calling as an *Extra-Skriver*.

Consider just a few fragments: Judging never enjoys the comfort of calculation but is constantly exposed to the "anxiety" and "fear" (*angoisse, effroi*) of a certain uncertainty.[26] Deciding must pass through undecidability's "ordeal," which is the category of Job and father Abraham. It must endure the oscillation of a still more onerous either/or, one that can never be put to rest, in order to make the Abrahamic "cut" of a decision. Again, judging belongs to a mad economy, even as the madness of justice confounds the rational stockbrokers of the finite with whom the madness of father Abraham is constantly juxtaposed in *Fear and Trembling*.[27] Finally, judgment is faced with three problemata which beset it. Will Derrida turn out to be another "supplementary clerk"— an *Extra-Skriver* extraordinaire—of father Abraham named by de Silentio? Was Johannes de Silentio taking over the role of prophet here and predicting the future, the coming of a deconstruction to come?

Events press hard upon us and demand a decision, a finite cut in the flow of events, a response to an ambiguous turn of events, here and now. This is not decisionism, not—for all of its rhetoric, which is considerable—an arbitrary leap or flip of the coin. Judgment is not only, not even primarily, I would say, anything I do. Judgment is not reducible to the capricious "I will" (*ego volo*) of decisionism, but constitutes a response that is made to what is happening to me, to what overtakes me. Judging always has to do with "the other's coming as the singularity that is always other."[28] This is not autodecisionism, the caprice of subjectivity, but the deepest heteronomism or heterotropism, a gift of responsiveness to the idiosyncratic demands of the event, to the (almost) infinite demands that are placed upon us by events.

How, then, to judge? It is very difficult. Judging is a delicate negotiation between precedent and the unprecedented, equity and difference, law and justice. Deconstruction settles gently into the uneasy space between these two, quivering between the universal and the singular. It lives *inter-esse*, being-in-between, in the margins—and negotiates the difference between them. In deconstruction, which is justice, everything comes down to (good) judgment and know-how.

HOW TO JUDGE (NOT)

Knowing how to judge means knowing how to keep an eye on singularities while keeping a watch out for the eagle/laws that hover over them. Judging attaches itself to the incommensurability of the individual, to the exception, and knows how and when to lift the universal, to put it out of action, which is what is meant by a suspension or *epochē*. It is not a question of suspending judgment in order to find the *eidos* or the law, as in classical phenomenology, but of suspending the *eidos* or the law in order to judge what is happening. In this perversely deconstructionistic untranscendental

Urteilslehre (doctrine of judgment), it is not a question of the suspension of judgment but of judgments of suspension, of judgments suspended over an abyss.

The suspension in question is not Husserl's, but Johannes de Silentio's. The abyss into which father Abraham was led by the voice that called him, which he answered in his best French, *me voici*, is the abyss of the individual exception, the abyss that is opened by the "teleological suspension of the ethical." By this Johannes meant the suspension of the universal, a suspension which exposes us to an abyss of "distress, anxiety, paradox."[29] Far from granting us unlimited licentiousness, lifting the universal makes things more difficult, more paralyzing. Divested of the guardrails of the universal, the single individual—Abraham—enters a fearsome sphere of singularity, silence, and incommunicability, where there is no law to fall back upon. However fearsome a figure the law of the father may be, Johannes de Silentio maintained that the sphere outside the law, the sphere where Abraham found himself, is more fearsome still. The real fear and trembling begin, he said, when, stepping outside the law, Abraham is forced to make a go of it without the reassuring supports of the universal.

The difficulty that Johannes de Silentio was trying to create for philosophy—for Kant (on universalizable law) and Hegel (on *Sittlichkeit*)—the disturbance he was trying to provoke in "ethics" (as a supplementary clerk of Abraham, Johannes was "against ethics"), has its source in his very different conceptions of time and freedom and—dare I say it?—even of being, conceptions quite at odds with what Johannes called "the categories of Greek philosophy":

> For if the ethical—that is social morality [*Sittlichkeit*]—is the highest and if there is in a person no residual incommensurability in some way such that this incommensurability is not evil (i.e., the single individual, who is to be expressed in the universal), then no categories are needed other than what Greek philosophy had. . . .[30]

Johannes and the other Kierkegaardian pseudonyms were forging a different set of categories, jewgreek categories, which befit the situation of the "single individual." They proceeded on the assumption of the radical contingency of things, that events happen, and that the links from happening to happening are contingent, not necessitated. This *other* idea of being and time shows up in Descartes, not when he defines God as infinite idea, and certainly not when he says *ego cogito*, which was at root a very Greek thing to say for someone writing to Jesuits, but when he insists on the need for the world, once it has been created, to be continually conserved in its being—lest it lapse back into nothing. Descartes's assumption is that unless God does something, unless He takes an active and incessant interest in the world from moment to moment, the world would just cease to be. That was the almost perfect opposite of what was assumed by Aristotle, who was most certainly using the categories of Greek philosophy. Aristotle thought it was entirely beneath the dignity of the divine being (*theos*) to pay any attention at all to the world and that God ought properly to be occupied with God alone, while the world tended to its own business. In the world, things ran quite smoothly, thank you very much. The stars trek along set courses and in regular patterns; the unchanging species persist, however many individual things come and go. They always have and they always will.

Kierkegaard and Descartes—this is a Franciscan idea; you will find it also in William of Ockham—had inherited a variant strain of Western metaphysics, a kind of metaphysical mutation that had worked its way into the mainstream metaphysical tradition, amounting to a kind of jewgreek mutant or contaminant of the prevailing categories of Greek philosophy. The jewgreek idea of "being and time," which was handed down by father Abraham, not by father Parmenides (who would certainly have been scandalized by it), was not necessitarian and universalistic at all but turned on very different categories, such as creation, annihilation, and conservation; freedom and contingency; divine interest and even divine intervention in history; and the strange idea of the sacredness of every hair on your head, i.e., of the "single individual." Indeed the idea of history itself, one that was filled with eschatological crises and messianic promises, was a jewgreek idea. The jewgreek paradigm turned on events, on the contingency, idiosyncrasy, and singularity of what happens, and of what was going on in people's hearts, rather than on being, permanence, law, and universality. From the standpoint of Kant and Hegel, who employed the categories of Greek philosophy, the idea that the individual event is higher than the universal is the very *form of evil*, since according to them the *telos* of the individual is to make herself commensurable, to fall in line with the universal. But on the jewgreek paradigm, this incommensurability is the very form of faith (Kierkegaard) or of justice (Levinas, Derrida, Lyotard).

That is why judging is a much more slippery affair in jewgreek (quasi) philosophy, a more elastic, agile, flexible matter occurring in jewgreek time, and that is why you could talk about suspending the law, or lifting it, or finding ways to let incommensurable individuals slip past it. On the jewgreek paradigm, judging is constantly flirting with abysses, idiosyncrasies, proper names—and with fear and trembling.

Judging in jewgreek time is not primarily a matter of applying the law, but of lifting the law.[31]

I will give you a good jewgreek example. It may seem lighthearted to you, but be assured I am always very serious—allowing, of course, for certain exceptions, for those moments when I am feeling highly heteromorphic. The medieval masters debated the question of whether God could change past time.[32] This is not a well-known medieval debate, and it will be certainly used as more testimony to medieval *Seinsverlassenheit* and to its unforgiveable distortion of the First Beginning. (Who can forgive that? It is beyond forgiveness.) Still, to those of us who have no inside information on the History of Being, who, try as we might, can get no further than what happens, who have not the slightest idea of whether we are needed by Being or the Spirit, to us supplementary clerks picking up pieces of obligation here and there—to us it is an interesting little fragment. Stuck as I am between the two Beginnings, unable to budge an inch, surrounded on every side by evils that everywhere beset me, this is the sort of thing that occupies my mind and provides me with a distraction from my unhappy circumstance. For this obscure little *opuscula* is a sign of a small Semitic strain that disturbs medieval onto-theo-Greco-logic from within, like a little computer virus that threatens to throw a massive system into disarray, or like any other little bug that invites extermination. This odd jewgreek strain is interesting to me because it is framed in terms of events rather than of Being's mighty History.

For these Semitico-medievals, whose onto-theo-Greco-logic was perversely put into the service of explaining something very Semitic, which is why I am calling it jewgreek, and whose speculations were invaded and inwardly disturbed by Rabbi Moyses Maimonides, Ibn Roshad, and numerous other non-Greeks, which is an excessively heteromorphic state of affairs, if you think about it—these medieval masters wanted to know, e.g., whether God could restore lost virginity. Now no one, and I say this with (almost) apodictic assurance, will contest that such a restoration could in certain situations be extremely useful, on a par at least with restoring the ceiling of the Sistine Chapel (although it was, I would be the first to admit, not a little phallocentrically put). It is a very revealing *question* to raise, almost the perfect opposite of the sort the Greeks were wont to put. The Greeks set to wondering whether the contingency of the past does not harden into necessity the longer an event sits on the shelf of the past. But these Semitico-medievals (who were not Semitic enough for Luther) wondered, on the contrary, whether the contingency of the past, being contingent, could not be completely wiped out, erased, like a computer file, without a trace, just plain annihilated. They wanted to let the event go up in smoke, letting it disappear without a trace. They could say with a freedom never dreamt of by Nietzsche that "there are no facts" (or interpretations, either), since God is free to undo them, i.e., to see to it that what happened did not happen. That is a dream, of course, one more dream of being without *différance*, with no traces left behind, of perfect erasures and of not having to labor *sous rature*. But it is a very lovely Semitico-medieval dream, a tall tale of hyperbolic time.

It was in such very hyperbolic, jewgreek time that a dream of perfect forgiving took place, a dream of forgiving without leaving a trace of the past behind, without anything left to be sorry (*poena*) for, with nothing to repent.

To be sure, this is a metaphysical debate, and it should be denounced as such by everyone who has climbed a Schwarzwald peak and seen the End of Metaphysics. Still, it had a point (if not a peak), because a certain

amount of heterologic had worked its way into all this onto-theo-logic. This
medieval view is actually even a little "postmodern." Almost. Phrases happen. They fly up like sparks. The links between the phrases are contingent
and fortuitous and they may be "forged" (formed/faked) in any number of
ways. The links are leaps, transitions from phrase to phrase, little leaps
across an abyss. It is an illusion to think that the links thus formed fill in the
abysses, that the transitions are smooth and uninterrupted. Linking is
leaping, not backfilling. It is island hopping, archipelagous, not a smooth
discourse along a level course.[33] But if events are that contingent, could we
not link them up in a new way, tell a new story, one which eases the pain
(*poena*) of the past, the pain done to us, which just forgets an event or two?
Would not that rather old jewgreek idea be very postmodern?

(Phrases are events, occasions, and the philosophy of events has a
slightly occasionalistic ring [*glas*] to it. There is a linguistic occasionalism in
Lyotard that is the companion of a certain refreshing nominalism, all of
which is aimed at keeping the event as light as possible, at lightening up
and steering clear of deep verbal or even nominative essences that are supposed to steady the course of events.)

Forgiving occurs in jewgreek time. It does not attempt to "retrieve"
(*wiederholen*) the past, even if you reconceive the past as what "has been"
(*das Gewesen*) (Heidegger), or to recycle the past and say yes to its endless
return (Nietzsche), or to raise the past up to the eagle heights of the present
or coming *parousia* (Hegel). It just forgets the past. Forgiving is a movement
in the Levinasian time of creation and annihilation, the time of radical,
magical transformations between Being and non-Being. That was a *scandalon* to father Parmenides and the Greeks, a very scandalous idea of Being
and time, but it is the very element of Levinas and Kierkegaard.[34] I would
even say that Heidegger, who never tired of saying he found everything in
the Greeks, that he wanted to be as Greek as he could be, was in fact giving
the Greeks a closet jewgreek reading, one that he first learned from Luther
and Kierkegaard. So after expunging Jews and Christians from the First Beginning, Heidegger then "bootlegged"[35] them back into Being's history by
way of a "retrieval."

For the Greeks, change itself provoked something of a *scandalon*, over
which they fought vigorously and which they sought to explain as a transformation within Being, from one sort of Being to another. Whatever happens (*geschieht, arrive*) happens within the horizon of Being. It was unthinkable that there could be a transformation of Being itself, that one could
wipe away the horizon of Being as a whole. But forgiveness is a transgression of Being and its time, of the time of Being and the Being of time. Forgiveness requires the freedom to dispense with Being's time and time's Being, to dismiss them both, to send them both packing. Forgiveness is the
inverse side of creation, the movement in the opposite direction, the reduction to non-Being which made father Parmenides rend his garments.

Forgiving is just forgetting, not Greco-Germanic forgetting, the sort that is meant to come back on you, to repeat itself on you eventually, the sort that requires recalling (Heidegger) or interiorizing (Hegel), so that the deeper the forgetting, which is the danger, the more one needs the recalling, which is the saving. Platonic *anamnesis*, Hegelian *Erinnerung*, and Heideggerian *Andenken* as the transition between the two beginnings, are so many ways to elude the event-fulness of events, to steady their course. On this jewgreek scheme, it is the forgetting that saves us and the recalling that poses the danger. Forgetting means not circling back, cutting no eagle circles in the sky, no recircling or recycling, but just forgetting, just forging ahead and forgetting. It is like Nietzsche's active forgetting, making a point to forget, trying to forget; that is perhaps a point on which we can get a consensus between Dionysus and the Crucified.

Hannah Arendt, an important jewgreek philosopher, who had an acute sense of the frailty of action and of philosophy as a headlong retreat from this frailty, who had therefore a very interesting deconstructive attitude toward philosophy and events[36]—Arendt says that forgiving is the jewgreek "remedy" to the harshness and severity of the event, i.e., to the irreversibility of time, even as promising is the remedy for its unpredictability.[37] If we forget the metaphysical problem of whether God could actually change the past and focus on the irreversibility of events, then we get to the factical problem behind the metaphysical speculation. According to Arendt, Plato wanted to make *praxis* look like *techne*, to treat action as if it could be shaped and molded. That was, Arendt says, the founding moment of "political philosophy"—and it is what Lacoue-Labarthe calls *la fiction du politique*.[38] Political philosophy represents a flight from action, from judging, from its fragility and contingency and abyss-like quality, into the comfort of the universal, the security of law and order, of rules and structures. It is a flight from the anarchic singular into the search for the political *arche*, which is the Greek remedy (*pharmakon?*). This is a very deconstructive streak in Arendt, because she thinks that "political philosophy," which is philosophy, which is metaphysics, tries to contain action and that action cannot be contained. Political philosophy takes action as its subject matter but cannot deal with it, which is why it suffers deconstruction and why the expression "political science" is a serious misnomer. Political philosophy cannot digest action.

The jewgreek remedy for irreversibility was to just forget it ("just gaming is just forgetting"), to forgive and forget. "Trespassing," which is a daily occurrence, part and parcel of the "web of relations" that makes up factical life, "needs forgiving, dismissing, in order to make it possible for life to go on by constantly releasing" us from what we do to one another. Forgiving keeps the web of relations loose and open-ended, making it possible for people to "change their minds" and start all over again.[39] So if someone were to "trespass" (*hamartanein*) against you—now Arendt is commenting on an old jewgreek narrative—and then to say to you that he had a change of mind (*metanoia*), then you are to release him (*aphienai*), forgive him, forget it and release him, just the way you would want to be released if you changed your mind.[40] Cut the cord of the past; keep no record; do not keep it in your heart (kardia). Cut it loose, release it. The standard translation of metanoia as "repentance" rather misses the mark of the releasing, Arendt says, the opening gesture of forgiving (aphienai) and of the sense of being renewed one gets with metanoia. Metanoia is a category of the heart, not of the mind, because nous here means heart, not reason or intelligence. It means making a new start, turning over a new leaf, getting out from under old traps and old habits. It means to start up a new chain of events, to link in new and fresh ways, to let the past go. It does not mean "repent," doing "penance," causing oneself or others more (re-) pain (paena) but, as Hannah Arendt says, "almost the opposite"[41] —i.e., no more pain (un-re-pentant!).

The opposite of forgiveness is vengeance, retribution, paying back, getting even, not letting go, clinging to events with a fury, drawing the strings and constraints of events still tighter, settling accounts, evening the score. Vengeance and retribution operate within a closed economy, with zero-sum accounting, in which there must be a balance of payments, balanced accounts, getting "even." Retribution makes good economic sense. But forgiveness belongs to the generalized economy of giving without getting back, without a payback, without a return on your investments. Forgiveness is more madness and bad economics.

Forgiving lets the web of human relations hang loose. It cuts the event loose, gives the Other space, room to breathe, to try again. Forgiving is letting go, lassen, a kind of Gelassenheit, not in the sense of wesentliches Denken, because it is not thinking at all, neither calculative nor meditative, not a matter of nous or logos at all, but a matter of kardia. Forgiveness does not enforce the rules, does not exact payment. It does not let the law take its toll. It dismisses the law, suspends it, lifts it, lets it hang in midair, in order to answer the call that wells up from the abyss of the Other. If someone "turns to you saying (epistrepse pros se legon) 'I have had a change of heart (metanoo)'," then you (we) should suspend the law, lift it off his/her back. Release them. Lift the law. Let them be. Lighten up.

When someone turns to us and speaks, the law dissolves before our eyes, for the law is never anything more than a schema, a general rule, a universal, while the individual is what happens. The law can never be cut to fit the singular, or else there would be as many laws as there are individuals. The transition from the law to the individual is always a leap. Forgiving is a leap from the law to the one who "turns to you and speaks." His or her speaking—not the content of what they say, for they may not be very articulate, but the speaking (they might also write you a letter)— dissolves the law down into the one who speaks, for individuals were not made for the law, but the law for individuals. In the speaking the law is deconstructed.

But justice in itself, if such a thing exists, is not deconstructible.

In this case, justice is attained by judging not. Forget it.

HOW TO JUDGE HETEROLOGICALLY

Were I invited, as my next project, to write a logic book (never fear!), I would divide it into two parts: I. "Homologia" (this would include a section on homophobia), which would deal with judging situations that are always the same, and II. "Heterologia," which would concentrate on heterological judgments, judging situations that keep turning out to be different. Part I could also be subtitled "Greek Logic," which is somewhat redundant, while Part II could be called "Jewgreek Logic," which is absurd.

In Part II, I would have a section on fallacies in which I would make a special plea for the *argumentum ad misericordiam*, which I think has been badly treated by the logicians, to the point that I feel extremely sorry for it. I myself am of the view that the *argumentum ad misericordiam* is a good argument, one with a heart. It would occupy a special place in my *Logic*, a place of honor, a preferential privilege, as a way of compensating it for the extreme disadvantages and blatant discrimination it has suffered in the past. This is, I will be the first to confess, a very heterodoxical approach to take to logic, but I would do my best to defend myself and, were I to fail, I would plead for mercy on the grounds of my good intentions and my numerous children.

The law is a paradigmatic piece of homologic, by which I mean a logic of the same, a logic which makes use of variables whose values make no difference, or whose differences are of no value, or, to put it still another way, where it does not matter what your proper name is. All that matters is that, if you are a substitution instance for x, you be consistently substituted for x, so that if *x* is *F* you will always be *F* and you will not occasionally, as events dictate, change your mind and choose sometimes not to be *F*. This makes for consistency, uniformity, equality, in short, for *homologia*. You are always saying the same thing, no matter the time or the place. Now this has its advantages. I do not want to ban homologic; on the contrary, it is Part One of my *Logic*. It is, as a great (*grammato*) logician once said, never a matter of choosing between these alternatives.[42]

But homology is a hard saying and so the law, which is exceedingly homological, is mostly for the hardy, and I myself, heteromorph that I am, will tire easily of all this hardness. Homological laws (a pleonasm) befit the strong and able-bodied, everyone with the *Seinskönnen* to keep going. The law keeps the *ich kann* of the hardy in check.[43] *Phronesis*, which prefigured existential *Verstehen*, is one of the best attempts made by homologic to give the law a certain amount of give while keeping the unity of a homological schema in place. *Phronesis*, the *arete* of the best and brightest, the hale and the hardiest, *die Gebildeten*, makes the law a reasonable thing. Still, the law is for those who are able to keep it, who should and could have kept it. The law restrains the autonomy and freedom of the best, of those whose freedom could be dangerous.

But what about those who have been laid low, who lie too low for the law, who have not gotten as far as freedom and autonomy? Then the eagle of the law soars right over them, does not even notice them. That is where the *argumentum ad misericordiam* enters the court and makes a special plea to lift the law, in order to lift these people up, to give them a lift, to give them relief. By lifting the law, one reaches out to those who have no strength for the law, who are not yet strong enough to stand on their own and to have equal standing under the law, who have not quite gotten as far as the homologous situation that the law presupposes.

I intend to include a section on modal logic in my heterologic in which I will defend a slightly paradoxical (or heterodoxical) axiom: *du kannst* implies *du sollst*. In Kant's strictly transcendental, very universalistic scheme, where obligation is a fact as it were of pure reason, and reason is the sphere of universalizability—which is why the transcendental logic is through and through a transcendental homologic—the existence of obligation (*Sollen*) implies the existence of freedom (*Können*). "Ought" implies "can do." It is of the following form.

Kant!
Me voici.
Du sollst!
Ich kann.

(Certain Germans have reported to me that when they begin to feel an obligation, they speak French, being sure that they cannot make it with their own language.) Kant assumes, of course, that everyone who can do, as a transcendental matter, can also do under the factical circumstances in which they find themselves. But in a more factical, differential heterologic, which takes differences into account, which pays attention to everything idiosyncratic and differential, there are *de facto* circumstances that need to be considered. For heterologic is the logic of difference, taking difference (*heteros*) into account (*logos*).

Heterologic does not blind itself to the fact that there are those whose facticity deprives them of factical freedom and autonomy, those whom events have reduced to indigence and disadvantage, to a state beneath the law, where they do not get as far as the law. It is of the utmost importance in heterologic to notice the variations in the values of the variables. For example, there are those who have no property for the law to protect; no income for the law to tax; who do not vote because they are not registered; who cannot read the law, and who have never heard of their legislative "representatives" who are supposed to represent their interests. They first require the factical ability (*Können*) to play the game of the law in order to be a part of its system of obligations (*Sollen*). In short, in factical, jewgreek heterologic, *du kannst* implies *du sollst*. Q.E.D. Such people are not homologous but are incommensurable with the law, so the law does not protect them, or their rights, or guarantee them equality, because they have not gotten as far as equality, not yet. Once they do, then they will wear the law like a shield. At the moment, they have hardly anything to wear.

The law sets out to give all an equal hearing. That is the essence of the homological operation. It gives everyone an equal voice, and that is an important right that I have no wish to repeal. It will be pointed out in Part One ("Homologia"). But there are those who have not gotten as far as having a voice or a vote yet, whose appeals are not filed before a court, who have been deprived, *de facto*, as a factical matter, of voice and legal representation. They are muted, silent, even invisible. They do have more than their fair share of pain and misery, which silently appeal for relief, and which must be made, as Lyotard says, to sound like an alarm.[44] When the voiceless can make themselves heard and get as far as equality and the law, as far as a *litige*, beyond the *différend*, they will lay aside the *argumentum ad misericordiam* and leave their children at home. They will represent themselves or pay for good lawyers. Then they too will be assimilated to the homological operation. But their problem at present is that the law's homological register is not recording their complaints.

Left to itself (if it has an itself), the law is unrelenting; it never takes a break. The law is universal, uniform, sweeping, blind, relentless. That is why it is sometimes necessary to suspend the law, to bracket it with a certain merciful *epochē*, to lift the burden of the law, so that the law does not exact the price it requires. To lift the law is to offer relief from the law, to let the other loose from the grip of law. Acting affirmatively on behalf of those whom events have treated most negatively, preferring the needs of the most needy and most disadvantaged, making exceptions, responding preferentially, actively, to every one who has been laid low by events: those are all modes, not of applying or appropriating the law, but of lifting it, sending it on its way—temporarily, for now, in the here and now, in order to lighten the press of events just long enough to let those who are laid low regain their footing. Affirmative action programs, head starts for those who have been injured before the race began, massive special support for urban schools and schoolchildren, instead of funding every school and every child equally, however well-to-do—that all makes good heterological sense, although it is mathematically, homologically, unequal.

It makes sense if you switch into a heterological mode, which means to recognize the urgent needs of the differential. It is not illogical but heterological; not less than fair but more than fair. It does not produce something less than equality (which would be a homological flaw) but more than equality, which is a heterological virtue.

The more or less homological ideal of *phronesis* is to settle into the event and to bring the law to bear on the event. The more jewgreek heterological ideal is to let the weight of the differential, of the disaster, bear down on us and to lift homological requirements. The *phronimos* keeps his bearing, while the heterologist has been knocked off his pins. The law aims at sameness, equality under the law, while heterology is attuned to difference, the differential, individual differences and differentiating conditions, like disasters.

The *argumentum ad misericordiam* is a bit of a hermeneutic trickster. It has been known to slip into the homological camp and there assume the guise of a sound homological argument. For, in the long run, does it make sense for an economy bent on profits and good returns to keep a sizable portion of its population in poverty, out of work, in poor health, imprisoned, uneducated, and unable to play the game of exchange, beneath the law? Is it not more expensive—in constant, homological dollars—to maintain public welfare programs and prisons and hospitals than it would be to educate and aid people to stand on their own feet in the first place? And this quite apart from the "appeal to humaneness"?—which may be a way to reinterpret the *argumentum ad hominem* and may require still another section in my *Logic*! Does it not make perfect homological sense, from the point of view of capitalism's own powerful *grand récit* (free enterprise, freedom of opportunity, fair competition, a flourishing economy, etc.), to get everybody on their feet? That of course is a strictly logical or homological argument, a piece of homo-logo-economics. But if that is so, then is the *argumentum ad misericordiam* really a fallacy after all? Is it even a fallacy in homologic, the logic of the same, that treats everyone the same? Or is it only a fallacy in phallo-sophy, which wants to be very hard, a logic of hardness, and hence not a fallacy but a phallacy?

This may turn out to be a kettle argument (so I will perhaps then add a section on kettle arguments, which I may also need to rehabilitate): we should lift the law even though it does not make homological sense, and then again because it really does. Or again (another kettle): we need the *argument ad misericordiam* because it is necessary to supplement equality and fairness with a more merciful frame of mind; *and* then again we need the *argument ad misericordiam* because that really is exactly (*au juste*) what justice is, what equality and fairness are. We need to be more than fair, *and* that is only fair. *Plus de juste:* no more fairness/more than fair.

The disaster is to apply homologic in the field of heterology, to treat the poorest and neediest homologically, blindly, with (mere) equity, to give them (merely) equal standing under the law who are laid low. It makes homologic sense, under the law, to be color-blind or gender-blind or race-blind, but it is merciless and bad heterologic if you have been laid low by your color or your gender or your race. The latter situations require a more multicolored heterology for lovers of heterodoxy, heteronomy, and heteromorphism, of rainbows of many kinds.

I am not calling for more *phronesis*, which is a homological virtue that turns on hitting the mean mark of the *logos*—letting the law be flexible and applying it adroitly—but for a heterological, hyperbolic excess on behalf of disasters. *Phronesis* is the virtue of the hale and the whole, of the best, with those who deserve honor, the town's leading men (*sic*). But the *argumentum ad misericordiam* is directed at the worst, who excel at nothing. *Phronesis* is a mode of *nous*, a matter of practical intelligence, not exactly of having a heart (*kardia, misericordia*). *Phronesis* is primarily cognitive; to be sure, it is "practical" cognition but it is still primarily *logos, ratio*, and unconcealing. *Phronesis* means being sharp enough to see into the idiosyncrasies of the situation, the subtleties of a complicated and slightly unprecedented situation. The *argumentum ad misericordiam* is not a matter of practical intelligence but of a certain succumbing to the claims of the Other, a giving in, a melting, a surrender, a loss of self; not *nous* but *kardia*. *Stricto sensu*, it is (homological) foolishness. The *phronimos* knows what he (*sic*) is doing; he knows what is happening and knows his way around the world. He goes around concealing things and avoids being a fool, which is his opposite. But the *argumentum ad misericordiam* answers the claim that disasters put forward, which looks a little mad; and its opposites are the ones who are smart enough to take care of themselves, those who know who is number one, who go first class (*glas*).

What *phronesis* and the *argumentum ad misericordiam* have in common is that they are directed at the individual, the different, the singular, let us say the absolutely singular, but with a difference. The object of *phronesis* is the singular action that requires the discernment to see how the law is to be brought to bear upon it. But the *argumentum ad misericordiam* does not apply the law; it suspends it in favor of the singularity of one who falls beneath the law, one who has become inaudible or invisible to the law, one of whom the law is oblivious. The *phronimos* can see just how the law fits here and now, whereas the *argumentum ad misericordiam* concerns those whom no law fits, who do not fit in anywhere, who are misfits and out of joint, those whom the law has laid aside, or lost sight of, or just misplaced—the way a man misplaces a tie and does not even know it is missing.

Phronesis is what makes the laws work, their necessary supplement; it makes for a well-run *polis*. But the *argumentum ad misericordiam* is addressed to those who have never had a chance to take their place in the *polis*, who have been on the outside, or the underside, of the *polis* from the start. It responds to the call of those who call from beyond the law, before the law takes note of them, who are incommensurable with the law.

But the question of the law is more complicated than this, more ominous than the issues raised by "forgiveness" and judging "heterologically," which are in their way still very beautiful.

RESISTANCE

On March 18, 1980 soldiers of the Salvadoran government entered the little village of Santa Marta in El Salvador and shot to death or cut down with machetes: Miguel, who was 1 year old; Anibal, who was 5; Santa Ana, who was 9; Marina, who was 13; and their father, Juan Hernandez. The entire scene was witnessed by Florintina Mendez, the wife and mother of the victims.

The soldiers said the children and their father were guerrillas.[45]

That event—and a thousand others like it, which perhaps will get documented with time as the story of that unhappy place comes to light—did not call for forgiveness, and certainly not for forgetting, not then, not there, not at that point. Or for the "conversation of mankind." Or for putting one's hope in the belief that the forces of reason (homologic) and compassion (heterologic) would bring the governments of El Salvador and the United States to their senses.[46] It called for resistance—in the names of the children, which are the names of justice. It called for a war of resistance whose warriors would be priests and peasants and nuns and village officials, waging war against the massive brutality of the army, the wealthy capitalists, and the government. It called for a counter-violence to retard and perhaps even to put an end to state and military violence in this little country named for the Savior, whose citizens and cities bear the names of saints.

There are times—too many and too awful—when the law is not merely blind or wooden and in need of a more supple application or a more merciful frame of mind. There are times when the law is the very embodiment of malice and oppression. Then—when the law spills blood—the law requires violation, transgression, resistance.

Do not ask me for the rule that governs forgiveness and resistance, negotiation and rebellion, that decides for us when one is needed rather than the other. I have already confessed my limits, that I have no such head as is required to make such judgments. Ask Ethics.

Do not ask me for the rule that governs memory and forgetting. One of the many antinomies of obligation is this: forgive and forget; on the other hand, cultivate the dangerous memory of suffering. Do not ask me for the resolution of this antinomy. Ask Ethics.

It is misguided distortion of the concept of heteronomy, of the philosophy of the Other, to think that the notion of the Other, and of obligation to the Other, leads to absolute pacifism and to letting oneself or others become a victim or a hostage or a slave in a socioeconomic or political sense.[47] Nothing would please the masters of capital and the masters of war more than that. That is exactly what Marx thought religion would do to the peasants and why he opposed religion; he never imagined radical priests and nuns. He was too much an *Aufklärer* and not sufficiently jewgreek to see this—albeit very repressed—side of religion. It was Nietzsche, not Marx, who comprehended the revolutionary power of religion, the possibility of revolutionary priests and nuns, the potential of religion to take the side of the poor and to disturb the order of rank—which is why he (Nietzsche) opposed religion! Marx and Nietzsche were masters of suspicion of religion for exactly opposite reasons. Both were right and both were wrong, because religion does not mean one thing.

There is a simplistic mistake that is often repeated about deconstruction that needs to be rooted out. The mistake is to think that deconstruction cannot oppose cruelty or oppression because then it would be "excluding" or "marginalizing" someone, viz., the oppressors. The homicidal rapist, the plunderer, a violent military, all that is just the "Other" and deconstruction recommends openness to the Other. By the same token, when egalitarian and democratic forces are in power, so this argument goes, then deconstruction must conclude that this "power" is just more violence, violently holding opposing forces—say fascist, sexist, or racist forces—in check and so thereby "excluding" or "marginalizing" them.

The mistake here is to construe deconstruction in an excessively formal sense and to pay no attention to the substantive merits of what is in or out of power, i.e, to whether or not the forces that are in power are just forces. For deconstruction "is" justice and Derrida says (almost) that he knows of nothing more just—and he should know.[48] Exclusion and marginalization, thus, are never merely formal ideas; they always have to do with damaged lives and disasters. Vicious military leaders, exploitatious capitalists, oppressive, dishonest government officials, rapists (homicidal or not) are not victims but victimizers, and so the restraint of their victimization practices does not constitute their "exclusion" but simply a just law or a just order. By the same token, the overthrow of such brutal forces does not represent their "marginalization" but rather a just revolution. Respect for the Other does not mean a pacifist submission to wanton violence; it does not mean respecting people who produce victims, i.e., respecting people who do not respect others, which would amount to letting disrespect reign. People who produce victims are not the "Other" to whom we owe everything. The Other, as Levinas says, is always "the widow, the orphan, the stranger," that is, emblematically, the victim—not the victimizers.

Miguel, Anibal, Santa Ana, Marina, Juan Hernandez, Florintina Mendez: they are the "others" who command our respect. The others are the victims, the disasters, the ones who are laid low and so come from on high, the powerless ones, not the masters of death who make disasters and produce victims.

It is precisely in the name of the Other, of justice, of respect, in the names of the children, that resistance is called for.

The most perfect resistance is nonviolent. Philosophers are on the whole unable to imagine nonviolent resistance. It usually requires more prophetic people like Gandhi and Martin Luther King to shape those visions for us, let alone make them happen. The most perfect revolutions should be velvet.[49] When the people simply rise up, provoked here and there, by this or that, who knows how or by what, when they simply fill the streets and refuse to go to work, when they shield their leaders against the military's bullets with their defenseless bodies—that is the power of powerlessness and of nonviolent resistance. That is a rare and lovely flower.

But nonviolence is not always enough. Sometimes you get Tiananmen

Square instead. Nonviolence should be tried, but when it is tried and tried and then tried again, without success, then we have reached the point where violence has provoked counter-violence. That is the lesser of the evils that beset us on every side. The only measure is pain and pain is a measure without measure. (I never said I had a theory of the good but only of the minimization of evil.) That is why the demands of the white government in South Africa that Mandela and the African National Congress renounce violence before the government will settle its differences with the black majority is so ludicrous. This government *is* violence; it is the very name of violence, an international name, an international shame and ignominy, while the name of Mandela sounds an alarm around the world.

I do not believe it is possible to remove the violence from nonviolence, to decontaminate it, to have a pure nonviolence. Any serious shift in the balance of power, any serious reconfiguration of the networks of power, including those that are for the better, will damage someone's interests and is thus far violent.[50] Pure nonviolence is possible only logically, homologically, anemically. Politics will never be what Levinas calls ethics; what he calls ethics does not exist but is a kind of hyperbolic demand on existence. Johannes Climacus got it right: a logical system is possible, but an existential one is not. By existential he meant factical. Climacus meant, it does not happen.

Obligations happen, but sometimes the sea of obligations in which we are immersed threatens to overwhelm us, to inundate and drown us. That sea is what Foucault means by "power" and "normalization." That is when we need resistance, not obedience. There is nothing valuable in itself about obedience. Obedience is not necessarily responsible; it depends upon what you obey. Sometimes responding to the call of the Other requires the most searing, disturbing disobedience to the law. Sometimes it is anarchy that is the most responsible of all, viz., when the *arche* is intent on spilling blood.

Resistance takes many forms and can be very inventive.

Antigone is a classical heroine of resistance, of disobedience, her heroism being precipitated by Creon's lack of wisdom. Her "feminine operation" was not only to care tenderly for her fallen brother but to resist—unto death—an immoderate man.

Civil disobedience, defying bad laws, is good resistance in a modern form. It includes taking the consequences, perhaps using the time in jail to write a letter, say from Birmingham, Alabama, in 1953. When Rosa Parks took a seat in the front of a bus in Montgomery, Alabama, in 1955 she set off a massive revolution that will not fail, even though it has suffered systematic setbacks from successive administrations in Washington which drew their support from public resentment and race baiting. Marching down public streets, singing songs of protest, demonstrating one's outrage publicly: those are the voices of *dissensus*, Lyotard's love of the *agon*. *Dissensus* stirs the pots of democracy.

Without resistance, the rights of women and of homosexuals will succumb to bio-power, to fundamentalists, to all those who want to inscribe their private views of the Good on everyone else's bodies, and to cut off the right to be different (not to mention what else they would like to cut off).

Democracy loves dissent. At least, that is the idea; that is what democracy, in itself, if there is such a thing, is supposed to love.

Oh my fellow democrats, there are no democrats.

DILIGE, ET QUOD VIS FAC

Love, and do what you will.

That is the first and only law of judgment, the principle of my doctrine of judgment which I shall use on the frontispiece of my *Logic*. This is the *principium sine principio*,[51] the principle without principle, the principle for what is not subject to principle. It is not the law of law, but the un-law of law, the un-law that inhabits every law, the out-law in the law, the unbinding of the law, the only law recognized in the anarchic field of singularities and proper names. It is a confession of the breakdown of the law, of its own deconstruction, a profession that the only law is the law of the singular one, an admission that homology dissolves, deconstructs into heterology.

That is the sense—the only sense, which is really quite strict—in which "anything goes."

It is the jewgreek way to let events be, to let the Other be, to let go of oneself. *Dilige* and let events happen, let the Other happen, let them flow and swirl and dance.[52]

Dilige and do anything, whatever you want; that is the open-ended, heteromorphic good I defend. Do not let the good be restrained or contained by the rule of law. It is not the subject of the law. Let it be multiplied and experimentally varied, *ad infinitum*.

Dilige, et quod vis fac: that is more anarchic, heterological advice. This is not *phronesis*, because it is not driven by the search for a moderate mean; its only measure is to let things happen without measure. It is not offended against by excess (only by defect); it *is* excess. It wants to be as hyperbolic as possible.

Dilige, et quod vis fac: that is a quasi-transcendental principle that says that you do not need principles. It is the way one makes one's way around in an abyss, the way one negotiates among singulars.

This is not Greek philosophy but a jewgreek conundrum, a jewgreek way to love the abyss, good jewgreek advice.[53] It is not Greek philosophy, even though philosophy defines itself as a kind of *philia*. But the sort of *philia* philosophy is—*amor intellectualis*— goes well enough with a cold heart, because philosophical *philia* is a sort of *nous, intellectus*, wanting and desirous of *nous*, or of the Forms, or wanting and desiring the aboriginal fluctuation of *physis* or *aletheia*, or even Being's wanting and desiring a place for its clearing, without necessarily caring a whit about flesh and blood.[54]

Dilige, et quod vis fac: that is the heterodoxical, heterological doxology of my joyful wisdom, of my heterology, the fusion and confusion of heteronomy and heteromorphism. *Dilige*: answer the heteronomic call of the disaster—*et quod vis fac*: and do what you love to do, whatever you like, be as heteromorphic as you like.

That letting-be is a *skandalon*, a stumbling block and an abyss to philosophy, which, with disasters, philosophy leaves to Jews and other non-Greeks. This is the *skandalon* that father Abraham gives to father Parmenides.

Events happen. Let them happen. Let them be.

I do not deny that this is another dream of being without *différance*, without violence. I say it is a salutary, fabulous dream, effanineffable. I say, let it happen. Let events happen.

SIX

Almost Perfect Fools

LEVINAS IS NO FOOL

I have gone on record against ethics, against both the Categorical Imperative and *Sittlichkeit*, against Virtue and against Being's binding *nomos*, against Kant, Hegel, and Heidegger, against all ethicists and originary ethicists. I have even dared to speak against Levinas's ethics of infinity, against the absolutely, infinitely Other. I love Levinas dearly, but I would love him more dearly still if, instead of singing the praises of ethics and infinity, he would admit that it is necessary to deconstruct ethics, or better, necessary to see that ethics undergoes deconstruction, right before our eyes.

That he sometimes does, like it or not. If you can get him to talk about politics, about jewgreek ethics and Israeli politics. About the Palestinians. If you ask him about infinite responsibility to the Other, about being held hostage to the Other, about the infinite *me voici* which opens itself to the unconditional command of the Other, and in particular about whether there are any Others other than the Others defined by antisemitism. Then he talks very freely of the desirability of "a political unity with a Jewish majority . . . a State in the fullest sense of the term, a State with an army and arms, an army which can have a deterrent and if necessary a defensive significance." Then the Other to whom you are responsible turns out to be "[m]y people and my kin," my own. That is, the Other ends up being the same. As to the Other who is not the same, who is the enemy, then it is better to keep an army.[1] So what is new in this philosophy which loves novelty?

I am not trying to make Levinas look bad. I am just trying to situate his discourse, to mark off its limits, to delimit the discourse on ethics and infinity. The Other is absolutely infinite—up to a point. You have to be sensible. There are limits. For example, if the Other is shooting at you, then we say, that is not the Other. So we draw a circle around "ethics," marking off a domain of purity, and we point out that everything has its limits, including the ethics of infinity, which turns out to be relatively finite. In addition to being held hostage by the Other, one also keeps an army, just as a deterrent against hostage taking.

That is the prophetic word. From on high.

Levinas is no fool.

This interview with Levinas is a revelation—albeit not a very divine one—of the impossibility of ethics, the impossibility of drawing a line around ethics, of preserving an inner sanctum, a holy of holies, called ethics, and of the need for the deconstruction of ethics. In addition to obligation, there is also resistance and deterrence—and art and religion and technology and many other games, too many to nail down, each of which shades into the others.[2] Ethics is always already political, even as it would be a disaster were politics to inure itself to ethics. When I say I am against ethics I am saying that, rather than maintaining an impossible duality between a (pure) ethics and a (dirty) *Realpolitik*, I would rather have a more sensible, a more delimited, deconstructed idea of ethics to begin with, so that I will have as little as possible to retract when what I have said about obligation is quoted back at me in an interview.

Pure obligation is impossible. It demands that we annul the I, even though it is impossible to make the I disappear. The I is a principle of return, of getting something back. One invests oneself—one's time, one's substance—in order to reap a reward. But obligation tries to divest the I of itself. *Strictissime*, that is impossible. As the Philosopher—to use Aristotle's excellent medieval name—has well argued, the "agent" would never do it. The *agens*—and we cannot avoid being agents—always acts for its own good. Otherwise, what good would it be to act? Aristotle, who was always eminently sensible, always wary of excess (*hyperbole*), who was interested in flourishing and in being filled with genial spirits (*eudaimonia*), said that agents act in order to let good things happen. Even when what happens is bad, the agent must at least for a time be held captive by the notion that it is good. One acts *sub ratione boni*, under the *hermeneia* that good things are happening. Otherwise, who would ever do it?

If I had to have an ethics, if it were a matter of public decency, or more forcefully still, if my annual salary increment depended upon having an ethics, then, since ethics is philosophy and philosophy is Greek, I would be a kind of radical Aristotelian, but very jewgreek (not very aristo-cratico-telian). My jewgreek ethics would include an idea of *eudaimonia*, of a certain *fröhliche Wissenschaft*, of a certain self-love[3] and self-interest, which goes along with a sense of obligation, the two together, in heteromorphic-heteronomic tension.

When we do something, Aristotle said, we get a return or a repetition. There is a line that leads out from the agent to the action and then back again, forming a circle or a loop, a ring or chain, a self-enriching hermeneutico-ontological link, so that the action always belongs to the circle of agency (*Sorge* as the *um willen seiner*). Even the gift, the pure gift—and the purer the better—belongs to this circle, because when I send a gift out, gratitude comes back, whether I want it or not.[4] In the strictest sense, obligation, making a gift of yourself to the Other, without encumbering the Other with your gift, without getting something back, is impossible. Even if I get no gratitude, if I am greeted with ingratitude, which is very painful, how can I not secretly congratulate myself on being such a selfless giver?

In obligation we are supposed to twist free of agency and become a patient; the I is supposed to make itself a hostage of the Other. That at least is the way it is put by Levinas, who is fond of Platonic and Neoplatonic *hy-*

perbole and *hyperousia*, of infinite excess and exceeding essence, of absolute transcendence and invisibility. Obligation presents a paradoxical paradigm, very jewgreek, and—when it has to do with the good of someone I do not know (the stranger) or do not like (the enemy)—not a little foolish. Yet that is what "responsibility" means, *stricto sensu*: to give up your Greek autonomy and agency and to submit to jewgreek heteronomy and patience, to respond to what comes to you from on high and to look a little foolish by treating yourself as an obstacle, a threat to the Other.

That I cannot (quite) do. I cannot (quite) hate myself. That is simply destructive, self-destructive. I must love myself (a little). Even Levinas admits that, if you can get an interview and ask a few pointed questions.

The problem with Levinas is that he has made ethics into a holy of holies, an inviolable inner sanctum, pure and uncontaminated. The problem, as Lyotard says, is that he is too monotheistic, insufficiently pagan—or Dionysio-heteromorphic. He talks as though there is a game of all games, one true game from On High, which assimilates all the other games, and that everything else is a graven image. But I myself subscribe to the (un)principle of contamination and find the distinction between the sacred and the profane one more *grand récit*. If Lyotard confesses that he betrays Levinas when he cites him, I must own up to being a coconspirator:

> In his [Levinas's] view, it is the transcendental character of the other in the prescriptive relation, . . . that is, in the (barely) lived experience of obligation, that is truth itself. This "truth" is not ontological truth, it is ethical. But it is a truth in Levinas's own terms. Whereas for me it cannot be *the* truth. . . . It is not a matter of privileging one language game above others. That would be something like saying: The only important game, the only true one, is chess. That is absurd. What is pagan is the acceptance of the fact that one can play several games, and that each of these games is interesting in itself insofar as the interesting is to play moves.[5]

There is more than one game to play, or more than one game playing us: that is what I mean by heteromorphism. In addition to ethics there is also politics, and these are not simply different essences or regions whose "relationships" are hard to work out; they always already bleed into each other. What happens is an indiscriminate mix, even a mess, of many different categories. The categories, on the other hand, are simply shorthand, simplifications which make it easier to think about what happens. They give us a vocabulary.

When the prophetic word that comes down from Levinas, the word about the Other who comes from On High, about the Infinite Other and the Other's infinity, when that word is that, in addition to being held hostage to the Other, you should also keep an army, to discourage an invasion, I do not disagree. I just want to make it plain that things are much more polymorphic and not quite as monochromic as Levinas lets on, that there is no such thing as "nonviolence" or "ethics," not even for Levinas.

I just want to make it clear that the Other is infinite—but only up to a point. After all, there are limits and one must avoid excess. I am just trying to show that there is more than one game in town—obligation does not have a monopoly—and that one never quite twists free of the Aristotelian point, that whatever I do—insofar as I do anything and insofar as the I is anything more than a field in which many forces play themselves out—it is done for a return. I cannot give pure gifts. I always act *sub ratione boni*: what I do is what I want, or what I think I want, or what "it" wants in and through me, or what something wants (because something is wanting).

One is always inside/outside obligation, on its margins. On the threshold of foolishness. Almost a perfect fool for the Other. But not quite; nothing is perfect. One is a hostage of the Other, but one also keeps an army, just as a deterrent.

FOOLS

That makes it all the more amazing, quite fabulous really, when something foolish actually happens, when fools occasionally appear and actually do something impossible, hyperbolically speaking. Obligation is impossible, but that is not to say that it does not happen, here and there, now and then. Being impossible is not a conclusive objection, inasmuch as the most interesting things are often impossible. It is only to shift the scene from philosophy to poetics, from Greek reflection on what is possible and necessary (or fated and ill-fated) to a jewgreek poetics of what "happens," or from Greek modal logic to jewgreek postmodal logic.

The task of poetics is precisely to grapple with the impossible, not in order to see how it may actually be possible after all, to unearth its most hidden conditions of possibility, but in order to proclaim that it happens, as a matter of factical fact, and to provide it with a suitable idiom. The idea behind jewgreek poetics is to be on the scene, like a part-time poet in residence, a poetically inclined freelance writer, in order to tell the story, or sing the song, when something fabulous happens.

From time to time, here and there, it happens that men and women respond, answer a call, spend themselves, using themselves up entirely for the Other. They spend years, maybe a lifetime, serving others, giving themselves up for the good of others. Sometimes, at the end, they are honored for their service, and we weep over their lives, which are recorded in a stirring biography, an excellent film, or a moving testimonial. At the conclusion of such experiences, although we were highly moved—quite shaken, really—we invariably find the wherewithal to regain our composure and the courage to go on with life, as if nothing had actually happened. We wonder aloud why there are not more such excellent films, the result being that nothing actually changes.

Or sometimes they are just killed or they die in prison. Then they are like a star dying in a distant, unheard of galaxy, of which we know nothing. Either way, it happens.

It is a kind of madness, a sort of *folie* not mentioned in Foucault's *Histoire*. We are confronted here with a paradigm switch, from the *phronimos* to the fool, from the Greek paradigm of the man who knows what he is about, who knows what is happening, to another more jewgreek paradigm of the fool.

Fools give up everything (almost) and (seem to) get nothing back. I would say that fools give an (almost) pure gift, that they (nearly) cut the chain by which a gift always comes back to the giver and puts the recipient in the debt of the benefactor; that they are almost perfect fools. But I will not say it. No one is perfect.

From a rigorous, homological point of view, we would say that if they do it, if it actually happens, then it is, *stricto sensu*, not impossible, in virtue of the principle *ab esse ad posse valet*. That is a humdrum homological point, to be greeted with a yawn; it is not very interesting or poetic. That is just more Greek logic, which is preoccupied with conditions of possibility; more modal logic, or transcendental homologic, whereas what is interesting is a postmodal heterologic. What is interesting is that what they did is a paradox, *folie*, madness; they made themselves fools, or they let themselves be made fools of. *Ab esse ad posse valet, quia absurdum est*: that is the first "principle" of my postmodal logic. They do it because it is foolish, a scandal, absurd. The whole thing is fabulous, which is not a category of Greek philosophy, not an element to be found in Greco-onto-logic, but a bit of jewgreek poetics.

Fools spend their lives working to feed and house the poor, or teaching in crime-ridden schools, or protecting defenseless wildlife; they lead a celibate life serving the peasants in Central America, only to be dragged out of bed one night and shot to death by right-wing gangsters; they spend the better part of their adult life in prison, refusing to cut a deal with a racist government, trying to make a point.

In general (since this list can go on indefinitely) fools consume their lives, their flesh, in the service of others, of other flesh, and they do not keep an army (just as a deterrent). They make themselves foolish, or, more precisely, the call of obligation makes fools of them. It happens. It is foolish, without why, a kind of Abrahamic scandal, a fabulous, mad, paradoxical event. We grope for poetical, heterological categories in a frantic effort to find an idiom for such foolishness, an idiom for which we lack the logic, the grammar, and the poetics.

Fools make a gift of themselves. They enter themselves in an economy without reserve, where to expect a repetition is madness. They make mad investments, which guarantee no yield, which even promise a loss. They enter their lives into the history of another madness, turn themselves into a song in praise of another folly. Fools do what is unlikely, unreasonable, impossible, at least not very sensible.

But that is what they want, their *bonum*. This is the Aristotelian point, and why I call it jew*greek*. Do not try to get in their way; they will not let you stop them. They will fight you like a cat. They are not will-less but very self-willed, maybe even a little difficult to get along with. They are smart, these fools are, and willful and tough. They know exactly what they are doing and no one can stop them. They are doing what they want, what something in them wants. That is their *bonum*. It does not matter what they intend or think they are doing. What matters is the amazing grace, the amazing gift they make. They have their faults, their meannesses, their impossible side, but it is amazing what they do.

They are not saints. Who is? Even saints are not saints. When we retell their stories we leave out a telling detail or two, because the story is supposed to be fabulous, a *fabula*, hyperbolic, hagiographic. A "postmodern saint" is a saint of the Other, a practitioner to excess of responsibility to the Other, a virtuoso of the moral life—this is Edith Wyschogrod's wonderful account in *Saints and Postmodernism*.[6] But "hagiography" is a form of *écriture*, a way of writing that succeeds by creating the impression—the impressive effect—of something pure and uncontaminated, holy and set apart, *hagios*, in an inner *sanctum*. That is the dream of being without *différance*, an im/possible dream of purity, of a pure cut, of pure being, or pure otherwise-than-being, of pure purity—very beautiful, quite fabulous. But as even Wyschogrod will concede: "Still another factor, the factuality of hagiography, precludes the notion of *full saintly realization*."[7] The fullness of the realization is always deferred; the fact is only a fact as it were. The deconstructive stylus tip in hagiographical *écriture* is inserted here. My postmodern saints are contaminated, demythologized heroes, warts and all, where something fabulous happens, who are not quite perfect (fools), who are quasi-transcendental, factical fools.

They do fabulous things and we poets of obligation write stirring "lives of fools" (hagiography), making them into the subject matter of an im/possible, effanineffable tale, of a wonderful *fabula*. What better way to bring home the point?

Or more likely we forget and ignore them, since the likelihood is they will in fact pass their lives in utter obscurity and oblivion, quite forgotten both by the History of Being and the History of the Spirit and, when this little star dissipates in entropic dissolution, quite forgotten altogether, in cosmic oblivion.

Their light flickers for a moment, for the twinkling of an eye, in a vast dark distant sky; then it is extinguished. Like a falling star (a disaster). Then they go under.

That happens.

SEVEN

A Happy Event

I had reached just this point in my work when I was visited by a remarkable piece of good luck. I had set about in search of a text or group of texts that would bring home to the reader what I had in mind by a "poetics of obligation," something to illustrate what this task of serving as obligation's poet or supplementary clerk actually meant, when events took the most felicitous turn, for which I can claim no credit whatsoever nor offer any explanation. I was scouring the books in my personal library, visiting all the best libraries in the area, and in general poring through tomes old and new when, as I say, the most curious thing happened to me. It was, I insist, not my own doing, nothing I had intended. It just happened.

I received in the mail, anonymously and wholly unsolicited, a parcel, for which I signed only with some suspicion. The package, thin and neatly wrapped in brown paper, contained several typescripts which bore a disproportionately long and very odd title:

SEVERAL LYRICAL-PHILOSOPHICAL DISCOURSES
ON VARIOUS JEWGREEK PARABLES AND PARADIGMS
WITH CONSTANT REFERENCE TO OBLIGATION
Johanna de Silentio, Editor

I cannot describe the effect upon me of seeing the name "Johanna de Silentio" looking back at me from this page. The experience was utterly uncanny. It was as if I were seeing a ghost, as if someone had come back from the dead. I had been reading the work of Johannes de Silentio with such devotion and for so long that I felt as though he had come back on earth, this time in a feminine form, for some as yet undetermined reason. Was it to correct my mistakes, to offer me counsel? Were it to admonish or punish me for my impudence about ethics, that would be an incomprehensible fate, for it was he who first put the idea in my head. He was back, but I knew not why. Was this perhaps the famous man's sister, or the man himself in a feminine disguise?

It was only after some moments had passed that I came to my senses and realized that Johannes de Silentio did not exist, that he was only a Kierkegaardian pseudonym, and that I had perhaps been working on this book too long. Even so, that did not diminish the mystery of my anonymous benefactor who chose to sign his name as the feminine counterpart to the famous Kierkegaardian pseudonym. But why do I say "his name"? Was this not indeed a woman? Or was this perhaps a man using a feminine pseudonym? My brain was awash in the most uncontrollable perplexities.

Upon further examination I discovered that there were eight typescripts in all, each of a modest length and neatly printed out. Each typescript bore an unusual title and an equally unusual signature—like "Felix Sineculpa" or "Magdalena de la Cruz." Such signatures, I hasten to assure the reader, I did not for a moment take to be true proper names. They were the inventions of a very poetic, albeit also slightly philosophical personality. Though I am fool enough in other matters, I was not fooled by these names, which I pronounced at once to be—quite unmistakably—pseudonyms also, of the same sort as Johanna de Silentio, although no less enigmatic. Indeed, the names were highly suggestive and I would subsequently pass many interesting hours meditating on the hidden hermeneutic significance of each name, my wits having been sharpened by many years of studying the most advanced hermeneutic theories. I was resolved that these authors would slip nothing past me. On one point, however, I confess failure: whether all of these authors are the same as the editor, Johanna de Silentio, or the same as one another but different from Johanna de Silentio, or whether each name is the name of a different author, as is *prima facie* suggested, I have to this day been unable to determine.

The discourses took as their subject matter topics ranging from the classic to the contemporary, from Antigone and the Hebrew and Christian scriptures to Nietzsche and a famous poem by Paul Celan. The author or authors did not compose treatises with a proper argument of the sort to which philosophers are accustomed, but highly imaginative narratives, or retellings of old narratives, such as the story of Abraham and the binding of Isaac, with which I myself have been extensively occupied, or even slightly farcical "treatises." They leave it to their readers to educe for themselves such philosophical substance and consequences as these discourses might contain. These are disarming discourses—even for the very heterologically inclined.

To this day I do not know whether we have to do here with one author or several, with men or women or both, with monks or laypeople, with rabbis or Dionysians, or even whether the authors are in all cases philosophers, which I rather doubt.

The relevant point for my present purposes is that the discourses all severally addressed the question of obligation and the associated questions of differences, disasters, proper names, the law, and judging—in other words, precisely the matters that I had been pursuing in the present work. The authors were furthermore clearly familiar with the writings of Kierkegaard, Nietzsche, Heidegger, Derrida, Lyotard, and Levinas and numerous other contemporary and classical authors. It was as if someone had been reading over my shoulder, had followed my line of argument very closely, and had seen fit to send me a little gift that exactly fitted my needs. I had been distributing printouts of various versions of this work to some friends for comment. Perhaps they had fallen into the hands of some person or persons of a very poetic disposition, eager to continue the line I was developing and to offer me unsolicited help. In any event, it was a pure gift for which I am extremely grateful (although I do not know where to direct my gratitude), and a piece of the most amazing good luck. It was like receiving my own *carte postale.*

My cause was prospering, but not by me.[1]

This little mailing proved to be a breakthrough that greatly facilitated my work. I felt like a man who had been pressing his shoulder mightily against a door that had suddenly been sprung open from within. It was all I could do to keep from falling on my face. Here was an important chapter of my book, sent to me from an anonymous benefactor, finished before I had opened a single file on my computer. The parcel provided me with a series of imaginative texts to offer to my reader which nicely illustrated the poetic category of which I have spoken in the previous chapters.

I feel obliged to warn the reader that what follows is an odd medley of voices: poetic, philosophic, and prophetic; always humorous and satiric but sometimes mixed with the most church-dark solemnity; at times atheistic, at times religious; both Greek and Jew; both male and female. This was (almost) more heteromorphism and miscegenation than I had bargained for. If we have to do with just one author here, and I for one do not think so, although I also cannot prove it, then he or she must be of a most alterable disposition, given to the most amazing fluctuations of mood. The authors everywhere oppose what Heidegger calls the "piety of thought," and some will think with an excess of impiousness. I do not deny that there will be some who would demand a more uniform, sober, and reserved mode of expression. Be that as it may, this is not my doing and the reader cannot hope to take me to court on charges on impiety or expect me to bear the consequences. My principal aim in the present work is to present my views and to escape with as little responsibility as possible. Were it possible to do so, I would write a preface in which, after acknowledging the help of many others, I would assign all responsibility for my views to them and accept no responsibility for myself.

The typescripts, as you might imagine, were wholly devoid of documentation, and so the principal obligation visited upon me by their arrival was, like a good editorial clerk, to supply them with a scholarly supplement. After all, a reader has a right upon picking up a book, particularly one she has paid for, not to be cast into utter confusion. So I passed many hours searching my library for the omitted references. I supplied the missing footnotes, and I added to each discourse a short commentary, all this with the aim of making these sometimes whimsical texts presentable to a sober philosophical public. As time went by, I became more and more convinced that I had been singled out by the authors as their anthologizer, handmaiden, and even at times it seemed as their housekeeper. In short, I was to be their supplementary clerk and bookkeeper, the *Extra-Skriver* who would put their books in order. They undoubtedly thought me, a professional academic, just the sort of dull person to do the plodding scholarly work for which they had neither the time nor the temperament. They are lively writers and I suppose they were convinced that I was bore enough to give these discourses academic respectability. I trust I have dutifully answered their call to boredom.

Far be it from me, however, devout heteromorph that I am, to deny that there are other ways to gloss these discourses than the ones I here propose. About the authorial intentions of these writers I have no privileged information. I have not "the remotest private relation to them."[2] These authors are quite unknown to me, I who do not know who I myself am.

I feel obliged, too, to comment in advance on the prevalence of humor in these pieces, especially given that their topic is suffering and disasters. This may seem improper, even irreverent, and perhaps it is. But to discuss suffering, to produce a discourse about it—instead of actually doing something about it—is a delicate matter that constantly verges on impropriety, as I think Johanna de Silentio has very eloquently explained. The authors employ humor in the spirit of Kierkegaard, Derrida, and Lyotard, all of whom are in their various ways comic writers and all of whom have evidently gotten into the pen of the authors of these discourses. They agree with Kierkegaard, who saw the comic as the mask of the religious, as the only way that the religious has of not wearing its seriousness on its sleeve. They exemplify what Lyotard says in *The Differend* when he writes of respecting the law "with humor because it cannot be completely respected," lest the law acquire the dangerous prestige of "total Being." The point behind the humor is to insist upon "the heterogeneity which persists beneath and despite legitimation." The idea is that the "respecting of the event which comic laughter is should be granted its ontological dignity," which belongs together with "the tragic tear." "Book II of the *Poetics* did this, only for that book then to be lost."[3]

Modesty forbids me from pointing out that this was exactly the sentiment with which I concluded my own *Radical Hermeneutics*. So it was not at all averse to me to come across several "tragic-comic" discourses on suffering and disasters. This highly miscegenated genre, this crossing of the lines and mutual contamination of heterogeneous styles and genres, is precisely what I think is called for by the question of obligation. The countenance of one whose face is never crossed by a smile is, I think, the face of terror itself.

Although the treatises were arranged in order, neatly typed, entitled and signed, I did find one loose page, written in a most beautiful and elegant hand, with neither title nor signature. I found it lying—or had it been carefully inserted?—in the fifth discourse, the one entitled "Temples." I dared not take the editorial liberty of assigning it a place in the sequence of discourses. But I did not wish to omit it entirely from the presentation of the discourses, as even this indecision would have been a decision. Furthermore, the piece seemed clearly to me to function like a "preface" to the discourses that follow, and quite a suitable one at that. Whether this is the purpose intended by the author(s), or by some hidden hand that has gathered them together like some Victor Eremita and seen fit to mail them to me, I cannot tell. How am I to decide these matters? How am I to judge? I lack the criteria. One would need to be a Dupin or a Persian detective. Be that as it may, I reproduce here this short fragment *in toto* as a way of introducing the reader to the letter and the spirit of the discourses to follow. I have supplied a title and a signature to the fragment in accordance with its obvious provenance, the passage from *Fear and Trembling*[4] from which I acquired my own vocation:

A WISH

The present author is by no means a Thinker. She has not understood the History of Being, whether there is one, whether it has come to an end. It is already enough for her weak head to ponder what a prodigious head everyone must have these days when everyone has such a prodigious Thought. The present author is by no means a Thinker. She is *poetice et eleganter* a freelance writer who neither hears the First Beginning calling nor is in a position to make any premonition about an Other Beginning. She writes because to her it is a luxury that is all the more pleasant and apparent the fewer there are who buy and read what she writes. She easily envisages her fate in an age when an author who desires readers must be careful to write in such a way that her book can be conveniently skimmed at the book display at the most recent conference on Postmodernism. She foresees her fate of being totally ignored; she has a terrible foreboding that zealous Thinkers will declare her abandoned by Being, in irretrievable Oblivion. I throw myself down in deepest submission before every *Seinsdenker*: "This is not the History of Being; it has not the least thing to do with the History of Being. I invoke everything good for the History of Being and for all the American shareholders in this omnibus, for it will hardly become a tower. I wish them all, each and every one, success and good fortune."

Respectfully.
Johanna de Silentio

The author had clearly seized upon the same passage from *Fear and Trembling* from which I have drawn my inspiration and had pushed it to a satirical extreme, making of it a statement of implacable and ironic opposition to Heidegger's Originary Ethics, concerning which I have stated my own incredulity. Here was my favorite text from *Fear and Trembling* being read back at me in an amazing gift in the mail, announcing that in what follows there is to be found another poetics, a way of poetizing differently, otherwise than with the *denkendes Dichten* of the Originary Thinker.

I am happy thus to present to the philosophical public these scattered fragments and loose pages, which I have tried to present as an orderly whole, as something like the work of serving as obligation's poet I would have offered had I not been so wondrously preempted.

September 1992
Villanova University
Villanova, Pennsylvania

Several Lyrical-Philosophical Discourses on Various Jewgreek Parables and Paradigms with Constant Reference to Obligation

The Parable of the Game

By Felix Sineculpa

In the beginning was Being and Being was unimaginably black and dense. Being clung to Being without void or division, without light or manifestness. Being was without non-Being, undivided, without difference or otherness. Resting within itself, in perfect concentration and self-identity, Being was wholly gathered to itself, altogether without strife or movement.

But Being was unable to keep this pact with itself, unable to retain its almost perfect self-compactness, unable to contain itself within itself. Accordingly, the aboriginal unity burst asunder in an explosion that cannot be measured by the laws of physics because it was of such aboriginality as to antedate the laws of physics. In an event that is older than time, in accord with laws that are older than law, in a world that antedates the cosmic order, Being swirled outward in vast concentric rings, forming a vast, smooth, seamless sea. Swirling around and around, sweeping and circling, the vast sea at length began to differentiate and divide itself, to cluster here and there in spectacular arrangements, thickening here and thinning there, producing space and multiplicity from out of itself.

After a stretch of time for whose measurement we lack the measure, after a time that produced time, Being had become a flowing movement, racing outward in every direction, more Becoming than Being. After a time for which there is no clock, the swirl of events had settled into certain regular patterns. These patterns, which It had itself produced, would come to be called laws, though they are not the laws Being obeyed but the laws Being produced, the patterns of its drift, the lines and directions Being forged when It first loosened its grip on itself.

The aboriginal energy of Being's great beginning, of the great dense blackness, was now redistributed across multiple centers of energy, divided into innumerable smaller clusterings and configurations of forces, into events that competed endlessly with one another in a great cosmic Game. The forces vied with one another for supremacy in endless strife, the weaker forces succumbing to the stronger, the stronger forces themselves falling before forces stronger still, the whole growing strong from the struggle of all with all.

Being had become a Great Game.

There was no meanness in Being, no ill will, no will at all, and hence no guilt. There were only the various victories and defeats, all of which belonged to the same vast economy, the one great innocent Game, which did not add or subtract an iota from the whole. Growing larger and stronger and more concentrated in one place took place at the expense of growing smaller and weaker and more dissipated elsewhere; forces declined here but grew stronger there. But it was all good sport, all part of the perfect innocence of the Game, of the round dance of events, of the Game that Being, which had become a play, played with itself, without rancor or sorrow.

The play was without care. When one force went under, that was a part of the total economy of forces, the justice of the whole. The whole was just, just because there was no justice of an invidious sort. The play was all and all was just. This was a justice without equality, a justice of unrestricted giving and taking, going over and going under, augmenting and declining, in a total economy without loss. If Being robbed and stole from itself in one place, it was only in order to give and restore to itself in another. If some forces lived off others like predators, that was only in order to allow certain forces to shine with beauty and splendor and so to justify the whole. Coming to be and passing away, in incessant becoming and strife, the whole played an innocuous Game, an innocent war, a war without victims or injustice. There is nothing unjust in the little victories that the forces win, nothing unfair in their harshness with one another, nothing cruel in their little contests. Being itself is not cruel or benevolent; It is without good will or bad; It is without any will at all unless the forces themselves constitute an army of little wills, of multiple micro-willings and strivings, struggling with one another in endless, innocent war games. But war is the father of the events and it bears no ill will toward its own offspring.

The Game was really quite beautiful in those days. It had made itself beautiful by making itself over into a beautiful swirling dance, a magnificent pageantry of lights, of battles and clashing swords whose sparks illuminated their play, whose thunderous noise filled the air with the music of their play. Everything was charged with the energy of the Game, everything laughed with the exuberance of the events as they danced and played. The forces glowed with beauty, going over and going under in a brilliant display of power and energy and good health.

When a long time ago—although countless aeons after the commencement of the Great Game—in a far-off corner of the universe, naked men wrestled under the shining Aegean sun, their luminous forms matched in contests that tested them to the limit, it was as if the Game had forged an image of itself. It must have seemed then that Being had cleared a space for itself in which It could present itself as It is in itself, in which It could celebrate itself and shine in naked radiance. Once long ago, there was a time and a place where it seemed as if the Great Game found words to express itself, temples to enshrine itself, a language and a people to call its own, where all its wondrous beauty could find a home. It must have seemed that the Game gave itself with a marvelous generosity that made the people—its people, its own people—who celebrated the games rise up in wonder.

At length, one of the forces drew up lame, no doubt too much abused by the harshness of the Game. It soon became weak and ill and seeing how the other forces prospered in the play it withdrew within itself and became quite ugly. It curled around itself and hissed its tongue. It grew black and filled itself with vile humors; it became sullen and sneaky, malicious and humorless, and it began to smell quite bad too so that it was not pleasant to be around. Instead of singing and dancing, it began to crawl and lay traps. It crept across the surface of the other forces, leaving behind a gossamer net in which the forces would get themselves trapped and become themselves sick and motionless. It grew more and more angry and spiteful and filled itself with seething feelings of rancor and ill will toward everything that flourished so in the Game.

"The Game is Evil," the sick forces hissed. "War is a cruel father. Going under and going over are unjust. More and less, stronger and weaker are unfair. Becoming is unjust. Life itself, for life is becoming, is unjust. Movement (*kinesis*) is wicked and causes pain. Be still. Pain and suffering are a refutation." "Evil, unjust, unfair, negation, stop, no": large, black, bloated words crawled into the throats of the healthy forces and choked them, suffocating them, making them ill. This was a very cunning stratagem on the part of the lame forces, cunning and clever. For they had found a way, despicable though it might be, to win at the Game, a way to undo the healthy, dancing, stronger forces. They had invented a fiction for themselves that served their interests well. The lame had invented a way to make the healthy forces trip, to trap them in their web and then poison them with their fatal bite. That was very shrewd. They had invented a way to cope with the Great Game, but it was a base and mean way, which cursed the Game.

This was a bad time, but it was only a time, a short time, and it had to pass away. The Game has all the time It needs, for Being produces time and Being suffers no loss that It cannot regain in time. The Great

Game that Being plays, indeed which Being is, cannot experience defeat. The Game is itself made up of victors and vanquished but It cannot itself as a whole be defeated or suffer a loss. Being plays on and on, swirling and rolling, configuring itself now this way, now that, in an endless, innocent cosmic dance.

Soon enough, the sick, twisted, ugly, ill-smelling forces would themselves submit to their cosmic fate, would themselves go under according to the rule of the Game which governs the events, which rules over everything that happens, everything that comes to be and passes away. Soon enough, the little bit of cosmic dust on which the sick forces made their home would vanish. For it too had been spun off by the Great Swirl and was no more than an infinitesimal speck that revolved around a tiny little star in a distant, wholly insignificant galaxy far off in a remote corner of the Great Swirl.

"War is Evil," the sick little forces shouted from the surface of their tiny little spot of space, their hands cupped to their twisted little mouths. The Game laughed and danced another round. "Murder is Unjust," the sick forces shouted all the more loudly, growing even more infuriated at Being's insouciance. But the Game gave no answer. Being laughs and dances, plays and frolics, rolls and swirls in great cosmic sweeps—but It does not listen. It gives, but It does not hear. It has no ears to hear. There is no one there, no one to listen. The Game does not know the forces are there. It does not know them at all, does not care to know them, does not care at all. Indeed one could speak of the Game's great stupidity, its great, stupid swirl. It plays because It plays, without why.

So long after the sick forces perished, for aeons and aeons, the Game continued its mighty swirl. The venomous black words disappeared without an echo, leaving behind not the slightest trace. All that remained was the laughter of the Game as It danced and played across an endless space.

* * *

Commentary: The Disaster. This little treatise has caused me many a sleepless night and I do not wish to pause over its disturbing story any longer than I am obliged. This man Felix formulates my worst fears, puts into words the midnight thoughts I do not permit myself to think. I would like to have avoided the responsibility of commenting on it at all, were that possible. It is a coldhearted account and this Felix fellow, this fearsome, menacing figure, is no one I wish to meet soon.

Felix frames Nietzsche's doctrine of the will to power—rather, the more merciless version of it to which I myself have said I subscribe, although I am having my doubts about that now—in terms of a narrative that has very oddly assembled elements of the "big bang" theory, presocratic cosmology, and Nietzsche's doctrine of the forces—along with an unmistakable admixture of a certain Heideggerianism about Being and the Greeks. Running together Nietzsche's play of forces with the *Spiel* of Being in Heidegger, Felix's tale turns on the opening sentence of "Truth and Lying in the Extra-Moral Sense," the result being a merciless reduction of the idiom of obligation—of suffering, injustice, responsibility—to a passing lameness, a bit of ill will, within the forces. Obligation happens—this is the Nietzschean genealogy—when one of the forces draws up lame. As for the idiom of obligation, that is portrayed by Felix as black, bloated, venomous words, like the black serpent that crawled down the throat of the shepherd in Zarathustra's vision.

Felix—the joyful one—is a poet of a dangerous wisdom, the wisdom that, for the forces, there is no Evil (he always capitalizes this), no injustice, no guilt (*sine culpa*). O, happy innocence![1] Suffering happens, but it is not "unjust" or "evil," not a condemnation of life, but simply part of the cost of life, of the total cosmic economy. Suffering is everywhere a part of what happens, but it is not "wrong" or "against nature." On the contrary, it belongs to the oldest and most merciless conception of nature, about which Nietzsche will not allow the philosophers to lie. Suffering belongs to the fury and violence of existence, something well understood among the "tragic" Greeks. It is part of the sheer, unbounded happening of the forces, which play themselves out in one configuration after another, achieving here and there, in rare moments, figures of transfixing beauty and delicacy. The goal, if it is a goal, is to prevent the best from succumbing to the worst, to prevent what is harsh, ugly, depressing, heavy, diseased, and dying from acquiring dominance over what is joyous, delicate, and beautiful.

The joyful wisdom of Felix/Nietzsche is aimed at preventing suffering from becoming the judge of life, the tribunal that judges whether life is something to be affirmed. Life is innocent, without guilt (*sine culpa*), the way the wolf is innocent, the way the waves that beat against the ship or the shore are innocent, however much destruction they do. Life is justified as a whole—as a total economy of life and death, joy and sorrow, pleasure and pain, high noon and darkest midnight. The justification—this is a hard justice—consists in letting a part justify the whole, in letting one moment, fleeting and fragile though it be, of transfixing joy or beauty justify the rest, justify the entire wheel of becoming. The justification is to see that there is no injustice, that nothing really is "unjust" in the "moral" sense,[2] that "injustice" does not "happen," does not mean anything, does not seize upon anything in the forces that the forces themselves recognize or that matters to them. "Injustice" is but a curse on life, a curse on the whole, a curse on the world, crawling out of the mouths of the lame-footed. "Injustice" in the moral sense is an idiom invented by the sick as a way of making others ill too. "Injustice" and "guilt" are bilious words secreted from morbid and moribund mouths, hisses given off by sick and coiled forces.

Let the forces play, let Being be, let becoming happen, and do not make the forces sick. That is the happy (*felix*) wisdom, the joyful phrasing, that dances off the lips of Felix.

The cold wisdom of Felix, his tragic knowledge, hovers constantly in the background of the other discourses, disturbing not only my sleep but the sleep of the other authors as well, of that I am sure (if I can be sure of anything about these authors about whom I know nothing). That no doubt is why it has been placed first—whether by the editor Johanna de Silentio or by some hidden hand serving as an anonymous editor. The spectre of Felix's *fröhliche Wissenschaft* haunts the other authors and gives them no rest.

Felix announces a primordial disaster, a star-crossed destiny that threatens always to undermine the discourse on obligation and justice. It is not that Felix's "parable" is true. That has never been a demand placed on parables, or the point of a parable. It is enough that it hovers over the discourses as a possibility, as the outline of a possibility, for it to let "obligation" and "responsibility" tremble in undecidability. The fearsome phantom of Felix returns—"*revenant*"—in the final discourse, in the merciless message of "Rewriting the Disaster," when Felix is provoked to respond to Rebecca Morgenstern's remarks on the abominable name of Auschwitz. That is when his joyful wisdom becomes most unendurable, when I am tempted to have recourse to Johannes de Silentio's remark that a life so devoid of consolation could not, for that reason, be true.

As their first and last voice, the terrifying laughter of Felix can always be heard in the background of the other discourses, disturbing their moving tributes to obligation.

DISCOURSE NO. 2

The Story of Sarah

By Johanna de Silentio

Side by side, shoulder to shoulder, they rode off toward the mountain. Isaac did not suspect a thing. It never so much as entered his mind. There were no reasons to suspect it, no words to say it, no thoughts to think it. Had anyone even suggested it, communicated it in the most oblique way, Isaac would have laughed—were it not so serious even to mention it.

They rode off, early in the morning, when the soft rays of the sun are cooled by the chill that still clings to the earth. They talked and talked, about the work that was still to be done back home, about the broken strap on Abraham's saddle that needed to be mended when they returned home, about the approaching harvest. Small talk between a father and son, of no consequence beyond the tender love betokened by such words.

Abraham kept talking because he could not say a thing, could not even think about what he must do, about what he had been called to do. A man must do what he is called to do, and he must not flinch. If the Lord calls, a man must respond. A man cannot say he loves and serves the Lord and then shrink back when it comes time to draw the knife, even if it be to slay his son, his seed, his hope, his pride, the future of a whole generation. Loving the Lord and spilling blood go hand in hand; they are a man's business. Otherwise religion would be a matter of womanly sighs and softness, of covered heads bent in suppliant prayer. But a man must bear the fear and trembling, the thunderstorm and the earthquake. He must venture upon the fifty thousand fathoms, brave the abyss. Faith is hard.

Isaac kept talking because he could not say a thing, because he was utterly ashamed of what he was thinking. He hated and loathed what they had to do, but he dared not say so lest his father think him no son, lest his father think he lacked the stuff to serve the Lord. Isaac hated the moment when the knife was drawn, when the innocent ram would look up at his father, unaware, until the moment the knife struck, of his hopeless condition. Isaac dared not reveal his thoughts, lest his father curse the day he was given a son who was a man in form alone but a woman within. Still, it was beyond Isaac how the Lord of Hosts was served by all this. Surely the Most High had no need of spilled blood; nothing was served by a burnt offering. Quite the opposite: it seemed to Isaac that a man could offer a sacrifice every day in the temple and have no justice in his heart. In that case the ram was a way of deflecting attention from the man, of putting the blame for the man's injustice on an animal with soft, innocent eyes. So the sacrifice was of no advantage to the man, and even less to the ram. The Lord was served by justice, not by the blood of the ram.

Isaac wished Abraham could get over this thing, that he would not put such stock in blood offerings, that he would listen to Sarah. Isaac knew his mother hated this business, too. She had never told him that, not in so many words, but he knew. She would never dispute Abraham, never try to put him in the wrong, especially not in front of Isaac.

Sometimes Isaac thought that Sarah should have more say in things, but that too was an unthinkable abyss and a sign that he was too soft, that he would never be a true man of God. He loved the God of Abraham, but he wished the God of Sarah could be a little more important.

Abraham stared straight ahead. He talked to Isaac all the while, keeping up a busy chatter, but he did not let Isaac see the look of terror in his eyes. He was afraid his eyes would betray him, afraid that Isaac would see the panic, the heartbreak, the abyss in his eyes. Abraham had entered a solitude in which no mortal man could any longer communicate with him, an abyss in which nothing could be understood, in which he had been stripped naked. Although he talked incessantly, he had become absolutely incommunicado. He had closed himself off from all human contact, had withdrawn within himself, lest the thought of Sarah, or the conversation of the two men carrying the necessities of the trip, not to mention his gentle son riding beside him, would dissuade him from what the Lord called for.

He was sure of what he must do and he must above all refuse human contact lest his resolve weaken and his courage flag. They would tell him that he was imagining things, that it was only a dream, and a very bad one at that, that no one in his right mind would conceive anything so hideous, that he had too severe an idea of what the Lord wanted. He alone understood that the harder it was, the more the Lord wanted it. This was a leap into an abyss, into a world of absolute solitude, without other faces, without other eyes, where there was no contact between man and man.

Uncanny. Abraham could feel it, the moment he knew that he must do what he must do, that this was the Lord calling, the moment he said "Here am I." He could feel for the first time in his life—and he prayed this would be the only time—what it meant for the law to be lifted. He hoped the Lord would never again ask him for such a thing, because he would be no match for it. It was as if he had been lifted from the earth and was floating about in empty space, but with unbearable freedom. This was a world without others, a world without the law. Only Abraham and the voice that called him into the abyss. He had been taught to observe the law all the days of his life, every waking hour. But now here he was, an old man, who had served the law faithfully, being told that the law had been lifted. The Lord himself had spoken. He was sure that this was the voice of the Most High; this was no finite voice, no mortal call. This voice spoke words of elemental power, words which were no words, and it spoke them with absolute authority. He always knew when the Lord wanted something. This was a region of utter and absolute strangeness, a region that was absolutely other, absolutely unknown, absolutely unknowable and ineffable. Stranger even than the strangeness that overtook him when he left the land of Ur.

As his eyes scanned the road ahead, looking for the mountain of which the Lord had spoken in his dream—was it a dream?—he thought the uncanny thought that he was the only man on the face of the earth to whom the law did not apply, whom it did not cover. One might think that such a suspension of the law would be like lifting a burden from one's back; instead it was like being hurled into an abyss, or abandoned in a desert, like having the ground that holds you up violently pulled out from under you. When Isaac was a child, and he would call "father, father," Abraham would appear in a flash. "Here am I, Isaac" he would say, and all was well. Now, for the first time in his life, Abraham knew that Isaac had lost that power. No one could call to him now, no one would come make him answer. He had one, absolute, immutable call to answer, one incommutable command to heed. This world without the law was a world without others, without words, without dialogue, without communication and human responsiveness. It was not a human world at all: both the call and the response transcended human ken and ability.

At length they reached the mountaintop, unpacked their beasts of burden, while the two men who had accompanied them waited below, at the foot of the mount.

"Father, father," Isaac said. The words floated across the mountaintop like the words of the Lord himself, and Abraham could see a little boy running across a field, his eyes red and swollen with tears. He could see the father stoop and comfort the child and, taking him inside the house, bathe and bandage the boy's bruised, bleeding arm.

"Father, father," Isaac said again, wondering at Abraham's distraction and unresponsiveness.

"Here am I, my son." Abraham answered.

"Behold the fire and the wood, but where is the ram for the burnt offering?"

"God will provide himself the ram for a burnt offering, my son." So they continued to work together, father and son, preparing the altar.

Abraham must do what he must do. He must answer his call. He stood atop the mountain with nothing between him and God, no intermediaries, no other contact. With untrammeled, abysmal freedom. Then he seized the boy in a flash and bound him to the altar, the strong, coarse rope cutting the boy's arms and causing them to bleed.

The father had descended upon the son with such lightning speed, and with such intentions as the boy could still not fathom, that he had offered no resistance. He could only lie there, not even terrified, still uncomprehending of the fate that had overtaken him. Then his father stood over him, prayed silently for a moment, and drew his knife.

Isaac looked at his father, unable to say a thing. And Abraham, for the first time in three days, looked into Isaac's eyes. Father to son, man to man, face to face, flesh to flesh.

Abraham looked for a moment that lasted an eternity into Isaac's still trusting, still utterly uncomprehending face, his eyes meeting Isaac's look of love and filial faith. Then he caught sight of Isaac's bleeding arm and he heard again the voice of a child from long ago.

"Do not lay a hand on the lad," said the voice of the child from long ago.

And Abraham wept bitterly.

Yet even after so terrible a lesson, even after the madness of the blood economy had been so painfully visited upon him, Abraham still insisted on spilling the blood of the innocent ram caught in a thicket whom he chanced upon.

Abraham and Isaac never spoke of this day atop Moriah, not to one another, not to Sarah.

But Sarah knew.

Isaac, who was faithful to his father all the days of his life, knew that he had been saved by the Lord, that the countenance of the Lord had somehow stayed his father's hand. He resolved henceforth that while he would always obey his father it was the soft voice and gentle caress of Sarah that he would keep in his heart.

* * *

Commentary: Against Abraham. Far be it from me to criticize Abraham. Far be it from me to raise my voice against the father of faith, the likes of whom I will never meet, as whose supplementary clerk I would be glad to serve. But it is evidently not so far for the woman—my guess is that this author *is* a woman—who here takes on the great patriarch. She is, unlike me, not intimidated by patriarchy or Knights of Faith. Here is the story of Abraham told not by a Johannes but by one Johanna de Silentio; indeed, not the story of Abraham, but the story of Sarah! Am I to understand that this is a feminist rewriting of Kierkegaard himself? Is this supposed to be a new version of *Fear and Trembling* (one written by someone with a mother)? Or even of the story of father Abraham himself? Can people simply rewrite great books or even the Sacred Scriptures if they have a mind to?[3] What is going on here? Is there no objectivity left? Do texts just mean anything at all so that, if they do not say what you want, you simply rewrite them yourself? Events in hermeneutics are outstripping me.

The scandal provoked by the story of Abraham—both Lyotard and Kierkegaard say it is a scandal—is that the "structure" of obligation revealed by the story is one of "blindness," of the cognitive density or unintelligibility of the obligation. If a command is intelligible, then it is a cognitive phrase whose authorship I can assume, in which case it is mine, something I want, and so not an obligation. If it is not intelligible, then it is arbitrary and irrational. You cannot neutralize the transcendence of the obligation. But then I cannot distinguish the command Abraham received from the commands of Nazi executioners, which are structurally alike: "That Isaac die, that is my law." "That the Jews die, that is my law." I cannot, in short, distinguish the command which founded the Jewish people from the command intended most heinously to put an end to them. The one is no more or no less a paradox than the other. Occupying the position of an addressee puts one in the position of a certain structural blindness. Lacking the universality and intelligibility of the law, Abraham's obligation becomes an idiolect incomprehensible to himself and to anyone else. The scandal is the source of Abraham's greatness for Johannes, but it is a matter of great concern to Johanna.

Lyotard tries to resolve this dilemma by breaking down the analogy between Abraham and the Nazis: "Did God want to test the SS's faithfulness to Him? . . . And did the SS love the Jew as a father does his son?"[4] Were the SS making a sacrifice in executing the Jews? Lyotard deeply resists referring to Auschwitz as a "sacrifice," which is to drape the obscenity in theological robes, which is how he means to repel the analogy with Abraham.

Lyotard in effect takes the same tack as Johannes de Silentio in resolving this issue: we need have no fear that the faithful, upon hearing this story from the pulpit, will rush out and start sacrificing their sons, or, by extension, other innocents. For such a deed can only be carried out in fear and trembling, in a *horror abyssi* from which everyone will shrink, in an ordeal to which only the father of faith can be expected to measure up. But both Kierkegaard and Lyotard are leaving it open that someone could indeed carry out such a sacrifice, whether against one's son or a whole race—so long as he acts in fear and trembling, against the deepest inclinations of his nature and affections, gritting his teeth and trembling from the vertigo of such solitary heights. But Johanna de Silentio takes this to be so much phallic aggressiveness and *Kampfsreligion*. Johanna is inclined to agree that Abraham was being tested, but she thinks that the great patriarch and father of faith failed the test, that he missed the point, kept on missing the point, and that the only one who has it right in the story is Sarah, the absent mother who is almost never mentioned and certainly not consulted by Abraham. Johanna turns this story on its head by retelling it from the point of view of the violence and sacrifice, by reading it as a story of the end of sacrifice, rather than of how much steely male machismo it takes to be willing to spill blood in the name of God. In *Fear and Trembling* Johannes de Silentio offers four variations on the story of Abraham, each one a different way to understand what cannot be understood.[5] Only the third variation approaches Johanna's version: Abraham comes down the mountain wondering whether he has sinned because he was willing to take the life of Isaac, even though the Lord stayed his knife. But all four variations offered by Johannes de Silentio center around the central idea that the whole thing was an ordeal meant to test the steel of the Knight of Faith and the Knight of Faith passed the test in an exemplary manner, for which he has been known ever since as the very father of faith itself, the father of us all.

Johanna switches the perspective of the story from Abraham to Isaac, or to put it in Lyotardian terms, from the addressee of the command to sacrifice Isaac (Abraham) to the content of the message (that Isaac die). But this shift of perspective—from Abraham to Isaac—effects a still more radical shift from Isaac's massively present father to Isaac's almost absolutely absent mother. The ironic title of this fragment—which identifies the ultimate shift of reference effected by Johanna—reminds us, as Mark Taylor has recently reminded us about Kierkegaard himself, that Isaac also had a mother or, as Taylor writes, a "(m)other," although Kierkegaard's texts are one long commentary on the massive presence of his father and of the law of the father. On Johanna's telling, the point of the story is not how much virile faith it takes to obey a command from the Lord to sacrifice your son, or how much manly courage it requires to maintain still your faith in the

Lord's promise to raise up a new generation from your seed in the face of an absurd command. Johanna uses a little maidenly trepidation before the Knight of Faith — precisely in order to unhorse him.[6] For Johanna, the binding of Isaac is not a story about manly courage and manly seed at all but about the movement beyond the virile violence of sacrificial religion, beyond human sacrifice in particular but beyond blood sacrifice generally, to a religion of mercy, beyond the God of Abraham to the "God of Sarah." The point is not far removed from René Girard's general thesis about violence and the sacred.[7]

Johanna clearly gives a Levinasian twist to the story by making it turn on the "face" of Isaac, which turns it accordingly in the direction of avoiding violence. The blindness of the command remains, but its knightly machismo is unseated. Obligation happens; it gives obligation, and we do not know what "it" is. We know only that in practice obligation comes down to the sparing of flesh, to the lesser evil and the least violence.

But Johanna also pushes beyond Levinas — whom she may well regard as another intractable knightly patriarch — by exploring what a feminist version of Levinas's ethics would look like.[8] She allows the ram, too, to have a face. The animal too is "flesh," suffers, and is accordingly a locus of obligation. This dismissal of the animal, this carno-phallo-centrism, Derrida says, is a mark of metaphysical humanism in both Levinas and Heidegger.[9] Above all, Johanna criticizes Levinasian absoluteness and the notion that we can reach a point that is somehow or another above or beyond the flux of interpretation (*hermeneia*). The encounter with the "absolutely other" (defended by Levinas and Kierkegaard), with one capable of issuing a categorical call, leaves one in a state of absolutely ineffable obedience, which is the structure of pure or absolute violence which makes the Nazi analogy possible. That opens the door to the wildest fanaticism and blood-spilling. That is why religion can inspire the worst extremisms and fan the most murderous movements. When people are convinced they speak in the name of God, then it is time for the rest of us to head for the doors. Every time we are told that something is thought or said "without mediation," Derrida says, then we are visited by the most massive and violent mediation.[10]

So then, prescriptions happen, but that does not mean that obedience follows. Obligation means the obligation to the other, to one who has been laid low, to victims and outcasts. Obligation means the obligation to reduce and alleviate suffering, not to produce it, not to augment it, not to spill blood in the name of the voices one hears. Sometimes prescriptions are to be followed by disobedience.[11]

I am compelled to point out, however, that the piece by Rebecca Morgenstern which appears below is an ironic reminder that nothing is innocent, nothing is pure and uncontaminated by violence — and hence that the vision of Felix is never expunged. The name of Sarah is also the name of violence. In order to protect the heritage of her son, Isaac, Sarah had Abraham take Hagar, Abraham's concubine and the Egyptian slave of Sarah, and Ishmael, the illegitimate son of Abraham and Hagar, out to the desert and abandon them. The descendants of Ishmael, the "Ishmaelites," became a wandering tribe of nomads, the outcasts, the others, the disasters who should enjoy the Lord's special favor. Rebecca, the biblical wife of Isaac, the honored and legitimate heir of Abraham, testifies to the line of legitimacy and lawfulness that runs from Abraham and Sarah, a line made possible by the violent exclusion of Ishmael and Hagar which preserved the purity of Abraham and Sarah's seed.[12]

DISCOURSE NO. 3

Before the Law: A Parable

By Magdalena de la Cruz

One day Yeshua went up to the Law. Before the Law there stood several guardians of the Law, doorkeepers who keep watch over and protect the Law, and also a man with a withered hand who had gone up to the Law seeking relief. The man had been sitting there for many days and years. During this time he had made many importunities of the Law for help, but always without success. He had made numerous offerings to the Law, having sold everything he had, but always for naught, for the man mattered very little to the mighty keepers of the Law, who had many other important duties. Yeshua asked the guardians whether, according to the Law, it was lawful to do good or to do harm on the Sabbath, to save life or to kill. He was making a distinction between the Law (the Sabbath was the Law) and Justice, and he was saying that the Law is deconstructible, but Justice, if there is such a thing, is not deconstructible. The guardians of the Law adjusted their long robes and stroked their long thin Tartar beards, which hung handsomely from beneath their huge pointed noses. They huddled together and took hurried counsel among themselves, but to Yeshua himself they would not say a thing. They wanted to tell him to wait until later, that it might be possible to heal this man if he were willing to defer this Justice and wait for another day, but they were afraid to say a thing. So they simply looked at Yeshua and kept silent. That made Yeshua all the more angry with the guardians of the Law and their hardness of heart (*porosei tes kardias auton*). For Yeshua wanted to lighten the yoke of the man with the withered hand, to lift the weight of the Law from him before he died, for the man was now very old and Yeshua had to bend before him in order to hear him speak. So Yeshua told the man to stretch out his hand. Thus it happened that the man's hand was healed on the Sabbath and the Law was deconstructed in the name of Justice. After that the keepers of the Law were convinced that Yeshua was an outlaw, a threat to the Law. So they spread the word among the other doorkeepers to watch out for this outlaw whose intent it was to destroy the Law and the Temple, and to see what he might be accused of in order that he might himself soon be brought before the Law.

* * *

Commentary. Magdalena's little "parable" is an outrageous concoction, a patent forgery, forged from Kafka, Mark 3:1–6, and Derrida. It is an outlaw text itself, a violation of a sacred text and of a famous contemporary classic, written in defiance even of Derrida.[13] I am sure that it will scandalize not a few among the faithful (faithful Christians and faithful deconstructionists alike). The piece is a model of impiousness, a pure type and a paradigm of jewgreek miscegenation.

Magdalena has effected an unbelievable fusion (confusion, profusion) of incommensurables—of deconstruction, biblical ethics, and Kafka. She has worked together the question of judgment—*das Urteil*—with Derrida's conception of an anarchic or hyperbolic justice, with a famous biblical figure, the man with the withered hand. She does this not by way of an argument about justice or jurisprudence, but by way of a story. She has no more hesitation in rewriting the Christian Scriptures than did Johanna de Silentio in revising the story of Abraham. Like Johanna, she practices a hermeneutical audacity for which I myself lack the nerve. Add to this the further audacity that the Law "should never give rise to a story" because of its pure, categorical authority; the "law of the law" is that it does not derive from or bend before a story.[14] Magdalena doubly compromises the Law—by giving it the form of a story, and of a story in which the Law is deconstructed. But that of course is what a poetics of obligations is all about, having lost its moorings in anything categorical. In this poetics, laws are not "illustrated" by stories, but rather stories have the final word on laws.[15]

The choice of the name "Yeshua," which is the original Aramaic version of the name of Jesus,[16] reflects what Mark Taylor might call Magdalena's "a/theological" disposition.[17] The point of this usage, in my view, is to stress the historical figure, the rabbi and teacher of justice, not the founder of an institutional religion from which Magdalena is keeping her distance. She is looking for the right tone to speak of a figure deeply steeped in institutional authority whom she wants to treat as an outlaw poet. Magdalena's "Yeshua" is not the founder of Christianity but a poet of justice, an an-archical, anti-institutional jewgreek poet who consorts with outcasts and outlaws. "Yeshua" is not quite Jewish, because he is a critic of the Law,[18] and not quite Christian, because he has never heard of Christianity.

Indeed, were such an anarchic figure ever to appear in the midst of Christianity, all the institutional might of Christianity—all the power of the church's law—would be bent on bringing him down.[19] So he is on the slash, a "marginal" figure, as John Meier says.

Magdalena has formulated this famous story of Yeshua in so markedly Derridian a fashion that I find myself smiling. But she makes a serious point. She brings out both a prophetic tone in Derrida and a deconstructionist tone in biblical justice.[20] This, I wager, is part of what Mark Taylor means by "mazing grace."[21] The mediating term in this amazing mediation, of course, is Levinas, who communicates a strongly biblical motif to certain postmodern writers. It is Levinas who contaminates this thing called "postmodernism" with a foreign strain, with a bit of a biblical bug. Levinas has bugged postmodernism with a prophetic conception of justice, with a call for justice for the marginalized, the outcast, the stranger, the abnormal. That is why the mad, deviant, institutionalized figures that populate the works of Foucault resemble much more closely the marginalized figures in the biblical narratives than the mainstream bourgeoisie of Christianity who, as Kierkegaard said in his usually punishing way, have made a profitable business out of the crucifixion.[22] (I know full well that this will give no comfort to either Christians or Foucauldians.)

Like Levinas, Magdalena's strategy is also to expose philosophy to its other. That is what Kierkegaard, Nietzsche, Heidegger, Levinas, Derrida, and Lyotard have all been trying to do, each in his own way. The idea is to let the immanence of philosophy be inwardly disturbed by the shock of transcendence, to unsettle the philosophy of freedom and autonomy by exposing it to a heteronomic nemesis. Magdalena loves miscegenation. She is an outlaw intent on breaking the Law of Genre, of classificatory propriety.[23] She contaminates what is Greek with what is not Greek, philosophy with literary and religious texts, logic with poetics. Her predilection for religious texts has to do with the emphasis she finds there, which is not on the *arche* and the *aristos*, the empowered, the best, the mainstream, but precisely on the opposite, on everyone who is out of power, out of favor, out of luck. She loves the privilege that is placed on everyone down and out, everyone leprous and ill-constituted.

The bodies she explores are not the bodies of the Olympic athletes—not the bodies of Greek men wrestling naked under the Aegean sun, which is what the body is for Felix—but the body of the man with a withered hand, which is not a body so much as flesh, to anticipate a usage we will encounter in her discussion of the *Antigone*. Her "Yeshua" is a kind of poet of withered flesh, of leprous flesh and crippled bodies, a poet of the disempowered, the unfortunate.

The stories of Yeshua are rewritten as contributions to a poetics of obligations, not to an "ethics" or a "metaphysics" or a religious "apologetics." Magdalena's stories transpire in a strange, anarchic land, a "kingdom" (*basileia*) that is ruled by the rule-less, where the withered hand has all the power, where the kingdom is in the hands of withered hands. In this fabulous, anarchic, jewgreek realm, the withered hand has the primacy, not the Law. Justice hovers over the man with the withered hand, over the leper, over sinners and outcasts, while the keepers of the Law, and the rich and the powerful, are called to give an account of themselves. What authority the Law has in this kingdom is borrowed from the withered hand, for the Law is made for the withered hand, not the withered hand for the Law.

The lame and the leper, the blind and the hungry, have the power of powerlessness, the power not of a principle (*principium, arche*), but of something singular and anarchic, of a casuality, a remnant left over by the Law. It is a mad kingdom, a kind of inverted world where the outlaws and the outcasts displace the universal and principial. The *principium*/prince in this strange kingdom is a beggar, outcast, excrement, litter—which is why Drucilla Cornell is being very prophetic when she describes Derrida as a "ragpicker."[24] In this kingdom, ragpickers are very important. The power in this kingdom is lodged not in the force of Law but in the vulnerability of the flesh, in flesh laid low, in hungry, mutilated, withered, aching flesh. Judging and judgment in this world are governed not by *nous*—it is not a question of insight or intelligence, of grasping universal principles and of understanding how they apply—but by *kardia*, by whether one is hard of heart, indifferent to the fate of flesh, or susceptible to the call of flesh.

This is not to say that we do not need laws, which would be one more dream of being without *différance*. The Law should stand strong like a wall against the winds of injustice. That is what laws are for. But the Law is blind. The Law is the *arche*, the universal, which cannot, in virtue of its very structure as law, lay hold of its other, which is the singular. But the Law cannot be laid aside. That is a double bind. The Law gropes for the singular like a man feeling for a key in the dark. The Law, which is in the dark, is the Sabbath; the singular is the flesh, the withered hand. The flesh of the withered hand, the sensuous singularity of leprous, HIV-positive flesh, calls out from beyond the Law, before the Law, across the Law, barely audible in the midst of the noise of the Law, barely visible to its statutes and provisions. The poetical is the idiom for the flesh, the voice of the man born dumb. The poetical concerns the man who pushes his way through the crowd toward the leper and, reaching out the flesh of his hand, says "be clean." The poetical concerns the communication of flesh with flesh, of withered, leprous, AIDS-afflicted flesh with healing flesh, of withered hands with healing hands. The poetics of obligations is a poetics of flesh. It provides an idiom for the communication of flesh with flesh across the *arche* of the Law, a communication not of *arche* with *arche*, but of abyss with abyss—*abyssus abyssum invocat*—in a kind of jewgreek anarchy.

Nonetheless, Magdalena's parable inevitably suggests another reflection. She has chosen to situate her story within the margins of another story, to inscribe her parable within the borders of Kafka's famous parable, a parable with a somewhat more melancholy outcome, in which the man who has come before the Law gets no relief.[25] The man from the country spends all that he has and devotes everything—his possessions and his life—to an utterly futile search. He seeks access to the Law, let us say to Justice, but Justice is deferred and deferred, until it is too late. He knocks and knocks but it was not opened to him; he asks but it was not given to him. The door was his alone, but entrance was always deferred.

The door was a disaster for the man from the country.

Even as K. himself was a disaster, one of this century's most famous disasters, the very paradigm of a disaster, the most prescient paradigm of disasters to come, for whom judgment was an unintelligible *préjugé*,[26] an inexplicable condemnation in advance, which ended, absurdly, with a knife twisting slowly in his heart. Even as Yeshua himself was a disaster, was headed for disaster from the moment they seized him and brought him before the Law, before his judges, who sought to accuse him (*kategoresosin*), Mark says, to inscribe the categories of the Law on his flesh, and so to destroy him.

Magdalena has surrounded the story of the withered hand with another story, set the margins of another narrative around its borders, thus forming an ominous shadow around its edges which it cannot shake.

Enter Felix, who waits in the wings.

DISCOURSE NO. 4

Temples

By Magdalena de la Cruz

I love Heidegger's temple, the one at Paestum. Heidegger has captured something important here, something deep, something which, just as he claims, stretches across the epochs. Heidegger's temple is one of the things I love, *inter alia*, part of my pagan *joie de vivre*. I do not wish to raze his temple—if it is his. Deconstruction has nothing to do with knocking down buildings, especially not Greek temples. On the contrary, deconstruction is a kind of architecture.

But what if we were to exercise a little vigilance about Heidegger's temple? By that I do not mean keeping a vigil there, naively heaving and sighing about the First Beginning or the last God, while we all sit at the foot of the great edifice reciting the "Origin of the Work of Art." I will be the first to agree that the temple is very beautiful, very powerful, that it has the power to gather everything around it. But what would happen if we were a little more vigilant about all this beauty and power and gathering? Does not that much beauty and power make you a little nervous? Does it make you wonder at the cost and worry about what happened to the ugly and powerless, about the ones who do not get gathered? Where have they disappeared? What happened to them all?

What would be the result if someone were to dare break the spell of this beautiful discourse, to interrupt its very strong *pathos*? (Is this pathos not just a little without feeling? Is that not what Heidegger himself says?)[27] What if someone added a little twist here and there that would have the effect of exposing the poetics of the temple to another poetics, mixing it with a dash of something else, right in the middle of all this monomanic Greco-mania, this powerful mono-Greco-Ger-manic discourse, with other temples and other temple scenes? Does anyone dare such a thing? Do I dare?

Is there not more than one temple? Are we to believe that the gathering *logos* has gathered the *Wesen* of the temple into just one essential temple, into a *Gesamtkunstwerk*, a *Gesamttempelwerk*, and that there is only one essential temple unfolding its essential being wherever temples come-to-presence? Were there not three temples at Paestum? And what if we traveled a little, beyond *Magna Graecia*, say to Jerusalem or Egypt or China or India, would we not find other temples?

Do not be misled. I am not out to clear the ruins at Paestum. I am only raising questions, which is the piety of thought itself. I am just wondering out loud what would happen if someone came along—but who would dare?—and complicated the scene a little, cross-inseminating Heidegger's temple with another temple, one outside the First Beginning, downstream from the Origin. Would that result in a very de-rivative, contaminated temple, one that is not Greek at all, but a little Jewish, or a little jewgreek? Suppose another transmission were to interfere with this broadcast from Freiburg and another voice were somehow dubbed over Heidegger's phonograph recording of this famous lecture?[28] Suppose the singing of this song of songs to the Greek temple were disrupted by another song of songs? (Should I say by the *first* song of songs? But who am I to say what was first or whether that song of songs was not the echo of multiple other songs? I was not present at the Origin.) What would it sound like if Heidegger's powerful homophonic voice, all this powerful Greco-German *harmonia*, were disturbed by a little dissonance and jewgreek polyphony? Would that be the end of the gathering *logos* or would it just open up new possibilities for other, more polylogical *logoi* and what is otherwise than *logos*? Do you ever tire of all this *Klang* and *Anklang* which always plays the same tune and hears the same echoes? Do you ever get tired of hearing the same poem read to you again and again? Could a fugue be centrifugal, heading out in every different direction at once, which is, according to the astrophysicists, what we are all doing anyway?[29] Could that be done?

But who am I to put such questions to the Questioning of Being? What will come of all this interrogation? Where will it all end?

Could it not be objected that this would amount to scribbling on the majestic columns of a great Greek edifice, spray-painting graffiti on its massive, swollen, white columns? But then again it could be described as ornamenting the column with a little *graphire*, which is an ancient custom.[30]

My fellow democrats,[31] ought we to fear disrupting such an authoritative speaker, to intervene upon the solemnities of this *magister solemnitatis*? Does anyone dare? The stakes are high. For in this temple, Truth is set to work and Being comes to be. Greek truth. But if truth is *a-letheia*, does it follow that truth *is* Greek? And that the expression Greek truth, like Greek philosophy, is redundant? Then is "Greek Being" also redundant? Could Parmenides' dictum then be glossed, "It is necessary both to say and to think that Being is (Greek)"? Are these all tautologies, like saying *physis* can only be said in Greek, or *Sein* can only be said in German, or *graffiti* in Italian?[32] Does anyone get tired of these *Seinsgeschichtlich* tautologies and find themselves wishing for a little heterology and paralogy to enliven these temple pieties? Could piety ever admit of a little impiety, just a dash? What would that look like? I for one would like to know.

In the temple, we are told, truth is at stake, Greek truth, the truth of the Greeks, the truth of truth. In the temple everything essential is gathered together about the Greek way to be, everything originary about their *ethos*. The temple gathers together and concentrates the originary ethics of the Greeks. I do not say that *Seinsdenken* is solely the thought of Being, that it lacks an ethics. For Heidegger's temple is ethical through and through, if what is meant by ethics is the elemental force of the Greek word *ethos*, and if ethics means originary dwelling.[33] But suppose someone were to insinuate or intimate *another* ethics, an ethics that originary *ethos* leaves out, that it has banished from the Greek temple? What then? Better still, suppose someone were to insinuate something otherwise than ethics, something about suffering? Suppose someone dared propose not a poetics of originary dwelling but a poetics of everything lacking origin and lacking dwelling? What if someone came along with the outrageous declaration that she did not care a whit about "originary ethics" on the grounds that it is not sufficiently jewgreek for her? Would anyone dare twit the beard of the Thinker with the impudent suggestion that the waxing of ethics is the waning of thinking, but with the little supplementary note that this goes for Originary Ethics too?

I am, by training, sex, and inclination, always interested in what is left out—of ethics, of essential thinking, or of large temples. I spend what little time I have for reading with the writings of dissidents, heretics, heterodoxists, and other excommunicants. (If I had a world-historical or Being-historical destiny—be assured, I do not—I am sure that it would have to do with running a mission house for everything that is left out of Being's mission, a kind of ontico-existentiell soup kitchen for everyone who could not get a room in the house of Being.) I am thus left to ask, what would happen were one to take account of everything the Great Gathering Greek Temple leaves out? What would a postcard from Paestum look like then? Who would buy it or put it in the mail or dare sign their name?

* * *

The Greek temple juts majestically from the ground, a great stone in a valley cut out of stone.[34] Its long, strong, stiff, hard marble columns stand straight and tall, shining in the Mediterranean sun. The temple is regular and well-proportioned, a model of symmetry and grace, "proud and well constituted," Nietzsche would have said.[35] Inside, through the portico, one catches a glimpse of the statue of the god, a tall, towering, erect divinity who comes to presence in the marble and dominates the sanctuary. The temple shines brilliantly under the open sky, letting sun and light be what they are.

(They say nowadays that Athena is black! How would that color the First Beginning and the essential kinship between everything Greek and German?)[36]

The temple holds its own steadfastly against the raging of the storm, lets the storm manifest itself in all its violence. Rain and wind shatter against its steady, rock-hard (e)rectitude. Stone and storm: unshakable, solid, stiff stoney hardness which lets the fierceness of the storm stand out.

(They accused Yeshua of wanting to tear the temple down. Not one stone upon another, he said.[37] Is that what deconstructionist architecture is all about? Did Yeshua resent magnificent, tall buildings? Had he no eye, no taste, for architecture? Is this what Hegel meant about ugly Jews with no sense of beauty? Hegel did not at all appreciate that Yeshua is also an ugly Jew. Nietzsche would probably say that if Yeshua had lived longer he would have gotten to like big buildings.)

Everything Greek is gathered together in the temple, all the Greek paths—"birth and death, disaster and blessing, victory and disgrace, endurance and decline." In the temple, as in the Greek tragedy, a *battle* (*Kampf*) rages, the primordial struggle in which a decision is to be made

[about] what is holy and what unholy, what great and what small, what brave and what cowardly, what lofty and what flighty, what master and what slave. (cf. Heraclitus, Fragment 53)[38]

The temple is a scene of a great and primordial *Kampf*, of a great Heraclitean *polemos*, a tissue of tensions that holds everything together in and through their mutual strife. This *Kampf* settles once and for all what stands up the straightest, is the most erect; it determines what has position (*Stellung*), standing (*Stand*), rank (*Rang*).[39]

The master stands the straightest, like the god, like the temple itself, whereas the cowardly slave slumps, cowers, bent and cringing, like a fallen building, a broken statue, like ruins, human ruins, debris, not very erect. The temple gathers and ranks; its gathering is a ranking. So this *polemos* is very orderly. It establishes order, gives us *arche* and *hierarche*, hierarchy and patriarchy. Far from throwing us into turmoil and anarchy, it puts people in their place, establishes class, tolls the bell (*glas*) that signals who comes in first:

> Because being as *logos* is basic gathering, not mass and turmoil in which everything has as much or as little value as everything else, rank (*Rang*) and domination (*Herrschaft*) are implicit in being. If being is to disclose itself, it must itself have and maintain a rank. That is why Heraclitus speaks of the many as dogs and asses.
> This attitude was an essential part of Greek being-there. Nowadays a little too much fuss is sometimes made over the Greek polis. . . .

(Oh, my fellow democrats, does he mean democracy? Does he dislike Greek democracy? Does democracy make him nervous?)[40]

> . . . If one is going to concern oneself over the *polis*, this aspect should not be forgotten, or else the whole idea becomes insignificant and sentimental. What has the higher rank is the stronger. . . .
> Because being is *logos, harmonia, aletheia, physis, phainesthai*, it does not show itself as one pleases. The true is not for every man but only for the strong.[41]

(So truth, which is Greek, is for strong, straight, erect Greek men only. Are we then to understand that truth as *adequatio* is displaced by truth as *erectio*, emerging into unconcealment? Does this occur in a flash?)[42]

The Greek temple separates out people who are godlike and erect, who are allowed inside the temple, from the dogs and asses, who can at best look up at it from outside, who slink in its shadows. Everything Greek crosses in the temple, as if the temple were a complicated, concentrated, congested Athenian intersection.

Fixed steadfastly between heaven and earth, gods and mortals, the temple lets the Greek world "world," lets the world come to presence in all its worldly glory, and lets the earth recede in all its density and solidity. In the temple, sun and air, light and dark, wind and rain, warmth and cold come to be what they are, come to shine, come to presence. In the temple, marble comes to be marble; we experience its earthly texture and solidity, its rich veins of color, we experience it for what it is.

Hard, cold, solid, massive, smooth, straight, strong, upright, invulnerable, towering, ageless, without crack or fissure, without the rift of pain, without frailty or feeling, its smooth, white, shining marble skin washed clean by roaring wind and rain.

"A stone is worldless,"[43] yet out of the stone, a world rises, emerges, stands forth, shines, comes to presence, the way the temple juts out of the valley, the way the god within juts from the sanctuary floor. Inside the temple sanctuary, inside its hidden parts, the statue of the god "bands erect."[44] What gathers and concentrates itself is called in Greek *physis* and *polemos*: an order of presence, an order (odor) of rank, of what stands tall over against what sinks low; standing tall *and not rather* sinking low.

* * *

Does this not make you nervous, all these Greek erections? I find myself wondering about the figures—never mentioned in the famous lecture—who soil the surface of the shining marble steps. Refused admission to the sanctuary, refuse to be swept away, loiterers, litter (literally). Shit (so to speak). What about people who do not stand erect, who do not emerge into presence, but slump in the shadows while all those with rank and standing rush on in to the temple to say a little prayer (they are very pious) and then rush off to answer Being's call?[45]

What about—I am only asking—those who do not speak or go inside the temple to pray or offer sacrifice? What are we to do with Heraclitus's slaves, the people who come up short in Heidegger's *Kampf*, or who offend Nietzsche's nose? What about the ass, the leftover, the remnant, all those whom the original *polemos* has spun to the bottom, the sediments, which is perhaps why they sit on the ground and do not seem to want to come (to presence), why they seem unable to shine with glory? What of those who don't have much *physis* or *phainesthai*? No *Scheinen*, just shit. What then?

Rain and wind huddle them all the more closely to the wall. The earthly elements let their flesh stand out in all its vulnerability. In the evenings, when a chill settles on the cold marble steps, when temple guards and doorkeepers—with long, pointed Tartar beards—assume their evening watch and clear the temple steps of refuse, they drag themselves off to disappear into the night, to hover over jewgreek steam grates.

The "lame and the leper," a famous, fateful jewgreek alliteration (in English, at least). Have you ever seen a leper? I am not sure what leprosy is. Do your limbs really drop off? Do your eyes sink into your head and does your flesh turn black? Does leprosy smell? I imagine death running wild; uncontrollable, insidious infectiousness. Leprosy is not only contagious, it is contagion itself, if it has an itself. Would Plato grant it an *eidos*? Could there be an *eidos* of leprosy? or of contagion? Can contagion emerge into presence and shine with glory and participate in the form of Beauty? This is not the problem of the "third man" but of the "dead man"—or woman. Is leprosy real, or is it just a very powerful image, a poetic metaphor in the poetics of disasters, a vague, ominous emblem for dying flesh, for withering away, for consumed flesh, a representation of the unpresentable, a hyperbolic expression for the vulnerability of the flesh, for the disaster? Is AIDS a modern form of leprosy? Is leprosy an ancient form of AIDS? How are these black spectres related? Are they perhaps both species of the Black Plague? Was that real too, or just another phantom haunting our sleep? What is the hidden epistemology of epidemiology? Is leprosy really a disease that can be treated by modern medicine, or is it just a product of the jewgreek imagination,[46] a way jewgreek poets found to body forth the body's fated end and the wrath of a god intent on visiting trouble on those who trouble him? Leprosy is disease itself, mortality itself, fatality itself, contagion itself. It is everything loathsome, untouchable, unclean; everything that requires exclusion, confinement.[47]

This *other* temple, this temple of the other, the one that disrupts Athena's temple, this other temple at Jerusalem, was very beautiful, and it even had a gate called Beautiful. But this temple gathers to itself everything repulsive, misbegotten, sick. This beautiful and well-proportioned building gathers bodies out of joint, disproportioned, ill-constituted, diseased, uncomely, unwelcome, unclean bodies. It drew the lame and the lepers— like flies. Just so. That is an odd sort of "gathering," a rather loathsome *legein*. But should we really say that this is a scene of "gathering" by the "thing," joined by the juncture, collected by the gathering *logos*? Would you say that the rats scurrying in subterranean sections of great buildings have been "gathered" there? Can that be included in gathering, understood, of course, in a *wesentlich* sense? Are the lepers and the lame really "gathered," made to intersect there, like those who have standing and rank, those who come to pray (they are, you must understand, very pious) at the first sound of Being's bell?

Would it be better to say that this jewgreek temple is not a "thing"? Or better still to say that to the extent it is a thing, to the extent it gathers the high and mighty, it is just reproducing the exclusionary operations of the Greek temple, the one with all the erections? Or best of all, in order to include what this massive, powerful, and beautiful thing excludes, must we put forward the unthinkable idea that we need to think (or un-think) in terms of something otherwise than a "thing," even otherwise than Old High German things, to something unthingly, an *Un-Ding*? Would that result in *ein un-denkbares Un-ding*, which I translate as something un-thingly which is heeded by something un-thinking? Would that be highly undignified, entirely beneath the dignity of *dichtendes Denken* and the *Dingen* of the *Ding*—to put it all in the language that Being itself favors? I am trying to imagine what would result if someone proposed another paradigm, a paradigm for what is unparadigmatic; what would result if we tried to think in something otherwise than paradigms or tried to take up something otherwise than thinking.

I do not know where all this will lead, where it will all stop.

What interests me about the jewgreek temple is that it does not seem to "gather" the lame and lepers, the way we are gathered around a table for a meal. Rather, it seems to draw them like rats or flies or *Ungeziefer*, which would prompt a call to the exterminator.[48] Are these slumping figures the "gathered," or the rejected and the excluded, the ones whom we rush by without a glance on the way inside? They do not appear to found or make, disclose or unconceal a thing. Should we say they have being-in-the-world or being-on-the-margins, being-in or being-out? Are they projected into the world, or rejected by it? Do they have projection or abjection for an existentiale?[49] Do they live *in* the public places of the *polis* or *off* them? Do they ever get as far as being-there, or are they just out of it? Are they "parasites" on public space, infiltrating its gaps and smelly entrails, like rats, cut off from gathering, depending upon the rain to bathe, or perhaps a public fountain?[50] Should that be called their entrance into the space of the *polis*—or just a way of keeping them out?[51] Is this "gathering"? Can gathering gather all that? Or is it something otherwise than gathering?

You should wear gloves (*glaives*) if you touch them, Nietzsche warns,[52] clear, plastic prophylactics to protect against the disease, or give them bleach to clean their needles, or keep them at a sword's (*gladius*) distance. They do not smell like flowers (*gladioli*). You will not find these ominous figures in the left-hand column of *Glas* but the right. They do nothing to advance the movement of the Spirit. On the contrary, the Spirit spits them out, they are leftovers, scrap, crap, the Spirit's shit. Ram them down Genet's shithole.[53]

Is Heidegger's temple, on the other hand, not located proudly in the left-hand column of *Glas*: with the eagle and the critique of ugly Jews? Is it not another Greek family gathering under tall columns, no barbarians (no non-Greeks) admitted? But again I ask: what if Athena is black, or if she is seeing a black man? Will the family show up for dinner? Is there such a thing as black *phainesthai*? Can *aletheia* be black but beautiful? *Nigra sum sed pulchra*: can Thinking deal with that?[54] Is not the jewgreek favor with the characters in the right-hand column, with the bastards and the refuse, the fags with names like nuns? Is not the "kingdom" in the right-hand column, the column that scandalizes the good and the faithful? But what then? What is the origin of the work of art then? Or its non-origin? What if works of art were to be concerned with what is non-originary? What is the non-originary ethics, or anti-ethics, or quasi ethics, of that unseemly temple scene?

This much is clear. The lame and the lepers are made of flesh, not of stone. Flesh is soft and vulnerable. It tears, bleeds, swells, bends, burns, starves, grows cold, exhausted, numb, ulcerous. You cannot ulcerate a marble column. Flesh smells. Nietzsche is right about this: slaves smell. Nietzsche's nose, his (g)noseology, is the key to the theory of the will-to-power. Flesh smells, especially when it is deprived of rushing water, or when it burns, when it rises like smoke. Flesh is exposure, vulnerability, the ability to be cut and bleed, to swell and fester. And it needs to be sheltered from the rain and the cold, but no less from the eye. Flesh is life, not (only) shining exuberant *physis* but *zoe,* animal life, living things with a digestive tract, sweat glands, genitalia, and nausea.

Do you think this is grossly materialistic, all this concern about eating and nourishing, about hunger and clothing? Still, I know a rabbi with an answer to that: "The Other's hunger—be it of the flesh, or of bread—is sacred; only the hunger of the third party limits its rights; there is no bad materialism other than our own." Thus spake Rabbi Manu.[55] He distinguishes bad materialism, which is a function of the philosophy of spirit, from good materialism, which is a function of the poetics of flesh.

Jewgreeks are dubious of temples and predict their unbuilding (*Abbauen*).[56] On the other hand, they want to feed flesh. Is that the way jewgreek deconstruction works? Are jewgreeks all deconstructionists? Or are they just against geophilosophy?[57]

Flesh is feeling, sensitive and vulnerable, but stone is ageless. Flesh is penetrated by the elements to which it is exposed. Flesh is permeable, pervious, suffers exhaustion or hunger, disease, disability, distress. Flesh is pain. Flesh is the condition of possibility of pain. Can you even imagine pain without flesh, without feeling? What would that be like? A pain that nobody feels, a more essential pain?[58]

Is jewgreek flesh not an altogether different paradigm, another form of factical life, the subject matter of another poetics, of poetizing differently?

Are stone and flesh two different paradigms (one of which is very unparadigmatic) for two different kinds of poetics? But then can this poetics be gathered into one essential poem, one great Greco-German *Ge-dicht,* one glorious Greco-Germ-anthology. Are we to think—can this be thought—that there is more than one great gathering site for poetry? More than one great gathering essential *Ge-dicht?* Does anyone dare set foot in that abyss?

Suppose someone made the following impious proposal:

On the one hand, a poetics of glory, of shining beauty and the order of rank, of erections and *arete,* of excellence and honor. On the other hand, another poetics, not of glory but of humiliation, not of the strong and erect but of those who have been laid low, not of the great but of the small, not of the straight but of the bent, not of the beautiful but of the ugly, not of massive, beautiful buildings but of lepers crouched in shadows, not of marble but of flesh.

But then again if there are two great essential poetics, why not three? Or four? Would it ever be a matter of choosing among them? Where would it stop? What is to become of us? How would the god who is to save us ever be able to find us in all this confusion?

I love philosophy (as I love Heidegger's temple). Philosophy, which is Greek, has always had its eye on a poetics of honor, of making oneself, or one's *polis*, beautiful. But what about other poetics, the ones Heidegger wants to excommunicate, the ones from which philosophy has always turned away? What if someone were to propose a poetics of the outcast, of everyone an-archical: lepers, prostitutes, tax collectors, Samaritans, prodigals; the mad, homosexuals, blacks, Jews, the HIV-positive? "*Les juifs*" all. Could there be a jewgreek poetics of everything which is not great, of the disenfranchised, the remnants, the leftovers?[59] Is that not, in any case, something poetry has always been?

Does it not already exist? Or are the Jews incapable of poetry, as Hegel thought?[60] You may believe that Yeshua and the prophets had miraculous power—to heal the lame, to cure leprosy, to raise from the dead. You may take all those fabulous stories as manifestations of his glorious power, demonstrations of a divine miracle man (*theios aner*),[61] full of divine *arete*. That is your business. My idea of Yeshua is that he was a poet. The point of these fabulous stories for me is to see that the "kingdom" had nothing to do with kings and royalty and glory, with a *principium* or *arche*, but precisely with the opposite, with the way the *abba*—which I recommend we translate as the Mother—stood by those whom the *arche* was intent on doing in. The kingdom turns on *kardia*, not on the glory of *aristos*, *arche*, and *arete*. When jewgreeks speak of a "kingdom," they are speaking *ironice*.

Would that not make for a fabulous poetics?

Would any of this poetry make it into the Heideggerian anthology?

What would a postcard of the jewgreek temple look like? Would they first take the precaution of clearing the temple steps?

* * *

Commentary: Against Originary Ethics. This discourse can be confusing. It begins with a prologue in which Magdalena raises a persistent series of questions about Heidegger's idea of an originary ethics. Then, after the first asterisks, she stages a farcical scene in which Magdalena (as I think, although she alludes to someone even bolder and more daring than herself) seems to interrupt Heidegger, who actually appears to be delivering once again his famous lecture "On the Origin of the Work of Art" (generously punctuated with passages from *An Introduction to Metaphysics*). One might even imagine Magdalena in the back of the auditorium making easily audible asides to the annoyance of everyone around her. The farcical staging reminds one of *Glas*, of the little peepholes in the columns, like graffiti on the temple columns. Magdalena, I find, has a way of saying what Heidegger says, saying it with the same gravity and cadence that Heidegger employs, until at a certain point the reader becomes aware that the whole thing has an ironic, even satiric purpose. The final section, after the next asterisks, raises the question of another poetics, of poetizing differently, beyond Heidegger's "phainesthetics," which is I think the whole point of all the discourses generally. Magdalena solicits the phallocentrism of religion and philosophy and Heideggerian *Denken*. She is a revisionist reader of canonical texts, and, most important to me, a very poetic personality who has united into one what Johannes Climacus would have called the three stages of existence, the aesthetic, the ethical, and the religious. The point of her discourse—and also of Johanna de Silentio's—is a neo-kierkegaardian one, that the stages of existence do not have a decidable difference, that they pass into one another in undecidable slippage, forming a quasi aesthetico-ethico-religiousness.

Magdalena shows—she insinuates, she wonders, she asks, she intimates, with irresistible irony—that "originary ethics" is ethics all over again, but this time radicalized and pushed to its extreme. For her, Heidegger's "overcoming" of Western metaphysics, far from displacing the rule of metaphysics, only serves to strengthen the deepest metaphysical tendencies of the Western tradition, to let them regroup on a still more profound level. Heidegger's notion of *Wesen*, far from displacing or disseminating essentialism, in fact gives rise to a higher or deeper[62] essentialism, the effect of which is to raise essence up from a Latin-nominative *essentia*, a static quiddity, to a verbally understood *Wesen*, a still deeper principle of gathering and unity, which reproduces a higher Greco-German essentialism. Just so, Heidegger's critique of metaphysical ethics is undertaken in the name of a still more originary ethics which turns not on human choices but on Being's own *nomos*. His thought remains captive throughout to the deepest axiomatics of Western thought, to its love of radiant beauty and its intoxication with beautiful form, to its valorizing of *aristos, arete, arche* and its systematic exclusion of *les juifs*. The thought of *aletheia* does not represent a step back out of metaphysics but a great plunge forward into metaphysics' deepest longing for emergent beauty and gathering unity. *Ens et pulchrum et unum convertuntur*. The thought of *aletheia* gives rise to an aesthetics of Being that turns not on the subjective play of faculties but on Being's own radiant glow, a still higher hyperaesthetics, or "phainesthetics"[63] of Being's shining glow, a "national aesthetics"[64] linking Hellas and Germania in a myth of Being's First and Other Beginnings. But if it is a certain higher aesthetics, it is not without its own anaesthesia,[65] its own insensitivity to everyone who is ugly, homeless, nomadic, expelled, or excommunicated.

The problem is not, as is so often repeated, that Heidegger has no ethics. The problem that Magdalena sees is the ethics he has, that he has not deconstructed ethics but raised it up a notch. His is a certain classical ethics of beauty, which here takes the form of a hymn to a phantasmic "First Beginning" whose ruthless effect is the exclusion of whatever is not purely and exclusively Greek, which purges everything Latin, Roman or Romance, Jewish or Christian. In excluding the Jew, he has, in the same gesture, excluded *les juifs*. The task of thinking is to preside over the Forgotten, to be a constant memorial of the most immemorial oblivion. But what more fateful oblivion can there be, as Lyotard protests, than one which subsists in and defines itself by its oblivion of the Jews/jews, its heedlessness of the call that issues from fallen flesh?[66] Magdalena isolates the intractably hierarchizing, exclusionary, elitist tendencies of the "thought of Being," and with it its indifference to the fate of flesh in the History of Being, its neutralization of human grief and misery in the name of a higher or deeper phainesthetics. She satirizes its intoxication with the supermyth of Being's fantastical itinerary, which remains oblivious of the innumerable little narratives, the ones with specific dates and locations, in which the blood of history is spilled. In this higher or deeper, this more originary ethics of Being's own glory, the misery or well-being of concrete historical subjects, the subjugated subjects of history, the real factical victims of history, are of no consequence, not "in essence" (*im Wesen*). They are not at issue, not the issue, not the *Sache des Denkens*, not essential. The thought of Being erases the victim in the name of *Wesen*, of *das Wesen der Wahrheit und die Wahrheit des Wesens*.[67]

For all its *Seinsgeschichtlich* responsiveness and responsibility, the thought of Being does not respond to the alarm sounded by disasters, to the call ringing from afflicted flesh. That is a matter of indifference to the mystery of Being's concealment and unconcealment. The happening of Being has nothing—in essence (*im Wesen*)—to do with what happens to flesh. The happening of Being is the subject matter (*die Sache*) of its own poetics (*denkendes Dichten*), a poetics not of suffering but of Being's own shining splendor. The happening of Being is the stuff of a *Seinsgeschichteroman* that tells the tale of Being's long sojourn from the Great First Beginning in Hellas, and of its detour, two and a half millennia long, in and through that great errancy called the *Abendland*. Then it returns home again to native shores, finding once again a native tongue, giving rise to a New Dawn, to an Other Beginning, in which *die Sprache spricht* (*Deutsch*). But these First and Other Beginnings are Being's own matters, strictly matters of *physis*, *aletheia*, and *techne*. They have nothing to do with victims and disasters, disease and destitution, genocides and holocausts. On the contrary, considered more thoughtfully, true destruction, homelessness, and war have to do with the essential homelessness of Being, with finding shelter and protection for Being, not for the child. The child is not a disaster for the thought of Being. The disaster for *Denken* is always a more essential disaster, the disaster of a dimming glow, a *Dämmerung*, in Being's epochal economy. The child is lifted up into a more essential child, metaphorized into

Being's play.[68] The child herself, the real, factical child, is not a concern (*eine Sache des Denkens*).

Originary ethics is not the deconstruction of ethics[69] but the *extreme* of ethics, ethics driven to its most radical, originary extreme, to its consummating aestheticization and its aesthetic or phainesthetic consummation. Originary ethics results not in an aesthetic justification of life but in an aesthetic justification of Being without regard to life. Originary ethics shows an aesthetic indifference to life in the name of a higher, deeper, more essential phainesthetic event.

Phainesthetics is accordingly a higher, deeper, more essential an-esthetics, an an-aestheticizing of flesh and feeling, of suffering and grief, of misery and destitution.

Originary ethics obeys a deep logic of essentialization, the results of which appear again and again in Heidegger's texts in regular, almost coded formulations of a mythical "more essential" disaster that dwarfs the real factical disasters in which blood is spilled and flesh divided. Originary ethics obeys a logic of decontamination that purges itself of everything having to do with *les juifs*, that purges itself of the suffering subjects of concrete history. For *Wesen* cannot be touched, is not contaminated, by that of which it is the *Wesen*.[70] Originary ethics allegorizes the harshest of evils in the terms of Being's more essential withdrawal. By evil, I say again, I mean nothing profound. I have no head for profundity. I do not mean any one essential uppercase Evil that gathers all lesser evils into one antho-logic of evils. I mean the multiplicity of evils that surround us on every side, that maim bodies and break minds, that are written all over the surface of damaged lives.

As I read Magdalena's parodic, quasi-prophetic prose, I realize how little patience I have with the History of Being. I can barely tolerate it any more, all this hearkening to *Wesen* and *Anwesen* which turns a deaf ear to everything and everyone who calls out for help, while draping itself out as the very essence of responsibility. Is it responsible for a thinking that is so unresponsive to factical neediness to describe itself in terms of responsibility and to annoint itself as the thought that is called for by a time of need?

The *"real need [die eigentliche Not] of dwelling"* is not to lack shelter but to fail to think the *Wesen* of dwelling.[71] The really authentic neediness, the proper, true, essential lack is not to be found in the pain of those who hover over steam grates or are buried away in the stench of subway stations, but rather in the fact that the Greco-Hölderlinian myth of the *Geviert*, of the fourfold, is fading fast away.

As to "the complete annihilation of humanity and the destruction of the earth," that is not the real, authentic, essential danger, for "there is a far greater danger"—infinitely greater, no doubt—something more terrifying (*entsetzend*), which is that the Greco-Germanic "thing" will have been displaced (*ent-setzt*).[72] The prospect of the universal conflagration of all living species is less menacing than the destruction of the mythical space of the

Ding: that is thinking's word, a word from the heart of thinking, from the heart's core. I propose we settle this disagreement about the disaster democratically—which will certainly not satisfy the demands of *dichtendes Denken*, which is not at all convinced that democracy is the way. I propose we take a vote, but with this proviso: that all the other species be given a vote. My principle is, one living thing, one vote.[73]

Consider one final, very famous result of the logic of decontamination and essentialization: what happens in a "motorized food industry" is "in essence the same (*im Wesen dasselbe*) as the manufacturing of corpses in gas chambers and the extermination camps."[74] One must take every precaution in reading this infamous passage; one must give Heidegger every benefit of the doubt, making the assertion as strong as possible, trying not to make Heidegger into the devil himself; otherwise it is just a red herring. What is really happening in and with the "essence" of technology, what is really coming to pass in the age of the Enframing (*Gestell*)—which he says is not some neutral thing able to be used for good or ill—is the unrestrained attack upon the soil and the earth by modern agribusiness. That, he says, is in essence the same as what is really happening in the gas chambers, which means they are both automated techno-chemo-power. What really *is* (*west*) there, in both agribusiness and the gas chambers, what really comes to presence in the filthy smokestacks of food processing factories as well as in the hideous smokestacks of the extermination camps, is the same rule of Being as *Bestand*, as raw material. Which up to a point is true.

Up to a certain tactless, tasteless point.[75] The problem lies in the standpoint that must be attained in order to make such an observation, the soaring, eagle-high level of thinking and discursivity that must be reached in order to let such words slip from one's lips without choking on them. One has to wing one's way up to a standpoint—which is the standpoint of *Denken* and *Wesen*, of *wesentliches Denken* itself—that neutralizes the distinction between life and death, between feeding people in industrialized countries and killing them, between growing food and murder. Such a standpoint, by a fantastic gesture of Being-historical totalization, completely obliterates the possibility of explaining why this disaster is visited upon the Jews in particular, not exclusively, but in particular, why the proper names of Jews headed the list.[76]

The *deconstructive* point to make would have been that a distinction between a technological agriculture and killing is perhaps not so clear: that agribusiness is not only feeding but also poisoning—the soil, the water, the foodstuffs—with lethal carcinogens, that agricultural technology is a *pharmakon*. But unhappily that is not the point of originary ethics, which is in fact actually enhanced by keeping the distinction clean and uncontaminated. Indeed, the worst case, the most essential disaster of all for originary ethics, occurs when technology *works*, when it functions so smoothly as to withdraw into inconspicuousness. "Everything is functioning. This is exactly what is so uncanny, that everything is functioning and that the

functioning drives us more and more to even further functioning. . . ."[77]
The truly "uncanny" *Wesen* of the food industry is realized when "it functions," when it feeds millions of children, feeds them well, and does *not*
pollute the earth or poison the food, when the technology is efficient, inconspicuous, and clean. That perfectly functioning *Technik*, in which the
uncanny essence of *Technik* withdraws into its inconspicuousness, is what
is in essence the same as the gas chambers. That is because the "essence"
of Being or technology has nothing to do with flourishing flesh or dying
flesh but only with Being's shining glow. The *Gestell* has nothing to do with
the factical disasters that befall living things but with Being's inconspicuous withdrawal. It is—in essence—the same whether anyone is gassed to
death or not. The fate of flesh is not a matter for thought, not at issue.

What is so scandalous, then, is not the statement, which has its own perverse logic, but the standpoint, not the thinker but the thinking, for the
standpoint is reached only by a stupendous and terrifying neutralization of
factical life, by a scandalous suspension of obligation itself, which makes
the flesh and the disasters of the flesh invisible and inaudible. If deconstruction wants to contaminate life with death and death with life, originary ethics is made possible by neutralizing the difference and decontaminating itself of both.

But is the flesh made for *Wesen* or *Wesen* for the flesh?

What is *essential*, according to the most rigorous requirement of thought,
is the motorized equipment, not starving and ravaged bodies. Undernour-
ished bodies do not figure in the account. Hunger is (*ist*) but it does not
come to presence (*an-west*). The disaster never makes an appearance on the
scene of Being's history. To think the History of Being is to think a history
in which the death in the death camp does not figure, does not matter, is
not a *Sache* for Poetry or Thought. The dark night of Being's inconspicuous
withdrawal has nothing whatsoever to do with murder, no more than
dwelling in primordial *physis* has anything to do with justice. Victims do
not emerge into presence in the First Beginning any more than they figure
at the endtime of the history of metaphysics, when they are gassed to
death by motorized equipment. The victim is not a matter of thinking or
thoughtful poetizing.

Vis-à-vis thinking, the victim is a differend, unable to register her complaint about the damage that has been done her in a voice that can be recorded in Being's history. The cry of the victim has no say (*Sage*) in Being's
call. That is not the call that thinking answers. The rigor imposed by *Seins-
geschickliches Denken* and the methodological strictures imposed by Faurrison's historiography thus produce very much the same result. They deprive victims of an idiom. They put victims in a position of being unable to
show that they have been done a wrong. What Faurrison does on the level
of historiography, Heidegger does on the level of Being's history (*Seinsgeschichte*). Faurrison doubts that victims of the gas chamber exist (*sind*). He
demands, like a good scholar, that they come forward with the factual ev-

idence for their complaints, that they step forward—in the flesh—and show us that and how they were gassed to death. Heidegger submits the victim to a no less impossible constraint because Heidegger does not think that victims ex-sist (*wesen*), come to presence, that they amount to a *Sache* worthy of thinking's or poetry's concern. The victim has to show she "is" (*west*) and that victims call for thought or for poetry. But in Being's fabulous history, the victim is a matter of indifference. Victims make no difference in the matter of thought; they make no difference that is worthy of thought.[78]

Thinking is concerned with matters that are "infinitely greater" than murder because "other."[79] Thinking has left the scene of the murder, has sailed off to a blessed Greek isle.[80] That would be Heidegger's "heading," the direction set by this admirable admiral from Freiburg.[81] No less than Hegel's speculative leap, the thought of Being has taken leave of factical life and left the rest of us to face the worst. It has absconded and is unavailable for comment. From one point of view this departure (*Abschied von Seienden*)[82] may be fortunate, given the tastelessness of what "originary ethics" is prepared to say. For it may well be that from a *Seinsgeschicklich* point of view, this eagle-eye of Being's history, the whole thing, the genocide, all the genocides, would turn out to be a possible cause for celebration (*jübeln*), like the slaughter at Grodek,[83] "essentially" speaking of course. *Im Wesen dasselbe*. It may be that the *Seinsgeschichte* is casting off a bit of *Verwesung* in preparation for the Other Beginning and the passing-by of the last God, that the whole bloody thing is—*im Wesen*, of course—something we just have to pass through on the way to the New Dawn. You have to shatter against the *eschaton* before you get to the Other Beginning, which is a certain *Seinsgeschichtliche Resultat*, a result you get, not by thinking dialectically in terms of the History of Spirit, but by taking the step back to the History of Being. But if that is so, then what is the difference between these histories? What is the difference between these merciless results? There is almost no limit to the insensitivity of what originary ethics is prepared to say, given that it has abandoned the sphere of sensitivity to *les juifs* and set sail elsewhere.

As if this originary ethics knew what was essential and what was not! As if this whole distinction did not need to be troubled down to its core! As if there is something first or prior or more primordial than murder or suffering flesh! As if thinking could ever occupy a site from which it would earn the right to neutralize the distinction between murdering flesh and nourishing flesh, and hence to neutralize the happening of obligation! As if something were more essential or more important or more pressing than that! As if Heidegger—above all, Heidegger!—knew what that was!

Prompted by Magdalena's impudent gloss on Heidegger's temple, by her satire of the Admiral from Freiburg, I offer you another gloss on the *Beiträge: Seinsfügung: Seinsfuge: Seins-fuga*: the Flight of Being, the massive emigration of "originary ethics" from what happens. I even propose a cover for the English translation: Heidegger in his Admiral's uniform, standing on the bridge, a hand shading his eyes, straining to see What is Coming off in the distance, while a fleet of little ships trail faithfully behind, the *Gesamtausgabe (aus dem letzter Hand)* in tow, all heading off for the Blessed Isles.

I do not think it is a question of gaining a hearing for victims in the history of Being but of finding other ways of thinking about thinking, and of thinking something otherwise than (what Heidegger calls) Being and history, and of engaging something otherwise than thinking; and of poetizing in a way that is otherwise than Heideggerian. It is a matter of seeking a poetizing that heeds the calls that issue from flesh, of recognizing that outside of Heidegger's Greco-Germanic phantasmagoria, that is what poetry has always been. It is a matter of writing other histories, of telling other stories, of worrying over other oblivions, of answering other calls, calls that come in the lowercase and in the plural, the histories and the calls and the oblivions of *les juifs*—of jewgreeks—who contaminate and defile the First Beginning. It is a matter of finding other modes of *Andenken* which recall what has been repressed, which are devoted to the dangerous memories of suffering.

Magdalena confounds this Greco-German aestheticization and anesthetizing by contaminating it with another poetics, a patho-poetics of everything that has been excluded, erased, silenced, muted, or derogated by Heidegger, viz., the patho-poetics of *les juifs*, of the jewgreek or greekjew, of everything that belongs to the silenced beginning, the beginning (or one of them) Heidegger repressed/forgot/denied (how many others are there?). She provokes images of spray-painting jewgreek graffiti on the temple columns at Paestum, of contaminating the paradigm of Heidegger's phallophantasmic temple with other temples, turning the task of thought away from the splendor of marble erections to slumping flesh, defiling the paradigm of gathering unity with that of spreading vermin who invite extermination. She sounds an alarm every time Greco-German eagles spread their wings.

More power, more jewgreek power, to Magdalena.

DISCOURSE NO. 5

The Feminine Operation

By Magdalena de la Cruz

Antigone is a figure of tombs and shrouds, a watcher of bodies, a guardian not of the Law, but of flesh. That is her function, her "feminine operation."[84] She attends to her brother, to his sensuous immediacy, to his dead body, lest he/it become carrion (*caro*, flesh), food for the beasts. Her operation is to prepare her brother's body for the grave, to hand it over to the underworld, to assure it safe passage. She is assigned to the tomb. Her care (*Sorge*) is not for Being but for her brother's body. She would, if Creon did not forbid it, bathe the body of Polyneices, anoint it with balms and fragrant ointments, and wrap it lovingly in clean linens.[85] But the king, the *arche*, who wields the force of Law, forbids returning the body to the earth. He prohibits mourning and weeping; he will not let Antigone bathe the body of Polyneices with her tears.[86] Creon wants the body of Polyneices to become something edible, a "feast of flesh" for dogs and carrion birds.[87]

Antigone stands against the rule of Creon, against the *arche*. That is her most solemn obligation, her most sacred, anarchic operation. The punishment for her anarchy is stoning, which she received in an unexpected way by being entombed in a "rocky prison,"[88] stone against flesh, the triumph of stone over flesh. That is the final suffering of her who, having a most famous father, has shared with her sister every "pain, sorrow, suffering, and dishonor."[89]

In the name of God. That is her womanly work, her appointed role, her divinely appointed resistance. The divine law is the law of the flesh, not of the *polis*. From the flesh there issues the power of the divine command to bury the dead, to tend to fallen flesh, to anoint it and wrap it, to protect it from the beasts of prey. Nothing merely human, no man, can suppress this imperative of flesh, the divinity, the infinity of this imperative. Creon pits himself against the power of powerlessness, against a corpse, and he is no match for it. In the wake of this defiance, a horrible carnage ensues. All the royal authority of his *arche* shatters against a dead body left uncovered, laid low by the power of a defenseless corpse. Creon is the lord of day and sun, a sun king of *polis* and *agora*. But he foolishly, rashly opposes himself to what is lower, to what is laid low, to a dead man—and a woman. The manhood of this king falls before the womanliness of a woman who resists in the name of what is sacred, holy, divine.

"We'll have no woman's law here while I live," he said.[90] So he did not live. His solar rule succumbed to the powers of darkness, to the underworld, to Hades and its guardians. For flesh is sacred, and dead flesh no less so.

The domain of this sun king is the *agora* and public life, the sphere of political discourse and action. Creon is the lord of war and peace. But he transgresses the law of the *oikos*, of the household, of hearth and bed, of table and bath. Antigone's kingdom (*basileia*) is not of Creon's world (*polis*).[91] The *oikos* is the kingdom of nurturing and feeding, of shelter and rest, of growth and recuperation, of eating and sleeping, of birth and death. The *oikos* provides a place to be born and nurtured, a place to grow old, a place to die. It is the sphere of newborn flesh, living flesh, loving flesh, dying flesh. A sacred sphere upon which Creon foolishly, rashly intruded, to his great cost. Flesh for flesh, life for

life, the son of his own loins[92] — the flesh of his flesh — for the flesh of
Polyneices, the full measure of retribution for his infinite trespass, his
trespass against infinity. He tried to kill a man who was already dead,
to wound further one who was already fallen;[93] he entombed one who
was still living while refusing to bury one who was already dead.
Perfect, paired, symmetric retribution for the violation of the flesh. He
defiled the hearth by letting the dogs defile this defenseless body.[94]

The rule of Creon is the rule of war. Antigone does not wage war, but
tends to its victims, at least to those who belong to her care. She does
not kill, she buries, and for that she is buried alive and cut off from
marriage and motherhood. She does not give birth, but she assists at
death and is punished by death.

Just a sister, never more than a sister, an eternal sister who is executed
before she can marry, whose intended man willingly shares her fate. "No
wedding-day; no marriage music; death will be my bridal bower."[95] Never
a wife or a mother. More grandsons yet unborn.[96] A pure sister. She is
never endowed with the full divinity of the *oikos*, never gives birth. She is
never granted the plenitude of the full feminine operation. That is what
interests Derrida about her. She never quite reaches the stage of a fully
dialectical opposition; never becomes a woman opposed to man in full
dialectical contradiction.[97] Hence she never quite engages the oppositional
gears that drive the system forward toward ever higher dialectical feats,
toward *relève*, allowing it to soar toward the sun. She stands to the side of
the system, out of position, in transcendental ex-position, a certain quasi
transcendental:[98] not wife or mother, only a sister. So the march of the
dialectic slips over the sister; its gears do not engage; it misses. The
transcendental exposition of the sister turns on flesh which cannot be
transcended, lifted up.

Antigone is a being of flesh. She is tied to a man who is not her lover
and not her son, but who is only her flesh, her brother, while never herself
gaining entry to the sphere of *Sittlichkeit*, of social life. She is tied by a pure
family tie, by a slender sibling thread, the ligature of brother and sister, a
fleshly LiGature (*LiGare, obLiGatio*, LG/GL): that is her *glas*, her (*sa*) call. But
this thin thread is strong enough to bind her because it is absolute, divine,
infinite. An absolute thread that is strong enough to make a double bind:

> Oh, but I would not have done the forbidden thing
> For any husband or for any son.
> For why? I could have had another husband
> And by him other sons, if one were lost;
> But father and mother lost, where would I get
> Another brother?[99]

The orphan's brother is irreplaceable: that is a law of consanguinity, of
common flesh and blood, a law which was not made by Creon or any

man.[100] Creon's breach of the *oikos* cannot be mended. He opens up an abyss that cannot close. This is a cut that cannot heal. Flesh cannot grow over it and form healing, hiding scar tissue. Flesh cannot repair this wound. The flesh cannot mend or replace itself, cannot bring forth new brothers, no more than it can grow new limbs or new organs. This brother is irreplaceable; this violation is infinite; this wound is (doubly) fatal.

So Antigone's resistance must be absolute; it must constitute a sacred, anarchic defiance. To the tomb. *Usque ad mortem.*[101] She stands against the human *arche* in the name of irreplaceable flesh, of unmendable wounds. A pure sister; an irreplaceable brother. These are obligations imposed by the flesh, not by the will of man; they are sacred obligations, as sacred as the gods, as sacred as flesh. As the king, Creon enjoys all the advantages of the *arche*: all the power of the law, all the trappings of authority, all the glory of this world. Antigone on the other hand holds out for what is defenseless, tomb-dark, invisible, subterranean. She is laid low; she has no worldly advantages, no visible power, save a certain sacred anarchy. Her obligation is not of this world (*polis*); her kingdom (*basileia*) is anarchic, is for all the world lawless. The divine obligation is entombed in a woman, in the void of her vacant womb, in her flesh, in her nurturing powers, in her childless mothering, in her mourning.

The feminine operation is an operation of anointings and ministrations, of shrouds and sepulchres, of burials and cold tombs. And of resistance, unto death. To the tomb.[102]

Greek women or Jewish. They attend to tombs and wrap the corpse in clean linens, anointing it with sweet-smelling ointments. The woman is a figure of mourning, even and especially when she is forbidden to mourn.

In anarchic defiance. To the tomb.

At the tomb, in the early morning hours, while the men still sleep. "Mary."

"Rabboni."[103]

What else can a memorable woman be if not a reformed prostitute?[104]

Two women administering the feminine operation: ministering to flesh, wrapping and anointing it, washing feet and tending to the sick, tender words and tender hands, binding up the other and binding oneself over to service. The feminine operation is one of binding, of obligation.

Supposing obligation to be a woman, what then?

Was Yeshua, who also bent over and washed feet, who bent low before the man with the withered hand,[105] a little too womanly, maybe even a little androgynous? Was he really a man? In what column would you put Yeshua? Left or right?

Would Creon have been better off had he been a little more womanly and a little less of a man?

Were Antigone and the Magdalene, who were never married, who never assumed the full sexual-dialectical opposition of man and woman, were they not stronger than any men, braver and more loyal? Was Antigone's action not something public, political, manly?[106]

Man/woman, woman/man: should not both be crossed by the feminine operation, which is an operation of flesh, which crosses over and miscegenates men and women, by the anarchic, hermaphroditic operation against the law of the father?

Man and woman: *archai*.

Man/woman. Wo/man. Fe/male. S/he. An-archy.

Jewgreek anarchical androgyny.

Two jewgreek androgynous wo/men. Maybe more.

* * *

Commentary: Supposing Obligation to Be a Woman. This of course is another of Magdalena's outrageous forgeries, the result of which is to give Sophocles' famous Greek tragedy a jewgreek drift. After restaging Kafka's "Before the Law" and Heidegger's "Origin of the Work of Art," Magdalena now produces and directs a jewgreek tragedy, into which she has written parts for Derrida, Levinas, and the Christian evangelists. She also manages to sign her own name inside the text by way of her namesake, Mary Magdalene, whose story she seems also intent to rewrite.

The center of gravity (and of levity) in the text is her question, "Supposing obligation to be a woman — what then?" That is a citation to the third power. It repeats, while altering, a famous sentence of Nietzsche's, "Supposing truth to be a woman — what?" in the Preface to *Beyond Good and Evil.*[107] But it also cites the citing of the same sentence in *Spurs,* where it is directed by Derrida against Heidegger's interpretation of Nietzsche, as a failure to understand the woman truth (almost).[108] Finally, this sentence is grafted on to *Antigone* through the reading machine of *Glas.*

Magdalena is still airing her grievances with Heidegger. Her Antigone is one more woman whom Heidegger has missed, over and above Nietzsche's woman/truth. Her "Antigone" stands in sharp contrast with the ludicrously phallic "Antigone" in *An Introduction to Metaphysics,* in which Antigone's name is never so much as mentioned. Her Antigone is thoroughly jewgreek as opposed to Heidegger's attempt to extract from the drama the pure essence of being-Greek. Heidegger celebrates dangerous seas and death-defying brothers, everything terrible, terrifying, and most strange (*to deinatoton*) — all belonging to the chorus's commentary on the rashness of Creon — as the originary essence of being Greek and (therefore) being human (without a trace of being jewgreek).[109] The "sister" is never mentioned, as if the title of the drama were written in such large letters across the map of the play that Heidegger never noticed it. Everyone in

Heidegger's *Antigone* has gone into politics, gone off to war, as Derrida would say.[110] The brothers are not at home (*un-heimlich*). Heidegger never mentions the exposed body, the dogs and vultures, the feast of flesh, not to mention the sister whom he does not notice. Clearly, there is more to "the Greeks" than Heidegger's Greeks, more Greeks than Heidegger has counted, some of whom are actually women, including a few who are a little closer to "the J/jews" than Heidegger would like (us) to think.

What then, indeed, if obligation is a woman? Then so much the worse for earnest warriors everywhere, valorous knights of faith or knowledge or thinking, dogmatic knights all, and so much the better for mere maids, like Antigone and the Magdalene. But then does Magdalena effect a simple un-horsing, a simple reversal, from mounted knights and macho kings to modest maidens and ministering little sisters, replacing castration with an-ticastration, i.e., with more castration?[111] It is to avoid that result that Magdalena pushes forward, beyond reversal, to a displacement whose final figure is a disfigured androgyn, a hermaphrodite, a wo/man. For who shows more public, political, manly valor than Antigone? What is more womanly than Yeshua's lavaboes? Who is more utterly destroyed by being manly than Creon?

Magdalena—this is also true of the discourses of Johanna de Silentio and of Rebecca Morgenstern—announces a very different "operation," one meant to solicit the massive phallic aggressiveness of all these men—Creon, Agamemnon, or Abraham; Plato, Kant, or Heidegger; Paul, Luther, or Kierkegaard.[112] Supposing obligation to be a woman—what then? Then the "gruesome earnestness, the clumsy importunity"[113] of the Law falls before a being of no standing, a nobody who dares defy the *arche* itself. It comes undone under the hands of a woman bearing not a sword but oint-ments and clean linens. The mighty masculine power of the throne trips clumsily over a shrouded woman bent over a corpse.

Supposing obligation to be a woman, not an empirical woman but an ar-chi-woman, a quasi-transcendental woman, a "generalized" woman? The Greek woman (Antigone) is not only Greek but Jewish (Mary Magdalene), a jewgreek; and not only a woman but a hermaphrodite, a sexual hetero-morph, whose empirical sexuality is disseminated. The operation of the ar-chi-woman is obligation itself—of tending to flesh, to withered hands and dead brothers, in defiance of Jewish or Greek Law. The figure of the shrouded woman bent over the body of Polyneices is the figure of respon-sibility itself, if it has an itself. Magdalena bends the sword tip of *Spurs* be-fore the bodies of Polyneices and the man with the withered hand.

The cross-insemination of Mary Magdalene with the text of *Antigone* is a gesture borrowed from *Glas*. (Magdalena constantly uses *Glas* without of-fering a patient exegesis of it. That is as it should be. *Glas* is text made for using, not commentary.) "Mary" is a citation of the word spoken to the Magdalene by the man in the garden on Easter morning, a word of instant recognition of the rabboni. But it is also a citation of the citation of John in

Glas, of *Glas*'s numerous citations of the Johns (both of them, the evangelist and the apocalyptist). It is also a citation of the lengthy ruminations over the name "Mary," one of the most improper of proper names, and so of the whole issue of the im/possibility of proper names that, above all in this context, are not quite rigid designators. This Mary, the Magdalena, the pseudonym suggests, is not a reformed prostitute—that is just part of the massive phallo-theo-logic of the Hebrew and Christian scriptures and an unwarranted smearing of Mary's good name—but the violently suppressed name of a (maybe *the*) beloved disciple and still more generally the name of obligation itself.[114]

The name "Mary"—this most common/proper name—resonates uncontrollably. "Mary" is also the name of the mother of Yeshua (there is a confusing *mêlée* of Marys in the Christian scriptures). There are thinly veiled allusions scattered throughout the pseudonyms' discourses that Yeshua, who is a poet, not a Divine Redeemer, was an illegitimate child—why else the talk of him as an "outlaw" and an "outcast"? That would make Mary a teenage pregnancy, and, insofar as Yeshua bears a special gift, it would mean that the Most High has taken the side of a young unwed mother and her illegitimate son.[115]

But the "woman" in this discourse is not merely a miscegenated jewgreek, she is also described by Magdalena as an an-archic andro-gynous fe/male, or wo/man, a s/he: the *sa* (his/her) of *Glas*. That sends us scurrying across the columns of *Glas* to Genet's transvestites (in the right-hand column), who bear the names of flowers, virgins, nuns, of the Blessed Virgin, of the Immaculate Conception, of "Our Lady" herself. "Obligation" is a transvestite operation, which Magdalena and Johanna de Silentio represent in a series of transvestite figures: a shrouded Yeshua bent over and washing feet is as much a ministering woman as Antigone or the Magdalene; Antigone tending her fallen brother at the risk of her own life is every bit as valorous as any king or soldier; Sarah has ventured further out on the path of faith than the valorous Knight of Faith, even as Johanna's Isaac is more like his mother than his father.

That is the *opération différantielle* in the sphere of obligation, the operation that makes masculine and feminine pass into each other, that unsettles the distinction, that breaks down the borders or margins between them, so that we cannot make a clean break between them. Masculine and feminine are constituted historical effects, not ahistorical *archai*, as Magdalena suggests somewhat cryptically at the end of the discourse. A man or a woman becomes what he or she is, not by conforming to the empirical contingencies of gender—on the contrary that is precisely what leads Creon to disaster—but by letting the an-archic communication between the genders happen, letting gender disseminate and multiply freely, which undoes the archical violence of opposition.

Obligation happens in and as the happening of wo/man, as *sa*.

What "happens" in the feminine "operation" is a disseminating, miscegenating, androgynous *mêlée*, the *sang mêlé* of jewgreek men who wash feet and of jewgreek women who are braver than any Knight of Faith (Abraham), Knight of Infinite Resignation (Agamemnon), or king (Creon).

Supposing *obligation* to be a woman—then what?

The feminine operation is the deconstruction of the rock, of the Law, of the father, of laws of stone and rigid fathers, of petrine privileging and petrification. The feminine operation happens in flesh, in the mother, the (m)other. That is where obligation happens, its locus.

Flesh is the locus of obligation. Obligation happens in living flesh and rotting corpses, wherever the power of powerlessness surges up and touches us, for flesh does not have an identifiable gender, a proper family name, a national identity. On the contrary, obligation happens amidst nameless outcasts and homeless nomads and decaying cadavers.

Finally, a more distressing point. The *opération différantielle* is an operation of contamination, not of decontamination. Accordingly it cannot be an operation of absolute nonviolence. It does not insulate us from disaster. On the contrary, it exposes us to disaster, which the bloody, tragic conclusion of *Antigone* brings home.[116] The displacement of castration is the recognition that we are always already castrated, cut into and incised by *différance*, the concession that castration is a structural feature of consciousness, even as Derrida has already split the columns of *Glas* before it is attacked. He writes two texts at once, split down the middle, already cut in half.[117] The orphan status of Antigone is not a contingent fact but an irreducible structure.[118] Consciousness is always already the offspring of lost parents, of an unknown source, of unconscious origins, embedded in an absolute past, a past that was never present. Consciousness is always already cut into by the unconscious (*sa/Ça*), always cutable and culpable (*coupable*), always guilty,[119] and so incapable not only of the healing wholeness of Hegelian *Sittlichkeit*, which can unify the rupture of opposing laws, but incapable also of the purity of obligation, signaled by a naive appropriation of the stories of Antigone, Sarah, Yeshua, or the Magdalene. To decontaminate Antigone of any trace of Creon is no less a dream of being without *différance*, ruled out by *différance* itself, confounded by the play of traces.

Différance is what makes obligation possible, because it is in virtue of *différance* that obligation falls on the side of everything that is different, outcast and out of luck, incised and victimized. But *différance* also makes obligation impossible, because it sees to it that obligation can make no clean break with the power of the powerful. In virtue of *différance*, the power of the powerful and the power of the powerless cannot be insulated from each other. Obligation is always complicitous with systems of power and violence. Obligation inevitably produces violence and perpetuates evils, simply because whoever acts is woven into the texture of the world (*polis*) and implicated in worldly power. Whoever acts, whoever undertakes to meet an obligation, inevitably pulls the strings of power and creates new binds, creating new knots in the act of loosening old ones. The preferential option for the most oppressed causes injury to others, to those who are not as bad off.[120] Lending a hand to others is a way of inducing dependence and of reducing them to subservience. That is something we cannot help; it is built in. We inevitably produce new evils in trying to solve existing ones. But that is no excuse not to act, not to do whatever we can. The imperative to act, the power of obligation, is urgent, incessant. Obligation never stops happening. It cannot be bracketed or suspended. The chords of obligation keep playing in the background.

The good is at best the lesser evil,[121] and even that may be strictly local and temporary. The long-range effects, quite unknown and unintended, may be a disaster.

There is obligation. *Es gibt* obligation. "It" gives obligation. It—we do not know what—gives. We who cannot say we, we who are orphans all, we cannot grasp what the "It," which gives, is. Nothing can stop the slippage between *sa* and *Ça*. Magdalena cannot avoid the cross-insemination of Creon with Antigone, of human and divine, of politics and obligation, of Judas and the beloved disciple.[122] That irreducible miscegenation, that uncircumventable, hermaphroditic undecidability, is the more disturbing implication of her story.

DISCOURSE NO. 6

On Impropriety

By Johanna de Silentio

I hesitate even to begin.

The concern with suffering ought not to take the form of a discourse but of a silent deed, as Johannes Climacus might have said.[123] It is an impropriety to write about it, a violation of good taste. Those who concern themselves with suffering in spirit and in truth do not by and large write anything.

It would perhaps be better to write about something else, something that would not look like suffering at all, something entirely different, and then inform the reader at the end that all along the subject had been suffering and that the whole thing was a parable. Then one could beat a hasty retreat before the embarrassment set in. Such a book might look like one of those conversations in which one purports to seek advice about a friend who has an embarrassing problem, while all along the subject has been oneself. That at least has propriety.

The present discourses should be disowned from the start, not at the end. Their only excuse can be, as Climacus said, that it is better to write a book and then disown it than not to have written it at all.[124]

The discourse on suffering is too full of fine names and self-approval, too convinced that it has all the powers of good on its side, that it speaks with the tongues of angels. It is incapable of thinking against itself, of holding itself in question. It does not let itself tremble in insecurity.

That is dangerous and can cause more suffering and perpetuate still more evil.

The discourse on suffering requires the art of the indirect mode.

Making oneself questionable is an important element in getting under way. Hesitation is not the opposite of action but a condition of possibility of action.

* * *

Commentary. Johanna pushes the argument against ethics one step further, one I had not anticipated. She is not just against ethics but against books that are against ethics. That I had not seen coming. When it comes to obligation, she favors the silent deed. She puts both me and the other authors on the spot, puts us in the position of Judas, of betraying obligation with the kiss of writing about it, of providing a poetics for it, the very point reached at the very end of the previous discourse.

The difficulty is exquisitely Kierkegaardian—and Derridian.

This little discourse—which Johanna did begin, after all the indecision, and which she did write, thus getting snared herself by the trap of writing[125]—is perhaps the wisest of the discourses. It could serve as a general prolegomenon to all the other discourses and even to my own study. Why Johanna, who is editing these discourses, did not place it first I do not know. I have not the least firsthand relation to these authors and I do not know their authorial intentions.

It is an excellent preface in particular to the next discourse—which concerns the propriety of writing about Auschwitz.

It is also possible that Johanna might be writing not a preface but a conclusion, a concluding unscientific postscript of her own, as if to say that she has had enough of ethics and philosophy, of conferences and writing, including writing against ethics. I wonder if she is not a person who has left philosophy, or at least the academic life, and is presently very deeply involved in some sort of community service work. I had the same suspicion about Magdalena. I wonder now if Johanna *is* Magdalena. What is to stop an infinite play, a *mise en abîme*, of pseudonyms writing under pseudonyms? Whoever Johanna is, she is put off by talk.

Her message is accordingly ambiguous. Is the bearer of this name, de Silentio, issuing a call for *silentium*, for the end of philosophy, ethics, and writing generally, a call for silent deeds? But then is it not already too late? Has she not already assumed the name of a famous author, or of a feminine counterpart to the author of *Fear and Trembling*, which is a very famous book, albeit one in which silence is counseled? Is she then saying that the times are ripe for a new wave of feminist Kierkegaardian pseudonyms—and hence for still more writing—who are come to remind us that we have forgotten not that the I exists but that the *other* exists? Has the time come for someone to write a new, slightly surreptitious commentary on *Fear and Trembling,* one that would set its sights not only on the Hegelian eagle and the History of the Absolute Spirit, but on the Heideggerian eagle and the History of Being, on Greco-Germanic eagles everywhere?

I for one propose that such a commentary be written, that we start by organizing a conference featuring several quasi-Abrahamic figures—Levinas, Lyotard, and Derrida could be among the plenary speakers—all speaking "under the authority and protection of him whom, under the name of Abraham, the young Hegel attacks,"[126] who would advocate the incommensurability of the singular, of everyone laid low by suffering and disaster. This is an excellent idea and it should be done. The one qualification I have about such a work is that it should take a more imaginative form than a commentary, which would be very boring.

DISCOURSE NO. 7

Lament

By Rebecca Morgenstern

I

"To write poetry after Auschwitz is barbaric. And this corrodes even the knowledge of why it has become impossible to write poetry today."[127]

Black milk of daybreak we drink it at sundown[128]

"The danger that the disaster acquire meaning instead of body."[129]

we drink it at noon in the morning we drink it at night

The danger is that we will turn a disaster into a meaning, diminish the pain of the event with a philosophical or theological gloss, or give it an aesthetic glow.

we drink it and we drink it

To write poetry after Auschwitz would be a barbarism compounding a barbarism, a barbarism added to a disaster, an aestheticization of a disaster.

we dig a grave in the breezes there one lies unconfined

"To talk in terms of a holocaust is to signify (*on signifie*) that God commanded the hand of the Nazi butcher, with the Jewish people in the place of Isaac. It is admitted, though, that if the Lord of Abraham asked the father for the sacrifice of his son, it was in order to test Abraham's faithfulness to the Lord. Did God want to test the SS's faithfulness to Him? Was there an alliance between them? And did the SS love the Jew as a father does his son? If not, how could the crime have the value of a sacrifice in the eyes of its victim? And in those of its executioner? And in those of its beneficiary? Or else, was it God who offered up part of His people in sacrifice? But to what God could He offer them up?"[130]

A man lives in the house he plays with the serpents he writes

"It is also said that Israel had to be punished for its faults, or fault: pride. Not one of these phrases, which describe the divinity's intention (testing, punishing) with a view to explaining the sacrifice, is falsifiable (Referent Section). Not one of them can stand as an explanation of the order to kill, that is, as its legitimation."

he writes when dusk falls to Germany your golden hair Margarete

"The only way you can make a 'beautiful death' out of 'Auschwitz' death is by means of rhetoric."

he writes it and steps out of doors and the stars are flashing he whistles his pack out

The stars flash in a void. Heedless of us, they dance and dart in and out, across a blue black abyss, vast bands of them, mindless of what transpires below. *Es blitzten die Sternen. Es blitzen, weil es blitzen. Es spielet, weil es spielet.*[131]

he whistles his Jews out in earth has them dig for a grave

"Why is the great child playing—the one who plays the world-game which Heraclitus sees in the *aion*? It plays because it plays. The 'because' sinks into the play. The play is without 'why.' It plays for the while that it plays. There remains only play."

he commands us strike up for the dance[132]

Dance of death, play of death. It plays because it plays. The stars play without why. "The question remains, whether and how, hearing the movements of this play, we can play along with and join in the play (*in das Spiel fügen*)."[133]

II

Black milk of daybreak we drink you at night

But surely there is barbarism and there is barbarism. The one is unspeakable disaster. The other, if it be a barbarism, seeks to find an idiom, after the disaster, for the memory of the disaster, for what must not fall into oblivion. The oblivion of something not only otherwise than Being but more important than Being. Shall I say for something more essential than Being, for a more essential rift than the Essential Rift?

we drink in the morning at noon we drink you at sundown

" . . . a 'people' [the Jews] survive within [the West] that is not a nation (a nature). Amorphous, indignant, clumsy, involuntary, this people tries to listen to the Forgotten. It is no 'ultimate paradox' that the memory (and not 'the memorial') of this foreclosure [Heidegger's silence about the Holocaust] is 'guarded in the poem of a Jewish poet,' Celan, after his encounter with Heidegger. 'Celan' is neither the beginning nor the end of Heidegger; it is his lack: what is missing in him, what he misses, and whose lack he is lacking."[134]

we drink and we drink you

A poem is a wail, a cry. I do not imagine poems issuing from a common Origin, gathering themselves together in one great *Ge-dicht*, in the *legein* of a great Greco-German anthology, singing Being's praises, singing the beauty of the coming of another dawn (*Frühe*).[135]

(Schwarze Milch der Frühe)

I imagine instead poems springing up here and there in spontaneous combustion, like fires. I imagine poems breaking out like fires, caustic and holocaustic happenings. I do not imagine a Great All-unifying Origin that gathers together all essential works of art and poems. I imagine instead cragged surfaces to which poems cling like the tendrils of creeping vines. I imagines crevices in which poems grow like microorganisms: the poem as "culture," i.e., a bacterial growth, verminous culture.

A man lives in the house he plays with the serpents he writes

"the dangerous memory of suffering"[136]

he writes when dusk falls to Germany your golden hair Margarete

Writing the dangerous memory of the disaster, any disaster, of disasters, in the plural and the lowercase. Writing of the disaster, with both the subjective and objective genitive; the disaster's own writing.

your ashen hair Shulamith we dig a grave in the breezes there one lies unconfined

"Now, invoking *Mercury*, which strictly follows Adorno and other German European thinking, one knows finally where the barbarians are to be found."[137]

III

He calls out jab deeper into the earth you lot you others sing now
and play

ihr andern: You others. You, *les juifs.*[138]

he grabs at the iron in his belt he waves it his eyes are blue

Face to face, eye to eye: the eyes of the other through the iron eye of a
gun. "For the Other cannot present himself as Other outside of my
conscience, and his face expresses my moral impossibility of
annihilating. This interdiction is to be sure not equivalent to pure
and simple impossibility, and even presupposes the possibility which
precisely it forbids—but in fact the interdiction already dwells in this
very possibility rather than presupposing it; it is not added to it after
the event, but looks at me from the very depths of the eyes I want
to extinguish, looks at me as the eye that in the tomb shall look at
Cain. The movement of annihilation in murder is therefore a purely
relative annihilation, a passage to the limit of a negation attempted
within the world. In fact it leads us toward an order of which we can
say nothing, not even being, antithesis of the impossible
nothingness."[139]

jab deeper you lot with your spades you others play on for the dance

ihr andern: ihr Andern, you Others.

IV

Black milk of daybreak we drink you at night

It has always been barbaric to write poetry. After Auschwitz. After
Hiroshima. After the gulags and the killing fields.

we drink you at noon in the morning we drink you at sundown

It is never after Auschwitz. After Auschwitz, there is—*Es gibt*—South
Africa, Salvador, the West Bank, the South Bronx, Sarajevo. Auschwitz
goes on and on, in jewgreek time. Auschwitz is as old as *les juifs.* There
is always a holocaust somewhere, every day. Even today. After
Auschwitz, after the disaster—were such a thing possible—poetry
would no longer be necessary, because it would no longer be impossible
or barbaric. That is jewgreek postmodal logic.

we drink you and we drink you

It was never not barbaric.

a man lives in the house your golden hair Margarete

But it is also barbaric not to write poetry, not to make a record, not to cry out, which is to be deprived of an idiom. It has always been impossible to write poetry. Poetry is concerned with impossible events, with what could not possibly have happened, could not possibly be happening, must never be possible again. It must be a dream or a nightmare. The impossibility of poetry is its most powerful imperative.

your ashen hair Shulamith he plays with the serpents

Poetry is the wail produced by barbarism, the idiom of crying out against cruelty, the writing of the disaster. Poetry is the writing of those who have lost their way, without a star to guide them. "Barbarism" is a Greek category, coined on account of bad Greek ears which could not understand what is not Greek. Barbarism: whatever is not Greek, whatever does not even sound like Greek, whatever sounds like *bar, bar*. My son, my son. That sounds like Hebrew. Like *les juifs*. *Bar, bar*: the other, you Others, *les juifs*. That is their wail, the idiom of their cry. Poetry is fundamentally bar-bar-ic.

V

He calls out more sweetly play death death is a master from Germany

A word from thinking, from a master of thinking, from a master of fugues, from a master of Being's fugues. *Seinsfuge*: from *fuga*, flight. *Seinsverlassenheit*: the flight of Being and Being's thinking from the scene of a disaster. A hope, today, of a thinking man's coming word, in the heart. A line of hope. A hope for something to come from Thinking. Come, a word. From the heart. From the heart of thinking, if thinking has a heart. A word from a Thinker, from the heart. *Todtnaubergsfuge*.[140]

he calls out more darkly now stroke your strings then as smoke you will rise into air

The vile smokestacks of the camps, the sickening smell of smoking flesh. The filthy smokestacks of the food processing factories, the exhausts of the tractors ploughing up the soil, the smoke of techno-agri-business.

then a grave you will have in the clouds there one lies unconfined

You will climb, not like the eagle but like jewgreek smoke, Shulamith. Your ashen hair, "in essence the same," Shulamith.

VI

Black milk of daybreak we drink you at night

we drink you at noon death is a master from Germany
we drink you at sundown and in the morning we drink and we drink
 you
death is a master from Germany his eyes are blue[141]
he strikes you with leaden bullets his aim is true
a man lives in the house your golden hair Margarete
he sets his pack on to us he grants us a grave in the air
he plays with the serpents and daydreams death is a master from
 Germany

your golden hair Margarete
your ashen hair Shulamith

Disasters are places where poems cluster like leaves trapped in the fissures of windswept walls.

* * *

Commentary: Writing the Disaster. This disturbing discourse is all about propriety, the propriety of writing about disaster, of a literature of the Holocaust. It takes for its subject matter Celan's poem *"Todesfuge"* ("Deathfugue"), the most famous poem to have emerged from the Holocaust, one that is cited again and again, and a poem whose very history of publication enacts the debate about propriety, about writing such poetry. Rebecca's discourse takes the form of a commentary inserted between the lines of Celan's poem. The discourse is grafted on to the fugal structure of the poem, inserting, by my counting, five other "lyrical-philosophical" voices into the polyphonic play of the poetry. Withdrawn from later editions of his poems by Celan himself—because of its highly explicit character—*"Todesfuge"* is, as it were, here put back into print, republished by Rebecca in its entirety. The fugue is playing continuously, like music in the background that can be heard whenever there is a lull in the conversation. At the end, it is as if everyone—Adorno, Blanchot, Levinas, Lyotard, Heidegger (and Rebecca herself), the whole ensemble of voices—stops in order to listen to the music. Struck by the wail of the music, they stop to give the fugue their full attention, which plays its final strophe without interruption.

Rebecca's discourse is an extended debate with Adorno's famous pronouncement that writing poetry after Auschwitz would be barbaric, a barbarism of culture that would only compound the barbarism of Auschwitz. But with the continual playing of the poem in the background—while the philosophers debate the point in the foreground—Morgenstern brings home the point that poetry goes on after Auschwitz, that poetry "happens," whether or not the philosophers, cultural critics, and thinkers agree. Poems happen. They happen whether there is some account (*logos*) for them or not, whether there is some identifiable deep Origin for them or not. Poems happen not as *logos* or as meaning, but —at least here, this poem—as a wail, a cry, a lament, even or precisely where there is no meaning. "Lament" (*Klage*), the title of one of Trakl's late poems which Rebecca uses as the title of her own discourse, is then a poem about poetry, a poem that does what poetry is. Poems happen even or precisely where beauty is questionable, where it would be out of place, tasteless, where ugliness is more in order. If a poem could break with beauty and become ugly, it would not be less of an artwork, less of a lament.[142]

The poem has a very ironic history. Celan himself was so troubled by "*Todesfuge*," about whether its "terrible beauty" did not help to transform Auschwitz into a work of art, that he withdrew it from publication.[143] But even as Celan eventually withdrew the poem from publication, thus conceding in effect the force of Adorno's complaint, Adorno retracted his criticism of it, thus confirming Celan's original poetic intent.[144] Celan in turn published another poem, "The Straitening" (*Engführung*), which was a rewriting, a new edition, of "*Todesfuge*."[145] The history of the publication of this poem reflects the undecidability of Adorno's provocative pronouncement.

How could we tell the difference between the silence counseled by Adorno, let us say silence before Auschwitz, and the silence of Heidegger, let us say silence about Auschwitz; between the silence of respect or of hyperrespect and obscene or embarrassed silence?

For Rebecca, Auschwitz is an event of total loss, a disaster, and the poem happens as a way to give it "body," as Blanchot says—the body of a cry, a lament—not meaning, not beauty. To Adorno's and Blanchot's admonitions, about turning Auschwitz into a work of art, Rebecca adds the voice of Lyotard, who admonishes the theologians about turning the Holocaust into a sacrificial work. Who is sacrificing what to whom in the Holocaust, Lyotard wants to know. How can that phrase ever be parsed? The theme of sacrifice is thus solicited—made to tremble—for a second time by Rebecca, who, following the delimitation of the phallocentrism of Abrahamic religion by Johanna de Silentio, here rejects the idea that the Holocaust is to be conceived as a holocaust, as a burnt offering, that is, after the Abrahamic model.[146] If anything, the poem, this poem, arises as a way of protecting the disaster from both meaning and beauty. It saves the Holocaust from having something saving, redeeming, about it; it preserves it from being enlisted in a *Resultat*, preserves it as a pure loss. The poem protects the disaster from *classification* (*glas*), from assimilating the singularity of the disaster to some interpretative or explanatory category, be it philosophical, theological, historical, or Being-historical. The poem happens as a way of letting the disaster stand out, as meaningless loss, as the singular event that it is. Poems break out like fires in language that have themselves been ignited by the *holo-kaustus*, the mass burning, which is just that, a searing and a singeing, but not a burnt offering or a moment in the life of Being or the Spirit or an occasion for artistic transformation.

The poem happens not as a meaning-giving event but as an event of commemoration, as a way of keeping a record, of recording the date[147] of a disaster. The poem is a re-cording, *im Herzen*, in the heart, of a disaster. It does not bestow beauty on the event (aesthetics), or sense (theology), even though the poem itself embodies the paradox of being itself beautiful. It does not transmute the event into an occasion for a *Kehre* to an Other Beginning (essential thinking), or lift it up into the progress of the Spirit so that it has a *Resultat* (speculative thinking). Divested of both *Kehre* and *Resultat* the poem simply re-cords the event, writes it down—or lets the disaster do the writing—as a gesture of mourning and commemoration, not of Being's farewell to beings (*Abgeschiedenheit von Seienden*), of its abandonment of beings (*Seinsverlassenheit*), but of something otherwise than and more important than Being, of burnt flesh and the obscene smoke that rises up from it. The only thing you can do with Auschwitz is to commemorate it, to commit it to heart. The disaster happens, i.e., it always happens, always and already, and always will. There is no suggestion that we can put a stop to it, only that we can watch out for it or provide an idiom for its record.

Although continually testing and contesting Adorno's statement, Rebecca's discourse never quite disagrees with Adorno. Rather, she treats Adorno's statement as an ever-present admonition, a call to distrust beauty, a call for vigilance about the whole Greco-German ideology of *phainesthai*, of *Sein als Scheinen und Schönheit*, which characterizes both Hegel and Heidegger, both *Geist* and *Sein*, both speculative and essential thinking, both of which tend to enclose the disaster in larger wholes. Adorno describes the "hermeneutic situation" of poetry today, and indeed of every day, where there are killing fields on every side. Rebecca does not reject this but rather generalizes it. She thinks that Adorno describes the situation in which poetry always finds itself, before and after Auschwitz. Genocide was not invented by the Nazis. It was practiced by the European "settlers" of the "New World," by the native populations that preceded the explorers, and in innumerable other times and places. Adorno is describing what for Rebecca is the permanent hermeneutic situation of poetry. Adorno rightly warns us of the danger of the "aestheticization of Auschwitz," which would be tasteless and obscene, a barbarism of a different sort added to an original barbarism. But Adorno's salutary admonition is countered by an event, by the fact that, with or without Adorno, poems happen. They spring up like weeds growing through cement cracks, under the most inhospitable conditions, like leaves trapped in a fence or wall, like fungi growing in crevices. Language is a fence, a wall, a surface in which poems cluster, are trapped, or grow like an infection or a bacterial culture, which is not an image of high *Bildung* but of contamination and infestation (requiring extermination) meant to confound the phainesthetic imagery of *physis*. The poem is not *techne*, not a beautiful supplement of self-emergent *physis*, but an infection, a parasite, a bacterial growth. That is to say, poetry needs to be thought of in terms that are otherwise than *techne*.[148]

Poems happen with the spontaneity of a cry or a wail, like a response to an injury. They keep happening, the way Celan's poem keeps happening throughout Rebecca's discourse, whatever the thinkers think. Far from being prevented by Auschwitz they are forced to the surface by Auschwitz, driven like leaves tossed by the wind which snag on jagged fences.

The notion that the poem is a cry seems to derive from Lyotard, from the notion that the silence of the differend seeks an idiom and from the idea that the silence of the victim is an "alarm" that sounds, that calls us to the scene of a disaster, like the disaster's *glas*.

I come now to the question of Heidegger (and to Heidegger's "question"). Heidegger is given two voices in the polyphony of the fugue. Heidegger first appears in the commentary on the first stanza as a philosopher or thinker of the event, of the sheer happening of the event. This Heidegger thinks the starkest thought of all, the thought of the disaster, of the happening of a cosmic play which plays without why. *Das Ereignis ereignet*. It happens because it happens; it happens without why. There is — *Es gibt* — nothing to explain, justify, redeem, or aesthetically justify the event. But this Heidegger is displaced by another Heidegger, one who finds an aesthetic, or a phainesthetic justification of the event in the History of Being, for whom poetry is the song sung by and on behalf of Being's shining splendor. This other Heidegger does not overcome aesthetics but adopts a higher, more essential aesthetics, a Being-historical (*Seinsgeschichtlich*) aestheticization (or "phainesthetics") which sees in poetry the song Being sings to itself, a song to the tremulous and fluctuating beauty of *a-letheia*. Such a Heidegger neutralizes the distinction between murder and agribusiness. The smoke that rises from industrial agriculture, which pollutes the air, and the smoke rising from Shulamith's ashen hair, which is an obscenity, are "in essence the same." That is a Heidegger for whom the wail of the poet is always a metaphor for an Other Beginning, always an allegory of something else (*allos*), something happening in Being's fabulous journey. No matter how bitter the lament of the poem, Heidegger will find in it — with the same ease and detachment as Hegel noting the cunning of reason, and with the same enclosing, totalizing gesture — the signs of a Turning toward an Other Beginning. Heidegger thus neutralizes the lament, silences it, does not allow it an idiom. Far from making a re-cord of the event, the event is utterly mythologized and transcribed, transported to an utterly oneiric space. Essential thinking is the pre-venting of the event. The Event pre-vents.

Heidegger does not, as he claims, open up a dialogue of thinking and poetry, or expose philosophy or thinking to the otherness of the poet. On the contrary, as Veronique Foti has shown—I would say decisively and authoritatively—Heidegger is intractably resistant to the density (*dicht, dichtigkeit*) of poetizing (*dichten*). Heidegger constantly "deflects" what happens in poetry, Foti says. Heidegger "occludes transgression, excess, or loss and constrains the poetry to fit the exigencies of an *essential* if always 'polemic' (or differential) unification. . . . Heidegger's deflections and conflations have the fundamental character of an aestheticization of the political . . . [which] constitutes the key aspect of his involvement with National Socialism." This whole tendency of Heidegger's reading of "his chosen poets" comes to a head in "Heidegger's refusal to extend his interlocution to Paul Celan":

> What makes this refusal important is not only that Celan writes out of the experience of the Holocaust but also that he both situates his poetry in relation to Hölderlin and criticizes and repudiates the aestheticization of the political, whereas Heidegger develops his own aestheticization in dialogue with Hölderlin.[149]

Heidegger thus is put at an extreme removal from the poetics of suffering or of the disaster. His *denkendes Dichten* and *dichtendes Denken* are precisely the occlusion and deflection of the poetics of suffering, one might even say, its extermination in the name of phainesthetics, the extermination of everything jewgreek in the name of the higher, purer, more essential poetry of a mythical Greco-Germania. On this point, Rebecca and the pseudonyms are the sworn enemies of everything Heidegger says about poetry, and this precisely on the grounds that Heidegger does not take his own counsel, to expose thinking and philosophizing to the disruptive otherness, the density and opacity, the *Dichtigkeit* of *Dichtung*. Heidegger's infamous silence about the Holocaust is accompanied by an almost equally ominous silence about Celan's poetry. As Foti says, Heidegger's *Denkweg* is a remarkable case of what Levinas calls "the mode of remaining the same in the midst of the other." His scandalous silence about the Holocaust is situated at an extreme from the poetic silence before barbarity by which Adorno and Celan are troubled.

That is why the polyphony of Rebecca's fugue includes the voice of Levinas—which Rebecca introduces by grafting Levinas's image of the eyes of the Other forbidding murder (the eye which from the grave looks back at Cain) onto Celan's image of the eye of the SS man squinting, one-eyed—*sein Auge ist blau*—through the sights of his rifle. Heidegger's "deflection" of these poets is a function of his silencing of the call, the cry, the lament of the Other, which is Levinas's most constant thought. By allegorically transforming the event of suffering into an event of Being, Heidegger has cut out the tongue of the poets he reads and turned their most bitter laments into hymns to Being's coming dawn.

It is perhaps just as well that Heidegger kept his silence about Celan, which is not to be confused with the silence of which Adorno speaks. One can anticipate the tasteless commentary: "Black milk of the *Frühe* we drink it *abends*" — the Great Greco-German Thinking-Poet "names" the declining darkness of the *Abend-land*, which is but a bitter prelude to the *Frühe*, the coming Dawn, in Greco-German *Seinsgeschichte*.

Is Heidegger able to hear anything else?

Suppose we made him sit down and listen to Celan's lament?

DISCOURSE NO. 8

The Lament of the Lamb

By Felix Sineculpa

Auschwitz is not Evil, not Absolute Evil.

Auschwitz is not some great Archimedean point, not some moral absolute we can fall back upon, not an absolute at all. Auschwitz does not impose a new Categorical Imperative, one which cuts through the sensible world with commanding, supersensible force.[150] Auschwitz is not a transcendental signified, not some kind of being-in-itself of Evil. It is not an uninterpreted fact of the matter, not a pure "moral fact." There are no moral facts, only interpretations.[151]

Auschwitz is not a fact but a perspective. The condemnation of Auschwitz is made from the perspective of the lamb. "That the lambs dislike great birds of prey does not seem strange: only it gives no ground for reproaching these birds of prey for bearing off little lambs."[152]

Disasters are not Evil. Nothing is Evil.

Is fire Evil because it burns the wood and turns it to ash? Is the sea Evil because it smashes against the coast and levels the dwellings that are foolhardy enough to nestle themselves against the swellings of its massive breast? Is the wind Evil? Is the wolf Evil, which descends upon the lamb and tears it to shreds, which grows stronger on the weakness of lamb flesh, which feeds on the flesh of the lamb?

Forces happen. The forces are what they are and they do what they do. We cannot separate what they are from what they do, because what they are and what they do are one and the same. It is a "seduction of language" to think that the effect can be separated from the cause, the predicate from the subject, the deed from the doer. *Es blitzt. Es blitzen die Sternen.* "It is lightning." "The stars flash." But we seek in vain for an *es*, for some subject to blame that could have withheld the deed or done otherwise. It is an exercise in futility, a vanity of the moralists, to tell the wolf not to prey or the eagle not to soar and sweep down on some defenseless creature. We might as well tell lightning not to flash, or tell the stars not to shine, or tell strength not to be strong, as tell the forces not to discharge.[153]

Life is "*essentially* appropriation, injury, overpowering of the strange and weaker, suppression, severity, imposition of one's own forms, incorporation and, at the least and mildest, exploitation." One exploits because one lives. " '[N]o more exploitation'—that sounds to my ears like promising a life in which there are no organic functions."[154]

To speak of "disasters" is to take the perspective of the part, the point of view of just one element in the total concatenation. It is a strictly regional judgment which achieves the semblance of absoluteness by attaching itself absolutely and unshakably to a part. It is said that a disaster like Auschwitz is Evil because it is "against nature." On the contrary, disasters are regular occurrences, among the most familiar pieces of nature, part of its most ubiquitous, most "natural" rhythms. Seen from a wider, larger perspective, from the perspective of the whole, disasters are familiar elements in nature's mosaic, part of the severe landscape of natural forces, part of the gigantic fortuitous game the forces play, "a game in which no hand, not even a 'finger of God' took any part."[155]

I will tell you how I think the forces happen. I will describe my interpretation of the panorama of their movements, the steps of their cosmic dance: Stronger forces dominate and overcome weaker forces. The best and most noble forces subdue the worst, the ones fit only to follow, not to lead. Cunning, clever, agile forces subdue dull and clumsy forces. Ignoble but more numerous forces undermine beautiful but rare and fragile forces. Brutal and cruel forces subdue gentle, more refined forces. Despicable forces overcome more likeable, lovelier ones. Ugly forces overpower beautiful ones. Gross, hostile, and aggressive forces subdue peace-loving and intellectual forces. Forces everywhere feed off other forces and thereby grow stronger while the fed-upon grow weaker. What we call "life" or "nature" is nothing but a field of forces feeding on other forces or being fed upon, subduing and being subdued, exploiting and being exploited, rising and falling, combining and recombining, building up and tearing down, in ceaseless cycles, tracing unending spirals of going over and going under.

That, I would say, is the "law" of how things happen, the very law that rules over the discharge of the forces, of the happening of the events. I would say it is a law except that the forces do not "obey laws," which is a piety introduced by moralists and another seduction of grammar. For the forces are nothing but the discharge of their own force from within. Nothing rules them from without. Life, nature, the total constellation of natural forces: what is that except the forces discharging their power, growing, expanding, drawing into themselves, gaining the ascendancy? That is how life happens, "not out of any morality or immorality, but because it *lives*, and because life *is* will to power."[156]

To speak of "nature" is to take the perspective of the whole, of the totality of what happens, of the whole concatenated chain of events, the best and the worst, the most noble and the most ignoble, the most beautiful and the ugliest, the grossest and the most refined, the numerous all-too-many and the rarest flowers—all of these together in one great constellation. Nature includes everything, the most fortuitous constellations and the calamity, the lucky stars and star-crossed disasters. The disaster is no more or less natural than the flame that licks at the forest, than the lion that tears at the heart of the lamb, than the wind that roars, than the eagle that sweeps off with its prey.

The beast of prey is a disaster—for its victims. The disaster is a value judgment made from the perspective of the prey. But it is not "against nature," not an unnatural event, not out of order. On the contrary, it belongs to the hardest, coldest, most uncompromising and undisguised conception of order and nature, to an order of nature for which all too few have the stomach. To speak of the "disaster" is to take the perspective of the prey, not of the beast of prey, but it is not to speak against nature.

Do you love nature?

> You want to *live* 'according to nature'? O you noble Stoics, what fraudulent words! Think of a being such as nature is, prodigal beyond measure, indifferent beyond measure, without aims or intentions, without mercy or justice, at once fruitful and barren and uncertain; think of indifference itself as a power—how *could* you live according to such indifference? To live—is that not precisely wanting to be other than this nature?[157]

The disaster is just another constellation of nature, one not to the liking of the victim. It is an event of certain forces whose stars are marked for oblivion and extinction. But the perishing of one star is a matter of cold indifference to the galaxies as a whole. What does it matter to the great cosmos if this little globe is overrun by death and disease? Is not the disease of one organism simply the life of something else, of the microorganism or the parasite, one that we do not like? Is not the weed that suffocates the flower simply another plant, one that we do not like? What does it matter if organic life itself is extinguished by a great nuclear holocaust, by an opening in the ozone cover, or by a stray meteor that sets off a cataclysmic chain of events? Is that not but a new configuration, another constellation of forces, and does not the great cosmic game love that movement too? Is not the death or destruction of the one intertwined eternally with the life or construction of the rest? Is

not the death of our little star not just one more form the whole
assumes, one more step in its endless dance? Will it not come to that
anyway? Will not that too have its turn, eventually?

Auschwitz is the business of cruel forces that form no part of a man of
breeding or taste or delicacy. It is no business of forces that are made for
higher, more delicate matters. Auschwitz proceeds from bent and
distorted forces, filled with *ressentiment* and negative impulses. It is the
issue of forces twisted out of shape and deflected by reactiveness, which
do not discharge actively, cleanly, in an upward spiral, building newer
and higher and more beautiful configurations of force, more intoxicating
constellations of forces that lift our minds above the pain of events.
Such cruelty reveals a lower type, cheap, agitating forces, which stir up
and play on the horned beast in people.[158] Auschwitz is the issue of
lower forces that have not learned to sublate and sublimate the will to
cruelty, mastery, and exploitation in a higher, nobler direction.[159] Such
cruelty is the exercise of baser, still unsublimated forces.

But these forces too are part of the whole, part of what is, part of the
fatedness of what happens. Auschwitz is part of how the forces are
discharged, the way forces of a mean and ignoble type are discharged.
But you cannot separate the deed and the doer, the quantum of force
and the deed. The cruelty of Auschwitz is like the cruelty of the wolf or
the eagle, of the fire or the wind. Shall we tell the wind not to roar or
the eagle not to soar or the fire not to burn? Auschwitz is a happening
of forces that are what they do and that do what they are, that burn
because they burn. *Es blitzt, weil es blitzt.*

Auschwitz is a part of the whole, a piece of the fate that belongs to
the whole. Each thing is part of the whole and the whole is, as a whole,
innocent. What happens is innocent. There exists nothing outside the
whole in terms of which one could judge the whole. The whole is what
it is, does what it does. That is all. The forces discharge themselves as
the forces that they are.[160] *Und nichts außerdem!*

Auschwitz is what it is, a piece of fate, a constellation of base, cruel
forces. But there is no one or nothing to blame, no subject that can be
separated from its predicates, no doer separable from its deed. The
lament of lambs before the beast of prey is not the voice of Being, of
God, or of the Moral Order. It is no voice at all but simply the noise of
the forces as they go about their business, going over and going under.

There is no Evil here, just stronger and weaker forces, noble and ignoble
forces, hostile and peace-loving forces. There is no "obligation" here. The
happening of obligation is still another seduction of grammar, an invention
of the moralists, a perspective-judgment made from the standpoint of the
prey or the victim, a judgment of sympathy for the lamb.

One must see Auschwitz in terms of the whole, take the long look,
the longest perspective. The smoke of Shulamith mixes with the whole.
It disperses into the clouds, which fall to earth as rain and rise again as

vapor. It is entered into the cycle of the seasons until one day this little top stops spinning and falls back into the sun. Then the universe draws still another breath, continuing its cosmic dance across endless skies, unmindful of what has transpired off in some remote corner. The laments of the lamb, never very audible to the cosmic ear, disappear without a trace.

* * *

Commentary: Rewriting the Disaster. The pages of the women authors, which are a kind of hymn to obligation, are haunted throughout by Felix Sineculpa's cold vision, by the utterly merciless view he takes of suffering. Felix is a practitioner of what Nietzsche calls his radical "honesty" or "truthfulness" (*Wahrlichkeit*). Truthfulness is all that is left when one sees that Truth is the will-to-truth, a fiction, a function of grammar intent upon imposing order and sense upon what happens. Felix practices Nietzsche's virtue of the "extreme," the virtue of seeing ideas through to the end, without compromise, "without mercy or justice," without what philosophy calls virtue.

In the discourses of Felix the poetics of obligation are attributed to a perspective-judgment, the perspective that attaches itself resolutely to the part, that takes the part of suffering, oppression, victimization, all of which has been summarized by way of Blanchot's term "the disaster." Disasters have no absolute rights, no divine warranty, no trans-historical or metaphysico-ethical backups. Obligation is a perspective, a point of view that stands or falls on its own. The poetics of obligation is a function of a *hermeneia* of a radical sort, a grappling with an abyss, a kind of wrestling with shadows, in which it is resolved that suffering matters, but it does not arise from a deliverance from on high. Nothing comes from on high. We have no access to something Infinite, Categorical, Good, or Evil. We are divested of all categorical assurances, of all transcendent deep grounds that invite capitalization. We live our lives in the lowercase.

Taking the side of the disaster is a gesture that is constantly exposed to and held out against another, more Nietzschean perspective, which is the perspective of the whole, the longer, indeed the longest, hardest look. Nietzsche sees the disaster, the suffering of any individual, as a moment chained to other moments, an event linked to other events, in a vast tapestry which is, as a whole, beyond judgment, and which is, as a whole, simply what happens, which we are invited either to affirm or reject.

Viewed in this way, Nietzsche may be seen to represent still another "totalizing" gesture. To be sure, this is not a Hegelian totalization, which sees in the disaster the negative moment in the progress of the Spirit, thus constituting a teleological totality; nor a Heideggerian totalization, which sees in the disaster the *Abendland* that serves as both *eschaton* and prelude to a new *Frühe,* thus constituting an eschatological totality. It is rather—if this is not too paradoxical—a kind of postmetaphysical or antimetaphysical totalization, which sees in the disaster but a part of a whole that as a whole has neither meaning nor value but simply is what it is. Both Hegel's teleological totalization and Heidegger's eschatological totalization turn on some notion of a beginning and an end, whether that end be a *telos* or an *eschaton,* and what they each call "thinking" consists in making one's way from beginning to end. Hence each in its own way remains attached to a metanarratival explanation that finds an overarching organization in what happens. Nietzsche's totalization is more radical and austere. It is the function of an active nihilism that actively detaches itself from and wipes the horizon clean of any notion of purpose:

> *We* invented the concept 'purpose'; in reality purpose is lacking. . . . One is necessary, one is a piece of fate, one belongs to the whole, one *is* in the whole—there exists nothing which could judge, measure, compare, condemn the whole. . . . Thus alone is the innocence of becoming restored.[161]

The whole is innocent (*sine culpa*). The whole is rendered innocent, "redeemed," by wiping the horizon clean of purposes, intentions, goals, agents, responsibility. Auschwitz is a part of an innocent totality and it becomes guilty only by relaxing one's view, by constricting one's perspective, by attaching oneself to a part, by not maintaining the severity, the coldness of the longest perspective, which climbs to the mountaintops of strictness. The gay science (*fröhliche Wissenschaft*) is a strict science (*strenge Wissenschaft*), stricter than any science, because it maintains a "reduction," a neutralization—of an injured part—more severe, more indifferent and disinterested, than is demanded of any other discipline, because it steels itself against the disaster. The point of view of "obligation," on the other hand, is radically partial, irrevocably attached to the singular one, to the lament of the singular being, of the particular. It is held captive by the cry of the individual and is quite incapable of Nietzsche's merciless "reduction." The name of Levinas's earlier book, the book that declares the impossibility of this reduction, should have been *Totality and Partiality.*

It was no mere accident, nothing purely fortuitous, I am convinced, that the discourses of Felix were placed—by some cunning if hidden hand—at the beginning and then again at the end of these treatises. The intent was to make the merciless standpoint of Felix the frame within which the lyrical-philosophical discourses on obligation are set. The voice of Felix is their setting, indeed I would say the spectre by which the other authors are continuously menaced. Felix haunts the other authors like a ghost. That is the best word. He haunts them and makes their words tremble. His cold vision is the fear and the trembling they confront. He robs their poetics of its power, breaks its hold on them and us. This fear and trembling is even more ominous than that of Abraham.

Felix shows that there is no writing of the disaster, no idiom we can provide for it, that cannot be *re*written. No matter how salient the disaster, how heinous the crime, it is always possible to redescribe it, to recontextualize it, to make it part of another idiom, in which the heinousness, the crime, and the obligation dissipate, in which the lament of the other that calls upon us is made to resonate differently (*glas*). However necessary and compelling the writing of the disaster may be, the possibility of rewriting the disaster is permanent and uncircumventable. The words of Felix are a dose of cold truthfulness; they descend on us like a wind that chills us to the bone.

There are no uninterpreted facts of the matter in the matter of obligation. There are no moral facts. That is why I have employed throughout these pages the Kantian formula that obligation is a "fact as it were." Obligation is like a fact, happens as if it were a fact, but its facticity and factuality tremble in the wind. Obligation happens, but when obligation happens we do not know what is happening, or whether it is not simply a perspective-illusion, a kind of game of ventriloquy played by the forces.

* * *

A FINAL FRAGMENT

Where do I myself stand in the midst of these multiple authorial voices, I who have dared sign my own name to this book? The truth of the matter for me — the cold truth that I do know what obligation is — lies in the exchange and interchange among these discourses, like the firing and cross-firing across the columns of *Glas*, the space or distance (the *différance*) between them. I pass my time between Good and Evil, in pursuit of something that is otherwise than ethics, neither a saint nor a postmodern. I settle into the empty space down the middle of the page, the spacing between the authors, the between-space of *inter-esse*, being in between, being-in-the-midst of factical life. That is where for the most part we, or I at least, pass my days. We rarely venture out to the edge, to the extremes, to the stormy seas where radical thinkers like Nietzsche venture, or to the other extreme where radical altruists spend their lives.

Like the feminine authors of these discourses, I can get no further than the happening of obligation. No matter what Felix says, no matter what eternal thoughts have entered into his head, obligation happens. The pulse of obligation beats steadily. The song of obligation, like Rebecca's lament, keeps playing in the background, whatever transpires in the conversations of the philosophers, even the most radical, the most extreme of philosophers, like Nietzsche. Obligation waits at the door for the philosophers and the genealogists of morals to finish their debates. As for the sun's fate 4.5 billion years hence, and that of the cosmos as a whole, it will no doubt be some time before I am able to devote my life's work to offering an opinion on that problem. For the moment, I am unable to budge from this place, surrounded by the happening of obligation. *Justitia fiat, coelum ruat.*[162]

Nonetheless, the menacing figure of Felix Sineculpa is always hovering in the background and regularly disturbs my sleep. I have a dream in which he is puffing on his cigar of a Sunday afternoon in Fredericksberg Garden, a look of irony and an odd sense of detachment on his face. He seems to be quite interested in a piece in his Sunday newspaper, but all the while his ear is cocked discreetly to an agitated conversation at the next table about the problem of Evil. After a while I can see the merest trace of a smile begin to cross his lips—and I wake up with a start.

NINE

Jewgreek Bodies

AN ANTIPHENOMENOLOGICAL SUPPLEMENT TO THE LYRICAL-PHILOSOPHICAL DISCOURSES

AGAINST PHENOMENOLOGY

As I read and studied the little treatises sent to me in the mail, I had in mind to follow them up with an exposition of the "phenomenology of the body" of which the authors made an important if implicit and nonthematic use. But I have been slowly drawn to the reluctant conclusion that the lyrical-philosophical discourses, and indeed the poetics of obligation itself, make a fundamental break with phenomenology, not only with the classical phenomenology of Husserl, but even with the later phenomenologies to which I thought at first this poetics might be more congenial. I see now, with no little regret, that the poetics of obligation must take its stand not only "against ethics," "against originary ethics," "against the ethics of infinity," not to mention being against books that are against ethics—to all of that I might somehow have been reconciled—but that it also must pit itself "against phenomenology."

The little discourses have gradually persuaded me that phenomenology's "body" is very much a philosophical creature and is quite unsuited to the needs of this poetics. Philosophy's body—from Plato and Aristotle to Merleau-Ponty—is an active, athletic, healthy, erect, white male body, sexually able and unambiguously gendered, well-born, well-bred, and well-buried, a *corpus sanum* cut to fit a *mens sana* in the felicity of being-in-the-world and mundane intentional life. But the bodies of Polyneices, Isaac, and Shulamith, of the lepers and the man with the withered hand, are disfigured, diseased, unburied, sacrificial, and ashen bodies. These jewgreek bodies are not quite so philosophical. A little ugly and unpleasant, they fall outside the classical paradigm of propriety and comely form.

The task that now befalls me, as the supplementary clerk of the lyrical-philosophical treatises, is to venture upon these scenes of impropriety, of improper and unbecoming bodies, to examine the bodies that have always fallen before phenomenology's *epochē*. If phenomenology is the phenomenology of *le corps propre*, the discourses are implicated in an antiphenomenology of improper jewgreek bodies, of bodies that are neutralized by phenomenology's reduction to "good form." For the poetics of obligation sides systematically (as it were—this is not the System; it has not the least thing to do with the System) with disastrous, disfigured, ill-formed, ill-fated, star-crossed, damaged bodies—with everything that the discourses call "flesh."

Like classical thought itself, phenomenology has a predilection for the reassuring world of ordinary perception and ordinary life. It moves in easy commerce with the well-clothed, well-fed, and well-housed bodies that make their way about in everyday life. It directs its attention to the way that world is constituted and to the constitutive role played by the "agent body," which always seems to be in excellent health, quite well rested, fresh from a trip to the islands. Phenomenology favors the good form of *le corps propre*, by which I mean not the sphere of "ownness" but a "proper" body, a body with propriety and decorum, dignity and grace (with just a touch of tan).[1] But the lyrical-philosophical discourses move in a more shameful direction, into a most improper sphere, into shocking scenes of impropriety and disastrous bodies; away from beautiful Greek bodies to malformed, disfigured, diseased, disabled, miscegenated, and transvestic jewgreek bodies, bodies buried alive, or dead bodies left to rot unburied; away from processes of constitution and building up toward breakdown and deconstitution. The discourses traffic with the anti-ideals of *le corps impropre*, of a disordered, improper, unbecoming body, as the subject matter of a kind of *antiphénoménologie de l'impropriété*.

This is not entirely without precedent. In *The Phenomenology of Perception*, Merleau-Ponty singles out a *corps impropre*, poor Schneider, who suffered from a head injury caused by flying shrapnel. But Schneider is taken as an instructive example of certain perceptual, linguistic, and motor disorders, and is assimilated by Merleau-Ponty into a philosophical schema. It is interesting to Merleau-Ponty and very revealing, for example, that Schneider cannot apprehend simultaneous wholes.[2] Schneider is an occasion of instruction, an index—*modo privationis*—of the healthy, normal agent body. But it is never mentioned by phenomenology that these motor peculiarities are a source of misery and humiliation for Schneider, that they reduce him to an object of phenomenological gaze, not to mention the gaze of many others. The humiliation—which is a jewgreek category—is neutralized by the phenomenological reduction, bleached out by a strictly Greco-philosophical operation. The reduction requires a distantiating eye, a slightly voyeuristic, phenomenological "we," hiding inside the camera box of phenomenological *Anschauung*, peering through the unidirectional glass of a philosophical reduction. "We" are those Greco-philosophers who are not like Schneider, who are indeed defined by being not like Schneider, who even find his disorders secretly, ever so slightly amusing. Schneider is he who is not like us but who tells us who "we" are.

The discourses have recourse to another reduction, a reduction to flesh, which is an antiphenomenological reduction aimed precisely at accentuating the humiliation and the misery of the flesh. In this antiphenomenology, the healthy agent body breaks down; the vigorous intentionality of its being-in-the-world is jammed or clogged. Its gender and sexuality become confused. The clear lines of the classical ontophenomenology of the body are blurred by the unsettling figures and strange disfigurements of flesh. The flesh is an antiphilosophical category, a jewgreek sphere of disfigured bodies, bodies in pain or laid low. "Flesh" is not the site of the "intertwining" of being and sense, but the scene of a disastrous tearing asunder, a scene of senseless laceration, ulceration, incineration. Flesh is what happens to a body that is stripped of being and sense, that suffers the violent loss of its world.

That is why the "flesh" of these "jewgreek bodies" is the site of obligation. I do not say it is the origin of obligation, because I do not know what obligation is and I am, accordingly, at a loss to say what its origin is. I do not offer a genealogy of obligation but only a topology of its surfaces. Flesh is the surface to which obligation clings, like vines clinging to a wall. If, as Levinas says, the space in which obligation happens is curved, then it is jewgreek flesh that curves it. I can feel space bending under my feet when I encounter flesh. I can feel it in my bones, which means in my flesh. Obligation happens—in and with and as flesh. Obligations are events interwoven with the texture, with the tissue of flesh. Obligation clings to flesh—like an odor or a scar or an indelible stain.

The task that falls my way at this point, as the loyal clerk of these discourses, is to sketch several salient features of these jewgreek bodies, some dominant traits of their topography, to offer a sketchy topopoetics of the flesh.

TRAITS OF FLESH

Having abandoned, or been abandoned by, the phenomenology of beauty, form, order, and movement, by the level, oriented, sanitary space of ordinary life, the discourses take up an antiphenomenology of what is immobilized and laid low, a poetics of bodies filled with the soft tissue of living things, with a fleshy, vulnerable stuff. "Flesh" is a richly disseminated Anglo-Saxon word that ranges over palpability, sensuousness, sensuality, concreteness, weakness, vulnerability. I love this word "flesh" very much, although I admit it is a little embarrassing and does not sound nearly as high-minded as *Geist* or *Sein* or *aletheia* or the thinging of the thing. This can be seen at once, as soon we see that flesh is also the flesh of animals, which means the flesh that we eat. Flesh is *Fleisch*, which is extremely embarrassing, hardly a matter for *wesentliches Denken* or for transcendental philosophy.[3] Flesh is carnality, carnage, carnivorousness, carnivality. Flesh is highly polyvalent, the site of uncontrollable disseminations, suggesting simultaneously carnivals and sacrificial offerings, sensuality and obligation. It is a word made for a heteromorph with heteronomic proclivities.

I offer here a somewhat unsystematic, unphilosophical tour of some of these slightly seamy and unseemly scenes.

1. Flesh is a site of eating and drinking. Jewgreek bodies eat and grow hungry. Jewgreek narratives are filled with food and drink, with table fellowship and ritual meals, but also with starving, malnourished bodies, with miraculous meals offered to hungry crowds, with images of poisoned, black milk. Philosophical bodies by and large seem not to eat; or their meals are taken in private and go largely unnoticed by the onto-theo-logicians, who are, on the whole, taken up with thinking higher humanisms.[4] (Still, there is, as I will point out below, a repressed discourse on eating in philosophy, which constitutes, as it were, a metaphysics of absolute eating.)

2. Flesh is the site of sacrifice. The body of Isaac is bound to the stake and (almost) offered in sacrifice. The sacrificial body is flesh exposed to cutting and burning, killed and then turned to ash. There is flesh—*es gibt/il y a*—ashen flesh. Bodies act or are acted upon, but "flesh" is stuff for cutting and burning. Jewgreek bodies turn ashen, like Shulamith, although it is, as Lyotard says, an obscenity to treat Shulamith as somebody's "sacrifice." When Abraham substitutes the ram for Isaac, he modifies and deflects but he does not fundamentally reject the economy of sacrificial flesh, of ashes and burning. *Il y a là cendre.*[5] There, where there is flesh, there amidst jewgreek bodies there are ashes. It gives ashes. The play that plays without why plays with ashen hands.

"Thou Shalt Not Kill" says the law. But that law, which is so filled with exceptions that it is hard to remember that there even is a law, and even harder to see what the law prohibits, was never meant to include animals. Animal flesh is the flesh of the other (uncapitalized) which is not the Other (Other Human Beings). "Thou shalt not kill—except animals." It is perhaps easier to remember the law if you put it in the affirmative: "Thou Mayst Kill Everything—Except Other Human Beings." To this is added a little codicil, a dangerous supplement: "And Sometimes, When It Is Necessary, Thou Mayst Kill Other Human Beings" (or at least keep an army, should the occasion arise).

The Lord, father Abraham thought, can only be pleased by seeing something die, cut up, and turned to ash, which is how Abraham interpreted the Covenant he cut with the Lord. Abraham thought he had to offer the Lord a meal, that the Lord was carnivorous. The face of Isaac only deflected the blade of Abraham—from Isaac to the ram. If he cannot kill Isaac, then he will kill the ram, because he must kill something. In the name of pleasing the Lord, of propagating his seed, of fathering a whole generation, surely something must be killed, cut, and burned. What, after all, is religion all about? Presumably, the eye of the ram, unlike the eye of Cain, does not stare back at Abraham from the grave.

"We"—who "we" are is a matter of bottomless complexity—kill to eat; we kill to sacrifice; we kill when it is necessary. We feed off and sacrifice the flesh of the other. We are beasts of prey, (like) lions, wolves, eagles. "We" prey/pray.

This sacrificial economy—which Abraham would not sacrifice—is what

Derrida calls "carno-phallogocentrism," which is a Greco-Judeo-Christian economy. The phallic, sacrificial religion of Abraham—which in Derrida's view communicates with Greek phallophilosophy—turns on what Derrida calls the "schema" of "carnivorous virility," on man-centered, meat-eating acts of killing.[6] This schema, Derrida thinks, belongs no less to the modern notion of the "subject," of the autonomous *ego cogito, ego volo*, which effectively marginalizes vegetarians, celibates, homosexuals, and women. Our freedom and autonomy, Levinas says, are murderous. We restrict the protection afforded by the prohibition of murder to "our" "neighbor," i.e., to the "same." But who is our neighbor?[7] On this point, Derrida says, however vast their differences, Heidegger and Levinas share a common privileging of human life, a common devalorizing of the animal, and a common thematics of proximity and propriety.[8]

The attempt to make a clean cut between animal and human life breaks down. Killing tends to generalize itself. Killing (other) animals bleeds into killing other people. The dominant schema is a generalized anthropophagic, man-eating violence.[9]

But then again, if flesh disseminates over human and plant, how can we eat plants? Where does this all end? We have to eat and we have to eat something living. That is a law of flesh. It is not a matter of maintaining a rigorous purity and purism but of vigilance about the effects of these practices, about the waste and the cruelty of excessively carnivorous practices.

Torture and murder likewise belong to this same economy of carnivorous virility which cuts, burns, and sacrifices. In torture, the body of the other becomes flesh torn apart and dismembered, carved, butchered, burnt with fire. In war, human beings are "slaughtered like cattle"—unless they are themselves the butchers; or they are "sacrificed," that is, cut to pieces, for their country. The bodies of women, too, have always been meat for these virile carnivores; likewise the bodies of slaves and migrant workers, and Third World bodies.

3. The bodies of Antigone and Mary the Magdalene and the hermaphroditic bodies of healers like Yeshua are sites of the feminine operation, of flesh tending to flesh, sites of mending, not wounding; of tending to the dead and watching over tombs, not killing; of nourishing nurses, not the black milk of violence.

4. The jewgreek bodies of the lepers and, today, of the victims of AIDS are "consumed" and eaten away. The paradigmatic diseases are diseases of consumed flesh. We who as carnal beings are made of flesh are likewise consumed and eaten—by parasite and infection. We who eat are ourselves eaten. We who would like to think of ourselves in terms of autonomy and freedom, of *Sein* and *Bewußtsein*, in particular we philosophers who are accustomed to think of ourselves as a pure I or spirit, indeed we male philosophers who do not even breast-feed, we must confess to being flesh/ *Fleisch*, consumable, edible "meat." Heidegger was scandalized by Aristotle, whom he accused of zoologism for having defined Dasein as an

animal (*zoon*) equipped with *logos*, for not having thought the essence of Dasein "high" enough.[10] But what can be said in defense of the Thoughtlessness of edible Dasein?

Even after death—especially then—flesh provides a feast for birds and beasts of carrion (from *caro, carnis*: flesh). The wickedness of Creon, his sin against the flesh, was to flaunt this, to leave Polyneices exposed to the (other) animals, to fail to shelter this defenseless, dead flesh. In the end, in the grave, flesh is exposed to the final consuming, the most haunting, sickening, final *consummatum est*: worm meat. *Memento homo pulvis es*: remember, man—and woman, too—that thou art flesh which turns to dust, remember the ashen flesh of Shulamith.

Being consumed, eaten away: that is a deep fear, a hideous end for flesh. We dread the loss of our substance, the dark spectre of flesh consumed by disease or starvation, of being reduced to a point where the body is driven to feed upon itself. We dread the horror of a tumor, for which the body serves both as host and prey. Flesh feeding on flesh, on itself, until the flesh is consumed. In the biblical narratives "leprosy" is the emblematic disease of the human condition; Yeshua and the prophets move among leprous bodies. Leprosy or the plague, in the ancient world, cancer or AIDS today, are gruesome figures of consumption, of flesh being eaten away, hollowed out and consumed. Sunken eyes, limbs of skin and bones, without flesh, with withered, withering flesh. These are preeminently, paradigmatically diseases of the flesh. Heart attacks, on the other hand, seem to me like cleaner, crisper, more Greco-German deaths. We prefer to fall from our own exertion; death by *praxis*, the death of the agent body, struck down in the midst of a daring deed, shattering against Being in a moment of fatal, heroic exertion.

Withering away in a bed, the death of the AIDS victim/leper, is a jewgreek death, self-consuming, *unheimlich*, decomposing flesh, a disgusting *Ver-wesung*. For the lovers of good form and propriety, such a death is in league with sin and evil, with unnatural perversions. It represents the visitation upon perverse flesh of dark, ominous forces. Perversion punished by a sickening reversal and disfiguration. *Poena*/pain: pain is penalty and punishment for perversity.

The whole thing announces a haunting transformation and disfiguration of the flesh which never quite figures in *The Visible and Invisible*: to become flesh is to become consumable; carnivorous and *caro*; eating and eaten. That is a "reversibility," to use a term employed by both Derrida and Merleau-Ponty, of a more graphic sort, one that sends a shudder down our spine, that is central to the impropriety of the flesh, to *le corps impropre*. Flesh constitutes a great chain of eating and being eaten.

5. Flesh is the site of a metaphysical metaphorics that transports eating to the sphere of absolute eating, of absolutely carnivorous virility, which is, as it were, a definition of what metaphysics calls being, act, substance, spirit. There is, I said above, an implicit if repressed "metaphysics of eating" in

metaphysics. "Spirit," which wants to raise itself above flesh, is in fact a higher, more perfect, decontaminated flesh, a flesh that has been insulated against the possibility of being itself consumed. Eating offers metaphysics an excellent model for being. Being and eating belong together because the essence of being is a kind of eating. The metaphysical desire for "pure act" is the desire for a preying that is not preyed upon, for absolute eagle-like preying and *Greifen*, for a consuming that is not vulnerable to being consumed. That for Nietzsche is an impossible desire and a form of nihilism, the desire not to go under, i.e., not to be eaten.

Vulnerable, consumable flesh does not meet the standards of metaphysics for true being. Flesh succumbs to the radical reversibility of the carnivorous and the carnal, of consuming and being consumed. Flesh fills metaphysics with anxiety and makes the *Aufhebung* choke, inhibiting the breathing of the Spirit. That is why Derrida has consistently pursued reversibility effects, identities unable to maintain their identity, which never attain an identity to maintain. Derrida is interested in hand and glove, foot and shoe, head and hat (like the man who mistook his wife for a hat),[11] in hermaphroditic transformations, in the instability and contingency of every identification. His reversibles pass into each other, have always already passed into each other, are always already inside out (without our being able to get a sure footing about what is the reverse of what).[12] A reversible is something that, failing to be itself, fails to avert its reverse and so never allows the dialectical machine, which is driven forward by self-identical identity and the opposing difference, to sink its gigantic prods into the ground and to swing into action.

Flesh is such a reversible, just insofar as what eats is always edible, what is carnivorous is always carnality. On such flesh, Spirit would choke.

But the dialectic's absolute—*Sa, savoir absolu*—is all-consuming, infinitely free being, which means the fullness of absolute eating, biting, and *Be-greifen*. It leaves nothing outside itself, no remains or leftovers. It finishes up every last morsel. It eats everything—nothing is indigestible to it—while not being itself eaten. Preying without being preyed upon, a sovereign eagle-like predator, it is the fullness of *energeia*; it does not slip into reverse but moves forward, higher, including, incorporating, assimilating, subsuming, consuming everything in its path.

If I had the nerve to write under a pseudonym, which I certainly do not, I would adopt some very Germanic name, like Wolfgang von something-or-other. I would write a parody of German metaphysics entitled *Sein und Essen*—this is a possibility omitted by Heidegger in chapter four of the *Introduction to Metaphysics*—in which I would defend the thesis that the Absolute is absolute *Essen*. Absolute *Sein* or *Essen* means an eating that cannot be itself eaten, a swallowing that cannot itself be swallowed. That, I would venture, is the very definition of "Spirit" (from the point of view of flesh) and the deconstructed sense of the *nous noetikos*, which is a certain perfect digestion. *Es is(s)t*, absolutely. Spirit feasts on the flesh of others while remaining itself inedible. That would enable me likewise to define what is not spirit—flesh—as what can always be eaten, what is always haunted by the possibility, the figure of being consumed. Hence flesh is unable to attain the freedom of spirit, to mount the high ground of absolute inedibility. That would give a new sense to the image of Being as a well-rounded whole, a slightly plump and overround Spirit that grows ever larger, fuller, more and more whole, the self-certain consciousness which is sure that it will never be itself swallowed up, the absolute circle of ingestion and digestion. But flesh is always already liable to be consumed, is always already meat.

At the heart of my treatise I would place the axiom *das Wesen des Essens*: *das Essen des Wesens*: the essence of eating (which means the Being of the same) is the eating of essence (the consuming of the other, of the substance of the other.) Eating means lifting the other up into a higher more substantial self, into Spirit. Thus Spirit is not only breathing, which is very edifying, but eating. The becoming of Spirit is a most unbecoming figure—a mouth that breathes between bites.

It goes to the heart of the flesh, on the other hand, that it can never achieve absolute inedibility, absolute invulnerability, absolute freedom from consumability, absolute *Wesen/Essen*. Flesh is always liable to be consumed, already exposed, left open, in a kind of quasi-transcendental exposition of which the rotting flesh of Polyneices is the paradigmatic figure. The poetics of obligation turns on this ineradicable exposure, this quasi-transcendental vulnerability—the exposure to wounding, destruction, consumption—that defines the figure of the flesh. It turns on this most graphic and carnal reversal and turning inside out, which stands at once against ethics, against metaphysics, against phenomenology, although never in opposition *simpliciter*.

6. That means that flesh is a site of a certain fated reversibility. We have of course been taught a great deal about reversibility by Merleau-Ponty, who has conceived the project of a philosophy of flesh and who has given us a beautiful philosophy of reversibility.[13] Flesh for him is the chiasm, the intertwining of the visible and the invisible, the place where Being folds back upon itself, invaginates, turns itself inside out, and thus allows itself to appear as visible. The "invisible" life of seeing, hearing, touching, the whole ensemble of sentient life, cannot be deployed except from the site of a being which is itself visible, audible, sensible. The visible world and the eye share a common flesh; the flesh is their common being and belonging together.

But Merleau-Ponty's analysis is—for my taste, despite all that I owe it, despite how much I love it—too epistemic, too Husserlian, too Heideggerian, too much devoted to seeing and perception, visibility and invisibility, still too much an ocular phenomenology which moves within the range of light and *Erscheinung* and *phainesthai*. It is still too edifying, too beautiful, too concerned with propriety and good form. It is still too much taken up with an encompassing intertwining that ties everything together into an ontological totality. As such, Merleau-Ponty's analysis is still a form of the idealism[14] against which he always fought, which still takes the measure of the flesh in terms of light and opening. It is no wonder that it finally succumbs to the discourse on Being and brushes against phainesthetics.[15]

That is why I have contaminated this phenomenology with an *antiphénomenologie de l'impropriété*, with eating and the edible, and why the authors of the lyrical-philosophical treatises have switched their paradigm from eye and mind and breath to nose and mouth and teeth and swallowing; that is why they have abandoned good form for the improprieties of disfiguration. They are less interested in the visible than in the edible and consumable or even, to be very graphic again, the flammable. For after all, flesh burns and turns to ash, and the foul smell of burning flesh is central to its scandal. The pseudonyms want to shock Merleau-Ponty's phenomenology of flesh out of the horizons of *phos*, light—they are more interested in fire, *pyr*, than light—and its attendant phainesthetics. They want to jolt it into a more graphic order, to scandalize it with a more carnal, meaty materiality, a more "figural"[16] configuration. Not visibility, but vulnerability, tearability, searability, flammability, edibility. *Il y a là cendre.* Are ashes phenomena, beings that emerge into presence, or are they merely the ashen remainder of quasi beings, quasi-present, half being and half nonbeing, of the *me onta* of flammable flesh?[17] If these are phenomena, they are not very phainesthetic and chiasmic, but more caustic sunderings and holo-caustic happenings.

Il y a là cendres. There is/it gives obligation. Cinders make for obligation.

Chiasmic intertwining is still too Greek for the authors of the lyrical-philosophical discourses, too Greco-phenomenological, too onto-phenomenological, still too much a captive to the metaphysics of identity and propriety and of the belonging together of Being and thought, of *einai* and *noein*, to the gentle convergence and criss-crossing of the thinging of the thing. Intertwining has too little to do with flesh/*Fleisch* and ashen hair. Intertwining is not a scandal but a gift and a giving, full of *harmonia* and gathering *logos*, of propriety and very becoming forms. It does not follow up on the Greeks who interest these authors, the tragic Greeks who tore their eyes out—which is when ocularism is more interesting, more fleshlike—the Greeks who left their dead enemies unburied and buried their living enemies alive. What holds the attention of the pseudonyms is not intertwining but flesh torn apart, eaten up, or consumed in flames. They are not interested in this phenomenological reversibility, which ultimately trades on the belonging together of Being and thought and sits down to table with the dialectic, but in being turned inside out or torn apart. Flesh does not mean intertwining but tear (from the Sanskrit *ker*): flesh is what can be cut up, sliced and burnt—like meat.[18]

The lyrical philosophical discourses instruct us about the exposure of the flesh to being consumed, the movement that throws flesh into reverse and breaks it down. That, I would say, is the very nature of suffering, were it not that suffering is less a nature than a denaturing, a breakdown of *physis* and *bios* and *zoe*, an undoing of *Wesen* and *natura*. What is suffering if not this very vulnerability of the flesh, this unremitting unbecoming, this liability to suffer every breakdown, reversal, and consumption?

AN ANTIPHENOMENOLOGICAL REDUCTION

I have been distinguishing between "body" and the "flesh."

The "body" is the transitive operation of intentional life, an active, well-organized agent that is borne into the world by the organization of its intentional operations. Whether it takes the form of the *fungierende Intentionalität* of Husserl, of Heidegger's being-in-the-world, or of Merleau-Ponty's body-subject, this transitive agent body is carried beyond itself and buries itself in the world of its concerns. The "body" is a very Greek and very philosophical creature, something that has always been valorized in philosophy. And phenomenology is philosophy in the intuitive mode, philosophy's eyes and ears, which is why Heidegger found it more and more difficult to separate phenomenology from Greek philosophy.[19]

The jewgreek bodies of the lyrical-philosophical discourses, on the other hand, are disasters. Lacking transcendence and transitivity, their intentional lines are jammed, their transcendence blunted, clogged, and shut down. Their hands do not move with prereflective ease along the tracks of the *zuhanden* world, because their hands are withered, crippled, maimed, or missing. Jewgreek bodies have been reduced to "flesh." Their flesh has been exposed.

The body is a scene of transitive events while the flesh is the scene of intransitive events.

In philosophy, smelling—e.g.—is taken as a transitive, intentional act, as a way of intending the world, lifted up, like an eagle, into the privileged operations of consciousness or of being-in-the-world, both of which are equally if differently transitive, equally if differently privileged performances. Smelling in the transitive-intentional sense is the sensuous intending, say, of the bouquet of a fine wine, of a flower, of a perfume, of good food—all of which are very becoming. That does not disrupt the decorum of professorial discourse, of philosophy professors like me who are concerned with maintaining their dignity and propriety. Smelling in the intentional sense is still good Greco-onto-phenomenological form. (As far as I can see, onto-phenomenology privileges the eye first, then the ear, then the touch; tasting and smelling are tied for last.)

But suppose this intentional escape is cut off and the flesh is trapped in itself, confined, in this case, in its own odors and odoriferousness. If the eye which sees is also visible flesh, then the agent body that smells becomes the unbecoming smell of flesh. Flesh smells "in the verbal sense," not a transitive, Greco-German verb, but an intransitive, jewgreek verb. The smell of jewgreek bodies is embarrassing. Because it offends our sensibilities to mention the unmentionable details of this embarrassment, I will be as discreet and circumlocutious here as possible. (I do not have the cover of a pseudonym.) Smell means the smell of sweat; of unwashed flesh; smells which gag; the vile smell of wastes, of fecal material (the pseudonyms were more graphic); menstrual, genital smells;[20] the smell of rotting flesh; the odors of disease and death. Putrefaction, decomposition, degeneration. The smell of *Un-wesen* and *Ver-wesung* (understood verbally of course).

Nietzsche, one of the truly great philosophers of the flesh, the first philosopher to philosophize with his nose, whose genius is in his nostrils,[21] is one of the few philosophers to have a nose for the smell of the other and to have organized his thought around the odor of rank. Nietzsche ranks bodies from those who smell the most rank to the those who smell the best, who rank the highest. Christians smell the worst to him, and their Book is very rank, whereas his high-ranking yea-sayers are quite sweet-smelling. Far be it from me to challenge Nietzsche's nose, which seems to me the most formidable nasal operation in Western thought, but I am dubious about his sense of priorities, about the order of his odor of rank.

The lyrical-philosophical discourses do not seize upon the transitive-intentional operations of the body but linger in the non-intentional, immanent smell of smelly bodies, which smell in the intransitive, jewgreek sense. When the intentionality of the body breaks down, when the agent body collapses upon itself, curls up within itself, then you get to the level of the flesh. That is where the disaster is.

That immanent, intransitive smell—that intransitive event—is a figure of the flesh. But the structure of intransitivity which I think permeates the pseudonymous discourses can be multiplied across all the operations of the other senses.

"Feeling" is an active, transitive operation of the philosophical body, which sends its intentional probes out into the world like a man searching about for a light switch in a darkened room. The hand probes the surfaces of things that are smooth or rough, wet or dry, warm or cool, hard or soft. It feels the textures and contours of other bodies, of other living bodies. Better still, for this is still too cognitive, too abstract a model, the feeling body swings into action in the world of sensuous elements, in a world for which it has a working feel, without taking explicit, thematic notice of this or that felt quality, which would derail and distract its efficiency and effectiveness. The life of this dignified agent body is edifyingly portrayed in a series of proper philosophical discourses, first by Husserl and then still more elegantly by Merleau-Ponty.[22] It is all very beautiful and very edifying and we have all—I speak at least for myself—learned a great deal from it.

But the discourses focus on another figure, another feeling, a little more misshapen and disfigured, a feeling that is intransitive, nonintentional.

Their discourses turn on the feeling that arises from the short-circuiting of transcendence, when feeling curls up within itself in the agony and torment of pain (as also in the enjoyments, *jouissance*, and the ecstasies of pleasure). That is what I mean by the reduction of the body to flesh, which is another reduction, not phenomenology's but a more antiphenomenological reduction. Flesh is not the intentionality of consciousness, not the seat or site for consciousness, not an organic apparatus or instrumentality that consciousness deploys in order to carry out its worldly projects, its excursions and forays in and around the world. Feeling is more—or, better, less—than the intentionality of consciousness, and more or less than *Sorge* and being-in-the-world—both of which too easily and too readily surpass the flesh, both of which are equally heedless of the quality of flesh. Feeling is not only intending but the intensity that can eventuate in the loss of the world and of all intentionality. Flesh is the site of the breakdown and destruction of the world—in the blindness of pain, in the interiority of agony, in the solitude of misery, in the worldlessness of suffering.

Pain is not an intentional state.[23] It not only resists language, but when it is intense and concentrated enough it destroys language, reducing us to primitive shrieks that are prior to language.[24] Pain does not reach out to the world, but, rather, is the occasion upon which one's world is destroyed. In moments of extreme pain, Elaine Scarry says, "the created world of thought and feeling, all the psychological and mental content that constitutes both one's self and the one's world, and that gives rise to and is in turn made possible by language, ceases to exist."[25]

The experience of torture, so powerfully analyzed by Scarry, is very revealing. The world of the victims of torture is reduced first to a room, then to the interior dimensions of their body:

> World, self and voice are lost, or nearly lost, through the intense pain of torture and not through the confession as is wrongly suggested by its connotations of betrayal. The prisoner's confession merely objectifies the fact of their being almost lost, makes their invisible absence, or nearby absence, visible to the torturers. To assent to words that through the thick agony of the body can only be dimly heard, or to reach aimlessly for the name of a person or a place that has barely enough cohesion to hold its shape as a word and none to bond it to its worldly referent, is a way of saying, yes, all is almost gone now, there is almost nothing left now, even this voice, the sounds I am making, no longer form my words but the words of another.[26]

The torturer's "art" is to deploy pain like a pen to rewrite someone's world. He uses pain to lead us to deny everything to which we are attached, the one person or cause we most love and for whom we always told ourselves we would be willing to lay down our life. Pain severs every worldly tie, destroys the significance of every mundane thing to which one attaches significance, and then, like a sculptor's chisel, it refashions the world according to the torturer's design. The torturer writes on the flesh of his victim with the stylus point of pain. The operations of torture are conducted on the level of the flesh, a subcutaneous level situated beneath the intentionality of consciousness and active bodily life. At the exquisitely exact point of optimal torture, which falls just short of causing death while maximizing pain, nothing is significant except the pain and its cessation. At that point the victim of torture has no morals, no religion, no politics, no family, no world, no subjectivity, transcendental or empirical. The victim is only pain, that is, only flesh.

By the same token, and in an opposite direction, pain is also the site of the making of the world, of a *poiesis*, which finds an idiom for suffering in literature, religious narratives, and philosophy itself. That is the other half of Scarry's thesis. Her examples at this point are the Hebrew and Christian scriptures and Marx.[27] Pain is a certain "origin of the work of art."[28]

Feeling, understood intransitively, is a scandal. The blindness of the feeling, the loss of the world, the intensity of the pain, the reduction of a living, bodily agent to the indignity of fleshy *hyle* in the hands of the torturer—all of that is a scandal and a stumbling block to philosophy. The scandal lies in the reduction to flesh, in the victim become flesh before the body of the torturer.

The body thus is an active, organic, organized, intentional, deed-doing agency, emblematized in statues of powerful Greek gods and beautiful Greek athletes. Flesh is but the stuff of a body. One can reproduce the functions of the body with artificial organs and valves and electronic pacemakers. But the flesh is the body's palpable, living, sensuous, feeling stuff, the site of a purely immanent, nonintentional feeling. The suffering is situated in the reduction to flesh. The agent body supersedes its pain, is oblivious of it—and only later, after the exertion, realizes it, feels its throb or pulsation. That is when it sinks back into flesh. Athletes take painkillers—and sometimes do not even need painkillers—to mute the flesh so that they may give themselves entirely to the agent body and delay the relapse, the collapse into flesh. The disasters of the flesh are situated in the shattered, shipwrecked intentionality, in the breakdown and collapse of being-in-the-world. In suffering, the body contracts upon itself, curls up within itself in agony and blind pain, and turns itself into flesh. In suffering, the body contracts into the immanence of flesh.

The healthy, whole, athletic agent body transcends itself, is carried by the momentum of its agency into the world, is lifted up like an eagle by the life of the transactions it conducts with the world. As flesh disappears into the body, the body disappears in the life of agency and becomes an invisible, ever available instrument of transaction with the world. The agent body moves with ease and speed and would, were it possible—like the transporter in *Star Trek*—move with the ease and speed of light itself. The agent body wants to be light, weightless, transparent, fast, efficient, unencumbered by the flesh.

But the flesh is density and contraction, the weight of matter, the slow pulsating of life, the throb of sensuality, the intransitivity of feeling feeling itself. The flesh feels itself, is itself the feeling of itself, does not distinguish between feeling and itself, but is the sheer immanence of intransitive feeling.

The agent body is mobile and actively constitutes the world. But a body immobilized by pain or disease, by the torturer's chain or the constraints of a narrow, unlighted cell, is melted down into flesh. The body become flesh is deprived of the ability to constitute and synthesize, to assimilate what it encounters. The reduction to flesh is a reduction to chaos and confusion. This reduction is the unbecoming of the world, its breakdown and loss of organization, even as the organic body dissolves into the pulsations of limp flesh.

The scandal is the impropriety, the demeaning reduction, the unbecoming figure cut by flesh, the figure cut into flesh. The scandal is the immanence and intransitivity of feeling.

The flesh is not the function of seeing nor even the physical eye which sees — the organ of sight which is the seat of attention, perspective, backgrounding and foregrounding — but the eye that is torn out, the eye too many. The flesh is not the eye that sees but the eye that is hollowed out by hunger; that is blinded by injury or disease or genetic fault; the cancerous eye that submits to the invasive knife of the surgeon. This is not the eye of "eye and mind" but the eye of "eye and flesh." Not the eye of Cézanne but the eye of a man born blind. The flesh is not the ear that hears but the ear in pain, that rattles with the confusion of indiscernible sounds, the site of vertigo and nausea. The flesh is the ear of the man born deaf. It is not the eye of Cézanne, but the ear of Van Gogh, the missing one, the one he cut off — like a piece of meat or a caruncle (*caro, carnis*) — in a mad rage when all he could think to do was to turn a knife against his own flesh, to transform the hand that created haunting worlds into an instrument of his own dismemberment. The flesh is not the tongue which tastes but the tongue cut out by the torturer's or surgeon's knife, the tongue which is twisted or tied by a genetic defect, whose density and thickness in the mouth choke off the airy flow of *la parole soufflée*.

Flesh is not the dazzling complexity of the neurological system which the most advanced computers strain to reproduce, which they may indeed reproduce some distant day. The flesh is the brain that has been invaded by a tumor, leaving a man or woman in terror and confusion, causing disequilibrium, throbbing headaches, a humiliating loss of memory, of recognition of the most familiar objects, impairing speech, hearing, sight. Flesh is felt in the inflammation, the infection that reduces the brain to its fleshy substance, to its gross materiality. An infection divests a distinguished woman of her expertise, destroys her effectiveness, happiness, and dignity. It reduces a once brilliant or creative or generous person to an undignified shadow of her former self; it reduces her to the indignity of the flesh.

I do not say one might not one day artificially reproduce flesh. Flesh is not a pure primal order of nature. I just say that if and when that day comes one will have built a being of flesh, not merely a functioning organism; one will have built a being that can hurt and be humiliated by the indignity of its humble state.[29]

Flesh is exhaustion, which is the overtaking of the body by the flesh, the sinking back of the body into flesh. The healthy agent body—the preoccupation of the phenomenology of the body—finally succumbs to overexertion, to the excessive expenditure of force, and sinks back into a chair or bed, allowing the body to fill up with flesh, to become limp, swollen, saturated with flesh. To fall off to sleep is to fall back into the flesh, to let the body which has been sculpted from the flesh dissolve back into its fleshy elements.[30] To relax is to return to the element of flesh, to suspend the agent body and the *logos* in order to become flesh. The bodies of the bathers described by Camus, basking naked on Algerian beaches, as drenched with sun as are the sun-drenched rocks themselves, have become flesh, saturated with warmth and sun.[31] A disease reduces a person to an exhausted heap, sunk into a sofa or a bed, helpless, weighed down by the unbearable weight of the flesh, bone tired. Disease carries out the reduction to the flesh in a kind of eerie antiphenomenological *epoché*.

The flesh is not a body but is always being organized and lifted up into a body. As long as it sustains and maintains this organization whole, flesh fades into the background of the agent body. But there are operations—like injury, disease, and torture or like sleep, relaxation, or the caress of the lover[32]—whose chief function is to fill the body with flesh, to let it overflow with flesh, to reduce it to the flesh from which it has been sculpted.

THE ANARCHY OF FLESH

Far be it from me to deny that flesh and pain have a history and that the borders between body and flesh undergo continuous historical shifts. I am not trying to make flesh into an ahistorical principle. There is a difference between the experience of pain before and after the discovery of anaesthetics, inside and outside medical-technological civilizations, inside and outside of one religion or another. Pain is valorized, feared, and experienced differently, depending on the historical, linguistic, economic, social, cultural, political, military, or religious presuppositions within which it is situated.[33] Pain does not occur outside the frame of *différance*. Flesh is the not a field of being without *différance*. I am much more interested in "*différance* in the flesh."[34] Even the reduction to silence and prelinguistic shrieks effected by torture or intense pain is possible only within the frame of language. A being that lacks language cannot be reduced to silence; torture is an operation performed on beings who can be made to speak.[35]

There are even cultures that take a certain pleasure in pain, whose members practice shocking cruelties toward one another.[36] I have no idea how far this can go, at what point the drive for survival and the carnal protest raised by the body against pain would draw a line and contain such practices. I do not see how one can deny that it would be possible to socialize people into accepting very barbaric practices. My claim is not that the prohibition of such cruelty is written in the stars, or in nature. On the contrary, my embarrassment as such is to have admitted that there is no such Absolute Prohibition, coming from above or below. My claim is that such claims as afflicted flesh make upon us are frail and finite, and my supplementary poetic strategy is to lend these claims an ear, to provide them with an idiom, to magnify their voice, to let them ring like bells across the surface of our lives, and to discourage cruelty. After that, I do not know what else to do. We have to do with competing poetics, poetics of obligation and poetics of phallo-aggressive machismo, with the persuasive power of competing poetics.

Far be it from me, a heteromorph to the core, to deny the historical plurivocity of flesh. I am not trying to erect "flesh" into some kind of *arche* or *principium*, a kind of jewgreek principle of primordial presence. Like Magdalena, I make every attempt to avoid centering everything on (any such) erection. The reduction to "flesh" is meant to have precisely the opposite effect, an antiphenomenological effect, viz., to fill the *arche* of the philosophical body with anarchy, to soak the stiff and rigorous agent body with a liquid stuff that makes it soft and flaccid. This antiphenomenological reduction does not discover some stony transcendental *principium* or irreducible *residuum* but an amorphic un-principle, an element of contingency, disorganization, breakdown, and undecidability.

Flesh is not an *arche* but the anarchy that fills the philosophical body and disrupts its archic-organic functions. Flesh is not *morphe* but a kind of dissoluble *hyle*, a soft hyletic stuff susceptible to multiple forms that makes heteromorphic multiplicity possible.

The flesh is not a sexual *principium*; it is neither male nor female; it is both male and female—and everything in between. Sexuality is a function of an organized body, of sexual organs. But flesh is the stuff of sex. Men and women are equally flesh, without regard to their sexual differences—even if men are gendered away from flesh, taught to take their pleasure actively, never far removed from the agent body, or even from violence, while women are gendered into flesh, attached more closely to the nurturing of flesh, which sociohistorical gendering is the empirical correlate of what Derrida calls the "feminine operation." But the feminine operation is an operation of flesh, not of empirical women. That is why men too perform the feminine operation and thereby confound their sociohistorical gendering. Flesh is an undecidable, which means that it is both male and female, and neither male nor female. Flesh serves to make the sexual differences communicate with and melt into each other. Flesh makes a man as tender as a woman; it makes a woman as swollen as a man. In the sexual embrace organs are transformed into flesh; flesh clings to flesh, flesh envelops and engulfs flesh, flesh penetrates flesh, in a movement that awakens the flesh and transforms a "reproductive function," a sexual "principle," into the "pleasures of the flesh." Flesh is flesh, whether it is male or female, homo-sexual, heterosexual, or bisexual. Flesh is the stuff of sexuality without re-gard to the sexual organs that are carved out of flesh or the historical con-stitution of genders. Flesh is transvestic, hermaphroditic, androgynous. Far from constituting a principled sexual difference, flesh creates gender-anarchy; not *ein Geschlecht*[37] but too many *Geschlechter* to count.

Flesh is also not the *principium* of a species, not a natural kind, not spe-cies-specific, and it is certainly not the private property of human beings. The several species are a function of their organic bodies, of the organiza-tion of flesh into natural kinds. Flesh is flesh in human and nonhuman be-ings, wherever there is *zoe*. It is in virtue of flesh that the differences among the species are melted down. We also speak of the flesh of a plant, the soft pulp of a fruit or a vegetable, thus further skewing the identity of flesh, thus further disseminating flesh. A chain saw tearing through the trunk of a hundred-year-old redwood tree is tearing through the flesh of the tree, its living pulp. The flesh of marine life choking to death in waters poisoned by oil and toxic chemicals is no less flesh than human flesh. The flesh of ele-phants cut down in rapidly disappearing habitats, of animals dying in sci-entific laboratories—all of that and more is flesh, dying, wounded, dam-aged, diseased, suffering flesh. The disappearance and destruction of species in which the modern world is engaged is an undoing of flesh and of its heteromorphic possibilities.[38]

Flesh is not the *arche* of organic differentiation, the principle of organic articulation, of incorporation. The body is a principle of operation; the flesh is the stuff of the body, its feeling, pulsating *hyle*. The body is organized flesh—and, as such, is always vulnerable, always liable to be reduced to flesh. The flesh tends to vanish into the body, almost to disappear into the organization and active life of the body. It is only when a man or woman who has always been strong and active is laid low that we remember that he or she is made of flesh. It is only in extreme moments—of pain and suf-fering, but also of pleasure and ecstasy—that we become all flesh; only in moments of extreme exertion that we are all body and utterly heedless of our flesh, of the consequences for our flesh. For the most part we lead lives that negotiate the difference between body and flesh, lives of *différance*, in-habiting the distance between incarnation and incorporation. But body and flesh are separated only by a hair. The flesh sees to it that incorporation is always an operation of the most fragile sort, highly unstable, subject con-stantly to injury and destruction. The body is woven from a very delicate gossamer stuff. The flesh is not the principle of the body or of bodily life but the un-principle which exposes it to ignominious undoing and the oblivion of disease, dismemberment, diminishment, and death. Flesh is al-ways waiting patiently for the agent body to finish its work, after which the body slumps back into flesh and dissolves. Flesh is the anarchy inhabiting the bodily *arche*.

Flesh is not an *arche*, the primordial truth or *logos* of the body, an overarching, ahistorical, transcendental standard, the truly absolute subject to which a reduction can be made of all mundane forms of bodily life. Flesh is not Being in itself or a primitive contact with Being. On the contrary, flesh is a loss of contact with Being. It is not primal contact but contraction and loss, the unbecoming of the world. Flesh is not Being but the loss of Being. It is not the intertwining of visible and invisible but the severing of the optic nerves, of limbs and spinal cords. Flesh is what becomes of us when we are deprived of Being, world, language, and truth. Flesh is not the becoming-one, the gathering *legein* of intertwining, but brutal unbecoming.

The immanence and intransitivity of the flesh is not the perfect self-return of pure presence present to itself. It is not a perfect transcendental return to itself, because it wholly lacks transcendence and everything transcendental. It does not return to itself from the world in a transcendental presence to itself, because it never makes it as far as the world, never transcends to begin with. Flesh is what clogs the wheels of the dialectical machine, the thick gum of carnality that clings to every transcendental operation and holds it stuck in place, the glue that makes everything stick to itself. Flesh is a kind of sticky *hyle* which clings to everything and which never is found without form, which does not exist in itself, which is always already formed and constituted in some historical body. Flesh is not the principle of pure presence or perfect being or true *Ansichsein*, but what happens to a body that is trapped inside itself by paralysis or disease. Flesh is a vulnerable, dividable, undecidable, intransitive un-principle. It is not a principle of unity but the un-principle which sees to it that unity is transient or impossible. Flesh is the an-arche by which the body is invaded, the impossibility that the body can become a principle, that it can forge forward in dialectical ascent, or function smoothly in organic coordination with the soul whose organ it is meant to be, or lend itself to the universalizing, transcendentalizing operations of the ego, which seeks to lift itself up above sensuous particulars. Flesh is the glue that gums up every transcendental/mental operation, the web of carnality that clings to everything. Flesh is the thickness and density of the body that traps the body in itself, that makes it sluggish and slow, that clogs the transcendental operations, choking the transcendental aspirations of the spirit.

The reduction to flesh is not a return that bends back upon itself, modeled after transcendental reflection, in which the *reflectieriende ich* manages to hoist itself up above the empirical *ich* and to capture itself in a moment of transcendental truth. It is not a return to primal presence but a jamming and a clogging which never get as far as presence, a collapse and a breakdown before an object is reached, a failure of transitivity which leaves us not with the purity of a pristine element but with the confusion and density of something murky and gross robbed of the light of truth. Flesh is not pure presence but what a man or woman is reduced to who is tortured half to death, deprived of all his or her faculties, in the chaos of pain and the pain of chaos. This is not a reduction in the sense of the leading back (*re-ducere*) to a primal subject, but a reduction in the sense of a diminishing or subtraction or loss.

Flesh is vulnerability and the reduction to flesh is a reduction to naked vulnerability. It is in virtue of the flesh that bodies bleed and break down, are cut up and consumed, become diseased and disgusting, that they hurt and curl up in pain, that they perish and putrefy. Flesh strips the body of invulnerability, deprives it of immortality and statuesque beauty and permanence—flesh is flesh, not stone—and leaves it aching or exposed, like Polyneices, to the most gruesome forces.

If I were to invoke a classic sculpture of the body that would express in stone this jewgreek paradigm of the flesh, it would not be Greek but Renaissance, and even then not the *David* of Florence but the *Pietà* of St. Peter's, in which Michaelangelo makes stone sigh with sorrow. That is an almost perfect attempt to show the body sunk in the sorrow of flesh, a slumping form embraced by the feminine operation. But had I been Pope Julius II, I would have commissioned Michaelangelo next to do a statue of Polyneices, dead and rotting, being sniffed by a dog. Today, there are experimental sculptures that seek, *per impossible*, to give a kind of form to the anarchy of flesh; or experimental music, which you can barely hear, according to a classical phenomenology of the ear and its synthetic operations.

Flesh is not an *arche* but the *an-arche* within the body, its unprincipled undoing, not its overarching principle but what allows it to be torn to shreds or eaten alive.

I do not mean always to sound so grim, to dwell only on the seamiest sides of the flesh. I beg the reader to recall that my task here is to gloss the lyrical-philosophical discourses which have taken up the issue of a poetics of obligation. I myself hold that flesh is the seat and site of pain and suffering, but no less of pleasure and joy, of carnival and carnal joy. But my topic just now is disasters and the happening of obligation, and that is what demands my attention at present. I am, however, prepared, some other time perhaps, to addess the question of the figures of *jouissance*, of the pleasurability rather than the vulnerability of the flesh, which is its other, cheerier side. Remember my Dionysian rabbi is also a fellow of the very brightest moods and of the very sunniest disposition, a lover not only of a good *Requiem* but of a stirring *Exsultatio*.

The point, after all, is to minimize the disasters and to multiply the several possibilities of joy, at which point we can safely say *chacun pour soi*, which is a joyful anarchy that celebrates the multiple forms which flesh can take, its heteromorphic possibilities for pleasure, affirmation, and joy.

OBLIGATION'S BODY

We are now in a better position to understand something about the event of obligation, if not to plumb the depths of its origin, at least to get a sense of its topography, of how and where it happens. This is, I think, the point around which the lyrical-philosophical discourses turn and the reason they were sent to me in the middle of my work on obligation and the deconstruction of ethics.

In the economy of obligation, the I is always structurally an agent body while the other—which enjoys a place of primacy—is structurally flesh. However hale and whole, the other is always vulnerable, always structurally liable to be reduced to flesh, while the I is structurally a bundle of active forces, an agile aggressive agent. That is what we mean by the "I," even if we think the I is a grammatical fiction, a piece of shorthand—for it is shorthand for a constellation of aggressive, active forces. Structurally, the I always poses a threat to the flesh of the other. To take on an obligation is to make oneself out as being in the wrong, to concede that the being-for-oneself of the I spells trouble for the other.

The body of the other is not (only) a thing in space, not (only) an object, but also something filled with flesh, something charged and pulsating with flesh. That brings into view another face of flesh, as more *morphe* than *hyle*, more an element of vivification and sentient life than some passive stuff. Flesh is a carnal stuff that flows through the body, pulsating beneath the body's corporate agency. This fleshy *hyle* engenders an indefinite but active penumbral space around the body of the other. It is that active halo of power that gives me pause, that pulls me up short, that checks my agency. The other is not merely a thing but a fleshy stuff sensitive to my touch, my approach, my agency, my active force, a bit of pulsating life vulnerable to my being. The other sends me certain carnal signals that warn me to proceed with caution. The body of the other is not confined to its three dimensions, but rather constitutes around itself a charged space, a field of force emanating beyond its bodily boundaries. I am submitted to this carnal halo as soon as I enter the other's domain. "Violence" means to take this space by force (*vis*), to invade a prohibited domain.

I understand, in my flesh, by some immemorial carnal operation, by a transaction conducted entirely within the domain of flesh—of flesh with and against flesh—that the body of the other is of flesh, is carved from flesh. This transaction is not an operation the I performs—it is not what Husserl calls an "ego act"—by the magic of empirical empathy or transcendental transfer, which are redundant attempts to cross to a ground on which we already stand.[39] It is an operation that is always and already performed in me, inscribed in my flesh by the flesh of the other, an operation that is older and more antique than me. As soon as we open our eyes the other is already there, has always already been there. Before we open our eyes we float in a sea of flesh. The other comes toward us from of old, always and already, from a seat, from a site of flesh that belongs to a past at which we were never present, making a kind of irresistible carnal approach.

The flesh of the other is no mere *hyle* but an active power that commands my respect, that elicits from me a certain "regard" which I do not extend to anything else. The flesh of the other is inhabited by "powers," filled with little quasi gods, as a certain less warlike, more egalitarian Heraclitus might have said.

There are always "relations of power" wherever there is flesh, and we are accordingly always awash in a sea of powers. That is what interests Foucault, who, I think, is another great philosopher of flesh. The opening sentence of *Histoire de la folie* sets the framework for the entire book by invoking the haunted spaces in which leprous flesh was kept confined.[40] The opening pages of *Surveillir et punir* supply the most vivid, the most graphic figure of flesh in recent French thought. The king inscribes his royal power on the flesh of Damien, graphically.[41] Foucault's concern is with the more subtle, more "humane" forms of regulating bodies and he has brilliantly delineated the ways in which psychological interiority is invented as a way of normalizing and constituting bodies. Bodies are covered by a thin film of micro-bio-powers that constitute and regulate what and who the I can be, that demarcate the limits within which the "individual" may range about. The power of the same to normalize and regulate similarity is a massive, important domain for investigation.

But Foucault does not analyze *another power*, the penumbra of power that the *Other*, the marginalized one, *emits*, the battery of signals that the Other sends, which is not normalizing power but the resistant power of the Other, the power emanating from powerlessness. The power of vulnerable, powerless flesh checks and disturbs the normalizing aggression of the same against the Other. Foucault does not consider a relation of power that opens a space for being different. For it is the power of homosexual flesh, which is different, which cries out against being bashed, which protests the violence. Foucault does not analyze the power of the vulnerable body of the Other to *prohibit* (I do not say to stop) violence, to issue a command against violence, even though such a power is what is presupposed by all of his analyses, not just the most graphic ones, like that of Damien the regicide. It took a rabbi, not a genealogist, to start rooting through this archive. All of this would belong to another *histoire de la folie*, the story of another madness, and the fabulous story of another Damien—the one surnamed the leper.

Take the practice of courtesy, which is a very proper, very becoming, very well-behaved way to comport one's body, a classical function of *le corps propre*. Courtesy is an illuminating transaction between bodies— bodies communicating with bodies, bodies signaling bodies with a minimum of ego-intentionality. Courtesy dictates that I do not brush aside the body of another if my way is blocked. I do not pluck someone out of his or her seat if I have been forced to stand. Not if I am courteous. I do not go up and inspect the face of someone very closely if I am curious about a spot I see, unless there are in place particular rubrics—e.g., if I am physician. But even then there is a very delicate protocol to be observed (and we must not forget a syllable of what Foucault has written about the power of the medical gaze). Otherwise it would be very unbecoming! It would be rude, incipient or even overt violence: invading a forbidden space with force (*vis*), gaining forceful entry, overpowering—by force—the power of the Other, riding roughshod over the power sent forth from flesh, the power pulsating through the flesh of the Other.

What courtesy is on the lower, more elemental registers of the flesh, familiarity, intimacy, and erotic embrace are on its upper registers. Intimacy is a matter of being welcome to enter the most secret, the most hallowed spaces and sacred regions of the Other's flesh, of being welcome in a region of (almost) absolute prohibition.

The flesh of the Other is also and no less what triggers my blow. It becomes the target of flashing anger, awakens my brutality. The flesh of the Other is never neutral; it does not submit to a neutralizing *epoché* or to the methodic doubt. The irreducibility of the flesh, of the signals it sends forth, is why obligation keeps happening, why it cannot be put out of action. It is always soliciting something: courtesy or discourtesy, anger or affection, etc. The I has always and already taken a stand toward the carnal powers that inhabit the Other. Even to treat someone with pure indifference or neutrality is in fact very rude, i.e., not indifferent. It is the flesh of the Other that I want to crush, smash, wound. I want to injure, I may even want to extinguish the life that stirs in that flesh and which fills me with rage. When in anger I wreck a chair, I am profoundly frustrated because I cannot make the chair hurt. I strike a futile blow that cannot reach flesh. I must content myself instead with making myself hurt, with making the hand that smashes wood or glass hurt, for that at least is wounded flesh and I have succeeded in introducing (more) pain into the world, which is what I want. The immediate object of anger and rage is to produce pain somewhere, in someone's flesh, even—all else failing—in my own flesh. Murder is a blow meant utterly to extinguish the power that emanates from the flesh of the Other, to crush it, to eliminate those alien gods. But that, as Levinas likes to point out, does not always succeed (Macbeth is his favorite example). Being haunted, I would say, is not a matter of being chased about by ghosts but by the powers that still smolder in ashen flesh, that hover over slain flesh. That was Creon's problem: the rotting flesh of Polyneices still commanded respect, still pulsated with the power of flesh. That was a power Creon thought he did not have to heed—and it came back to haunt him.

The lines of force that emanate from the flesh of the Other bend everything in their path and curve the space the Other occupies, producing a poetically inverted world (*verkehrte Welt*). In classical phenomenology we said that the space and time of "objects" is homogeneous and Euclidean; it can be marked off and staked out by a classical Greek geometry. But such absolutely level space is an abstraction; such objects are to be found only in mathematics books. In the factical "lifeworld" (*Lebenswelt*) space is always heterogeneous and differentiated because it is always interwoven with bodies; space is "oriented" around valuable keepsakes, favorite chairs, homes and neighborhoods (or space is the habitat of other living species).

But it requires a special jewgreek geometry and topography to track the twists and turns of the radically inverted world of obligation, to follow the highs and lows of the paradoxically slanted space that has been curved by flesh. It requires a certain jewgreek topopoetics to stay with the fabulous somersaults of the flesh and its law of inverse proportions. For the lower laid the body of the Other, the more the space it occupies is curved and the more the Other ascends on high. The taller and more erect our agent body, the lower we need to bend. That sounds like a classical law of inverse proportions for which classical science is well prepared—except that it is a little mad (*fou*, *verrückt*).

What the lyrical-philosophical discourses show, I think, is this: the flesh of the Other supplies the site, the locus, the *topos* of a jewgreek poetics of obligation. The irreducibility of the flesh, the inextinguishability of its living powers, is the reason for the irreducibility of obligation. Obligation happens in and with the steady pulsating of the pulse of flesh, with the irrepressible powers that emanate from it. The giving of obligation is the giving forth of certain fleshy impulses, like the *eidola* of Epicurus, which travel across its curved space.[42] The obligation that issues from the flesh, that comes over me and overtakes my flesh, does not need me to legitimate it or back it up. On the contrary, it takes the initiative and pulls me up short or draws me out. Obligation is an operation that is conducted in the domain of the flesh, one of the things that clings to flesh, like an odor or a sticky glue.

It is likewise obligation that awakens "my" flesh (where "my" is understood here and throughout structurally, as the flesh "of the I"), that stirs it into life. In obligation, my flesh is "moved" by the Other, mobilized into action; this is a certain *kinesis*, a kind of carnal jewgreek kinetics. Or it is not moved and the I remains impassive, immobile. But that too is an operation of the flesh, a hardness of heart, which is also a kind of flesh, flesh in the privative mode, flesh that fails to have a heart or that has a heart of stone. In the medium of the heart, stone and flesh are opposite configurations.[43]

The flesh of the Other is the site of the disaster, of damaged lives, of the loss—which is what awakens obligation. The suffering of the Other is what solicits the I, solicits and awakens the flesh of the I and so transforms the I from agent body to awakened flesh. The suffering of the Other touches my flesh, melting my body down into flesh. The I undergoes a change of heart, from stone to flesh. The I becomes, from a strictly egological standpoint, a bit foolish.

Above all, it is suffering, which is situated in the flesh, that sends the signals that activate the networks of obligation. Obligation is a jewgreek paradox and foolishness—another kind of *folie*—centered on flesh laid low, which empowers it to come from on high, which means to be the site of obligation. Obligation consorts (the way one "consorts" with known criminals) with everything laid low and takes on by association the scandal of what is laid low. Obligation issues from the figure of disfigured flesh, from the whole array of wounds to which the flesh is subject, from every sort of gross dismemberment and disability, to the most subtle forms of exclusion and excommunication of the most able-bodied. It is precisely flesh in its several afflictions that is the most demanding, the most commanding, the most obliging. Afflicted flesh is the Other writ large, the otherness of the Other in its most graphic form.

That is why the lyrical-philosophical discourses love to be graphic. They do not mean to be rude. Their graphic portraits of foul-smelling or rotting flesh all have to do with the gods that inhabit the flesh, with the powers that pitch their tent in afflicted flesh, with the obligations that fly up like sparks from the figures of disfigured flesh. Given their humorous and ironic relationship with Heidegger, one might say they take themselves to be messengers of another (jewgreek) god, sent to announce a fateful destiny, that only a jewgreek god, only a god that smells, can save us now.

Obligation is a relation of flesh to flesh, a transubstantiation in which the flesh of the Other transforms my body into flesh. Under the touch of the Other the I becomes flesh. The I—which is structurally an agent body—is transformed from agent to respondent, from agent to patient, and becomes the patient of the Other's suffering. The *patiens*, the suffering, damaged flesh of the Other, becomes the transformative agency that by coming from on high, converts the I into flesh, becomes the agent of the conversion of the I. Conversion is transubstantiation—of body into flesh. Touched by the flesh of the one who suffers, the I becomes flesh and is (re)incarnated—as one who is a little "touched," a bit of a fool, a little mad (for justice). In this (re)incarnation of the I, "becoming flesh" means becoming mad, a little *verrückt* in the *verkehrte Welt*.

This way of becoming flesh does not mean that the I is laid low, that it is struck down by disease or injury. Nonetheless, given its foolish exposure to contamination, it does run the risk of coming down with leprosy—that is the other Damien I mentioned—or with AIDS, which is no small part of its madness. The I becomes flesh by being "touched." The I becomes the flesh of one who is touched. This being able to be touched is the vulnerability of the I, the vulnerability of my agent body, of my free and autonomous self-possession. Being touched is a transformation from autonomy to heteronomy, a reconfiguration of an autonomous agent into a heteronomous one. Being-touched is the foolishness of an aggressive agent become non-aggressive—for that is, *stricto sensu*, a paradox, since the I is always already—structurally—aggressive. It is the transitivity correlated to the intransitivity of suffering, the agency correlated to this *patiens*, the response awakened by this obligation. Being-touched is the vulnerability, susceptibility, or sensitivity of the I to the power that emanates from the Other. This is the vulnerability that Levinas describes, but it should be remarked that this is a secondary vulnerability, that it arises under the impact of the vulnerable flesh of the Other.

This vulnerability does not strike the I down, leave it limp and sighing, but mobilizes its active forces and swings it into action. (Body and flesh are not supposed to represent a new dualism but a cooperative interplay.) This is a paradoxical, mad agency in which the I expends itself on the Other, which is utter foolishness. Such is the sickness, as Nietzsche says, of an animal that has lost its instincts — or perhaps it constitutes the instincts of another jewgreek animal.

The foolishness of obligation means trafficking with the most unbecoming persons, inhabiting the most unseemly places. It means consorting with the most ill-constituted, with the lowest registers on the odor of rank. It labors among the poor and the homeless, the mentally and physically disadvantaged. It nurses the sick, tends to the terminally ill, works in the worst schools, the worst hospitals, the worst clinics, the worst slums — all of which is a feminine operation usually reserved for women. From the point of view of this madness, psychiatry and clinical psychology do not fuss over the interpretaton of "The Purloined Letter" (Lacan and Derrida), nor are they viewed primarily as ways to normalize dissidents (Foucault and Szasz). They constitute attempts to reach out to people who are tormented by demons all their own, who are driven painfully mad, who are on the verge not of producing a great work of art but of putting an end to their own flesh. The question of normalization is trumped by the question of pain.

It belongs to the structural possibilities of the flesh to remain "invulnerable" to the Other, to refuse to allow oneself to be "wounded" by the Other, to shield one's flesh from the power or the force of the Other. Instead of being "moved," "touched," "melted," "softened," one is "callous," "hard," or "stone cold" — i.e., heartless. Far from being mad, that is the essence of good sense and of avoiding paradox.

The madness (déraison) of obligation is not philosophy's longing for wisdom. Philosophy, which is Greek, has never considered the advantages of madness, which is a jewgreek strategy. Nor is it philosophy's way of being-moved (kinesis, Bewegtheit) but a jewgreek version of kinesis. For it is a matter of being touched, rendered susceptible or vulnerable to the being-laid-low of the Other. It is a mad form of motion in an inverted world and is activated not by the energeia of the Other but by the Other's deprivation (steresis) and reduction, by the Other's fleshy hyle. It is a jewgreek paradox of being-moved by the power of powerlessness, a jewgreek paradigm of being held "hostage" to the claim of the Other. It is easier to describe this figure of foolishness in jewgreek categories like hostage, captivity, and wounding, like disfigurement and defilement, and to inscribe them in the history of another madness, than it is to describe them in sensible categories of Greek philosophy that are organized around act and agency, autonomy and good form, beauty and propriety — the prized terms of metaphysics and ethics — all of which transpire in an upright world.

The whole economy of obligation, the obliging and being obliged, is a bit mad. Still, it happens. Here and there. Men and women sometimes answer a call, spend themselves answering a call. What they do is slightly impossible, because, as Aristotle says, every agent acts for the sake of the good, of the agent's own good. Otherwise it would not be sensible. If they spend themselves for the Other, that is what they want, so they are doing what they want, seeking their own good. Still, they make their own good the good of the Other, which does not seem very sensible.

It is not my assigned task to say that what they do is sensible or even possible or to pass judgment upon them at all. My work as obligation's poet and supplementary clerk is simply to record that it happens, to remark upon its remarkable quality, and to attribute the whole thing not to a modal but a postmodal logic.

Sometimes, at the end of their lives, these heroes of the impossible become quite famous. We weep over films made of their lives and we rush out to buy the videotape for our permanent collection, which we display in a prominent place, rejoicing to think that we are, in our living rooms at least, on the side of obligation. They become stars and virtuosos of obligation. But sometimes they labor in an almost perfect oblivion and are never heard from again; sometimes their stars are blocked from view or just knocked out.

Sometimes they are disasters.

TEN

Otherwise than Ethics, or Why We Too Are Still Impious

I turn now to say what—in sum—I have learned from Abraham and Johannes de Silentio, from the strange painting signed by Abraham of Paris, and from the lyrical-philosophical discourses of Johanna de Silentio, Magdalena de la Cruz, et al., by which I was so mysteriously visited. It has not been my task to write a *tractatus de obligatione*, to make obligation safe and to shelter it from attack, to provide it with the protection afforded by *episteme* or *Wissenschaft*. I have instead undertaken to make certain supplementary contributions to a poetics of obligation as an event that happens in the midst of a cosmic night, that regularly disturbs my sleep. In taking a stand against ethics, in never pretending to get as far as ethics, I have produced something that is otherwise than ethics, something a little too impious for ethics, while yet being very attached to its obligations. I move about in the difference between piety and impiousness, between ethics and the innocence of becoming, keeping up a correspondence with Dionysus while staying in constant touch with my rabbi.

ON MINIMALISM

My concern throughout has been to keep metaphysics to a minimum. The last thing I want is to set off another round of German metaphysics. So when I speak of an "event" as "what happens"[1] I am not putting on great metaphysical airs. I am writing from below and saying, in the most unrestricted, least imposing sense possible, that anything at all that happens is an event. I am also saying that I am not sure what is happening, even though things are happening all around me. I am like a man caught up in a swirl of activity who keeps asking "what's happening?"[2] Something is happening, but he cannot say just what, because so many things are happening. The point of talking like this is to find an idiom that carries a minimum of metaphysical baggage, that commits itself at most to a minimalist metaphysics. I am practicing a certain Ockhamism, which puts the razor to whatever I do not need.

We cannot just avoid or simply step outside metaphysics, which would mean to step outside the logic and the ontologic of our grammar and our intellectual habits. That would be a hypermetaphysical undertaking for which I lack the grammar, the logic, and the head. To speak at all is to have recourse to a way of framing and phrasing, to fall back upon a way of dividing up and parceling out, to mark the world up (*archi-écriture*) and to stake it out in one ontocategorial way or another. That is unavoidable. The idea is not to deny our presuppositions but to unfold them with greater penetration, staying on the alert as best we can to the ontocategories that shape our thought, troubling ourselves about them and worrying them a lot.[3] To speak at all is always already to be caught up in a certain amount of violence, of hermeneutic violence, of *archi*-violence and *archi*-incisions.

If you tried absolutely to neutralize metaphysics, to put it out of action *simpliciter*, you would get caught up in a metaphysics of neutralizing consciousness, in the metaphysical idea of a consciousness able transcendentally to neutralize real being. That is what Heidegger caught Husserl doing.[4] It is better to recognize the inevitability of metaphysics, to be vigilant about its omnipresence, and then to try to keep it to a minimum, to treat events as nonviolently as possible, with a maximum of *Gelassenheit*.

The time has come to overcome the "overcoming of metaphysics," or to make it plain that the point of overcoming metaphysics is to "not-be-overcome-by-metaphysics," by too much metaphysics, not to suffocate or to perish from the extravagant, totalizing tendencies of a maximizing metaphysics. A maximizing metaphysics is always too violent for events, which are very delicate and tender little growths; it is more violent than necessary, more violent than archi-violence, which is unavoidable. One cannot avoid some sort of metaphysics or another, but that does not mean that one needs to rush headlong into the most extravagant, totalizing, maximalist, metanarratival, in short, the most meta-physical forms of metaphysics, which are always organized around some Meta-event or other.

My minimalism is what is behind my affection for "anarchy," for the *arche* is always a stroke of violence, a violent incision, a cutting up and ordering about of events, of the singularity of events, by a sweeping principial power, by a *principium*/prince, by a Meta-event that orders everything around. The key to my idea of anarchy is to see that it is always on the side of keeping violence to a minimum. We need just laws and *archai* of various sorts, tentative, revisable *principia* (put forward in fear and trembling), for the point of the law is to protect the weak against the strong, i.e., to minimize violence. My anarchism is no street-corner antinomianism, but the cultivation of an eye for the singularity of events. Its aim is not to level the law but to keep the law honest, to keep the eye of the law on the withered hand, as Magdalena put it. I do not commit myself to pure anarchy or pure nonviolence. I avoid the metaphysics of purity and willingly embrace the mutual contamination of anarchy by the law and of the law by anarchy.

To affirm the anarchy of events is to embrace a polyarchy that concedes that events are indefinitely redescribable, indefinitely reconfigurable, that we lack the perspective from which to pronounce the meaning or pass the final judgment on the sense of events. Events belong to multiple, incommensurable, heteromorphic quasi systems in a kind of flat infinity that stretches out indefinitely in every direction. In virtue of such flatness, events never contain or attain an upright, order-giving, vertical infinity, the infinity of some absolute being—*l'infini*: the Infinite One—some Meta-event that dominates and organizes other events and serves as their *arche*. That would amount to vertical violence, the hierarchical violence of an overarching *arche* that takes itself to have full authority and to speak with authoritative power, which it is the point of minimalism to keep to a minimum.

Minimalism is a metaphysics without a Meta-event, a kind of decapitated metaphysics. Metaphysics in the traditional sense wants to keep its head. But I have no head for metaphysics and a metaphysics with no head.

Minimalism thus does not mean absolute simplicity but rather bewilderment before a tangled complex of events, a kind of amazement before the mazing grace of events, before the dense entanglement of what's happening. Minimalism is a philosophy that begins in a maze (*thaumazein*). The violence would be to erase the complexity, to simplify the quasi system, to dominate the textuality of the event with the simplicity of a single system, of an overarching principle or interpretation. The violence would be to stop the slippage, to erase the ambiguity, to take the play out of events, to put events out of play and into order, to hierarchize them, to erect principial authorities who would give authorized interpretations and definitive solutions and judgments.

Minimalism lets events happen, lets them be, lets them go, without imposing grand and overarching schemata upon them, without simplifying them. It has decided to come to terms with intractable plurivocity and heteromorphic proliferation, in the spirit of Abraham of Paris.

You cannot avoid linking one event to another and that to another, *ad infinitum*—again and again, and in different ways, over and over. But in this minimalist metaphysics or quasi philosophy of events you will never come up with some Meta-event that organizes all other events, that puts them to rest, that arrests their play, that sweeps over them all and gathers them to itself in a final "because" and gives them all a rest. I do not care if you call such a Meta-event *ousia* or *eidos*, *Bewusstsein* or *Wille zur Macht*, God or the gods, *abba* or *Jahweh*, the *logos* of the Dialectic or the all-gathering *logos* of the primordial Greek Beginning (*pace* father Abraham and the prophets, *pace* Hegel and Heidegger and Greco-German philosophy). Everytime somebody tries such a thing, we can show that this schema is always already troubled and disturbed from within. Every time an event is treated as a Meta-event, there is a power play afoot and the police are not far behind.

The most violent violence arises from thinking one can dispense with archi-violence and lay hold of some nonviolent thing-in-itself, some absolute, unmediated *arche*. It is just when people think they have gained access to the unmediated, Derrida says, that the rest of us are visited by the most massive, most violent mediations.[5] The point of a minimalist metaphysics of events is to avoid putting on the royal airs of the *arche,* to keep events in play, to lift the load the *arche* places on the back of what is happening, even while one recognizes the place of provisional rules. In minimalism, events are taken as tender shoots and delicate growths that need to be protected from such violence.

ES GIBT

"There is" (*es gibt*) is the minimalist way I have chosen to speak. It tries not to say too much, not to be too imposing a saying, not to impose itself on events. It tries to let events be.

There are (*es gibt*) events. They happen "because" (*weil*) they happen. They happen "for the while" (*dieweil*) that they happen. The "because" sinks into events, sinks off in what happens, fades away like an echo in space, leaving only the events.

Events happen without "why." There is no "why" outside what happens, no Meta-event that dominates other events, that serves as the point and purpose of what happens. Whatever is outside what happens is what does not happen. Events link on to other events, forming chains of events of various kinds, too many kinds to count or record. The "why" sinks into the "because" and is submerged in what happens; the Meta-event is submerged in the flow of other events.

What happens is what there is (*es gibt*). That is all. "There is" (*es gibt, il y a*) is the simplest, least encumbered way to speak of what happens. I have nothing up my sleeve; I am not trying to slip something past you. *Es gibt, weil es gibt*: There is because there is. That is a way of speaking that does not weigh events down with heavy ontological burdens or lift them up and carry them off with eagle wings to great mountain heights. "There is" (*es gibt*) is part of a minimalist metaphysics that is trying to travel light.

This very tautological way to speak in fact produces highly heterological effects. This minimalism is part of a corresponding maximalism in the sense that it allows for a maximum of pluralistic possibilities. That is because its very simple way of speaking is not very imposing, not too incisive.

Minimalism gives events some play, lets them play, allows for a maximum of heteromorphic multiplicity. *Es gibt* means *es spielt*: it plays. It plays because it plays. It plays for the while that it plays. It is all like a child playing who plays because she plays. The play is without why; the why sinks into the play.

Es gibt. It gives. What gives (*was gibt*)? *Es spielt*. It plays. What plays? What is the "it" which gives or plays?

Nietzsche has already warned us about this mistake, about the illusion, induced by grammar, of looking for some subject or agency or author when we use impersonal expressions like "it's lightning," or "it's raining" — or "it happens." Nietzsche is warning us to keep metaphysics to a minimum, to keep William's razor sharp. *"Es gibt"* means "there is" in the sense of "it is given that," "it happens that," "I am saying that." But there is no *"es"* which gives. The "It" is not a Meta-event. To say that what happens is like a child playing is actually a way of saying that there is no child, that nothing watches over what happens, that nothing anchors it down or lifts it up—not even a child. "It is raining" means "the rain falls." The "it" that "rains" sinks into the rain that falls. There is no "it," no agency implied. When we say "there is," "it is," we are conceding that nothing (we know of) is there, that no *thing* is there, that no one is there, behind or beneath or hovering over what is happening, no surpassing *arche* watching over everything. What happens is what happens. "There is" is a way of getting beyond the notion of a deep agency at the heart of what happens that is driving it somewhere, or of a deep *telos* at the end of what happens that draws it to itself. It is a way of speaking very simply, of saying that it happens, and that that is all. It is a way of declining to separate the "it" and the "happens."

Minimalism "declines" to say more. It does not deny that there is more, for how after all would it do that? *"Es gibt"* is a way of saying something happens, who knows what? It is a form of modesty. If that is so, then I do not know whether there is or there is not "any more." That is the region to which maximalist metaphysics proudly stakes its claim, the waters upon which religious faith ventures, full of fear and trembling. All I am saying is that minimalism is the horizon within which more robust assertions must be made, and that more robust assertions are on their own.[6] Minimalism is not a new overarching metaphysics. It is just one more perspective, a very modest perspective that arises when one asks, in genuine bewilderment, "what's happening?" When we say "there is" or "it is," that is a way of saying that nothing Overarching we know of is there, that it's just happening.

This is not a tautology but a heterology, because it does not indulge itself in the thought of a *to autos*, of something Self-same undergirding or overseeing what is happening. It does not try to gather what is happening into a unity and claim that "all is one," or claim that everything that is happening is really "nothing more than" such-and-such a Meta-event, or the history of such-and-such, or the giving and withdrawing of such-and-such, or caused by such-and-such. For any such undertaking I have confessed, again and again, I have no such prodigious head. *Es gibt* is not a way of sustaining or underwriting identity but of making space for difference, of making space for everything. To the extent that it does not indulge itself or impose itself, to the extent that it adopts a very simple, minimalist way to speak, very timid, its hat in its hand, the expression "there is" is very unimposing.

It does, however, impose upon itself a very severe, austere regime, self-effacing and without pretense.

"Es gibt/there is" is an impersonal, anonymous expression. If *es gibt* is a game playing, it is a game without a player, without an Overarching Someone or Something throwing the dice and trying to win. It is only a game. Or it is

not even a game, if by a game we mean something over and above the play of its elements, the play of events. Events happen. Phrases happen. The forces discharge themselves, or are discharged, in the middle voice—in between agency and passivity, in between causal agents and passive patients, without distinguishing the force and its discharge, the event and its happening. Events, phrases, forces happen (*arrivent*), one after the other, linking and un-linking and relinking, incessantly; that is what they are.

"*Es gibt*" is an austere way of speaking—it is our ascetic ideal—which confesses that we do not know what is happening. It is even a way of say-ing that nothing is happening, i.e., no *thing* is happening or making-hap-pen, over and above what is happening, no one Great Meta-event. It is a kind of plea which implores us to stick to what is happening; or a kind of confession that we are stuck in what is happening, and that it is impossible to get any further. It is a confession that we do not have such a prodigious head as is required for answering the question what is happening, that we cannot get on top of what is happening, that we are stuck in the middle of it, *in medias res, inter-esse*, amazed and bewildered. We cannot soar over what is happening with philosophy's eagle-wings. What's happening has clipped our wings.

No one we know of is there. No one we know of knows we are here, on the little star. We are like orphans—and widows and strangers. The stars do not care, do not take care of us. We are disasters, all.

"*Es gibt*" is a way of saying that we can lay claim to no star to guide us, no ground to found us, no deep core of *eidos* or *ousia, Sein* or *Geist*, to see us through the flux of events. It is a way of speaking of the "abyss," of the *Abgrund*. "*Es gibt*" exposes all to an abyss, lands us in a void, leaves us without support, with a minimum of foundations.

I have been speaking all along about obligation in minimalist terms. There is—*es gibt*—obligation. Obligation happens with and in terms of proper names, of the singularity of the individual. Obligation is a matter of being attached to a singularity, to something bearing a proper name. The lyrical-philosophical discourses were signed by curious proper names, strange names that provided a minimum of identification. That allows their readers a maximum of substitution; it allows these wondrous proper names to substitute for the names of us all, and in that way to speak to and of the obligations of us all, of each and every one of us.

But *es gibt* is neither a proper name nor a pseudonym but the very name of anonymity, of no-name, of no thing, of no one. It is a name for no one and for nothing, for the emptiness of the space between the stars, for a starless interstellar void. *Es gibt* is the name of the nameless, anonymous anarchy of what is happening. That is why it disturbs my sleep.

So to say *es gibt*/there is obligation, to say "it gives obligation," comes down to saying that when obligation happens it happens in a void, in an abyss.

Unlike Levinas, whom I love very much but whom I am obliged to betray, I do not think that anything can "deaden the heartrending bustling of *il y a*." I am more inclined to believe Levinas when he says that obligation comes "from I know not where" (*je ne sais d'où*). I am more inclined to believe that we cannot separate the *il* which is Him, God, which is God's own utter illeity, from the *il* of *il y a*, from the rumble of *il y a*. "God" is not the "apex of my vocabulary," something which would organize and stabilize my vocabulary, but another word that puzzles and disturbs my sleep. I am pursued by a more radical anarchy than Levinas's, one without an apex or a deep, founding, preoriginary ethics from which science and law and politics and institutional life can be derived and secured and can draw breath. I am haunted by a more disturbing diachrony, one with which I can never catch up. To say that this diachrony leaves its trace in obligation, and then to say that this trace is the trace of God, is that not to track this trace down, to catch up with it, to catch one's breath? That is too much for me, I who am permanently behind and out of breath and a terrible insomniac. If he— *il*, E.L.—"does not know from where" obligation comes, then why does he say a thing? Why does he say that it (*il*) is the trace of God? Why does he say that what he does not know can put an end to the haunting rumble of *il y a* instead of making it worse? For what else is *il y a* than being caught in the grips of I know not what, than being always already seized by what can never be present? My meditations on *il y a* leave me in a permanently anarchic state, tormented by the truth of scepticism. *Me voici*, here I am, called upon by I know not what, all my nouns and pronouns inwardly disturbed by anonymity.[7]

Il y a. Es Gibt. It happens.

When a proper name is used, when a proper name happens, it is like a voice crying in the void, like a prophet crying in a cosmic wilderness. Standing on the surface of the little star, our hands cupped to our mouth, we shout our proper names into the abyss. *Es gibt*: there are proper names. Proper names happen against the horizon of the impersonal, the improper, defying the anonymity of *es gibt*, rising up and sinking away.

If you press proper names, if you push hard enough against their surface, or probe with your stylus into their core, you will find a core of impropriety, of *différance*, for if they were truly proper they would not happen. So there is something slightly pseudonymous about proper names as well, and we are all slightly pseudonymous characters. The *différance* by which proper names are inhabited is the indifference, the anonymity, of what is happening that infiltrates their idiolect. The pseudonymous is the mask of the anonymous.

Proper names happen in the abyss. They happen for a while. They happen for the while that they happen. Then they die out like a lost language belonging to a lost time. In the long run, that is what they are and that is what our language is or will amount to. Eventually, as the little star grows cold, the noises of our language will disappear into the stellar night.

Eventually, we will all have spoken forgotten, dead languages.

Eventually, the memory of all these people and all these languages and all these proper names and the dates and places by which they are marked will be entrusted to faint and indecipherable traces on listing stones. Not even that.

Il y a là cendre. Not even that.

It gives—proper names. It—that is, nothing—gives them. They are given, but they are not given by anyone or anything. If they are gifts, they are gifts without a giver. If you insist that gifts must have givers, then you abandon minimalism and become pious. Proper names happen; that is all. The rigidity of their designation eventually withers, or it goes up in smoke, like Shulamith.

Es gibt/il y a/there is/it happens: that means there is nothing there that anyone can lay hold of. There is no Overarching agency or doer, no super-causal agent, no transcendent something or other, no *arche* we can grasp. Not as far as we know. It happens. There is no one there to thank or blame, no one archi-thing or archi-person doing it all, behind it all, responsible for it all, none we can grasp. It happens and it is innocent. It happens, for better or for worse. That is all.

Obligations do not derive from some central source of power. Obligations are strictly local events, sublunary affairs, between us. They are matters of flesh and blood, without cosmic import or support.

They happen.

AGAINST HEIDEGGER, OR, IN THE NAME OF ANOTHER HEIDEGGER

All along I have been settling accounts with Heidegger. The minimalism of the *es gibt* is my way of repeating Heidegger—carefully, selectively, warily, differently.[8] I have been repeating Heidegger while all along clipping Heidegger's eagle wings, reading Heidegger against Heidegger. It is a part of my love/hate relationship with father Heidegger (it is not safe to love Heidegger unless you also hate him), of following Heidegger while being against Heidegger. There is a certain Heideggerian tone to what I am saying here at the end, but I am trying to keep Heidegger to a minimum. I am a minimalizing Heideggerian.

I have been edged on by the lyrical-philosophical discourses, which were very irreverent toward Heidegger—who is the father of all of us who are deconstructing this or that, or talking about its delimitation. Like the discourses, I have been throughout as impious as possible toward Heidegger, because Heidegger is far too pious, dangerously pious, about the *es gibt*, about his *Sprache*, his *Volk*, his poets, and his Greeks. But my impiety has been, in part at least, minimally, in the name of another Heidegger. I will not say a higher Heidegger, because I have had enough of Heideggerian heights and the soaring of Greco-German eagles. But I will say of another, simpler and more austere Heidegger, the Heidegger of the *es gibt* and of the groundless play of Being's comings and goings, which is, I think, the austere setting within which obligations are given.[9]

I have been reading with you, vaguely and from afar, and contaminated with other texts, my favorite passage from Heidegger, from *Der Satz vom Grund*, a text which I have been reading for many years[10] and which keeps taking new turns on me, which keeps happening to me anew, again and again. But I have been simultaneously editing it all along, and with a heavy hand. I hold the text and read it with one hand, while in the other I hold my scissors. (That is how I read everything these days; my study is a mess.) That is because Heidegger, as I now think, could never maintain himself in the simplicity of the thought of the *es gibt*. Much as he loved the splendor of the simple, he could not contain himself, he could not hold back from the most extravagant, baroque adornments of *es gibt*. Whatever he may have said about *die Strengheit des Denkens*, he could never discipline himself to a rigorous minimalism. He always said too much about what's happening, even though he protested against the Gigantic in the *Beiträge*.[11] However provocative his meditations on *es gibt*, he always reduced *es gibt* to silence under his great Greco-German metanarratival outbursts, buried under the massive *Sprechen* of his *Sprache*—with disastrous effects on obligation. My view has been to take a minimal view of *es gibt* in order to maximize obligation. I have found it necessary to deny the History of Being in order to make room for obligation.

I have been reading Heidegger reading Heraclitus, as every Heidegger afficionado will have already noticed. Here is Heidegger "translating" a fragment of Heraclitus about a mysterious child-king:

> The mission of Being (*aion*), that is a child, at play, playing a board game; the kingdom is a child's. (Frag. 52)[12]

The "kingdom" (*basilein*), Heidegger comments, means the *arche*—the *principium* or, let us say, the "principality"—which gives the rule for the way Being holds sway in that time, in that epoch. The Being of beings (the *arche*) happens again and again, each time differently, in each and every epoch of Being—as *eidos*, *ousia*, *esse*, *Geist*, *Wille*, etc.[13] But what is the *arche* of the *archai*, the truth of truth, the unity of the manifold senses of Being, the rule that rules over the happenings of Being? That is the child. The *Seinsgeschick*, the giving or sending—the *Es gibt*—of Being, of the Being of beings, is a child at play. This great royal child, Heidegger says, is the "mystery of that play in which humans and their life time are caught up, upon which their essential being is staked." Heidegger asks, why is this great child described by Heraclitus playing his world-game?

He plays because he plays.

The "because" sinks into the play. The play is without "why." It plays for the while that it plays. There remains only play: the highest and the deepest.

Here is where my editorial work begins, where I brandish my scissors, where I cut the text off (like a rabbi): just at the point where Heidegger abandons the disaster and finds a lucky star to steer him through the groundless play:

> But this "only" is everything, the One, the Unique.

Here is where Heidegger starts heading for his star, where he gets very mono-astro-nomical. As he says elsewhere:[14]

> To head toward a star—this only.
> To think is to confine yourself to a
>   single thought that one day stands
>   still like a star in the world's sky.

You can see Heidegger starting to gather everything together, to collect what he has been letting be, letting go, letting happen. He cannot hold himself back; it is among his most fundamental gestures. Now a gigantic *logos* moves in, a single star that gathers the world-play together into the unity and simplicity and singleness of the *Seinsgeschick*, of the all-gathering One, of the Self-same. Like a great invading army, a massive metanarrative moves over the *es gibt* and assumes control of the play so that the play is no longer fully in play but rather gathers itself together under a Single Guiding Star. Something first flashed (like the morning star), for a moment, in the First Beginning, something great and aboriginal, for which we latecomers are too late. But this Something is not over but coming to us in the Other Beginning, for which we today wait and await, for which we are too early. In the meantime, the time of need, everything hangs in the balance. We latecomers, we *Abendländers*, we must wait to see if the evening star will transmute back into the morning star, if the gentle law of the *Es Gibt* (now in capital letters), the hidden law of benefaction in this giving and sending, is coming to save us. Still, we must do our part. The text concludes:

> The question remains whether and how we, hearing the movements of this play, can play along with and join in (*fügen*) the playing.

The question is whether we can join in the fugue (*Fuge*) by hearing the resounding of the First Beginning in the Other Beginning. The question is whether we have the ears to hear the Great Greek Beginning, to resonate with the Great Greek Harmony, the Harmony of these Greek Spheres.

That is the end of minimalism and the beginning of another tall tale, an astronomically tall tale. The austere play of the *es gibt* gets its star. The "It" acquires a proper name and a proper language and a proper home, a Beginning and a Future Destiny. The play is watched over by the mildness of a royal child who holds gentle sway over a Great Event. The goalless, anarchic anonymity of what happens gets filled in and filled out with the propriety of Being's own proper name and Greek tongue. That is why I have to edit this text rigorously, to edit out the Greco-German patronyms and astronyms, to take *es gibt* more austerely, more ascetically, more minimally.

That is also why I read *es spielt* in terms of *es gibt*, but not *es ereignet*. For *Ereignis* sets off an uncontrollable chain reaction of Heideggerian events. *Es ereignet* invites an irresistible Heideggerian gesture, promotes the most massive outburst of Heideggerian piety. At the sound of *Es ereignet* Heideggerian knees everywhere bend, their eyes cloud over, their heads laid against the breast of the Event of Appropriation. Then we are inundated by wave after wave of *eigen, eignen, Er-eignis, zu-eignen,* and *ver-eignen,* by a whole avalanche of *Eigentlichkeit.* That spells the end of minimalism and the *es gibt,* of its unadorned, impersonal impropriety, of the anonymity, the anarchy, the abyss.

Even *es gibt* itself is vulnerable to this Heideggerian chain reaction. For even if you avoid hypostasizing the *es*, as Heidegger does, you may not avoid pietizing the *gibt,* just as Heidegger does not. *Es gibt* can ignite another Heideggerian chain of *Geben* and *Entnehmen,* of *Denken* and *Danken,* of thinking as thanking for the gift that Being gives us to think. This massive piety brings *es gibt* under the rule of law, albeit of a higher, more elusive, more essential law, a gentler, eschatological, astronymical law than metaphysical teleology would enforce.

The modesty of my minimalism is not to know what is happening. For my part, the thrust of the *es gibt* or the *es spielt* is to divest us of the Gathering (*logos*) of the One and the Unique and the Single Star and to expose us to the wiles of plurivocity and polyvalent multiplicity, of a heteromorphic, anarchic abyss, of stellar oblivion and exploding stars. I am less inclined to bend my knee before the "mystery of the play" than to head for cover. That is why I stick to (or find myself stuck with) "it's happening," the mere happening of *Ereignis,* if you will. On a minimalist scale, the *Ereignis* is just an "event" (maybe even an impropitious event), and that is all, without the propriety and the appropriation, which you are more likely to hear in "*es geschieht*" or "*il arrive*" or "*il y a*." I am trying to stick to something a little more minimalistic, Ockhamistic, and occasionalistic, something a little more fortuitous and chance-like in *Ereignis*—without the flapping wings of the *Seinsgeschick.* Whenever I hear Greco-German eagles soaring overhead I head for shelter. I do not want to be saved by a Greco-German eagle. Far from waiting for such a bird to save me, I hope he never has a clue as to where I am hiding.

Heidegger has a way of seizing upon the sheer facticity of what is happening—that is what I love—and then of annulling or superseding it—that is what is dangerous. He has a way of "deflecting" what his favorite poets kept trying to tell him, Veronique Foti says,[15] even as he kept telling us to listen to the poets and to let them disrupt the complacency of our lives. I would say that Heidegger's entire path of thought is a kind of "deflection" of what he himself was continually reflecting upon, that Heidegger could never catch up with or come to terms with Heidegger, that Heidegger always lagged behind Heidegger. He takes to task the attempt of onto-theo-logic to dominate and totalize what is happening, only to find a higher, more essential way to dominate and totalize it all his own. He has a way of exposing the radical contingency of what is happening and then of covering it up.

Already in *Being and Time*, in the discussion of "truth," Heidegger said "there is" (*es gibt*) truth so long as "there is" (*es gibt*) Dasein. Truth happens, and it happens just because and just so long as and just for the while that Dasein happens. But why does it happen? Why must there be truth? Why does Dasein happen as the place where truth breaks out? To that Heidegger makes a minimalist response: "it is quite incomprehensible why entities are to be *uncovered*, why *truth* and *Dasein* must be."[16] The question "why?" already belongs to the horizon opened up by truth. The happening of truth, of uncovering, is the condition under which it is possible to ask "why?" so that the "why?" will never be able to circle back behind truth and find the condition under which truth is possible. Truth is the condition of the why; the why cannot find the condition of truth. Truth happens, without why, before why. But in the all-important chapter on historicity Heidegger found a way to take this minimalism back and to transmute the facticity of Dasein's being into a deeper necessity:

> The more authentically Dasein resolves . . . the more unequivocally does it choose and find the possibility of its existence, and the less does it do so by accident (*unzufälliger*). Only by the anticipation of death is every accidental (*zufällige*) and 'provisional' possibility driven out. . . . Once one has grasped the finitude of one's existence, it snatches one back from the endless multiplicity of possibilities which offer themselves as closest to one — those of comfortableness, shirking, and taking things lightly (*Leichtnehmen*) — and brings Dasein into the simplicity of fate (*Schicksal*).[17]

Here is where the need to get beyond the *es gibt* breaks loose, the need to "drive out" (*austreiben*) everything fortuitous and accidental, to drive what happens into the resoluteness of destiny, to force the *es gibt* into the destiny of resolving. That is to overload what happens and turn it into the stuff of a *telos* or a *Schicksal*. It says that what happens is not just what happens, that it has all along been ripe and rife with the future, that it groans and wails until it can bring forth the future.

This is exactly what got Heidegger into an enormous amount of trouble in the 1930s, when he thought that the "moment" had come, that it was time to seize the moment, which turned out to be a way of seizing power. This was all tied in with his love of difficulty and distrust of bourgeois ease

("taking things lightly," *Leichtnehmen*). If you make things difficult and la-
borious enough, you will drive the contingency out of things, and force a
destiny to the surface. After 1936, this love of destiny grew even worse,
even though it assumed a new form. It was no longer a matter of willing
and striving and resolving and forcing the contingency out of things, but of
poeticizing and thinking and waiting for the gentle law of the One and the
Unique to play itself out and send us back to the future, to send us the Future as the coming-back of the early Dawn. But it was still the same idea of
submitting what happens to higher or deeper laws, of finding some kind of
deeper unity or destiny to gather together the heteromorphic and heterologic plurality of what happens. He was still astronymical, still overloading
what happens with destinies, with evening stars and morning stars, and
with what is graciously giving and sending itself to us in what happens. He
was still organizing what happens into a higher or deeper whole, an eschatological or astronymical whole.

Heidegger would not listen to the poets he was reading, who kept trying
to break the bad news to him that what happens is what happens, that it
has a mean accidentality about it, and that it is not *unterwegs* to the Other
Beginning. His poets kept trying to warn him about soaring off with eagle
wings over what happens; they kept trying to tell him to stick to *es gibt*.

The *es gibt* means it's happening without why, which also means without
the eschatological turning of Being's errant destinings into the Truth of Being. The *es gibt* means you can't drive the contingency out of events and
force them into a destiny or a necessity, that you can't relieve the cold chill
of the *es spielt* with the thought that there is some why, some meta-why,
which is configuring everything and gathering it into an eschatological cli-
max. That would be to force events, to overload them with a gigantic metanarrative, to steer them toward a guiding star, to say more than we know,
to abandon the simplicity of thinking and minimalist austerity. That kind of
violence, which goes beyond the archiviolence advocated by a minimalism,
inevitably leads into onticoconcrete violence to enforce its *arche*.

The *es gibt* means there is no way to lift yourself up above what happens,
to soar over it with eagle wings—be they Hegelian or Heideggerian
eagles—and force it into a destiny, a *telos* or a *Seinsgeschick*. The *es gibt*
means it's happening without a deep destiny that overrides and mutes obligation in the pieties of *Andenken*. I have found it necessary to deny these
temple pieties in order to make room for obligation.

EXULTATIONS AND OBLIGATIONS:
BETWEEN NIETZSCHE AND ETHICS

This talk of being against ethics has put me in a delicate position. I am
trying to occupy a spot midway between Ethics, which (like Levinas) I too
love more than God, and Nietzsche, who (like Deleuze) I love more than

the death of God. I love Nietzsche and Ethics, to excess, really, but I lack the piety demanded by Ethics for its Good and its Infinity and its Categorical Imperatives, even as I cannot muster the lionhearted, macho courage required by Nietzsche's cold cosmic truthfulness. I am neither a Knight of the Infinite Abyss, ready to hurl myself into the Void, nor a Knight of *l'Infini*, the Infinite One who hovers over all. I am not a knight at all. I distrust favors from the Crown.

My Dionysian rabbi seems not to want to settle down in either Athens or Jerusalem but, if anything, to operate a shuttle between the two, a kind of jewgreek monorail that will allow him to move back and forth as the seasons and his moods dictate. He is not a man to stay where the climate is always the same. It is very embarrassing to lack identity like this, but I will try my best to make a case for such undecidability, to assume at least the appearance of respectability.

Minimalism means having been cut off from a guiding star and a Meta-event, a point outside of what happens that explains, legitimates, or gives meaning to what happens. What is outside of what happens is what is not happening. What happens is like a quilt: it has a pattern but it is not going anywhere. When you get to the edge of a quilt you have not found its *telos*, you have just reached the point at which the quilt ends. If you got to the end of what happens, to where it is going, you would have reached the point at which nothing is happening anymore.

What happens can only be taken for itself, for what it is. One can savor what is happening or not, or something in between. What is at issue is not the purpose of what happens but whether one rejoices in what is happening, whether what is happening is a joy or a disaster, or something in between; whether one is a hapless victim of what is happening or whether one is flourishing.

Events knit themselves together in a kind of middle voice action that is neither purely active nor purely passive. Events form patterns, configurations, or structures which may either lift us up or cast us down, or both; which may prove to be a source of joy or a curse, or something in between. Life is an accumulation of such patterns, of innumerable microlinks and microconnections, little linkages that weave our days and works together, that strengthen the fabric of life, that support life against the stress of events—or fail to.

Events give joy or they do not (or something in between). But they do not as a whole have a meaning (*sens*, direction). That gives my minimalism a melancholy look, but I beg the reader to be patient with me just a bit longer; I promise an (almost) happy ending. The point lies in the joy or the disaster, in the flourishing or the loss, not in the meaning. The point is not where events are "going," or where we are going with them, because the only place we seem to be going is stellar oblivion. We are, from that point of view, all disasters, lost stars, lost in space.

Astronomy is the most philosophical of all sciences.

Events do not admit of a *Resultat* that explains or legitimates them, but of an *exsultat*, which allows us to rejoice in them.

The point is not the "meaning" of events but rather the *joie de vivre*, the joy of ordinary life, of our days and works, of the finite, immanent, intermediary goals of daily life, the surpassing joy of the day-to-day, of work and companionship, the exultation in the ordinary, which is, after all, what there is. Great Events and surpassing *Übermenschen* are relatively rare — and certainly beyond me.

The Kingdom of God is here, now. Not in the First Beginning or the Other one; not in History or the Spirit; not in the surpassing discharge of some Greco-German *Übermensch* who prides himself on his feeling of distance from ordinary life. The Kingdom of God is found in daily pleasures, in ordinary joys.

Events happen. They happen for better or for worse. There is nothing outside of events that you could accept in exchange for what happens, that would be better than what happens.

Exultation is the joy one takes in what happens, in the patterns that events forge of themselves, the pleasure of events that one savors with fondness, that give deep, quiet, lasting joys — or loud and oft-repeated ones. *Chacun à son goût*. We do not need Greco-Germans to rank-order the order of joys. Let many joys happen. Let them happen with heteromorphic delirium, delight, and multiplicity. Exultation is the particular course of pleasures and pains, joys and sorrows, that flow our way, that arise in the course of events, whatever form they may happen to take.

When events are torn asunder, when the loss is beyond repair, when events leave us in shreds, in "tears," then you suffer a disaster and you lose your lucky star. That is what activates the lines of obligation, what gives obligation a sense of urgency.

It does not take much for the tenuous gossamer web of life to come apart. A stray bullet, a stray chromosome, a stray virus, a wanton cellular division — and the flesh is hopelessly ruined. Events strike a very delicate balance; they form frail, fragile, vulnerable configurations and microconnections. They are easy prey to chance and misfortune, to mis-hap. Joy is sustained on a tissue-thin surface, a tissue of flesh.

To speak of what happens is to give up thinking that events make sense all the way down, that there is some kind of *eidos* behind appearances, some kind of *Geist* or rule or principle with a deep if elusive grip on things, some *logos* or *nous* keeping what happens in order and holding events mightily in its sway. To speak of what happens is to be willing to take events for themselves, to hope for the best, to make the best of them.

To speak of what happens is to give up looking for the Meaning of events, because while events give joy or sorrow they do not, as a whole, have Meaning. While there are numerous meanings *in* events, there is no meaning *to* events overall, no overarching Meaning which is their point, their *logos* or *telos*, their sum and their substance. The sum and substance of events is nothing other than the events themselves.

There is no deep structure that sustains what we believe or cherish, what we savor in life, none at least that we know of. That is my *docta ignorantia*, the product of my research and numerous sabbatical leaves.

You see how minimal are the resources I marshal against Ethics.

Beneath the surface of ordinary life—the surface of productive, functioning, busy lives—there lurks an abyss. Beneath the surface of healthy agent bodies the abyss of flesh stirs, an abyss of vulnerability that can swallow up every joy. The abyss is forced to the surface—by the desperate circumstances in which one lives, by a personal crisis, by a moment that drives us to the rail of life, that forces us to ask what is going on, what is happening. Sometimes a physiological event, a microscopically slight chemical imbalance, hurls someone into an abyss of depression and melancholy, of torment and pain. The bottom can fall out from the world in a thousand ways. That is the disaster, the danger of irreparable loss, the trigger that sets off the networks of obligation.

My concern in these pages is almost exactly the opposite of Heidegger's in *Being and Time*. Heidegger's concern is with people who are so immersed in daily life that they need an exposure to the abyss in order to break the thoughtlessness of their lives and get their active agent life in gear. My concern is with people whose lives are torn to shreds, or nearly so; who have been consumed by the abyss, or nearly so. My interest lies with people so exposed to the abyss by which events are inhabited that they cannot get as far as ordinary life and its ordinary joys and sorrows.[18]

My concern in these pages is almost exactly the opposite of Nietzsche's. Nietzsche looked with distance and disdain upon the small joys and little sorrows of ordinary people. He made everything turn on the massive discharge of force of a great tragic artist, the overwhelming energy of what is great and overflowing. I regard massive discharges of energy with some suspicion, even with fear and trembling, and I am considerably more interested in the fate of ordinary people. I am inclined to let tragic artists fend for themselves. I do not think that life as a whole, including great quantities of suffering, is justified by an Ionian column or a Greek tragedy. Nothing justifies great quantities of suffering; that is what I mean by a disaster.

My concern in these pages is almost exactly the opposite of Hegel's. I do not think it is worth sacrificing a hair on the head of the least of us to advance the cause of the History of Spirit. The History of Spirit—like the History of Being or the *Überfluss* of the *Übermensch*—is a dangerous invention of Greco-Germans who do not blush to let innocent flowers perish for the advancement of their phallosophical phantasies. I take my stand with Johannes Climacus and the lyrical-philosophical treatises against the System, against the History of Being and the History of Spirit, against Ethics and Metaphysics (although I wish all of them well).

Beware of philosophers: they are too much occupied with strong or healthy people, with autonomous agents and aggressive freedoms. They miss the disasters. They pass right over those who are laid low by the cruelty of events. They take no stock of those who cannot get as far as freedom and autonomy or the origin of the work of art. They pay no mind to people who are crushed by what happens, whose lives are not knit together but in shreds, people who are hap-less, who fall victim to what happens. It is these unhappy, hapless, joyless people who call out when obligation happens. Joylessness is a loss, a disaster. There is nothing one can be offered in return for joylessness. The only response that is appropriate, the only response that is called for, is to offer to repair the loss, to lend a hand when the damage threatens to run beyond control, to help restore the possibility of joy, the rhythms of ordinary things. That is what obligation amounts to.

Obligation proceeds on the assumption that what happens is all there is, that there is nothing to legitimate the destruction of what happens, so that the role of obligation is to help restore the joy to what happens, to make exultation possible, or possible again.

Ethics is intended to answer the scandal of deep and utter joylessness, of utter misery, of unspeakable, unwarranted suffering. The idea behind Ethics is to subject the disaster that befalls the child or the deportees to infinite valorization, to treat their fate as absolutely Evil, as Evil incarnate, Evil in itself. Ethics seeks a deep backup for our condemnation of Auschwitz, one that would make it impossible to redescribe it. But it is always possible—to the chagrin and scandal of Ethics—to adopt a Nietzschean idiom in which the Nazis are taken to be wolves or eagles, parts of a cruel but "innocent" economy, in which the cry of the child dies out like an echo in empty space, in which the smoke of Shulamith dissipates in the air, in which events move on and everything is forgotten. Ethics is intended to counter the abyssmal thought that everything is innocent, that there is a dumb anonymity at the heart of things, that the fate of the deportees is absorbed without remainder into what Nietzsche calls "this mighty realm of the great cosmic stupidity."[19] Ethics wants to find the infinity of the personal at the core of events—that is Levinas, that is Ethics—but instead finds itself up against the anonymity of the *es gibt*. Ethics requires infinity of some kind, if not the infinity of the Law, which is instantiated in the person (Kant), then the infinity of the person (Other), which is the Law (Levinas).

Ethics is piety. It cannot abide the impious thought that events happen, the simplicity, the scandal, the asceticism of the thought that events happen, and that the sources of joylessness and misery go unpunished. The sworn enemy of Ethics is the anonymity and innocence by which things are inhabited.

But we who have had the impiousness to take our stand against Ethics, which means to take a stand between Nietzsche and Ethics, between Evil and the Innocence of Becoming, we must confess to having no cosmic backups for our condemnation of Auschwitz. That is our embarrassment and scandal. We have to live with the anonymity that insinuates itself into obligations. But if it is not possible to expel anonymity with infinity, it is at least possible to *defy* the anonymity of the *es gibt* and its cosmic dice game and to attach oneself, almost blindly, with a hypervalorization, with a hyperbolic valorization, to proper names. My stand against Ethics—but for obligation—comes down to taking a finite but hyperbolic stand—without Infinity and its assurances—on behalf of restoring joy and the possibility of exultation. I embrace justice, the jewgreek myth of justice, the hyperbolic emphasis, the conscious exaggeration, the stress and hyperstress on justice—for the least among us, for the widow and the man with the withered hand—the salutary jewgreek savoring of the singularity of the *me onta*. I try to be prepared to face the worst, to deal with the abyssmal thought that if you probe deeply enough you will find, at the heart of obligation, the mute anonymity of *das 'es'*, the raw givenness of obligation, the fact, as it were. *Es gibt*, there is, obligation. That is all. Obligation happens in the face, in the facelessness, of Anaximander's anonymous cosmic justice, the *dike* of Nietzsche's cosmic dice game. Obligation rises up as an anarchic, hyperbolic resistance to this *dike*, taking sides with the singularities that come-to-be and pass away in this Greek agonistics.

Justitia fiat, coelum ruat.

The eagles of philosophy soar over disasters, lifting them up and putting them in larger relief, while the jewgreek heroes of obligation, who never leave the ground, hasten instead to their relief (*relève*). Either way, the stars play heedlessly overhead.

Obligations happen for the while that they happen and then fade away. That is all there is to them. But that is enough. They do not need to last forever. Obligations require proper names, not, *pace* Lacoue-Labarthe, sacred, everlasting names,[20] nor, *pace* Levinas, infinite ones. If Ethics needs Sacred or Infinite names, obligation is willing to get along with simple, proper names. Obligations happen with or without sacred names, with or without the Infinite. To follow the way of obligation means to be stirred by the appeals, to answer the calls of lowly proper names, of what is laid low. The right response to what is laid low is not the invocation of a sacred name but offering relief, lending a hand. Without why. Because. Because flesh is flesh, because flesh calls to flesh, because to promote flourishing and joy, in particular that of the least among us, of the *me onta*, is its own form of life—*pace* Nietzsche.

Flesh flourishes—or it does not—under starless skies, and then it goes under, leaving its memory behind in faded traces on weather-worn stones.

But for the while that it flourishes, for the while that flesh is flesh, flesh calls and makes its needs felt, and the needs of flesh are all you need for obligation.

To say *"es gibt/il y a/*it gives" obligation is to situate obligation within an impersonal "it." The "it" is not an entity but the pregiven, encompassing, impersonal horizon of the "it is," "it happens." The "impersonal" is not the opposite of the personal, its opposing genus or antagonistic type, but rather the encompassing matrix and ever-present horizon of the personal, like the night on either side of the day. It is that from which the personal arises and to which the personal returns. Dusk to dusk. Dust to dust. *Cendre des morts: il y a là les cendres. Lethe to lethe*, to cite another Heidegger.

By the personal I do not have in mind any grand metaphysical gesture, anything transcendent or transcendental, infinite or sacred or supersensible, either Being or Otherwise than Being. I am trying to keep the metaphysics to a minimum. I am happy enough to grant that it is mostly a matter of grammar; I do not feel the need for a grand metaphysical backup. I mean, very minimalistically, something which is mostly a matter of phrasing. "You" say; "we" or "I" hear; "he," "she," or "they" are spoken about. Personal phrases happen. There are happenings of a personal kind.

By a person I do not mean an autonomous metaphysical subject but a subject of obligation, something that makes demands on me, that asks for a hand, for the flesh of my hand. A person is a place where obligations happen, where "someone" says "I" to "me," where "you" call upon "me," where "they" call upon "me" or "us." A person is a place where the eyes of the other come over me, overtake me, pulling me up short. From obligations a whole network of interpersonal relations springs up; in persons a whole network of obligations takes root.

Obligations spring up in a void, like grass in the cracks of sidewalks. The personal is a web woven over the impersonal, a filmy, gossamer surface across a dense mass. A name in the midst of namelessness. A bit of light and warmth in the midst of a surrounding darkness and cold, like the window of the house in Trakl's *Winterabend*, lit up within and come upon by the weary traveler or stranger. The person is always the wayfarer, the stranger, like Abraham or Ishmael.

Personal events happen. *Es gibt/il y a*/it gives persons—they, you, we, I—for the while that it gives them, because it gives them, without why. The why sinks into the because, into the bonds that spring up among persons, into the internal connections and inner constellations that they weave among themselves. Obligation is an operation introduced by life to mend its wounds, to let the links of life form their own spontaneous combinations.

For a while, for the while that they last. Cut off from the stars above, obligations form their own earthly microconstellations, knitting themselves together across the surface of our little star.

Flesh flickering under a starless sky; the exultations of flourishing flesh; the cries of joy; the calm cadences of quiet conversations among friends; the quiet repose of solitary thought; the laughter of lovers fading into dark, starless nights. Those are all the stars we have, all the stellar direction we are likely to come upon.

An Unscientific Postscript on a Disaster

I conclude, but without the benefit of a conclusion, of a closure, lacking the support of a mighty Meta-event to set everything aright. I run the risk of looking like an experienced speaker who, having reached the end of his lecture, is unable to find a way to inform his audience that he has nothing more to say. He shifts from one foot to the other and begins awkwardly to back off the stage, all the while mumbling something inaudible and smiling foolishly, until at last the audience realizes that, as he has now disappeared from view, the lecture must be over.

I have at my disposal only fragments and singularities, which are what Ethics calls "cases." So it is fitting that I bring these remarks to a close not with a grand conclusion but with a fragment, an example, with a bit of a problem—which is big enough, a disaster really—if you are caught up in it, viz., the problem of suicide or self-destruction. This is a problem that interests me for itself, but also because a good deal of what I think about obligations and events, about exultation and damaged lives, converges here and takes a palpable form.

From time to time the abyss shows through, the anonymous void by which we are inhabited breaks out and we are swallowed up, or very nearly. The tenuous links that events form among themselves give way. We are driven to the edge, or over the edge. The abyss bleeds through the cracks and crevices of ordinary existence; the void peers out from behind the minimalia of everyday life.

The disaster breaks out and we are gone.

Once again, by the abyss I do not mean anything profound or romantic, any dark and mysterious realm upon which only *Denkers* or *Dichters* may venture, a space reserved for heroes of the void. I say again, I am no Knight of the Infinite Void, no knight at all. Far be it from me, minimalist that I am, to venture out on bottomless, uncharted seas. I have no heart for the Abyss. I leave that to the warriors of Being, the Knights and Admirals of Greco-German phallosophy. As for me, I may be seen rowing timidly some distance behind, looking about for the remnants that may have floated to the surface from disasters in the deep.

The abyss is just another name for what happens, for the happening of events, for the fact that events happen because they happen, cut off from the comforts of a deep and reassuring ground. The abyss is the decapitation of events, the loss of the Meta-event. But that can be disturbing.

After all, life is through and through questionable, and to be "disturbed" or to lack "balance" at such moments is not, or is not merely, "psychological." It is life's imbalance, the world's disturbance. We suffer not only from mental imbalance—from the inability to ride out the misfortunes and setbacks of life, to laugh off the limits life sets—but from a certain cosmic disturbance, the world's imbalance.

From the disaster. We are a little mad because the world is a little mad.

I do not think that people who are driven to the edge are getting things all wrong so much as that they are unreasonably right, right to an excess. That is their imbalance. (And mine or ours—for their *déraison* is nothing

"other.") They pay too close attention to life. They are scrupulously, infinitely attentive to life and—to their misfortune—they see through its
masks, the very structures that have been put in place for our own protection. They do not know how to ignore, forget, forgive, repress, move on.
They are too demanding of life and life just cannot deliver on their demands. Life is not whole, not reasonable all the way through; it is no match
for their expectations.

After all, things do tremble in insecurity. They happen because they happen. They are not propped up, down deep. If you press events tightly
enough, you will not seize hold of some necessity in them; events will instead squeeze right through your fingers.

What happens *is* a little mad—a little violent, a little cruel, a little meaningless, a little hopeless, a little unfair.

A little. But enough. Sometimes too much.

There are people who see that, or who are pushed into seeing that, who
are not protected from seeing that, and they will not give themselves or the
world a break. They will not let it pass. They will not let up until they force
the abyss out of hiding and then the abyss gets the better of them.

Those who dare set foot in the space of self-destruction are not always
mired in falsity so much as they have overexposed themselves to the truth,
to the cold truth, "harmful and dangerous in the highest degree,"[21] to the
sort of knowledge that destroys, to the disaster, that the universe is a com-
fortless place, that we do not know who we are, not if we are honest, and
that we huddle together for warmth in this cold night. Self-destruction
seems to me often a function of overexposing oneself to something from
which most of us have the prudence to take shelter. It is like staying out too
long in sub-zero temperatures, like not having the good sense to come in
out of the cold.

One gets pushed to a brink, to the edge of the "why?" which sinks into
the because, pushed into the discovery that there is nothing deep to sustain what we most cherish, no guardrails around existence, no net to catch
us. The web comes undone, the links are broken, the tissue is torn asunder, the immanent system of meanings collapses. There is no sustaining
ground beneath what happens, no transcendent aim beyond what happens to explain it. Events are not going somewhere; they are just happening.

The rhythm of everyday life goes limp and loses its purely immanent
sense and interwovenness. The individual is cut lose from the world of her
involvements and is set adrift, in a dangerous detachment from work,
loved ones, friends and companions, drifting on the edge of the world,
flirting with world-lessness. In such a state, events undergo a monstrous
magnification. People become inordinately afraid of ordinary perils. They
experience as sheer terror the world that most of us take in stride. They
become compulsively, obsessively preoccupied with matters that hardly
matter to others. They translate ordinary defeats and losses into occasions

of massive self-contempt and self-hatred. Adolescents take the ordinary setbacks of teenage life to heart, and what to one young person is just a bad day or a bad date or a bad break, which they greet by a shrug or a laugh, takes on truly tragic dimensions. They are filled with fear, anxiety, insecurity, hopelessness, terror, distrust, disgust, or despair by events that most people brush off or just ignore or at least know how to cope with.

They lose the ability to say "that happens," "such things happen," and instead they succumb to what happens, are destroyed by it. "That happens" is not a magic incantation but a formula for keeping one's balance in the midst of what is happening. The medium sized bumps and chinks in ordinary life become enormous hurdles, gigantic obstacles which throw them into confusion. What happens in ordinary life undergoes a process of magnification and exaggeration that makes it literally larger than life.

Events become monstrous, de-monstrations of the abyss.

Everyday happenings become occasions of utter terror, of insuperable depression, irredeemable self-hatred. People lose their resiliency, their capacity to rebound, to forget, to move on, to put things behind them, to erase the past, to link up in new ways, to re-create themselves, to laugh at themselves and the follies of being human, to take the course of life in stride. Such people have among other things lost the power of genuine (not hysterical) laughter, which was the wise remedy that Zarathustra recommended in the face of the abyss. The order of rank (the best and the toughest), Nietzsche said, is "almost" determined by the ability to suffer. What truly determines the order of rank is the capacity for laughter, which means for him an ability to affirm the endless cycle of joy and suffering: "I would go so far as to venture an order of rank among philosophers according to the rank of their laughter—rising to those capable of *golden* laughter."[22]

Events have their own particular, limited, internal linkages inside the chain, but they do not have ultimate or transcendent purposes. Events are not on the whole going anywhere. They happen. The little planet will eventually grow cold. The will to power will eventually reconfigure and we will all be quite wiped away. For that is what we are, you and I and all things. *Und nichts außerdem!*

The joys that life has to offer are entirely internal. Life is like a game we enjoy playing. One desires life for the sake of life. "If someone asked life for a thousand years, 'why do you live?'" Meister Eckhart said, "then if it could answer, it would say nothing other than 'I live because I live.'"[23] One is not trying to *get* somewhere with life, and it would make no more sense to offer someone help in getting where life is going—death—than it would to offer a jogger a lift in one's car. In fact there are laws against offering such help.[24] There is nothing that one could trade life *for*, nothing that would make a good exchange for life. It is the very joy one feels in one's work, one's companionships, one's surroundings, one's activities that gives life its savor, or in which the taste of life turns sour. Events are self-justifying, self-legitimizing, and self-sustaining. If we take no joy from events, we take no joy from life, for events make up all the life there is; they are what we mean by life.

But the fabric of events is a delicate knit. It does not take a lot for the momentum of ordinary life to wither, for its fabric to unravel. It can unravel in a moment of tragedy from which one never recovers, even as it can deteriorate slowly over time as love or friendship or the ability to work wane. Ill health, a sudden and irrevocable reverse of fortune, or even ordinary misfortunes that other people deal with handily, can send one spinning into the abyss. There are disasters that drive one to the limit, in extremis, beyond the bonds and boundaries of ordinary life. The abyss peers out from behind the cracks of daily life, the way a great ravine becomes visible between the tracks of a railroad if we let ourselves look down. There is nothing deep and firm to sustain us, not if we look down, not if we ask why? and demand an ultimate response, a final answer. What sustains the elements of life is only their internal connectedness and inherent worth. When that is shattered—whether by misfortune, terminal illness, or simply by a serotonin imbalance[25]—life is shattered and it is extremely hard and often impossible to knit it back together again. Indeed, too often it is not even knit together to begin with; people never even really get the fabric of ordinary life started, and their lives seem shattered right from the start; they are simply born into desperation and neglect and never escape it.

Despite my recommendation to take up reading tombstones, I am not resurrecting the familiar existentialist line on death or suicide. I have no interest in macho confrontations with the abyss, in heroically hurling myself into a void, in "glamorized masculine anxiety." These heroic, übermenschlich ruminations on my impending death are always focused on the meaning of "my" life, "my" death, or taking "my" life. My concern has been all along the alarm sent out by others. My standpoint is that of obligation, of the demands made on us by the fortunes and misfortunes of the other. From the standpoint of obligation, the I is always, structurally, the sane, healthy, well-constituted agent body, while the other is flesh laid low. It is always the "other" who is drawn to or "succumbs" to self-destruction. This is not an aggressive phallic operation, a problem for the "lone phallus," out there all alone, without maternal protection.[26] It is a question of activating the feminine operation, of listening to the alarms that are sounded by other flesh.

Once again, we must beware of the philosophers. Philosophers like Hume too often entertain the illusion that the question of self-destruction concerns rational, autonomous agents deliberating the pros and cons of a course of action, rather the way one deliberates about an investment. That is the suicide of the I, the suicide of an Aufklärer.[27] While political suicides may be something like that, or the reasoned suicides of honor in Greece and Rome may have been something like that, the fact of the matter is that acts of self-destruction are usually not acts of reason and phallogocentric lucidity. When they are, so be it. But philosophers are too inclined to think that suicide is simply or even primarily a matter of freedom and reason, whereas a good many acts of self-destruction are hardly exercises in philosophical thinking or existential resoluteness. A good many, perhaps most, suicidal people are in a state of ambiguity and undecidability about death, not lucidity. They fear death as much as they fear life; they want life as much as they desire death. Their actions are ambiguous, often inconclusive, steeped in undecidability, usually not meant to be conclusive or unconditional, so that many "successful" (= completed) attempts at suicide are really accidents, and the attempts were a call for help that went too far. Suicidal people are in pain and they are calling upon us to respond.

The gestures of self-destructiveness of the Other are a call for help, alarms sounding, the *glas* of obligation ringing in our ears. What has gone wrong with such lives is that the thousand little links, the microconnections of ordinary life have come unstrung. The complex, sustaining networks of life, the minimalia and the microlinks that make up ordinary life, have collapsed.

But what are we called upon to do? What can one do? What is our responsibility?

There is no "answer," no cognitive solution, to the questions that self-destructive people put. They are, I think, putting questions before which philosophers no less than their analysts (if they can afford one) are struck dumb, the difference being that the philosophers' ignorance comes cheaper. Moreover, self-destructive people do not require an answer so much as companionship. We are all children of the same dark night, inhabited by the same demons, haunted by the same spectres. We are all equally beset by the inscrutability of what happens, and none of us, philosophers or analysts, have a hotline which feeds us special information about the *eidos* or *ousia* or *Geist* or *Wille* that is behind what is happening. No one can lay claim to having the *logos* of the abyss. There are no "professionals" in the field of what happens, just laity in various states of being de-laicized.

Professional "therapists" are not to be construed as people who have the *episteme* that governs these matters. That illusion, which does more harm than good, has been mercilessly exposed by Foucault's histories of madness. Therapists are or should be, on my accounting, people who have professed an allegiance to those who suffer lives of enormous and sometimes unbearable pain. (The "unconscious" is an important notion because it is a source of inestimable pain, not because it offers the occasion for provocative literary theories or because it has the structure of a language—if it does.) Therapists and clinical psychologists and counsellors of every stripe belong, on this view, to an ancient but very unscientific jewgreek paradigm, the paradigm of the "healer," people who "drive out devils," usually by "laying on hands." I imagine what is behind such old jewgreek stories is the power of a man or woman of compassion to calm a troubled heart, to take the hand of the troubled one in their hands, literally to lend them a hand, to be on hand. They did not have anything special to say to them or the miraculous power to suspend the laws of nature. They did not know anything special. Who does? But they talked with their troubled friends through long nights or lonely days, hand in hand, flesh in flesh. It is not what they said (*le dit*) that matters but the saying (*le dire*)—and the flesh of their hand. That was the miracle of what they did.

What healing they could do, they did in virtue of the power of companionship and friendship, which awakens the power of the flesh to knit itself back together. The healer tries to reactivate the spontaneous bonds of everyday life, to set in motion once again the process by which life heals itself, to reactivate the growth and formation of the protective tissue of life, the web of flesh, the microconnections that everyday life knits around itself. The healer is a healing presence, a "help," someone who is "there," a voice in a world of silence, compassion in a world which has become merciless, support in a world without grounds. In the matter of obligation, "being-there" means being there for the other, for someone who calls out for help.

We are all fellow travelers on the little star, fellow participants of the same cosmic play. What we have to offer one another is our voice, our healing hand, our laughter, ourselves. The hand heals of itself, because it is a hand, because it is flesh. We all have the hands of healers and we can all heal by laying on hands. Our golden laughter is wiser than any words. That is the feminine operation. It is not a question of finding an answer to the night of truth but of sitting up with one another through the night, of dividing the abyss in half in a companionship that is its own meaning. I follow the excellent advice to put in the place of "the fear and trembling of a paternal Abraham or a solitary Nietzschean subject . . . that of a trembling people, a trembling community."[28]

It is not a question of introducing a solution from without, or from above. Life is healed only by life. There is nothing outside life that one can introduce as a remedy or solution to its sorrows, even as there is nothing outside life that grounds it or founds it or gives it a transcendent sense. The wounds of life can be administered to only by more life, life pressed against life; life in life, hand in hand, siblings of the same dark night.

Even a religious belief in a purpose transcendent *to* life can function only if it takes root *in* life. Faith must be a living faith, a significant form *of* life, a living spirituality, a spiritual life. Faith must knit itself into a rich and immanently rewarding pattern of life. Far be it from me to make trouble for religious faith, I who am a devoted admirer of father Abraham, a devout reader of Magdalena's stories of Yeshua, a lover of jewgreek narratives devoted to flesh and healings, a lover of saints and mystics. I am only trying to draw the parameters within which faith happens. A man or woman of faith is not one who knows nothing of the abyss but rather one who has looked down this abyss and construed it in terms of the traces and stirrings of a loving hand, who finds in the abyss of suffering an infinity, who sees

the Other as the trace of the Infinite.[29] Faith is a matter of a radical hermeneutic, an art of construing shadows, in the midst of what is happening.
Faith is neither magic nor an infused knowledge that lifts one above the
flux or above the limits of our mortality. Faith, on my view, is above all the
hermeneia that Someone looks back at us from the abyss, that the spell of
anonymity is broken by a Someone who stands with those who suffer,
which is why the Exodus and the Crucifixion are central religious symbols.
Faith does not, however, extinguish the abyss but constitutes a certain
reading of the abyss, a hermeneutics of the abyss. Faith is not a way of es-
caping what happens, but a way of interpreting it and coming to grips with
it.

THE ANONYMOUS

What haunts my days and disturbs my sleep is the thought of the anonymous, of cold lunar surfaces or an uninhabited deep, of frozen polar regions inhospitable to life. I lie awake imagining a world that consists of
nothing other than a certain cosmic rumble, an incessant, dull, inarticulate
roar.

My peace is disturbed by the mercilessness of a certain Nietzscheanism
according to which there is no one there, nothing within or beyond the
stars, no Aristotelian gods inhabiting them and steering them safely about
the heavenly vault, nothing but the charging and the discharging of forces,
firing and misfiring. *Und nichts außerdem!* Nietzsche and his delegate Felix
Sineculpa have cost me considerable sleep.

Imagine a world in which no one is there. Or in which we are alone. A
world without proper names, without names at all.

The discourse on obligation is a treatise on proper names, on the affirmation of "someone," something more or less proper, personal, over and
beyond or within the cosmic hum. By "someone" I do not mean anything
deep or profound, some permanent presence beneath the flux of time,
some transcendental *ich* organizing a complex assembly of faculties, habits,
and acts, something Infinite or Sacred or Supersensible. On the contrary, I
mean the most fleeting and transient of things, the most tender growth, a
flickering light, very delicate and fragile, vulnerable to the elements. I
mean the several possibilities of joy or sorrow, of pleasure or pain, of exultation or humiliation, attached to proper names, the memories attached
to proper names. By "someone" I mean persons long ago, barely remem-
bered now, their names barely legible on weather-beaten stones. The stuff
of memory and stories. I also mean the ones who tell the old stories, who
understand that they are themselves the stuff of future stories, who anticipate what they themselves will have become.

Were I able to find the time I would write a book on old cemeteries, and
I would cultivate the art of making rubbings to save the names that have

been effaced by time. Remember my theory of *Seinsvergessenheit*: people who do such rubbings do more to recall the meaning of Being than all German philosophers combined.

Obligations shatter the silence of anonymity with proper names, if only temporarily, shooting proper names into the night-dark sky like darts of light, like shooting stars, fleeting moments of illumination. We send up small, tiny, limited little infinities into the night, as if there were something Infinite that contracts the vastness of the sky, as if there were an Infinity that shrinks the seas and dwarfs the mountaintops, that makes all of nature bow down.

As if these proper names really were infinite and not themselves moments in the life of the seas and the stars and the mountains, as if they were not woven of the same flesh, the same mortal stuff and fragile flesh as the earth.

As if. As it were. Facts as it were. There are no facts, only interpretations.

Obligations are fleeting, finite victories over the anonymity which is older than us, which is stronger and higher and deeper than us, which is before we are. Obligations are our hyperbolic act of affirming infinite worth, of attaching hyperbolic significance to the least among us, of answering infinite demands, within the frail, finite, fragile bounds of our mortality.

Proper names are our temporary triumphs, and passing protests against the anonymity of *il y a*, against the transciency of *es gibt*, against the namelessness that surrounds us.

Obligations forge the links of "you" and "I" and "we" and "he" and "she," forming little links that spread tenuously across the surface of the little star, weaving a thin tissue of tender, fragile bonds and multiple microcommunities. Obligations form a delicate gossamer surface across the face of the little star, like a thin snowfall in early spring covering the thawing ground, providing just the slightest cover of white, and vulnerable to the first rays of the warming sun.

The anonymous is the incessant rumble of events, while obligation is the event of someone, of something personal in the midst of this inarticulate hum. Events happen anonymously, like the roar of the surf, while obligation is like the cry of a small child who has lost his way on the beach calling for help.

The anonymous is the roar of wind and rain on a dark night, while the personal is the voice of a fair and delicate young boy, shivering in the rain, who would rather die than live without his love.

In the Trakl poem "A Winter Evening,"[30] a traveler comes upon a warmly lit house, an inviting table within, set with bread and wine, visible through the window. The anonymous is the winter night, the stellar cold of the winter sky, the frozen earth, the lifeless, lightless night without, while the house within affirms the realm of the I and you and we and they. The house within is a small corner of light, warmth, and companionship in the midst of winter's harshness, a brief respite of relief from pain and of shelter from cold and hunger. The house offers a tenuous, temporary hold against the fierceness of the night.

The snow falls on the house, on the fields around the house, on the churchyard over the hill, on the whole region, covering the whole country.[31] At length the whole earth is covered by the snow, through which, here and there, little houses are barely visible, warmly lit, with tables set with bread and wine, inviting weary travelers to their hospitality, offering welcome to wayfarers of every kind. The traveler comes within and shares the bread, and afterwards tells a story of a delicate young boy she once loved, now dead. Travelers weeping over their joys, laughing over their misery and mortality. The next morning they are on their way again.

We are all becoming shades, shadowy spectres of bygone life, vanishing almost without a trace, except for the memory inscribed in barely legible names on listing tombstones.

Flesh clings to flesh in the anonymity of the night. The day is a temporary respite from unrelenting night. Night is the mother of us all: an almost perfect anti-Platonism.

The snow falls on the house, on the churchyard beyond the house, on the sea beyond the churchyard, covering the whole earth, covering the proper names on gravestones and houseplates, covering the whole island, the whole world. Tombstones barely visible through the snow, listing and crooked, the name of young Michael Furey, of all the dead, hardly legible through the drifting snow:

> Yes the newspapers were right: snow was general all over Ireland. It was falling on every part of the dark central plain, on the treeless hills, falling softly upon the Bog of Allen and, farther westward, softly falling into the dark mutinous Shannon waves. It was falling, too, upon every part of the lonely churchyard on the hill where Michael Furey lay buried. It lay thickly drifted on the crooked crosses and headstones, on the spear of the little gate, on the barren thorns. His soul swooned slowly as he heard the snow falling faintly through the universe and faintly falling, like the descent of their last end, upon all the living and the dead.[32]

Obligations happen, bonds are formed, tables are set, while the earth is covered in cold white snow, while the surf roars, while the stars dance their nightly dance, while worms inch their way toward forgotten graves.

(In the Place of a) Conclusion

Obligations happen, like faint flickers of flesh against a black expanse, lights against a great night.

Obligations happen; they happen because they happen; they happen for the while that they happen. Then the cosmos draws a few more breaths, the little star grows cold, and the animals made of flesh have to die.

The snow falls faintly through the universe on all the living and the dead.

Life is justified not as an aesthetic phenomenon but as a quasi-ethical one.

NOTES

One. Against Ethics

1. Still, there is precedent for impious talk like this: Paul Feyerabend, *Against Method: Outline of an Anarchistic Theory of Knowledge* (London: Verso, 1975); and Theodor Adorno, *Against Epistemology: A Metacritique*, trans. Willis Domingo (London: Blackwell, 1982), although this is an innovation of Adorno's English translator. I am in full agreement with the epigraph from Epicharmus that Adorno used, "A mortal must think mortal and not immortal thoughts." Ethics is too immortal a thought, which is, incidentally, also the reservation about ethics that the theologian Karl Barth voiced in "The Problem of Ethics Today" in *The Word of God and the Word of Man*, trans. D. Horton (Pilgrim Press, 1928), pp. 136–181.

2. John D. Caputo, *The Mystical Element in Heidegger's Thought* (Athens: Ohio University Press, 1978; reissued with a new preface: New York: Fordham University Press, 1987), pp. 254–257.

3. John D. Caputo, *Heidegger and Aquinas: An Essay on Overcoming Metaphysics* (New York: Fordham University Press, 1982), ch. 8.

4. John D. Caputo, *Radical Hermeneutics: Repetition, Deconstruction, and the Hermeneutic Project* (Bloomington: Indiana University Press, 1987), ch. 9.

5. See "Dialogue with Jacques Derrida," in *Dialogues with Contemporary Thinkers*, ed. Richard Kearney (Manchester: Manchester University Press, 1984), pp. 120–121; and John D. Caputo, "Beyond Aestheticism: Derrida's Responsible Anarchy," *Research in Phenomenology*, 18 (1988): 59–74. This essay is the earliest version of the present study. I approximate my present views somewhat more closely in "Hyperbolic Justice: Deconstruction, Myth and Politics," *Research in Phenomenology*, 21 (1991): 3–20.

6. *Kierkegaard's Writings*, VI, *"Fear and Trembling" and "Repetition,"* trans. H. Hong and E. Hong (Princeton: Princeton University Press, 1983), p. 15.

7. I am toying a bit with Jacques Derrida, *The Other Heading: Reflections on Today's Europe*, trans. Pascale-Anne Brault and Michael B. Naas (Bloomington: Indiana University Press, 1992), pp. 14–15.

8. Martin Heidegger, "A Letter on Humanism," trans. Frank Capuzzi in *Martin Heidegger: Basic Writings*, ed. David Krell (New York: Harper & Row, 1977), pp. 232–233.

9. Heidegger, *The Question Concerning Technology and Other Essays*, trans. W. Lovitt (New York: Harper & Row, 1977), p. 34.

10. On the myth of the passing by of the last or ultimate god, see Heidegger, *Gesamtausgabe*, B. 65, *Beiträge zur Philosophie: Vom Ereignis* (Frankfurt: Klostermann, 1989), pp. 405–417.

11. I set forth these criticisms of Heidegger in detail in John D. Caputo, *Demythologizing Heidegger* (Bloomington: Indiana University Press, 1993), which is a companion piece to the present study; and *Radical Hermeneutics*, chapters 6–7.

12. See "Only a God Can Save Us: *Der Spiegel*'s Interview with Martin Heidegger," trans. Maria Alter and John D. Caputo, *Philosophy Today*, 20 (1976): 282. As Derrida rightly says, one can only imagine this scene, which is both wildly funny and highly dangerous, imagine who these unnamed Frenchmen are, and in what language they confessed the poverty of their native language. See Jacques Derrida, *Of Spirit: Heidegger and the Question*, trans. G. Bennington and R. Bowlby

(Chicago: University of Chicago Press, 1987), pp. 68–70. Can the poverty of French be expressed in French? Or is this poverty too inexhaustible, too deep, for an impoverished language like French?

13. For all citations in this paragraph, see Jacques Derrida, "Passions: 'An Oblique Offering'," trans. David Wood in *Derrida: A Critical Reader*, ed. David Wood (Oxford: Blackwell, 1992), pp. 13–15.

14. Which it is, in the sense of Michael Jackson, who has not as far as I know addressed the question of deconstruction.

15. On the whole problematic of the "difficulty of life" and of its relationship to Aristotle's *Ethics* and Heidegger's thought, see Caputo, *Radical Hermeneutics*, pp. 1–7; and John D. Caputo, *Demythologizing Heidegger*, chapter 2, "Heidegger's *Kampf*: The Difficulty of Life."

16. See below, chapter 8.

17. Kierkegaard, *Fear and Trembling*, p. 6.

18. The gesture is Heideggerian: There is something in metaphysics (here: ethics) which metaphysics (here: ethics) is not *up to* (able to think, manage). One might also say, as Edith Wyschogrod has suggested to me, that there is something "ethical" in ethics which ethics cannot contain. A similar project can be found in Charles Scott's challenging work *The Question of Ethics: Nietzsche, Foucault, Heidegger* (Bloomington: Indiana University Press, 1990): "the question of ethics arises out of ethical concern" (p. 1).

19. Kant, *Critique of Practical Reason*, trans. Lewis White Beck (Indianapolis: Bobbs-Merrill Co., Library of Liberal Arts, 1956), p. 166.

20. Jean-François Lyotard, *The Postmodern Condition*, trans. G. Bennington and B. Massumi (Minneapolis: University of Minnesota Press, 1984), pp. xxiii–xxv. I say "so-called" because it would be just more world-historical or Being-historical thinking to think that one speaks for an age, particularly one that arrives after the end of this or that. I who do not know about origins have no more knowledge about endings.

21. Derrida says (*The Other Heading*, p. 9) that if "we" have an "identity" it is one that prevents us from saying "we."

22. Derrida, *Of Grammatology*, trans. G. Spivak (Baltimore: Johns Hopkins University Press, 1975), p. 162.

23. *Es gibt* is a central Heideggerian expression, not for obligation, but for Being. See "Time and Being," in *On Time and Being*, pp. 5ff. *Il arrive* is a basic expression for Lyotard about "phrases": "*Une phrase, 'arrive'*" in *Le Différend* (Paris: Éditions de Minuit, 1983), p. 10 (hereafter "LD"); *The Differend: Phrases in Dispute*, trans. Georges Van Den Abeele (Minneapolis: University of Minnesota Press, 1988), p. xii. Kant, *Critique of Practical Reason*, p. 48: "Moreover, the moral law is given, as an apodictically certain fact, as it were (*gleichsam als ein Faktum*), of pure reason, a fact of which we are *a priori* conscious, even if it be granted that no example could be found in which it has been followed exactly." I will come back to the Levinasian expression below. I am continually running these positions together into a single view of obligation (for which I hope to assume no responsibility whatsoever).

24. The ease with which *Befindlichkeit* can accommodate "obligation" reveals the background of *Being and Time* in Aristotle's ethics, even as it reveals the way Heidegger let ethical obligations get formalized out of the existential analytic. On the re-implication of *Being and Time* in a certain originary ethics, see Robert Bernasconi, "'The Double Concept of Philosophy' and the Place of Ethics in *Being and Time*," *Research in Phenomenology*, 18 (1988): 41–58.

25. *The Differend*, No. 170 and "Levinas Notice," No. 1, pp. 109–112 (LD, pp. 162–165).

26. I take the expression "blindness" from Lyotard, *Differend*, Nos. 165–166, pp. 108–109 (LD, pp. 160–161). For an insightful, if critical, appraisal see Martin Jay,

"Lyotard and the Denigration of Vision in 20th Century French Thought," *Thesis Eleven*, 31 (1992): 34–67.

27. The anti-Enlightenment argument is that ethical laws acquire depth, density, and binding power only from the thickness of the tradition; otherwise they are paper-thin intellectualisms. That has been MacIntyre's claim ever since *After Virtue* first appeared (Notre Dame: University of Notre Dame Press, 1981). For an argument that it is Gadamer, not MacIntyre, who can best defend this view, see P. Christopher Smith, *Hermeneutics and Human Finitude* (New York: Fordham University Press, 1990). In *Radical Hermeneutics* I argued that Heidegger thinks something of the same sort (pp. 240–248).

28. The last two possibilities are reductionistic. I am saying that there are no knock-down theoretical arguments against reductionism.

29. Jean-François Lyotard, *Heidegger and "the Jews,"* trans. Andreas Michel and Mark Roberts (Minneapolis: University of Minnesota Press, 1990), p. 84. This wonderful remark, which I follow without exception, in this very powerful book, which I also follow without exception—with the exception of certain remarks about Derrida—should be directed by Lyotard against ethics, but not against Derrida, who is, I think, a very Abrahamic figure, always already circumcised; see Jacques Derrida, *Glas*, trans. John P. Leavey and Richard Rand (Lincoln: University of Nebraska Press, 1988), pp. 41a–42a.

30. Johannes de Silentio himself offers us at least four different versions, not to mention the unpublished versions in the *Journals*. See Kierkegaard, *Fear and Trembling*, pp. 9–14, 267–271; and below, chapter 8, for still another retelling which seems to me a rather bold challenge to father Abraham, one I myself would have never ventured alone.

31. See the three problemata in *Fear and Trembling*, pp. 54ff.

32. Lyotard, *The Differend*, No. 176, p. 117 (LD, pp. 172–173).

33. Kierkegaard, *Fear and Trembling*, pp. 16–17.

34. This is Derrida's point about "undecidability" and infinite recontextualizability. My thanks to Edith Wyschogrod for her help with this reflection.

35. The story of the "binding of Isaac" is found in Genesis 22:1. For the *me voici*, see Emmanuel Levinas, *Otherwise than Being or Beyond Essence*, trans. Al Lingis (The Hague: Martinus Nijhoff, 1981), pp. 141–152; for a commentary by Jacques Derrida, see "At this very moment in this work here I am," trans. Ruben Berezdivin, in *Re-Reading Levinas*, eds. Robert Bernasconi and Simon Critchley (Bloomington: Indiana University Press, 1991), pp. 17ff.

36. Hegel, "The Spirit of Christianity," in *Friedrich Hegel on Christianity: Early Theological Writings*, trans. T. M. Knox (New York: Harper & Row, 1961; Copyright University of Chicago Press, 1948), p. 187.

37. Hegel, "The Spirit of Christianity," p. 187.

38. Hegel, "The Spirit of Christianity," p. 196.

39. I am clearly following here both the spirit and the letter of Derrida's *Glas*, which contains an illuminating gloss on "The Spirit of Christianity." See *Glas*, pp. 34a ff. and *Glas*, p. 53a. For an indispensable glossary which contains the cross-references to the French text, see John Leavey, *Glossary* (Lincoln: University of Nebraska Press, 1986). *Glas* too is an exemplary text for me, a provocation whose effect can be felt throughout this study; it is certainly one of the texts of Derrida I would blame were I accused of anything immoral.

40. I am here running two texts together: Friedrich Nietzsche, *Twilight of the Idols* in *Twilight of the Idols and The Anti-Christ*, trans. R. J. Hollingdale (Baltimore: Penguin Books, 1968), pp. 40–41; and *Kierkegaard's Writings*, VII, *Philosophical Fragments*, trans. H. Hong and E. Hong (Princeton: Princeton University Press, 1985), especially pp. 9–22.

41. For two recent studies showing the proximity of Kierkegaard and Kant, see

Edward Mooney, *Knights of Faith and Resignation* (Albany: SUNY Press, 1991); and Ronald Green, *Kierkegaard and Kant: The Hidden* Debt (Albany: SUNY Press, 1992).

42. Hegel, "The Spirit of Christianity," p. 211. See *Glas*, pp. 57a–58a; 131a ff.

43. *The Differend*, Kant Notice 2, No. 2, p. 123 (LD, p. 181).

44. "I have therefore found it necessary to deny *knowledge* in order to make room for *faith*." *Critique of Pure Reason*, trans. N. Kemp Smith (London: Macmillan, 1963), Bxxx (p. 29).

45. Heidegger talks like this quite a lot: "philosophy is metaphysics" or "philosophy is Greek," etc. See Heidegger, "The End of Philosophy and the Task of Thought," in *On Time and Being*, trans. Joan Stambaugh (New York: Harper & Row, 1972), p. 55. Hegel would agree with Heidegger about the Greek essence of philosophy, but he thinks that Christianity is even more Greek than the Greeks, which is what set Kierkegaard's pen in motion. I am embroidering on these remarks to say: ethics is philosophy, which is metaphysics, which is Greek. So being against ethics is like de-Hellenizing ethics or coming up with a "jewgreek" ethics.

46. Nietzsche, *Twilight of the Idols*, p. 41.

47. *The Differend*, Kant Notice 2, No. 5, p. 125 (LD, p. 184).

48. See *The Differend*, Declaration of 1789 Notice, pp. 145–147 (LD, pp. 209–213).

49. See "Loving the Torah More Than God," in *Difficult Freedom*, trans. Sean Hand (Baltimore: Johns Hopkins University Press, 1990), pp. 142–145.

50. By "piety" I mean not only a discursive style but a discourse which is centered and homological, which makes everything turn on something central, unique, and one, like the Other (Levinas) or the *Ereignis* (Heidegger). Eccentricity is no less a form of centering than concentricity. Levinas's piety is centered not on the True but on the Good and can be seen in the monopoly of ethical discourse, its hegemony over other discourses. See Lyotard's discussion of Levinas in *Just Gaming*, trans. Wlad Godzich (Minneapolis: University of Minnesota Press, 1985), pp. 60–61. See also Lyotard's search for an "impiety with justice" in *Instructions païennes* (Paris: Galilée, 1977); "Lessons in Paganism," trans. David Macey, *The Lyotard Reader*, ed. Andrew Benjamin (Oxford: Blackwell, 1989), pp. 122–154.

51. See Levinas's remarks on Derrida in "Wholly Otherwise," trans. Simon Critchley, *Re-Reading Levinas*, pp. 3–10. This volume is an excellent compilation of investigations into the complexities of the Derrida-Levinas relationship which are based on the later texts of both Levinas and Derrida. I myself do not think that Levinas intended a breach of metaphysics in a "postmetaphysical" style, as in Derrida. I think he intended a more Neoplatonic or "hypermetaphysical" radicalizing of metaphysics, in the style of Plotinus or Meister Eckhart. Still, I am not here trying to settle the hash of these intricate problems, much less of the subtle scholarly treatment given to these formidable difficulties in these careful studies. For a fuller expression of my views see Caputo, *Demythologizing Heidegger*, chapter 10.

52. *Fear and Trembling*, p. 15.

53. Nietzsche, *Beyond Good and Evil*, trans. R. J. Hollingdale (Baltimore: Penguin Books, 1972), No. 39, p. 50.

54. *Philosophy and Truth: Selections from Nietzsche's Notebooks of the Early 1870s*, ed. and trans. Daniel Breazeale (Atlantic Highlands: Humanities Press, 1979), p. 79.

55. Lyotard, *The Inhuman: Reflections on Time*, trans. Geoffrey Bennington and Rachel Bowlby (Stanford: Stanford University Press, 1991), pp. 8–11.

56. Unless, of course, anticipating such a disaster, we will have come up with a way to think without a body or the earth, which is the question Lyotard poses to himself.

57. Friedrich Nietzsche, *The Will to Power*, trans. W. Kaufmann (New York: Vintage Books, 1968), No. 1067, pp. 549–550.

58. Friedrich Nietzsche, *Daybreak: Thoughts on the Prejudices of Morality*, trans. R. J. Hollingdale (Cambridge: Cambridge University Press, 1982), No. 130, p. 130.

59. See Kant, *Critique of Pure Reason*, A671 = B699.

60. See my "Hyperbolic Justice."

61. This is also a lesson from Derrida, *The Other Heading*, pp. 41 and 118n.5, who is deeply interested in the possibility of what is impossible, which is above all what is interesting and important.

62. *Fear and Trembling*, p. 49.

63. *Fear and Trembling*, p. 27. *Repetition* was published by Kierkegaard on the same day as *Fear and Trembling*.

Two. Between Good and Evil

1. *Fear and Trembling*, p. 7.

2. *Extra-Skriver* (literally "extra-writer") is a neologism of Kierkegaard's which is translated by the Hongs as "supplementary clerk"; by Hannay as "freelancer" in *Fear and Trembling*, trans. A. Hannay (New York: Penguin Books, 1985), p. 43; and by Lowrie as "amateur writer" in *"Fear and Trembling" and "The Sickness Unto Death,"* trans. W. Lowrie (Garden City, N.Y.: Doubleday Anchor, 1954), p. 24. It means someone who does not earn a serious living by his writing but who writes on the side, for the pure love of it, with no hope of making any money or even of being taken seriously. See Mark Taylor's excellent discussion in *Altarity* (Chicago: University of Chicago Press, 1987), pp. 327–330. My thanks to Elsebet Jegstrup for her help with this wonderful word.

3. *Fear and Trembling*, p. 15.

4. See Drucilla Cornell's wonderful description of Derrida as a *chiffonnier* (ragpicker) in her *Philosophy at the Limit* (New York: Routledge, 1992), chapter 3.

5. Derrida, *Of Grammatology*, p. 162. This of course was also the problem Johannes Climacus had with the System: he could never find a place to make an absolute start: *Concluding Unscientific Postscript to the "Philosophical Fragments,"* trans. D. Swenson and W. Lowrie (Princeton: Princeton University Press, 1941), pp. 101–106. I am running together the projects of *Glas* and the *Postscript*.

6. *The Differend*, No. 165, p. 108 (LD, p. 160).

7. See Lyotard's analysis of the groundlessness of the authority of the "Declaration on the Rights of Man," *The Differend*, pp. 145ff (LD, pp. 209ff.); and Derrida's analogous analysis of the American founding fathers in "Declarations of Independence," trans. Tom Keenan and Tom Pepper, *New Political Science*, 15 (1986): 7–15.

8. The groundlessness of a law or a phrase is the thrust of the word "mystical" in Derrida's "Force of Law: 'The Mystical Foundation of Authority'," trans. Mary Quaintance, *Cardozo Law Review*, 11 (1990): 919-1078. Rorty says much the same thing: if someone's "final vocabulary," her frame of reference as a whole, is challenged, all one can do is go around and around, using some parts of this vocabulary to support other parts, and the latter to support the former, until one finally draws a line in the sand and insists that this is, after all, one's final vocabulary. It is what, as a whole, I always presuppose. That, says Rorty, is not all bad; one should just understand the contingency of one's final vocabulary. See *Contingency, Irony, and Solidarity* (New York: Cambridge University Press, 1989), pp. 3–22.

9. Descartes, *Discourse on Method*, trans. L. J. Lafleur (New York: Library of Liberal Arts, 1960), Part III, p. 18ff.

10. Gadamer also points out the unthinkability of deferring ethics in Descartes in *Truth and Method*, 2nd rev. ed., trans. rev. Joel Weinsheimer and Donald Marshall (New York: Crossroad, 1991), p. 279.

11. *Summa Theologica*, Ia, I, 1, ad 2m. For the distinction between theology and philosophy, see *Summa contra gentiles*, Bk. II, c. 4, no. 5. In terms of this distinction, Enlightenment metaphysical systems, which have *principia* and try to begin at the

beginning, are very "theological," while Derrida, who urges us to begin where we are, is very "philosophical."

12. Walter Kaufmann, *Nietzsche: Philosopher, Psychologist, Antichrist*, 3rd ed. (Princeton: Princeton University Press, 1968), p. 67.

13. Philippe Lacoue-Labarthe, *Heidegger, Art and Politics*, trans. Chris Turner (Oxford: Blackwell, 1990), p. 31.

14. "Problem of facticity—the most radical phenomenology, which *begins* in the genuine sense 'from below'." Martin Heidegger, *Gesamtausgabe*, v. 61, *Phänomenologischen Interpretationen zu Aristoteles* (Frankfurt: Klostermann, 1985), p. 195. By "radical" I do not understand "foundational," but rather "racinated," rooted in a dense and inextricable system of roots, of factical pregivenness, which antedates me and my attempts to disentangle it; see Derrida, *Of Grammatology*, pp. 101–102.

15. When Rorty says that anything can be redescribed, and Derrida says that every signifier is caught up in the slippage of *différance*, they are saying pretty much the same thing. Either way, obligations keep coming in. Could someone be socialized so as to feel no obligations at all? Colin Turnbull's *The Mountain People* (New York: Simon & Schuster, 1972) is a sociological study of the Ik, a people who seem to have been socialized into an easy brutality toward one another. I would say that the body always offers a carnal protest against pain, against torture, mutilation, deprivation, or even murder itself, but I would not underestimate the capacity to redescribe such practices or to socialize them into acceptability. The point of a poetics of obligations, as Rorty would put it, is to make such practices look bad.

16. See Derrida's excellent discussion of the "epoch of judgment" in his opening remarks at the Cérissy conference on Lyotard. Derrida asks "How to Judge Jean-François Lyotard?" or "How to Judge, Jean-François Lyotard?" We live in the epoch of the *epoché* of judgment, he says, one which tried to bracket judgment (Husserl) or to render it secondary (Heidegger, Freud). But then Lyotard told us: you cannot leave judgment behind; it will give you no peace. "Préjugés: Devant la loi," *La Faculté de juger* (Paris: Minuit, 1985), pp. 87–99. I return to these matters in chapter 5, below.

17. Jacques Derrida, "My Chances/Mes Chances: A Rendezvous with Some Epicurean Stereophonics," trans. Irene Harvey and Avital Ronell in *Taking Chances: Derrida, Psychoanalysis, and Literature*, eds. J. Smith and W. Kerrigan (Baltimore: Johns Hopkins University Press, 1984), pp. 27–28.

18. Lyotard came to criticize the Wittgensteinian notion of a language game that he used in the 1970s as excessively subjectivistic. See *The Differend*, No. 188, pp. 137–138 (LD, pp. 199–200). His later position is more like Gadamer's, except that Lyotard thinks of this game as having a dense rhetorico–pragmatic force, not as bearing the truth of the tradition. Cf. Hans-Georg Gadamer, *Truth and Method*, pp. 101–134.

19. Even the obligations we have to ourselves come as if from without; they pull at me against the grain of the I. The question of suicide turns on the question of the obligation that I receive from my own flesh, *le corps propre*, which weighs heavily upon me, like the call of the other, forbidding murder yet pleading for relief. In suicide I am put in a double bind by my own flesh, at odds with myself, wanting both to live and to die.

20. *Just Gaming*, p. 59.

21. There is, I think, an important (quasi)philosophy of religion in deconstruction; for a little start on it, see Charles E. Winquist and John D. Caputo, "Derrida and the Study of Religion," *Religious Studies Review*, 16 (January 1990): 19–25.

22. I am extending the discourse of Derrida's *The Other Heading*: to be philosophical is to live under the regime of numerous European capitals and large cities, from London to Paris to Berlin.

23. In chapter 8, below, Johanna de Silentio retells the story of Abraham from Isaac and Sarah's point of view.

24. *The Differend*, Nos. 197, 214.

25. The various, very famous proposals of Nietzsche, Heidegger, Hegel.

26. *The Differend*, Second Kant Notice, No. 2, p. 121 (LD, p. 178). Later on in the text, Lyotard distinguishes the merely "apathetic pathos" of the feeling of respect which "accompanies" obligation in Kant's ethics, where pathological feeling can never be the determinant of action, from "enthusiastic pathos," which is stirred by the infinity of the Idea, which has "aesthetic validity"; see Fourth Kant Notice, No. 4, pp. 166–167 (LD, p. 240). The difficulty is that the one who calls upon us in obligation is not very well described either as physical or metaphysical and our being obliged is not well described either as feeling or more than feeling. The difficulty is metaphysics' problem, not obligation's.

27. "Ethics prohibits dialogue. . . . " See *The Differend*, Levinas Notice, 1, pp. 111–112 (LD, p. 165). Lyotard is glossing Levinas's critique of Buber.

28. In the sense of Levinas's materialism of the other person; see Levinas, *Difficult Freedom: Essays on Judaism*, trans. Sean Hand (Baltimore: Johns Hopkins University Press, 1990), p. xiv; and of Adorno's "materialism," which is a concern with the material suffering endured by others, where "materialism comes to agree with theology"; see *Negative Dialectics*, trans. E. B. Ashton (New York: Continuum, 1983), pp. 192–207. The opposite of such "materialism" is an idealism that always finds a way to explain or justify the sufferings of others. See also Cornell, *Philosophy of the Limit*, ch. 1. I am not unaware that to speak, with Lyotard, of obligation as a feeling is to invite the elementary objection that one remains within a simple reversal of the *nous/pathos* binarity. But, as these remarks on "materialism" and "idealism" show, I am seeking the displacement of this distinction. If "obligation" is not accommodated by what metaphysics calls the sensuous or the supersensuous, body or spirit, feeling or more than feeling, which would be to make of it either too little or too much, then so much the worse for metaphysics. Obligations happen, with or without metaphysics. See above, note 26.

29. *The Differend*, No. 22, p. 13 (LD, pp. 29–30).

30. *Glas*, pp. 154b–157b. Heidegger's *Beiträge zur Philosophie: Vom Ereignis* are organized around the *Klang* and the *Anklang*, which resonate between the First and the Other Beginning. See §§50ff.

31. Maurice Blanchot, *The Writing of the Disaster*, trans. Ann Smock (Lincoln: University of Nebraska Press, 1986), p. 2. For a critique of Blanchot's depoliticizing tendencies, which evolved from his rather disastrous right-wing politics in the 1930s, see Allan Stoekl, *Politics, Writing, Mutilation: The Cases of Bataille, Blanchot, Roussel, Leiris, and Ponge* (Minneapolis: University of Minnesota Press, 1985), pp. 22ff. For illuminating commentaries on the work of Blanchot, see Mark Taylor, *Altarity* (Chicago: University of Chicago Press, 1987), ch. 8; and Jacques Derrida, *Parages* (Paris: Galilée, 1986). Translations of parts of *Parages* are to be found in "Living On: Border Lines," trans. J. Hulbert, in *Deconstruction and Criticism*, ed. Harold Bloom (New York: Seabury Press, 1979), pp. 175–176; "Title (to be specified)," trans. Tom Conley, *Sub-stance* 31 (1981): 5–22; and "The Law of Genre," trans. A. Ronell, *Glyph* 7 (1980): 176–232. Most of Blanchot's short but dense novels have been published in English translation by Station Hill Press.

32. *The Differend*, No. 113, p. 70 (LD, p. 109).

33. Martin Heidegger, "The Fieldpath," trans. T. F. O'Meara, *Listening*, 8 (1973): p. 39. Heidegger's remark might be inspired by a sentence from Nietzsche cited in *What Is Called Thinking*, trans. J. Glenn Gray and Fred Wieck (New York: Harper & Row, 1968), p. 80.

34. See Caputo, *Demythologizing Heidegger*, chapter 2, "Heidegger's *Kampf*."

35. *The Differend*, Nos. 152ff., pp. 86ff. (LD, pp. 130ff.)

36. The quarter-century that Nelson Mandela spent in unjust imprisonment is from our standpoint a disaster that called out for international protest and redress;

but from Mandela's standpoint, from the standpoint of his freedom, his suffering is a price he was willing to pay for his people, for the "we" to which he belongs, and then the cost was—for him, not for us—bearable. Such an economy governs death itself: "The 'reason to die' always forms the bond of a we" (*The Differend*, No. 156, p. 100 [LD, p. 149]). The extreme disaster occurs when one's suffering or death cannot be raised up to a reason, which is the case at Auschwitz, where death comes not as a "die rather than . . . [be defeated or enslaved]" but simply as "die." That—and not the technologization of death (Heidegger)—is why the deaths at Auschwitz are not "beautiful deaths." Derrida has written about the Mandela case in "The Laws of Reflection: Nelson Mandela, in Admiration," trans. Mary Ann Caws and Isabelle Lorenz, in *For Nelson Mandela*, eds. Jacques Derrida and Mustapha Tlili (New York: Seaver Books, 1987).

37. That is what Nietzsche understood better than anyone and that is the thrust of his whole idea of "affirmation."

38. I am running together Bataille's notion of expenditure without reserve, Blanchot's *désastre*, and Lyotard's critique of Hegel.

39. The groundlessness of Being is discussed in Heidegger's *Der Satz vom Grund* (Pfullingen: Neske, 1957; Eng. trans. *The Principle of Reason*, trans. Reginald Lilly [Bloomington: Indiana University Press, 1991]), a text I have been meditating upon for many years. See John D. Caputo, *The Mystical Element in Heidegger's Thought*, rev. ed (New York: Fordham University Press, 1986); and below, chapter 10, where I bring to a head the course of these reflections on obligation in terms of groundlessness. What Heidegger says in this text needs to be translated—deconstructed, demythologized—into a discussion of disasters. Heidegger's own discussion of it as a feature of the history of Being is for me a mystification.

40. *The Differend*, No. 236, p. 171 (LD, p. 246); see also "A Memorial of Marxism: For Pierre Souyri," trans. Cecile Lindsay in *Peregrinations: Law, Form, Event* (New York: Columbia University Press, 1968), pp. 45–75 (a translation of "Pierre Souyri: Le Marxisme qui n'a pas fini").

41. It is necessary to distinguish avoidable from unavoidable disasters. The ravages of a storm, of a cataclysm of nature, are disasters even though they are no one's doing; but it is quite another thing to be lured to an early death by the tobacco industry. It is part of Nietzsche's cold wisdom to think that at bottom there is no real difference even here, that it is all part of the wheel of becoming, part of a larger cosmic economy, which is for him a cosmic innocence. That for me is a truly challenging thing to say about obligation and it is the sentiment with which I am always wrestling. That is why any discussion of obligations and disasters is always implicated in an analysis of the political and social structures that produce disasters, structures which are contingent, revisable, and avoidable.

42. Religion (*re-ligare*) attaches infinite value to obligation (*ob-ligare*). Religion is a discourse on the Infinite (*l'infini*) (which is not "infinity," *infinité*), an infinite Someone to whom one is obliged. That is why Levinas's discourse is religious while Lyotard and Derrida are not quite religious, or a/religious, on the slash between religious and irreligious.

43. See, e.g., Augustine, *City of God*, XI, c. 9; Plotinus, *Enneads*, 3, 2, 5.

44. The countertradition, according to which evil has a life of its own, a being or force of its own, is found in the Manichaeans and then later in Jacob Boehme, through whom it passes into Schelling. It is upon this streak in Schelling that Heidegger is commenting in his Schelling lectures: Heidegger, *Schelling's Treatise on the "Essence of Human Freedom,"* trans. Joan Stambaugh (Athens; Ohio University Press, 1985).

45. "The time of the 'System' is over." Heidegger, *Beiträge zur Philosophie*, p. 5.

46. *The Differend*, No. 182, pp. 135–136 (LD, p. 197).

47. Nietzsche, *Twilight of the Idols*, "How the True World Became a Fable."

48. *The Postmodern Condition*, p. xxiv. "Incredulity" is an interesting word; the great metanarratives have not been "refuted" but have simply withered away and lost their power to command our belief.

49. Although they have profoundly different concerns and perspectives, Heidegger, MacIntyre, and Bloom share a common alarm over the fragmenting or withdrawal of what is handed down by tradition, a decline which comes to a head in the dominance of "value theory." See MacIntyre, *After Virtue*, chs. 2–6; Heidegger, *Basic Writings*, pp. 238–239 and *An Introduction to Metaphysics*, trans. Ralph Mannheim (New Haven: Yale University Press, 1959), 196-199; Allan Bloom, *The Closing of the American Mind* (Chicago: University of Chicago Press, 1987), pp. 141ff. and 194ff., and on Cornell, see pp. 313ff.

50. Nietzsche was inclined to attribute various high-minded philosophical views to the intestines and sundry dietary disorders; see *Ecce Homo*, trans. R. J. Hollingdale (Baltimore: Penguin Books, 1979), "Why I Am so Clever," sec. 1, pp. 51–54.

51. I would say of obligation what Jean-Luc Nancy says of community: it is not a work (*dés-oeuvrée*), not a product, but a given. Far from being "lost," it is, as Nancy says, impossible to lose it, to shake it loose. See Jean-Luc Nancy, *The Inoperative Community*, trans. Christopher Fynsk (Minneapolis: University of Minnesota Press, 1991), pp. 34–35.

52. Levinas's ethics is a metaphysics of the Good, of the Good beyond being; his disruption of modernity, in my view, is carried out more from a premodern, Neoplatonic standpoint, than from a postmodern one.

53. MacIntyre's account of a hypothetical "catastrophe" at the beginning of *After Virtue* (pp. 1–5) brilliantly captures and explains historically the situation of incommensurability which "modernity" eventuates in, against its will, and which "postmodernity"—if this word still means anything—simply assumes as a starting point. That was also my starting point in *Radical Hermeneutics*, ch. 9, "The Ethics of Dissemination."

54. Aristotle, *Metaphysics*, II, 1 (993b8). Heidegger's notion in *Being and Time* that the hermeneutics of facticity should begin with what is *zunächst und zumeist*, what is "proximally and for the most part" familiar to us, is very likely a translation of Aristotle's notion of beginning with what is more manifest to our batlike eyes, although less manifest in itself. See *Being and Time*, trans. J. MacQuarrie and E. Robinson (New York: Harper & Row, 1962), §15. I have the same sort of gesture in mind by beginning with being-obligated.

55. "*Der letzte Gott*" is a somewhat puzzling figure, a kind of end-time appearance of the divine which will signal the lost awaited other beginning, in Heidegger's *Beiträge* (pp. 405–417).

56. On Meister Eckhart's negative theology, see Caputo, *The Mystical Element in Heidegger's Thought*, ch. 3. James Bernauer sees a certain analogy to negative theology in Foucault, in whose work he hears an analogously apophatic claim: however human beings are constituted, that is not true; but however they are not constituted, that is what is always true. See his first-rate analysis of Foucault in Bernauer, *Michel Foucault's Force of Flight: Towards an Ethics for Flight* (Atlantic Highlands: Humanities Press, 1990), pp. 175–184. I have pursued a comparable interpretation of Foucault in "On Not Knowing Who We Are: Madness, Hermeneutics and the Night of Truth," in *Foucault and the Critique of Institutions*, eds. John D. Caputo and Mark Yount (University Park: Pennsylvania State University Press, 1993).

57. On the resonances of "come" (*viens*), see Jacques Derrida, "Of an Apocalyptic Tone Recently Adopted in Philosophy," trans. John Leavey, *Semeia: An Experimental Journal for Biblical Criticism*, 23 (1982): 91–95; and "The Force of Law," pp. 969–971.

58. See Lyotard, "Lessons in Paganism," *The Lyotard Reader*, pp. 122–155.

59. *Heidegger, Art, and Politics,* p. 31.

60. Foucault, *History of Sexuality,* Vol. 2, *The Use of Pleasure,* trans. Robert Hurley (New York: Pantheon Books, 1985), pp. 10–11; Johannes Climacus noticed the same thing: as opposed to the stunted creatures who concerned themselves with which German university offered the best livelihood, the Greek philosopher made his personal existence into a work of art: *Concluding Unscientific Postscript,* pp. 268–269.

61. I will use the expression "jewgreek" throughout this study to signify, emblematically, everything miscegenated and impure and hence subject to expulsion, decontamination, extermination. I also use it to say that whatever I say here is always already Greek, philosophical, metaphysical, that one cannot simply walk away from our inherited Greek conceptuality, nor would one want to, as both Derrida and Levinas insist. The expression of course is taken from James Joyce's *Ulysses* ("Jewgreek is greekjew. Extremes meet."), and it received a now classic gloss in Derrida, "Violence and Metaphysics," *Writing and Difference,* trans. Alan Bass (Chicago: University of Chicago Press, 1978): "Are we Greeks? Are we Jews? We live in the difference between the Jew and the Greek . . . " (p. 152).

62. Siegfried Lenz, *The Training Ground,* trans. G. Skelton (New York: Holt & Co., 1991): "Never trust anyone who preaches genuineness and purity. The apostles of purity bring us nothing but disaster." Cited by Theodore Ziolkowski, "Beware of the Purists," a review of *The Training Ground* in *New York Times Book Review* (January 5, 1992): 3.

63. This is the sort of disagreement I have with James Marsh in *Modernity and Its Discontents,* eds. James Marsh, John Caputo, Merold Westphal (New York: Fordham University Press, 1992). The main contribution of Habermas himself is to supply us with a paradigmatic case, one no postmodernist could ever surpass, of how *not* to read the so-called postmodernists.

64. I learned that from a Jesuit; see Robert Henle, S.J., "Prudence and Insight in Moral and Legal Decisions," *Proceedings of the American Catholic Philosophical Association,* 56 (1982): 26-30; and my use of Henle in "Prudential Insight and Moral Reasoning," *Proceedings of the American Catholic Philosophical Association,* 58 (1984): 50-55.

65. Whether this cold truth has a warm heart is the point of Jacqueline Brogan's superb discussion of *Radical Hermeneutics* in "Eradication/Reification: Or What's so Radical about *Radical Hermeneutics?*" *Diacritics,* 20 (1990): 74-84.

66. Making indifference and cruelty look bad is the way Richard Rorty would put it in *Contingency, Irony and Solidarity* (Cambridge: Cambridge University Press, 1991), Part III. Although I like Rorty's turn to literary and narrative portraits of the cruelty we inflict on one another, I am not uncritical of his views. See my "On Not Circumventing the Quasi-Transcendental: The Case of Rorty and Derrida," *Working Through Derrida,* ed. Gary Madison (Evanston: Northwestern University Press, 1992).

67. This is not "intuitionism," since it is not something "seen" by the "I," nor "emotivism," because it is not describing a feeling of subjective preference, like a taste—but a disruptive shock received by the I which shatters everything intuitional, emotive, and egological. It is not "decisionism," because it is nothing I decide but something that comes crashing down on me, disrupts the sphere of the *ego volo* and draws me out of myself, much against my will. "Decisionism," a view originating in the work of Carl Schmitt, and one of the most familiar Habermasian critiques leveled at Lyotard and poststructuralists generally, means the reduction of choice to the "arbitrary" affirmation of one "value" over another. Decisionistic models are the opposite of technocratic models. See Jürgen Habermas, *Toward a Rational Society,* trans. Jeremy Shapiro (Boston: Beacon Press, 1968), pp. 62ff. But decisionism turns on a theory of a free subject arbitrarily positing its own values, a framework deeply at odds with both the deconstruction of the "subject" and the Levinasian conception of the "exteriority" of obligation which are at work in the

present study. The disaster that besets the other is anything but a "value" posited by the "I" and anything but arbitrary.

68. *Totality and Infinity*, p. 269, and the discussion of "fecundity," pp. 274–277, with the proviso that fathers *and mothers* have sons *and daughters*. For a defender of anarchy, Levinas is stupendously patriarchal.

69. Johannes Climacus said that existence itself—the existence of a poor existing spirit—keeps being and thought apart, even if they are the same in a German philosopher. The greatest embarrassment would ensue, Climacus adds, were an enthusiastic disciple to inform Herr Professor that he wished to apply this excellent doctrine, it never having occurred to Herr Professor that any one would actually try what he has merely imagined and written books about. *Concluding Unscientific Postscript*, pp. 170–171. In *Identity and Difference*, trans. Joan Stambaugh (New York: Harper & Row, 1969), pp. 27ff., Heidegger reads the Parmenidean doctrine that being and thought are the same by glossing *to auto* as "belong together," but with results which are no more helpful for poor existing spirits.

70. This is Johannes Climacus's argument in the *Philosophical Fragments*, trans. H. Hong and E. Hong (Princeton: Princeton University Press, 1985).

71. This is Lyotard's argument in "Answering the Question, What is Postmodernism?" in *The Postmodern Condition*, pp. 71–82.

72. Rorty's idea of inventing new vocabularies and reinventing oneself is similar, but he casts this in terms of "autonomy," where on my approach the *autos* is itself highly disseminated and pluralized. There are too many selves for me to keep track of.

73. I return to this theme of exultation again in chapter 10, below.

74. See my discussion of Kierkegaard's concept of repetition in *Radical Hermeneutics*, ch. 1.

75. *Philosophical Fragments*, pp. 18–19.

76. Augustine, *Commentary on the First Epistle of John*, in Migne, *Patrologia latina*, v. 35, p. 2033. For an insightful commentary, see Étienne Gilson, *The Christian Philosophy of St. Augustine*, trans. Lawrence Lynch (London: Gallancz, 1961), pp. 140–141, including n. 50. I have organized a good deal of *Radical Hermeneutics* around this text, which I do not believe commits one always to have a Bishop for one's guide.

77. My fondness for Latin in this text is meant as a strategic twitting of Heidegger's nose, as a disturbance to all the bowed Heideggerian heads and bent knees, which flex every time they hear Greek. One ought to be disabused of the foolishness that there is an order of rank of "Greco-German" and Latino-Romance languages (or Indo-European, for that matter), which is a dangerous bit of linguistic hierarchizing which understands nothing about *différance* and hence about language (or its "languaging") and which keeps company with a consumately disastrous politics.

Three. Dionysus vs. the Rabbi

1. *The Will to Power*, No. 983, p. 513.

2. As Lyotard quips in *Just Gaming*, p. 94, " 'Always act in such a way that the maxim of your will may,' I won't say 'not be erected,' but it is almost that, 'into a principle of universal legislation.' Into a principle of a multiplicity. . . .''

3. *Fear and Trembling*, p. 8.

4. The thematic of the undigestibility of difference, of the undigestible bit, the fragment, is central to Derrida's *Glas*, p. 1a, which opens with the question "What, after all, of the remain(s), today, for us, here, now, of a Hegel?" and to Kierkegaard's *Concluding Unscientific Postscript to the "Philosophical Fragments,"* whose epigraph is from the *Greater Hippias*, 304a: "But really, Socrates, what do you think

this all amounts to? It is really scrapings and parings of systematic thought (*logon*), as I said a while ago, divided into bits." *Sa* is the name of the System, of *savoir absolue*, although that is only a fragment of its polysemy and polyphony in *Glas*.

5. *Fear and Trembling*, p. 8.

6. *Savoir absolue*: one of the many senses of *Sa* in *Glas*.

7. Edmund Husserl, *L'origine de la Géometrie*, Traduction et introduction par Jacques Derrida (Paris: Presses Universitaires de France, 1962). *Edmund Husserl's "Origin of Geometry": An Introduction*, trans. John Leavey, ed. David Allison (Stony Brook, N.Y.: Nicholas Hays, 1978). Gilles Deleuze, *Nietzsche and Philosophy*, trans. Hugh Tomlinson (New York: Columbia University Press, 1983).

8. I take poststructuralism to turn on relatively narrow and technical questions about the delimitation of structuralism, whereas postmodernism is a much broader, more amorphous cultural phenomenon which includes everything from "thirty-something" to Andy Warhol. On "Postmodernism," see Ihab Hassan, *The Dismemberment of Orpheus: Toward a Post Modern Literature* (New York: Oxford University Press, 1971) and "The Question of Postmodernism," in Harry A. Garvin (ed.) *Romanticism, Modernism, Postmodernism* (Lewisburg, Pa.: Bucknell University Press, 1980). Lyotard seems to have taken the word over from Hassan. For the history and range of the term, see *Postmodernism: ICA Documents*, ed. Kisa Appignanesi (London: Free Association Books, 1989).

9. This is where a good deal of the criticism of "poststructuralism" is focused, leaving its critics with the impression that it is an apolitical aestheticism. See John Ellis, *Against Deconstruction* (Princeton: Princeton University Press, 1989); J. Claude Evans, *Strategies of Deconstruction: Derrida and the Myth of the Voice* (Minneapolis: University of Minnesota Press, 1991); John McGowan, *Postmodernism and Its Critics* (Ithaca: Cornell University Press, 1991); Allan Megill, *Prophets of Extremity: Nietzsche, Heidegger, Foucault, Derrida* (Berkeley: University of California Press, 1985). The critique gets nasty in David Lehman, *The Sign of the Times: Deconstruction and the Fall of Paul De Man* (New York: Simon and Schuster, 1991), who rightly complains that the word "deconstruction" has become a buzz word, but who goes on to link it with fascism on what I regard as *ad hominem* grounds. The most influential but deeply misguided critique, of course, is Jürgen Habermas, *The Philosophical Discourse of Modernity*, trans. Frederick Lawrence (Cambridge: MIT Press, 1987).

10. Deleuze, *Nietzsche and Philosophy*, p. 181.

11. *Nietzsche and Philosophy*, p. 184.

12. Nietzsche, *Thus Spoke Zarathustra*, trans. Walter Kaufmann (New York: Viking Books, 1966), "On The Three Metamorphoses" pp. 25–28.

13. Notice the symmetry of re-sentment, re-activeness, re-sponsibility.

14. Martin Heidegger, *What is Called Thinking?* trans. Fred Wieck and J. Glenn Gray (New York: Harper & Row, 1968), Part One. On Kierkegaard, see *The Question Concerning Technology*, p. 94.

15. *Nietzsche and Philosophy*, p. 220, n.31.

16. *Nietzsche and Philosophy*, p. 185.

17. *Nietzsche and Philosophy*, p. 186.

18. Edith Wyschogrod registers a similar complaint about Deleuze's work, which is for her a kind of Neoplatonism and a "myth of the plenum." See her *Saints and Postmodernism: Revisioning Moral Philosophy* (Chicago: University of Chicago Press, 1990), pp. 208–217. *Saints and Postmodernism* can be profitably read alongside the present chapter.

19. *Thus Spoke Zarathustra*, "The Drunken Song," no. 9, p. 322.

20. I indulge here in a bit of autography: "Gilles" is the French translation of *Aegidius*, which means shield or protection (as in "aegis"). Gilles's philosophy shields the will against being and otherness in order to let willing proceed under its own aegis.

21. *Nietzsche and Philosophy*, p. 188.
22. *Nietzsche and Philosophy*, p. 190.
23. *Nietzsche and Philosophy*, p. 189.
24. *Nietzsche and Philosophy*, pp. 25–27.
25. *Nietzsche and Philosophy*, p. 176 (my emphasis).
26. *Nietzsche and Philosophy*, p. 190.
27. *Nietzsche and Philosophy*, p. 190.
28. *Nietzsche and Philosophy*, p. 198.
29. For a helpful delimitation of Deleuze's interpretation of Nietzsche, see Ronald Bogue, *Deleuze and Guattari* (New York: Routledge, 1989), p. 16 and p. 33.
30. *Thus Spoke Zarathustra*, Part III, "The Wanderer" and "The Vision and the Riddle," pp. 154–156.
31. Nietzsche says that "my judgment is *my* judgment: another cannot easily acquire a right to it." *Beyond Good and Evil*, No. 43, p. 53. Ergo, my Nietzsche is mine, etc.
32. *The Will to Power*, No. 749, p. 396. For an account of Nietzsche that does not back off from the extreme of Nietzsche's "immoralism," see Philippa Foot, "Nietzsche's Immoralism," *The New York Review of Books* 38, No. 11 (June 13, 1991): 18–22.
33. *The Will to Power*, No. 3 (p. 9). So when Nietzsche says that truth is a lie, he is telling the hard truth, and he is making it hard to make an easy distinction between truth and lying. See "On Truth and Lies in a Nonmoral Sense," pp. 79–97.
34. *Beyond Good and Evil*, No. 39, p. 50.
35. Jünger moved from this aesthetic justification of life to an "aesthetics of horror." Karl-Heinz Bohrer, *Die Aesthetik des Schreckens: Die Pessimistische Romantik und Ernst Jüngers Frühwerk* (München: Carl Hanser Verlag, 1978). See Michael Zimmerman, *Heidegger's Confrontation with Modernity* (Bloomington: Indiana University Press, 1990) for comments on Bohrer's thesis (p. 53) and on Jünger's relation to Heidegger (pp. 46ff.). I do not think it is possible to "decontaminate" Nietzsche of such scandalous connections, which is the effect of Deleuze's proposed rehabilitation. Derrida showed better than anyone the "heterogeneity" of Nietzsche's text, its excessive polyvalence, that it is written in many styles, and that it cannot be mastered by the left or the right, by Heidegger or Walter Kaufmann, or by anyone else, including Nietzsche himself. Jacques Derrida, *Spurs: Nietzsche's Styles*, trans. Barbara Harlow (Chicago: University of Chicago Press, 1978), pp. 95–101. But it is of no little interest that later on Derrida went on to insist that this very polyvalance means that it is not possible to decontaminate Nietzsche's texts, to sanitize them of everything we find offensive or scandalous about them, of every "embarrassment" of our "democratic" sensibilities. There are serious and important discursive veins in his text that lend themselves precisely to the several appropriations of his thought, including the fascist one. "There is nothing absolutely contingent," Derrida wrote, "about the fact that the only political regimen to have *effectively* brandished his name as a major and official banner was Nazi." Derrida, *The Ear of the Other: Otobiography, Transference, Translation*, ed. Christie McDonald, trans. Peggy Kamuf and Avital Ronell (New York: Schocken Books, 1985), p. 31. See also Christopher Norris's interesting review of *The Ear of the Other*, "Deconstruction Against Itself: Derrida and Nietzsche," *Diacritics*, 16 (Winter 1986): 61–69. Robert Detweiler, *Nietzsche and the Politics of Aristocratic Radicalism* (Chicago: University of Chicago Press, 1990) has amply documented the extensive textual foundation in Nietzsche for the most oppressive and reactionary political views; it seems to me foolish, if not downright disingenuous, to try to persuade oneself that Nietzsche did not hold such views.
36. *Will to Power*, No. 749, p. 396.
37. *Will to Power*, No. 1060, pp. 545–546.

38. *The Will to Power*, No. 1067, p. 550.

39. I am pointedly using Levinas's term.

40. In *Différance et Répetition* (Paris: Presses Universitaires de France, 1981), Deleuze defends a new concept of the Scotist conception of the univocity of being: everything is the same, that is, different. But that is just what Nietzsche denies: only the best are different and they must learn to cultivate their difference from the common and the mediocre, who are all the same. Deleuze also makes use of *haecceitas* in *Mille plateaux: capitalisme et schizophrénie, II* (Paris: Minuit, 1980), p. 318.

41. *Thus Spoke Zarathustra*, "The Song of Melancholy," No. 1, p. 296.

42. See Derrida's comment on the governing power of the axiomatics of nausea in Nietzsche's valuing in *The Ear of the Other*, pp. 23–24, note.

43. *Ecce Homo*, p. 126, emphasis in the original.

44. *Nietzsche and Philosophy*, p. 82, emphasis in the original.

45. See Eric Parens, "From Philosophy to Politics: On Nietzsche's Ironic Metaphysics of Will to Power," *Man and World*, 24 (1991): 169–180. Nietzsche has an excellent insight into Judaism and Christianity: they are, or ought to be, emancipatory, so that the expression "liberation theology" should be (but is not) redundant. But he counted that an objection to religion, instead of one of its finer moments. Parens, who wants to preserve the tensions in Nietzsche's thought, does a good job of dispatching Mark Warren's claim in *Nietzsche and Political Thought* (Cambridge: MIT Press, 1988) that we can dismiss what Nietzsche has to say about politics, that is, trim the text around the edge and put Nietzsche out in a new, decontaminated edition with clean margins.

46. For a superb collection of poststructuralist interpretations of Nietzsche, see *The New Nietzsche: Contemporary Styles of Interpretation*, ed. David B. Allison (New York: Delta Books, 1977).

47. *The Closing of the American Mind*, pp. 217ff.

48. *The Will to Power*, No. 416, p. 223.

49. I rely upon my memory. Did Nietzsche write this or have I read it somewhere else? I cannot find the text.

50. *The Will to Power*, No. 293, p. 165; No. 331, pp. 180–181; No. 584, pp. 314–316. Alexander Nehamas offers an intelligent and subtle commentary on the theme of the interwovenness of all things in his *Nietzsche: Life as Literature* (Cambridge: Harvard University Press, 1985).

51. *The Gay Science*, trans. W. Kaufmann (New York: Viking Books, 1974), No. 341, pp. 273–274.

52. See Nehamas, *Nietzsche: Life as Literature*, pp. 81–83, who shows that the play of forces is analogous to the play of differential signs in Saussure. But Nehamas omits the crucial disanalogy: while Saussurean signs are totally arbitrary and without positive content, the forces are essentially positive powers which are inextricably woven together with one another. Saussurean signs reduce to their difference from one another; Nietzschean forces produce their differences from one another.

53. *The Will to Power*, No. 1067, p. 557.

54. *The Will to Power*, No. 639, pp. 340–341; No. 712, pp. 379–380.

55. Ironically, Nietzsche's concept of the forces was importantly influenced by a physicist, R. G. Boscovich (1711–1787), who became a Jesuit priest!—whose more Leibnizean, anti-Newtonian frame of mind Nietzsche admired. Boscovich argued that an atom is to be understood as a center of force, not as a bit of mass. Nietzsche mentions him in *Beyond Good and Evil*, No. 12, trans. W. Kaufmann (New York: Vintage, 1966), p. 20 and n.16. See George Stack, "Nietzsche and Boscovich's Natural Philosophy," *Pacific Philosophical Quarterly* (1981): 69–87.

56. *The Will to Power*, No. 632, pp. 336–337; No. 634, pp. 337–338.

57. *The Will to Power*, No. 639, pp. 340–341.

58. "I was the first to *discover* the truth, in that I was the first to sense—*smell*—the

lie as lie. . . . My genius is in my nostrils." *Ecce Homo*, "Why I Am a Destiny," No. 1, p. 126.

59. See *Beyond Good and Evil*, No. 263, pp. 183–184. See Dan Conway's interesting paper in which he says that Nietzsche appreciated that he ended up as resentful a figure as any of the thinkers he criticized, and that he chose to deal with this by way of a self-parody. Conway, "Nietzsche's Vow of Silence: Affirmation and Resentment in *Ecce Homo*" (unpublished).

60. Wyschogrod's Levinasian critique of Nietzsche is that Nietzsche's perpetual self-overcoming implies a body that is always awake, a kind of metaphysical insomniac, invulnerable to fatigue or sleep. *Saints and Postmodernism*, pp. 103–104.

61. See *Radical Hermeneutics*, ch. 9.

62. In *The Anti-Christ*, No. 52, p. 169, Nietzsche complains of the theologians' incapacity for philology, their inability to read texts or events honestly. Nietzsche recommends a merciless, cold hermeneutics.

63. Foucault is on the slash. He is very close to Nietzsche and Deleuze, of course. But his account of the marginalized, the criminal and the mad, does that not arise from a response to the call of the other (*alter*)? In *Saints and Postmodernism*, Edith Wyschogrod argues that there is a "fault line" in postmodernism which divides philosophers of difference such as Levinas, Derrida, and Blanchot, from philosophers of the plenum, such as Deleuze, Guattari, and Genet (pp. 191, 223, 229). This corresponds to an analogous distinction I am making here between heteromorphic and heteronomous theories of difference, but with this exception, that, as I will show in the next section, Derrida and Lyotard should be situated on the line between heteromorphism and heteronomism. One should mention also Bataille, who, as a philosopher of excess *par excellence*, belongs on the side of pure overflow and expenditure which characterizes the heteromorphic model. In an interesting discussion, Wyschogrod shows how Bataille's excessive expenditure can be brought into alliance with Levinasian desire of the Other, "expenditure in the interest of the Other," i.e., with heteronomy, by being made to answer the questions: "To what or to whom is the subject of expenditure indebted?" "How does this indebtedness come about?" See *Saints and Postmodernism*, pp. 142–148, 154.

64. *The Will to Power*, No. 654, p. 345.

65. *The Will to Power*, Nos. 630–634, pp. 336–338.

66. In the "Prologue" to *Thus Spoke Zarathustra*, p. 9, the sun is the model of the Overman, of giving of its overflow and overripe fullness: "You great star, what would your happiness be had you not those for whom you shine?" The same image recurs at the end, "The Sign," p. 324.

67. In *Saints and Postmodernism*, pp. 210–214, Edith Wyschogrod likewise finds a certain Neoplatonism in Deleuze. But does not Levinas also conceive the absolutely Other in terms of Neoplatonic infinity? Both Deleuze and Levinas are philosophers of infinity, of infinite excess, and both seek to deploy a kind of Neoplatonic infinity to throw the dialectic out of gear. Deleuze affirms the infinite excess of the same; Levinas affirms the infinite excess of the Other. I have never gotten as far as the infinity of the Other, and I do not have the stamina for the infinity of the same.

68. *The Genealogy of Morals*, trans. Walter Kaufmann (New York: Viking Books, 1967), II, 2, pp. 58–60.

69. To each his own.

70. Like Johannes Climacus, I assume that one is better off if one is not convinced one has a mission—either to announce the end of philosophy or "to divine the coming of a matchless future." *Concluding Unscientific Postscript*, p. 210.

71. Heidegger argues that the subject remains at least the implicit model for such an *autos*. See "The Age of World Picture," in *The Question Concerning Technology and Other Essays*, trans. W. Lovitt (New York: Harper & Row, 1977), pp. 115–154.

72. For an excellent study of the question of the other in this sense see Michael

Theunissen, *The Other: Studies in the Social Ontology of Husserl, Heidegger, Sartre, and Buber*, trans. C. Macann (Cambridge: MIT Press, 1984).

73. In "Violence and Metaphysics," Derrida argues that such symmetry is inescapable. See *Writing and Difference*, trans. Alan Bass (Chicago: University of Chicago Press, 1978), pp. 125–131: if I do not concede that the *other* person (*alter* ego) is an alter *ego*, my *fellow* human, I reduce him or her to something mundane or neutral, which is the very gesture of violence.

74. The path from Deleuze's affirmation of affirmation in *Nietzsche and Philosophy* to the schizorevolutionary desiring machines of *Anti-Oedipus* (1972) seems to be a straight one. In *Saints and Postmodernism*, chapter 5, Wyschogrod raises the same sort of difficulties with *Anti-Oedipus* that I raise with *Nietzsche and Philosophy*. She sees in it a "myth of the plenum" which denies the reality of lack and sees desire as totally affirmative, a dream of plenitude without *différance* (p. 214). *Anti-Oedipus* represents a kind of postmodern Neoplatonism in which the pure unrepressed desire finds ever new ways to flow and overflow, unchecked by Oedipal structure and the law of castration. While such overflowing is a good model for conceiving of a certain excess of generosity and for a Levinasian "desire" for the good of the Other, "producing the alleviation of suffering" (p. 209), it is fatally flawed in that it leaves no room for the limit that the Other puts upon my willing, the check of "obligation" and "responsibility." In this view, the Other is a completely absent absence which does not impinge upon the self at all, not an absence present in the traces of language which calls upon us, as in Levinas (pp. 216–217). This shows up in Deleuze's treatment of the face as a despot rather than as vulnerable. Constantin Boundas responds to Wyschogrod's critique in his "The Ethics of the Event: A New Stoicism," *Joyful Wisdom: A Journal for Post Modern Ethics*, 2 (1991). Boundas claims that Wyschogrod is looking in the wrong place for a Deleuzean ethics; she should look to the notion of making oneself worthy of an event in *The Logic of Sense*.

75. Derrida criticizes the thematics of a "pure cut" in favor of the "logic of parergonality" in *Truth in Painting*, trans. Geoffrey Bennington (Chicago: University of Chicago Press, 1987), pp. 83–118.

76. In both *Altarity* (Chicago: University of Chicago Press, 1987) and *Tears* (Albany: SUNY Press, 1990), Mark Taylor effects a remarkable mutual infiltration of postmodern and religious motifs.

77. *Concluding Unscientific Postscript*, pp. 210–215.

78. *The Differend*, No. 208, p. 144 (LD, 208-209).

79. See Derrida, "Préjugés," *La faculté de juger*, p. 94, on the undecidability of the double bind and the need to make a judgment. Derrida does not turn deciding into decisionism but provides the only sensible way to avoid turning a choice into a technical calculation.

80. That is why Drucilla Cornell has recently redescribed deconstruction as the "philosophy of the limit." Although I love this book, which lays to rest a whole nest of confusions about Derrida and, like the present study, moves in the space opened up by Derrida and Levinas, I still prefer the word "deconstruction." The language of limit and finitude—like the word "creature"—belongs to the most traditional metaphysics of infinity; it suggests that it is to be followed up by a philosophy of the unlimited. (The old Jesuit curriculum used to have two courses: metaphysics of finite being [creatures]; metaphysics of infinite being [God].) See Cornell's "Introduction: What is Postmodernity Anyway?" in *The Philosophy of the Limit* (New York: Routledge and Kegan Paul, 1992), p. 1. "Limit" is a better word for Gadamer's Heideggerianized version of Hegel than for Derrida. See Dennis Schmidt, *The Ubiquity of the Finite* (Cambridge: MIT Press, 1988). That is why Derrida writes that "the return to finitude" does not take "a single step outside of metaphysics." "*Différance* is also something other than finitude." *Of Grammatology*, p. 68.

81. Wyschogrod's enlistment of the pure expenditure one finds in Nietzsche, Ba-

taille, and Deleuze into the idea of an expenditure of altruistic service to others, of Levinasian desire for the Other, is an example of how the wires between hetero-morphism and heteronomism can be crossed. See *Saints and Postmodernism*, p. 209.

82. *The Differend*, No. 202, p. 142 (LD, p. 206).

83. In one of its pronunciations, Mark Taylor's *Tears* rhymes with "cheers."

84. *The Differend*, No. 173, p. 116 (LD, p. 171).

85. *The Differend*, No. 173, p. 116 (LD, p. 171).

86. Medieval respect for *auctoritates*, earlier masters.

87. "Outside the church there is no salvation." An early theological slogan from the Church Fathers.

88. See Stephen Houlgate, "Power, Egoism and the 'Open Self' in Nietzsche and Hegel," *Journal of the British Society for Phenomenology*, 22 (1991): 120–138, for a sal-utary reminder to postmodern readers of Nietzsche that Nietzsche is profoundly critical of any giving or surrender that would involve surrendering to what is other. Even the "gift-giving virtue" is not "an attitude of genuine responsiveness to, or humility before, the matter at hand, but rather an attitude of emphatic self-affirma-tion in the act of self-giving" (p. 127). Gift-giving is always overflow of magnanim-ity, never a response to what comes from without.

89. Mark 12:41-44.

90. In giving, Levinas says, I make a present of my presence and I become "a hostage delivered over as a gift to the other." *Otherwise than Being*, p. 151.

91. Wyschogrod, *Saints and Postmodernism*, p. 34: the saint is "one whose adult life in its entirety is devoted to the alleviation of sorrow (the psychological suffer-ing) and pain (the physical suffering) that afflicts other persons without distinction of rank or group or, alternatively, that afflicts sentient beings, whatever the cost to the saint in pain or sorrow." Wyschogrod claims that "only . . . postmodernism [of the kind influenced by Levinas] can provide a language and interpretive context for saintly existence" (p. xxiv).

92. I am deploying Mark Taylor's idea of "altarity."

93. I have heard this talk of "trickling down" in some other context, but I cannot recall where. Perhaps it was in a previous existence.

94. "[E]verywhere we must read 'so to speak.' " Plotinus, *Enneads*, VI, 8.13. Cited in Wyschogrod, p. 213. That, I think, is also the upshot of deconstructive analysis. That is the Derridian sense I give to the "fact as it were" of obligation.

95. After referring to the "Chandala morality" of Paul, the apostle of revenge, Nietzsche asks: "*What follows from all this?* That one does well to put gloves on when reading the New Testament. The proximity of so much uncleanliness almost forces one to do so. One would no more choose to associate with 'first Christians' than one would with Polish Jews. . . . Neither of them smell very pleasant." *The Anti-Christ*, No. 46, p. 161.

96. *Concluding Unscientific Postscript*, p. 161.

97. See Kierkegaard's *Repetition*, p. 175.

Four. In the Names of Justice

1. *Concluding Unscientific Postscript*, pp. 210–215.

2. I am making use in this chapter of some of the more technical features of Ly-otard's discussion of the proper name in chapter 2 of *The Differend*, "The Referent, The Name," pp. 32–58, which I have worked together with Derrida's notion of the proper name. I also use Lyotard's discussion of the ethico-politics of proper names, the names which rise up against the great philosophies of history, No. 257, pp. 179 (LD, pp. 257–258), and what Derrida thinks is the "central" name of Lyotard's dis-course, the name "Auschwitz," which is the subject of the central chapter, "The Result." The whole of *The Differend* can be seen as an explication of the name

"Auschwitz." Then, in *Heidegger and "the jews,"* almost in response to Derrida, that name is generalized. On the whole, Lyotard seems to have a more unproblematized idea of the proper name, to emphasize our pragmatic success in using proper names, and to locate the value of a name as a sign of protest. Derrida is more troubled by the philosophical possibility of proper names and the valorizing of propriety, although I think he shares Lyotard's pragmatic, or pragrammatological, conviction that (glossing over the difficulties) proper names certainly "work." But Derrida also points out the role proper names play in systems of social control (*Of Grammatology*, p. 111). Genet himself and Genet's characters are "anthonyms," but the flowers are cut when the court clerk calls out Our Lady's and First Communion's legal names, returning them to the "first classificatory violence," the "taxinomic rigor" of the law and the courts, which will lead to execution (*Glas*, 99b).

3. *The Differend*, No. 113, p. 70 (LD, p. 109).

4. Derrida's decentering of the name "Auschwitz," *Les fins de l'hommes*, p. 311.

5. The Vietnam War Memorial in Washington, D.C. Contrariwise, an absolutely comprehensive list of everyone alive, stored and easily accessible by powerful computers, would make for a system of perfect terror.

6. Heidegger warns us against the "gigantic" in *Beiträge*, pp. 97–98 *et passim*, but his history of Being seems to me quite a bit gigantic itself, and in its own way, and despite itself, not a little totalizing. I give more detailed support for this claim in my *Demythologizing Heidegger*.

7. I borrow these excellent expressions from Theodor Adorno's *Minima Moralia: Reflections from Damaged Life*, trans. E. F. N. Jephcott (London: NLB, 1974).

8. I support these complaints in *Demythologizing Heidegger*, chapter 7, "Heidegger's Scandal," and chapter 8, "Heidegger's Poets."

9. See Hegel on the slaughter bench of Reason/History in *Reason in History*, trans. Robert Hartman (Indianapolis: Library of Liberal Arts, 1953), pp. 27ff.

10. I have examined this claim in some detail in *Heidegger and Aquinas*, chs. 4 and 8.

11. But we cannot forget that, in virtue of *différance*, that could also provide for a system of perfect terror.

12. The best recent work done on the classical problematic is Jorge Gracia, *Individuality: An Essay on the Foundations of Metaphysics* (Albany: SUNY Press, 1988).

13. See Jean-Luc Nancy's distinction between an individual and a singularity in *The Inoperative Community*, p. 27: the individual has a kind of enclosedness which mimes infinity, whereas the singular being is finite and exposed.

14. *Nicomachean Ethics*, I, 3 (1094 b 12–15).

15. See Lyotard, *The Postmodern Condition*, pp. 59–60, who refers us to Paul Watzlawick, Janet Helmick-Beavin, Don D. Jackson, *Pragmatics of Human Communication: A Study of Interactional Patterns, Pathologies and Paradoxes* (New York: Norton, 1967).

16. Derrida, *Margins of Philosophy*, p. 328.

17. The dream of Rousseau, dreamt again by Lévi-Strauss, and criticized by Derrida in *Of Grammatology*, pp. 101–140.

18. Heidegger, *Being and Time*, §§32–33.

19. In "How to Avoid Speaking: Denials," in *Languages of the Unsayable*, eds. Sanford Budick and Wolfgang Iser (New York: Columbia University Press, 1989), pp. 3–70, Derrida argues for the inseparability of prayer, praise, and predication in a dispute with Jean-Luc Marion, whose *God without Being*, trans. Thomas Carlson (Chicago: University of Chicago Press, 1991), contains an interesting critique of *différance* as a still higher idolatry beyond onto-theo-logic. For a commentary, see John D. Caputo, "How to Avoid Speaking of God: The Violence of Natural Theology," in *Prospects for Natural Theology*, ed. Eugene Long (Washington D.C.: Catholic University of America Press, 1992), pp. 128–150.

20. For a full account and the sources of these remarks, see Caputo, *The Mystical Element in Heidegger's Thought*, ch. 2. As Derrida says, negative theology is a "certain form of language, with its *mise en scène*, its rhetorical, grammatical, and logical modes, its demonstrative procedures—in short a textual practice attested or rather situated 'in history' . . . " "How to Avoid Speaking," p. 3.

21. This is more true of *Otherwise than Being* than of *Totality of Infinity*. See Stephan Strasser, *Jenseits von Sein und Zeit: Eine Einführung in Emmanuel Levinas Philosophie* (The Hague: Nijhoff, 1978), who regards this as a kind of *Kehre* in Levinas.

22. See the interview with Richard Kearney, "Deconstruction and the Other," in *Dialogues with Contemporary Continental Thinkers*, ed. Richard Kearney (Manchester: Manchester University Press, 1984), pp. 105–126, which clears up this and other recurrent misconceptions of deconstruction. See also Rodolphe Gasché, *The Tain of the Mirror* (Cambridge: Harvard University Press, 1986), pp. 280–282.

23. I am here combining Lyotard's more upbeat pragmatism and Derrida's pragrammatology discussed in "My Chances/*mes* Chances: A Rendezvous with Some Epicurean Stereophonies," trans. Irene Harvey and Avital Ronell, in *Taking Chances: Derrida Psychoanalysis, and Literature*, ed. J. H. Smith and W. Kerrigan (Baltimore: Johns Hopkins University Press, 1984), pp. 27–28.

24. For Lyotard, a proper name is a "linchpin," "an empty and constant designator," the pin which holds on the axle of the name all the ostensions and descriptions which belong to the name. But its reference to reality is never certain, never equal to 1.0, since the name can keep changing and gather new—even counter-factual or counter-sensical—ostensions and descriptions. See *The Differend*, Nos. 66-67, pp. 43–44 (LD, pp. 71–73). Derrida's delimitation of proper names is based on a direct critique of the notion of propriety itself. Lyotard is adapting Kripke's notion of a "rigid designator." For a critique of Kripke from the standpoint of Wittgenstein and Derrida (which unfortunately does not mention Lyotard) see Henry Staten, "The Secret Name of Cats: Deconstruction, Intentional Meaning and the New Theory of Reference," in *Redrawing the Lines: Analytic Philosophy, Deconstruction, and Literary Theory*, ed. R. W. Dasenbrock (Minneapolis: University of Minnesota Press, 1989), pp. 27–48. Staten also appreciates the importance of cats.

25. T.S. Eliot, "The Naming of Cats," *Old Possum's Book of Practical Cats* (New York: Harcourt Brace Jovanovich, 1967), p. 2. The only truly proper name, I think, is the one described by Eliot, the name which is known only to the cat itself (not even to any other cat), which the cat carries around with itself, privately and singularly, in absolute monological consciousness—so that this name could never function in the absence of the cat. The cat carries this name to its grave and this name will not be found engraved on its tombstone, if you are in the habit of visiting animal cemeteries on your day off. This is an absolutely secret, ineffable name which is truly the cat's very own proper name. This, the great poet poetizes thoughtfully, is very likely what cats are thinking about if you come upon them of an afternoon, seeming to catch a little nap on a sunny, curtained windowsill, but actually lost in meditative thinking. It is an excessively humanistic prejudice, already adequately criticized in numerous places by Derrida, to deny that cats have monological consciousness or that they engage in meditative thinking (*besinnliches Denken*). That is what it would take to have a truly proper name. But this is somewhat more of a statement about cats than about names, a bit of hyperbolic praise of cats, and something of a tall tail.

26. Indeed he makes prophecy a philosophical issue in *Otherwise than Being or Beyond Essence*, pp. 149ff. If he is a postmodernist, as I do not think he is, it is with a kind of prophetic postmodernism.

27. Derrida plays thus with Levinas's initials—which also spell the name of God in Hebrew (is this further testimony to the inner spiritual alliance of French and Hebrew?), thereby raising the questions of the "it" and of Levinas's valorizing of

fathers and sons—in "At this very moment in this work here I am," trans. Rüben Berezdivin in *Re-Reading Levinas*, pp. 11–48.

28. Heidegger's jug; see *Poetry, Language, Thought*, trans. Albert Hofstadter (New York: Harper & Row, 1971), pp. 166ff.

29. The concept of "the absolute" throws us into endless paralogies. In the Middle Ages, Thomas Aquinas held that the absoluteness of God absolved God of any relation to us but that we remained related to God, which is something that even very good Thomists cannot accept; see W. Norris Clarke, "What Is Most and Least Relevant in St. Thomas' Metaphysics Today?" *International Philosophical Quarterly*, 14 (1974): 411–434.

30. When Johannes Climacus spoke of having an absolute relationship to the absolute, that is what he meant: decisive and unequivocal. See *Concluding Unscientific Postscript*, pp. 347ff.

31. This is the sentence of Eckhart cited by Derrida in "Violence and Metaphysics," *Writing and Difference*, p. 146. For the whole sermon, "Quasi stella matutina," see *Meister Eckhart: An Introduction to the Study of His Works*, trans. and ed. James Clark (London: Nelson and Sons, 1957), pp. 205–211. In this sermon Meister Eckhart says a number of beautiful things about the morning star; the disaster is to lose such a beautiful star.

32. A standard piece of the wisdom of Zen, which corresponds somewhat to Eckhart's idea of my being in the mind of God before I was created.

33. For texts and commentary see Caputo, *The Mystical Element in Heidegger's Thought*, pp. 103–109.

34. Maurice Merleau-Ponty, *The Phenomenology of Perception*, trans. Colin Smith (London: Routledge & Kegan Paul, 1962), p. 242.

35. Derrida, *Truth in Painting*, trans. Geoffrey Bennington and Ian Macleod (Chicago: University of Chicago Press, 1987), pp. 326–327.

36. *Fear and Trembling*, p. 28.

37. Moses Maimonides was a central figure for Meister Eckhart and a source for the elements of negative theology found in Thomas Aquinas.

38. As Drucilla Cornell puts it so nicely, "The possibility of the ethical lies in its impossibility; otherwise the ethical would be reduced to the actual, to the totality of what is." *The Philosophy of the Limit*, p. 83.

39. See above, note 25.

40. That is also Meister Eckhart's view. When he was called on the carpet by the Curia for the "excesses" of his sermons, he said he was speaking excessively, *emphatice*. See Caputo, *The Mystical Element*, p. 125, and Alasdair MacIntyre's critique of me and Meister Eckhart in *Three Rival Versions of Moral Enquiry: Encyclopedia, Genealogy and Tradition* (Notre Dame: University of Notre Dame Press, 1990), pp. 167–169. Levinas says that his own analyses proceed by way of "hyperbole," but by hyperbole he does not mean an operation of *différance*, which is what I mean, but rather the infinite excellence and transcendence of the Other; see *Otherwise than Being*, pp. 183–184.

41. It requires something of us. That suggests another way to read it, the way Josiah Thompson reads the "paradox" in Kierkegaard, viz., as a way of setting limits to thought so as to discourage thought from any further thought in order to make the transition to action. See *Kierkegaard: A Collection of Critical Essays*, ed. Josiah Thompson (Garden City, N.Y.: Doubleday, 1972).

42. Kristeva has an interesting essay on Thomas Aquinas in which she supports Thomas's (Aristotelian) position that self-love is a condition of loving others. See "Ratio diligendi, or the Triumph of One's Own: Thomas Aquinas, Natural Love and Love of Self," in *Tales of Love*, trans. Leon S. Roudiez (New York: Columbia University Press, 1987), pp. 170–187.

43. Deconstruction collects loose fragments and rag-tails, whence Drucilla Cor-

nell's praise of Derrida—she dedicated the book to him "in friendship"—as a rag-picker. *The Philosophy of Limit*, ch. 3.

44. See the powerful "Preface" which Nietzsche added to *Daybreak*, No. 1, p. 1.

45. *Ecce Homo*, "Why I Am so Clever," Nos. 1–3, pp. 51–58.

46. See Heidegger, "The Pathway," trans. T. O'Meara and T. Sheehan, *Listening*, 8 (1973), p. 39.

47. See Jean-Paul Sartre's distinction in the *Cahiers pour une morale* (Paris: Editions Gallimard, 1983) between an *"exigence,"* which is the violence of the categorical imperative (pp. 225–285), and an *"appel,"* which is transacted in freedom (pp. 285–306); for a commentary, see Monica Hornyansky, "Exigence and Choice," *Joyful Wisdom: A Journal for Post Modern Ethics*, 2 (1991).

48. "Force of Law," p. 945.

49. "Force of Law," p. 957. "And so I will not say it, at least not directly, and not without the precaution of several detours." But is it not already too late? Has he not already said it, in deferring saying it?

50. The very idea of *différance* disturbs the idea of the "in itself" or the "as such" or even the "very idea." See *Margins of Philosophy*, pp. 25–26.

51. John Rawls, *A Theory of Justice* (Cambridge: Harvard University Press, 1971), p. 131. Rawls goes on to say that, unfortunately, in *Ontological Relativity and Other Essays* (New York: Columbia University Press, 1969), Quine has deconstructed (I am not sure if this is Quine's word!), or troubled, the ideas of definite descriptions and general properties, but that he, Rawls, begs leave to "avoid" these difficulties—in the name of justice.

52. Whereas Lyotard says almost exactly the opposite—but about justice, not the law (*Just Gaming*, p. 94), which implies that the maxim of your will would—"ideally"—never be a universal ideal but the property of a proper name.

53. It would clear things up a bit if we distinguished between legal justice and deconstruction's justice, which is, I will not say "prophetic" or "ethical" justice, but a quasi-ethical almost prophetic justice. Deconstruction's justice is like the justice that would reign if each case, which is always different, were judged on its own merits without the weight of the law.

54. Whence the wrongheadedness of critics of deconstruction like Thomas McCarthy, "The Politics of the Ineffable," *Philosophical Forum*, 21 (1989–90): 146–168, who would expect a full-blown political theory, complete with empirical analyses, to issue from Derrida. Deconstruction is a quasi theory about what political theory ought to look like, one which problematizes the idea of theory in the strong sense, and which gives an orientation or direction to a political or legal theorist working from a Derridian point of departure—such as Drucilla Cornell. It is a politics of the quasi or almost ineffable, which recognizes, which is famous for insisting, that we are always already enmeshed in writing, rules, and laws—against Rousseau and Lévi-Strauss, e.g.—and that ineffability is the dream of being without *différance*. Deconstruction is related to political, legal, or literary theories rather the way Gadamer's "philosophical" hermeneutics is related to specific hermeneutic methods: it is a (quasi-) philosophical reflection *on* them, not an example *of* them. The same rejoinder applies *a fortiori* to Nancy Fraser, "The French Derrideans: Politicizing Deconstruction or Deconstructing the Political," in *Unruly Practices: Power, Discourse, and Gender in Contemporary Social Theory* (Minneapolis: University of Minnesota Press, 1990). In addition to Cornell's *The Philosophy of the Limit* see also her *Beyond Accommodation: Ethical Feminism, Deconstruction and the Law* (New York: Routledge, 1991). This sort of work is the proof of the pudding for the issues raised by McCarthy and Fraser.

55. A Jesuit, who is not a deconstructor, said that. See Robert Henle, "Prudence and Insight in Moral and Legal Decisions," *Proceedings of the American Catholic Philosophical Association* 56 (1982): 26–30.

56. This is Heidegger's gloss of the *Nicomachean Ethics*, 1106 b 28, which I use as a constant motif in *Radical Hermeneutics*.

57. I do not protest this. Recent tax "reform" laws in the United States are riddled with obscure *ad hoc* exclusions, filled with "rigged definite descriptions," which unfairly favor wealthy contributors to congressional campaigns.

58. *Glas*, 1a, 1b.

59. See *Parmenides*, 130c–d.

60. "It is possible to see deconstruction as being produced in a space where the prophets are not far away." *Dialogues with Contemporary Thinkers*, ed. Richard Kearney, p. 119.

61. I support this usage, which I borrow from Louis Mackey's description of Kierkegaard as a kind of poet, in "Derrida: A Kind of Philosopher," *Research in Phenomenology*, 17 (1987): 245-259.

62. See Derrida, "The Principle of Reason: The University in the Eyes of Its Pupils," trans. C. Porter and E. Morris, *Diacritics*, 13 (1983): 3-20.

63. In *Faith in History and Society*, trans. D. Smith (New York: Crossroad, 1980), pp. 109–115, the theologian Johann Baptist Metz speaks of "the dangerous memory of suffering." That, I think, is where all *Andenken* and recalling from oblivion should begin.

64. These are the excellent terms in which Heidegger speaks of openness toward death in *Being and Time*, §53.

65. See Lyotard on love in *The Differend*, No. 232, pp. 159–160 (LD, pp. 229–230).

Five. The Epoch of Judgment

1. I borrow the term "events" from Lyotard, for whom an "event" (*événement*) is what happens (*il arrive*) in the singularity of its occurrence. It is the idiosyncratic complex of time, place, circumstance, objects, etc., in what is happening. It is not an immediately given object or referent, but always something "presented" in "phrases" or sentences. Indeed phrases or sentences are themselves quite important events in their own right. Events have an intensity that breaks in upon us, whence the "date" of an event—Berlin, 1953; Budapest, 1956; Poland, 1980; Sarajevo, 1992—is the sign of a disturbance that impinges upon us, that demands phrasing. Events are irruptions that cannot be absorbed or smoothed over by flowing narratives. *The Differend* is organized around an event, Auschwitz, which is mentioned in every chapter and is the subject matter of the middle chapter. Events are often disasters in search of an idiom; the idea behind Marxism, e.g., is to find an idiom for the suffering produced by capitalism. The differend is an event of suffering deprived of an idiom. Events are characterized by their intensity, singularity, disruptiveness, multiplicity, heterogeneity, irreducibility, and open-endedness (one ought to keep a kind of experimental openness to events to come). The best account of the event is to be found in the last chapter of *The Differend*. For an excellent account of Lyotard's notion of events, see Geoffrey Bennington, *Lyotard: Writing the Event* (New York: Columbia University Press, 1988). There is also a philosophy of events in Gilles Deleuze, *The Logic of Sense*, trans. Mark Lester and Charles Stivale, ed. Constantin Boundas (New York: Columbia University Press, 1991), which centers on Deleuze's interpretation of the Stoics. For an interesting account of Deleuze which is comparable to the use I am making of Lyotard in the present study, see Constantin Boundas, "The Ethics of the Event: A New Stoicism," *Joyful Wisdom: A Journal for Post Modern Ethics*, 2 (1991) (St. Catherine's, Ontario). See below, chapter 10.

2. I borrow the excellent metaphors of the parliament and of pandemonium from George Johnson's review of Daniel Dennett, *Consciousness Explained* (Boston: Little, Brown & Company, 1991) in *The New York Times Book Review* (November 10, 1991), p. 58.

3. The history of metaphysics is filled with many variations on this idea: the

classical idealist or rationalist thesis about innate ideas or principles maintains that the mind or the soul comes equipped with certain heavenly, supratemporal inscriptions; the various ways of defending knowledge of the Good; the idea that the categorical imperative cuts through the sensible world and whispers a supersensible command in our supersensible ear. Etc.

4. See the essay "Time and Being" and the accompanying protocol in *On Time and Being*, trans. Joan Stambaugh (New York: Harper & Row, 1972), pp. 1–54. I have argued this point in detail in *Radical Hermeneutics*, chs. 6-7, and *Demythologizing Heidegger*, chapter 1, "*Aletheia* and the Myth of Being."

5. "Comment juger—Jean-François Lyotard?" Derrida asks in "Préjugés," *La faculté de juger*, p. 87, making Lyotard both the addressee and the subject of the question.

6. Derrida, "Préjugés," p. 94.

7. Lyotard, *Just Gaming*, pp. 15, 14.

8. Derrida, "Préjugés," p. 94.

9. Derrida, "Préjugés," pp. 96–97.

10. See *Nicomachean Ethics*, III, 7 (1115 b 15–20).

11. Lyotard is leaning heavily, I think, upon Aristotle's discussion of *epieikes*, the equitable, and he uses a citation from this discussion as an epigram to *Just Gaming*, "For when the thing is indefinite, the rule also is indefinite, like the leaden rule used in making Lesbian moulding; the rule adapts itself to the shape of the stone and is not rigid, so too the decree is adapted to the facts" (Bk. V, c.10, 1037 b 25-35). See *Just Gaming*, pp. 2, 26-29. I do not know if Lyotard's recourse to Aristotelian prudence at this point is entirely prudent. Derrida expresses some reservations in "Préjugés," p. 94.

12. Kant, *Critique of Pure Reason*, A133 = B172.

13. In "Préjugés," p. 98, Derrida says that one of the things he is *not* going to speak of is the question of "Derrida and Lyotard." To some extent that is just what I am speaking about.

14. See *Radical Hermeneutics*, p. 262. The incommensurability of competing schemas does not imply their incomparability. Ptolemaic and Copernican astronomies were incommensurable but the scientists of the day were able to compare them and choose between them.

15. Ever since Kant and Hegel, the Latinate "morals" has suggested something more ahistorical than the Greek "ethics."

16. *Radical Hermeneutics*, ch. 9.

17. The name of Aristotle is invoked through the prism of medieval Aristotelianism in order to name an ahistorical human nature. It was in the name of rescuing Aristotle from all that, that Heidegger undertook his "destruction" of Greek ontology. A similar ambiguity surrounds the interpretation of Gadamer on understanding: you may emphasize either his deep debt to a Hegelian conception of truth and its historical unfolding, or the influence of Aristotle and *Being and Time*.

18. After hearing Lyotard's "After Auschwitz," Derrida said that he had never felt so close to Lyotard. *Les fins des hommes*, p. 312. On the other hand, Lyotard says he sees no reason to attribute a "mystical profundity" to the abyss in which judging is caught up. *Differend*, No. 178, p. 128 (LD, p. 187).

19. The context is a conference organized by Drucilla Cornell on the topic of "Deconstruction and the Possibility of Justice" and held at the Cordoza Law School.

20. Derrida, "Force of Law," p. 959.

21. Derrida, "Force of Law," p. 961.

22. Derrida, "Force of Law," p. 963.

23. Derrida, "Force of Law," p. 965.

24. All citations in this paragraph are from Derrida, "Force of Law," p. 965.

25. Derrida, "Force of Law," p. 967.

26. Derrida, "Préjugés," p. 94.

27. Ordeal: *Fear and Trembling*, pp. 52–53 (Abraham's); *Repetition* (published the same day as *Fear and Trembling*), p. 210 (Job's). Economics: *Fear and Trembling*, p. 5, 49; madness: *Fear and Trembling*, pp. 106–107.

28. Derrida, "Force of Law," p. 965.

29. Kierkegaard, *Fear and Trembling*, p. 63.

30. Kierkegaard, *Fear and Trembling*, p. 55.

31. I am not saying that legalism is not massively present in the Jewish and Christian traditions. I am simply siding with the counter-traditions in those traditions, the ones who think the law was for the individual, not the individual for the law. I do not think that "jewgreek" means one thing. When Jesus pitted love against legalism, he was just siding with one form of Judaism against another; he was not trumping Jewish legalism with Christian *agape*, as Hegel thought. See E. P. Sanders, *Jesus and Judaism* (Philadelphia: Fortress Press, 1985).

32. Peter Damiens, "On the Divine Omnipotence in Remaking What Has Been Destroyed and in Undoing What Has Been Done," in *Patrologia Latina*, ed. Migne, v. 145 (Paris, 1867), Opscula XXXVI. For an illuminating commentary, see Robert McArthur and Michael Slattery, "Peter Damiens and Undoing the Past," *Philosophical Studies*, 25 (1974): 137–141.

33. See *Differend*, Kant Notice 3, No. 1, pp. 130–131 (LD, pp. 190-191) on the "archipelagous" nature of judging.

34. See, e.g., the "Interlude" in Kierkegaard's *Philosophical Fragments*, pp. 72–88. See also the editors' copious notes to the "Interlude" for the history of ancient opinions on the necessity of the past.

35. My thanks to David Crownfield for using this magnificent piece of American English to describe Heidegger's relation to the Greeks and the Jews. This implies that if you read the Greeks the way Heidegger wants, if you try to be very Greek or even more Greek than the Greeks, you will touch bottom on Semitic or jewgreek time, much to Heidegger's embarrassment. The later Heidegger's preoccupation with time and history, with decisive moments, with first and other beginnings, was all part of a massive bootleg operation and Heidegger's persistent silence about his early Freiburg period, including his original unwillingness to have these lectures included in the *Gesamtausgabe*, was part of the coverup. This is argued very nicely in John van Buren, *The Young Heidegger* (Bloomington: Indiana University Press, forthcoming). See also Derrida's portrait of Heidegger as a Judeo-Christian thinker in *Of Spirit*, p. 116.

36. From the time of Plato and Aristotle ethics has mainly consisted of building guardrails and protective shields around action so that action is not exposed to the cold, left unguarded, unprotected, in all of its frailty and fragility. There is a basic deconstructive impulse at work, I think, in Hannah Arendt's notion of the "frailty of action" which "political philosophy" tries to counteract; see *The Human Condition* (Chicago: University of Chicago Press, 1958), pp. 188ff. and Caputo, *Demythologizing Heidegger*, ch. 10. Lyotard thinks that "deliberation" about what "we" ought to "be" or "do" is very "fragile," exposing and exposed to the abysses between phrases, whereas "narratives" (and *a fortiori* metanarratives) tend to fill in the abysses. See *The Differend*, Nos. 210-217, pp. 147-150 (LD, pp. 213–217). See also Martha Nussbaum's notion of "Luck and Ethics" in *The Fragility of Goodness* (Cambridge: Cambridge University Press, 1986): "luck" is what *happens* to us; "ethics" is the domain of the "controlling power of human reason"; luck is the riskiness of life, ethics tries to make life safe (p. 3).

37. Arendt, *The Human Condition*, pp. 236–237.

38. Arendt, *The Human Condition*, pp. 192–197; Philippe Lacoue-Labarthe, *Heidegger, Art and Politics* (Oxford: Blackwell, 1990), pp. 77–99.

39. Arendt, *The Human Condition*, p. 240.

40. Luke 17:3-4.

41. Arendt, *The Human Condition*, p. 240, n.78.

42. Derrida, *Margins of Philosophy*, p. 135. It goes to the heart of the deconstructive gesture, after making a distinction, to unmake it. That is what Derrida likes about Austin. It is always a matter of how-to-do-and-undo at the same time, writing with both hands.

43. One problem with Heidegger's existential analytic, as Levinas pointed out, is that everybody, even inauthentic Dasein, is hale and whole, a well and able-bodied *Seinskönnen*. The existential analytic valorizes hardiness. So even though its doctrine of *Jemeinigkeit* is an exemplary piece of heterologic, by maximizing existentiell differentiations, the failure of the existential analytic as a heterologic is that it has no corresponding analysis of *Jedeinigkeit* and so it makes no provisions for the *argumentum ad misericordiam*. On the contrary, it is worried more about robbing people of their anxiety.

44. *Differend*, No. 22, p. 13 (LD, pp. 29–30).

45. James Lemoyne, "Out of the Jungle in El Salvador: Rebels with a New Cause," *The New York Times Magazine* (February 9, 1992), p. 29. Lemoyne is discussing the fragile peace treaty that was signed in early 1992 and the need to "forgive" but to "never forget," as one rebel leader put it, in order to make the treaty last.

46. And the Soviet Union. The fighting subsided when the cold war ended and the superpowers ceased fueling the fires of the war in the names of their competing metanarratives and with no regard for proper names like Miguel or Marina.

47. The other is the enemy as well as the friend. When asked whether "for the Israeli, isn't the other above all the Palestinian?" Levinas answers, " . . . in alterity we can find an enemy, at least then we are faced with the problem of knowing who is right and who is wrong, who is just and who is unjust. There are people who are wrong." "Ethics and Politics," in *The Levinas Reader*, ed. Sean Hand (Oxford: Blackwell, 1989), p. 294. I do not dispute Levinas's point but, as regards the Palestinians, his judgment. The question of the Other is always the question of the victim; the problem of judgment is to judge who is producing victims.

48. Derrida, "Force of Law," pp. 945, 957.

49. The name given to the Czechoslovakian revolution led by the playwright Vaclav Havel. These Eastern European revolutions are steeped in undecidability, fluctuating between velvet and blood, between peaceful popular uprisings and Sarajevo.

50. See the argument of Ernesto Laclau in "Community and Its Paradoxes: Richard Rorty's 'Liberal Utopia' " in *Community at Loose Ends*, ed. by the Miami Theory Collective (Minneapolis: University of Minnesota Press, 1991), pp. 83–98. This volume is a first-rate collection of papers which grope for a postmodern notion of community. For me, community means being-bound to one another (heteronomism, obligation) while preserving a postmodern space for diversity (heteromorphism). A postmodern community is a "weak" or "negative" community; it has no positive, binding, common idea of the Good, but only a negative idea of our obligations to those who are laid low.

51. That is what Eckhart called God. Angelus Silesius's couplet "Love Is Without Why," upon which Heidegger commented in *Der Satz vom Grund* (Pfullingen: Neske, 1957), pp. 63–75, recapitulates Eckhart's doctrine of groundless grounds and principles without principle, without why or wherefore, in terms of love. This belongs to the *Wirkungsgeschichte* of Augustine's saying. For a more extensive commentary, see Caputo, *The Mystical Element in Heidegger's Thought*, ch. 3.

52. I am rewriting Heidegger's notion of *Gelassenheit*, here, by directing it more generally to other persons as well as (and not just) toward jugs and bridges. This is what I called in *Radical Hermeneutics* (pp. 264–267) a "generalized *Gelassenheit*."

53. "To love what happens as if it were a gift, to love even the *Is it happening?* as

the promise of good news. . . . " *The Differend*, No. 232, p. 159 (LD, p. 229). That is how Lyotard sums up the jewgreek advice of the New Testament, the problem being for Lyotard that this became both a commandment and the basis of a new meta-narrative.

54. Love in Heidegger is either thought's hankering (*orexis, philia*) for Being; see *What is Philosophy?* trans. William Kluback and Jean Wilde (London: Vision Press, 1962), pp. 51–53; or it is Being's hankering for thought, its "favoring" (*Mögen*) us; see *Basic Writings*, p. 196. That, and another human being, will fill many a lonely night. In *What Is Called Thinking*, pp. 138–147, Heidegger wants to assimilate thinking, thanking, and the heart (*Gemüt, Herzengrund*), but I do not think this is very successful given the fact that this heartfelt relationship is between thought and Being and given the indifference of this heart to other human beings (or animals).

Six. Almost Perfect Fools

1. *The Levinas Reader*, p. 292.

2. Up to a certain point, Levinas does not mean to deny this. He makes it clear that the ethical relation of the subject to the Other, of my unlimited responsibility to the Other, is always already limited by others, by the third man, which introduces the necessity of calculations and the equal distribution of my obligations, i.e., of philosophy, law, and rationality. See *Otherwise than Being*, pp. 153–162. But keeping an army is something more than the even distribution of my being a hostage to the other of the other; it is something more like *Realpolitik*. It is a recognition, like it or not, of the equiprimordiality of the *conatus essendi*. In the view I am working out, which is more Lyotardian than Levinasian, interest and disinterest happen together, equiprimordially. The "subject" for me is all at once, synchronously, pluralistically, both active and passive, autonomous and heteronomous, aesthetic and under obligation, religious and atheistic. It is the solemnity and piety of an absolutely diachronous and absolute passivity that Levinas is forced to retract when it is pointed out that, in addition to being-for-the-other the subject is also, at the same time, *in* the same time, synchronously, being-for-oneself and interest. That makes *Totality and Infinity* and *Otherwise than Being* not nonsense but great works of prophetic hyperbole, which I love very dearly, with all the wisdom of love, but which I do not quite wholly believe, and about which I preserve a certain rhythmic scepticism. When one says "obligation happens," that means it just happens, that it happens along with a lot of other things that also happen, that it does not have the deep status of an archioriginal, preoriginal founding event, that it never has, never had, the depth structure, the infinity — "thanks to God" — that Levinas attributes to ethical substitution. In the view defended here, in this work, the ethical, the political, the aesthetic, etc. belong to a grammatological surface, to an extended, polymorphic, anarchical field without hierarchy, to a multiplicity of collateral, intertwined, not easily distinguishable events, simultaneously conditioning one another, not derivable one from one other; not equiprimordial, but equisuperficial. Interest is contemporaneous with disinterest. Disinterest does not somehow come first, is not earlier than interest. Nobody was there at the beginning. When I am obligated, I do not know by whom; the order comes *"je ne sais d'où."* (*Otherwise than Being*, p. 150.) In this Lyotardian betrayal of Levinas, both saying and the said are swept up in the play of multiple language games. With Lyotard, however, I have the complaint that there is a tendency, particularly in *Just Gaming*, to suggest that the language games are self-contained, insular minisystems unto themselves. It is true that the transitions between them always involve a leap, but this cannot be a "pure" leap across an utter discontinuity. An oceanographer will tell you that wherever you see an archipelagous grouping there was once a single landmass. Merleau-Ponty's image of "ambiguity" is more successful, of an ambiguous inter-

penetration of one sphere by another, "the ambiguous setting of their intercommunication" (*The Phenomenology of Perception*, p. 166)—so that everything is sexual, economic, religious, political, ethical, etc. Undecidably, anarchically, synchronously so. See *The Phenomenology of Perception*, pp. 171-173, n. 1.

3. See Kristeva, *Tales of Love*, pp. 170–187.

4. See *Glas*, 242a-244a: "I give you—a pure gift, without exchange, without return—but whether I want this or not, the gift guards itself, keeps itself, and from then on you must-owe, *tu dois*" (243a).

5. Lyotard, *Just Gaming*, pp. 60–61.

6. See Wyschogrod, *Saints and Postmodernism*, pp. 150, 58.

7. *Saints and Postmodernism*, p. 150, my emphasis.

Seven. A Happy Event

1. This line of Johannes Climacus in the *Concluding Unscientific Postscript*, p. 225, perfectly described my feelings at this moment. Like Coleridge, my *Biographia literaria* would get a supplementary boost, *in medias res*, from a letter in the mail.

2. *Concluding Unscientific Postscript*, "A First and Last Declaration," p. 551 (unnumbered).

3. *The Differend*, No. 208, p. 144 (LD, pp. 208–209).

4. The whole passage is lifted, sometimes verbatim, sometimes with a strategic alteration, from *Fear and Trembling*, pp. 7–8, so that it applies *mutatis mutandis*, now not (only) to Hegel's System of the History of Spirit, but to Heidegger's Thought of the History of Being.

Eight. Several Lyrical-Philosophical Discourses . . .

1. *O felix culpa* is an expression from the old Latin liturgy: o happy fault (the Fall of Adam) that brought so great a redemption (the coming of Christ). Felix teaches an opposite wisdom: o happy innocence that has no need of a redemption.

2. The inversion of the order of rank, the slave revolt which subjugates the best to the worst, would be the one sense of "injustice" that Nietzsche would allow, injustice in the extra-moral sense.

3. After much research I have found a theory for Johanna's practice, a feminist scriptural scholar who recommends rewriting the Scriptures—so you would then read the story of the prodigal daughter, or pray "Our Mother, Who Art in Heaven," etc. See Elisabeth Schüssler Fiorenza, *In Memory of Her: A Feminist Theological Reconstruction of Christian Origins* (New York: Crossroad, 1986), pp. 60–64. In *Bread Not Stone: The Challenge of Feminist Biblical Interpretation* (Boston: Beacon Press, 1984), pp. 10–15, Fiorenza says that the Scriptures are a "historical prototype" (which admits of rewriting), not a "mythical archetype" (which does not). This sort of imaginative reinvention is what I mean by heteromorphism.

4. *The Differend*, No. 168, p. 109 (LD, pp. 161–162).

5. *Fear and Trembling*, pp. 9–14.

6. So the argument of Derrida's *Spurs* against the Knight of Dogmatic Truth applies, *mutatis mutandis*, against the Knight of Faith or the Knight of Infinite Resignation. The problem is: too many Knights, not enough trembling maids.

7. A good general presentation of his thesis is to be found in René Girard, *Things Hidden Since the Foundations of the World*, trans. S. Bann and M. Metteer (Stanford: Stanford University Press, 1987); see the enlightening commentary on Girard's work by Andrew McKenna, *Violence and Difference: Girard, Derrida and Deconstruction* (Urbana and Chicago: University of Illinois Press, 1992).

8. On "Levinas and the Feminine," see the pieces by Luce Irigaray, Catherine Chalier, and Tina Chanter in *Re-Reading Levinas*, pp. 109–146.

9. See below, chapter 9.

10. *Truth in Painting*, pp. 326–327.

11. Johanna's delimitation of the thematics of difficulty, hardness, and *Kampf* in *Fear and Trembling* applies *a fortiori* to Heidegger. The young Heidegger's interpretation of the ontology of Christian life, acquired from Kierkegaard and Luther, turned on the militancy of the Scriptures, on fighting the good fight and keeping the faith, on the readiness to put on the helmet of faith and the breastplate of hope, on the call to constant vigilance and keeping a constant watch, in short, on a certain Christian soldierism. Johanna bears a more nonviolent message. See Caputo, *Demythologizing Heidegger*, chapters 2, "Heidegger's *Kampf*," and 3, "*Sorge* and *kardia*."

12. Genesis 21:8-21. See Mark Taylor, *Altarity*, p. 221.

13. Derrida writes of Kafka's "Before the Law" in (his, Derrida's) "Before the Law": "If someone were to change one word or alter a single sentence, a judge could always declare him or her to have infringed upon, violated, or disfigured the text. . . . Anyone impairing the original identity of this text may have to appear before the law." In *Jacques Derrida: Acts of Literature*, ed. Derek Attridge (New York: Routledge, 1992), p. 211.

14. Derrida, "Before the Law," p. 191.

15. This is also what Wyschogrod argues in *Saints and Postmodernism*.

16. John P. Meier, *A Marginal Jew: Rethinking the Historical Jesus* (New York: Doubleday, 1991), pp. 205–208.

17. Mark Taylor, *Erring: A Postmodern A/theology* (Chicago: University of Chicago Press, 1984). A/theology means to hover on the borders between theism and atheism. For a commentary, see my review of *Erring* in *Man and World*, 21 (1988): 107-114.

18. In fact, of course, Jesus' critique of Jewish legalism was an eloquent representation of an antilegalistic strain within Judaism; he was not introducing something foreign into Judaism. This was a deconstruction, not a destruction. See E. P. Sanders, *Jesus and Judaism* (Philadelphia: Fortress Press, 1985).

19. In Dostoevsky's story, Jesus does make the mistake of reappearing again and is immediately summoned before the Law of the Grand Inquisitor.

20. I should say of a certain biblical justice because there is an unmistakable taste for violence in the Scriptures and the notion that God would take the side of just one people and treat everyone else so harshly is little short of obscene.

21. Taylor, *Erring*, pp. 149ff.

22. Søren Kierkegaard, *Attack Upon "Christendom,"* trans. W. Lowrie (Princeton: Princeton University Press, 1968), pp. 71, 117.

23. See Derrida's "The Law of Genre," in *Acts of Literature*, pp. 221–252.

24. Cornell, *The Philosophy of the Limit*, pp. 62ff.

25. "Before the Law" itself appeared both within the margins of *The Judgment*, trans. Willa and Edwin Muir (New York: Vintage Books, 1969), pp. 267–269, and outside these margins, as a separate piece.

26. Derrida's discussion of *"Vor dem Gesetz"* constitutes the body of "Préjugés," the paper he delivered at the Cerisy conference on Lyotard, and follows immediately upon his exploration of the question "Comment juger—Jean-François Lyotard?" See *Jacques Derrida: Acts of Literature*, ed. Derek Attridge (New York: Routledge, 1992), pp. 181–120.

27. See Derrida, *Truth in Painting*, pp. 262, 292, 320, on "the heaviness of the *pathos*," indeed the "pathetic collapse," that envelops Heidegger's commentary on Van Gogh. On Heidegger's dismissal of feeling as something merely psychological and anthropological, see *Poetry, Language, Thought*, p. 205; *On the Way to Language*, p. 181.

28. In the 1960s Verlag Günther Neske issued recordings of Heidegger's lectures *"Der Satz der Identität"* and *"Hölderlins Himmel und Erde,"* but not *"On the Origin of the Work of Art"*—unless Magdalena has access to a private collection.

29. The *Beiträge* (*Gesamtausgabe*, vol. 65) is organized around the musical motif of a fugue and of the *Klang* and *Anklang* that rings out between the First Beginning and the Other Beginning. This is Heidegger's *glas*.

30. The whole discourse turns on an allusion to Derrida's treatment of Hegel's discussion (in the *Aesthethics*) of the phallic columns of India, in which inscriptions are "notched out"; see *Glas*, pp. 2a-3a. The column, including the columns of *Glas* itself (which are themselves notched out with little inscriptions), is a central phallic signifier in *Glas* and Magdalena is assimilating Heidegger's temple to these phallic columns.

31. In the longer version of "The Politics of Friendship," *The Journal of Philosophy*, 85 (1988): 632-644, Derrida spoke of the democracy of the future, the democracy to come, varying the sentence from Montaigne to read, "Oh my fellow democrats, there are no democrats."

32. See Derrida, *Of Spirit*, p. 70.

33. See *Basic Writings*, pp. 234–235.

34. Magdalena now paraphrases Heidegger, *Poetry, Language, Thought*, pp. 41–43.

35. *Ecce Homo*, p. 134.

36. Magdalena is undoubtedly referring to Martin Bernal's controversial *Black Athena: The Afroasiatic Roots of Classical Civilization*, Vol. I: *The Fabrication of Greece, 1785-1985* (New Brunswick: Rutgers University Press, 1987); Vol. II: *The Archeological and Documentary Evidence* (New Brunswick: Rutgers University Press, 1991).

37. See Mark 13:1-2.

38. *Poetry, Language, Thought*, p. 43.

39. *An Introduction to Metaphysics*, p. 62.

40. In the 1966 *Der Spiegel* interview, "Only a God Can Save Us," trans. Maria Alter and John D. Caputo, *Philosophy Today*, 20 (1976), p. 276, Heidegger expressed his doubts about the value of "democracy."

41. *An Introduction to Metaphysics*, p. 133.

42. "To test the logic of antherection . . . I propose that one try everywhere to replace the verb *to be* with the verb *to band erect.*" *Glas*, pp. 132b–133b; cf. p. 148b.

43. *Poetry, Language, Thought*, p. 45.

44. Magdalena is taking this from the Rand-Leavey translation of *bander* in *Glas*, to be stretched taut, as in an erection.

45. Magdalena is probably referring to Acts 3:2: "And a man lame from birth was being carried, whom they laid daily at that gate of the temple which is called Beautiful to ask alms of those who entered the temple."

46. Perhaps a reference to the discussion of the Hebraic imagination in Richard Kearney, *The Wake of the Imagination* (London: Hutchinson, 1988), pp. 37–78; the Hebraic imagination, Kearney says, is mimetic, ethical, historical, and anthropological.

47. Leprosy is a "chronic . . . malady capable of producing, when untreated, various deformities and mutilations . . . skin lesions appear as light red or purplish spots [or] as yellow or brown infiltrated nodules. . . . This leads to numbness (usually of the extremities), contractures and ulceration. [But only] mildly infectious." *The New Columbia Encyclopedia* (New York: Columbia University Press, 1975), p. 1564.

48. In *Die Verwandlung*, Gregor Samsa is turned into an *Ungeziefer*, a noxious vermin, a cockroach. Of the "extermination" of the Jews Lacoue-Labarthe writes, "The Jews were treated in the same way as industrial waste or the proliferation of parasites is 'treated.' . . . As Kafka had long since understood, the 'final solution' consisted in taking literally the centuries old metaphors of insult and contempt—vermin, filth—and providing oneself with the technological means for such an effective literalization. . . . Nowhere else, and in no other age, has such a will to

clean and totally eradicate a 'stain' been seen so compulsively. . . . " *Heidegger, Art and Politics*, pp. 36–37.

49. Perhaps a reference to Julia Kristeva, *Powers of Horror: An Essay on Abjection*, trans. L. Roudiez (New York: Columbia University Press, 1982), especially ch. 4 on the semiotics of biblical conceptions of defilement. For Magdalena, the function of a literature of disasters is to find an idiom for the defiled. Edith Wyschogrod suggests the word *Auswurf* (as opposed to Heidegger's *Entwurf*) to cover this sense of being cast out; see *Saints and Postmodernism*, p. 247.

50. The Roman fountain mentioned in "The Origin of the Work of Art"?

51. On "rats" and "parasites" see Mark Taylor, *Tears*, pp. 123–127. Taylor is also making use of Michel Serres, *The Parasite*, trans. L. Schehr (Baltimore: Johns Hopkins University Press, 1982).

52. *The Anti-Christ*, No. 46, p. 161.

53. A series of references to *Glas:* on gloves, gladiators, and gladioli, all sheaths and all gl-functions, see *Glas* 50b-52b. On the Spirit's shit, see *Glas*, p. 1b, and Lyotard, *Differend*, No. 154, p. 91 (LD, p. 137): "We wanted the progress of the Spirit; we got its shit."

54. The Latin Vulgate translation of Song of Solomon, 1:5, "I am very dark, but comely" (*The New Oxford Annotated Bible*).

55. Magdalena has nicknames for philosophers. Heidegger is "the Thinker," presumably on an analogy with Aristotle "the Philosopher." Emmanuel Levinas, whom she loves but, like Lyotard, regards as very pious, is "Rabbi Manu." She is referring to Levinas, *Difficult Freedom*, trans. Sean Hand (Baltimore: Johns Hopkins University Press, 1990), p. xiv. See also Adorno, *Negative Dialectics*, p. 207: "At its most materialistic, materialism comes to agree with theology. Its great desire would be for the resurrection of the flesh, a desire utterly foreign to idealism, the realm of absolute spirit."

56. Mark 13:2.

57. "Geophilosophy" is Lyotard's term for the "sacralization of a territory," a philosophy of the soil and native soil, for Heidegger's *Germania* in particular—as opposed to "Freud, Benjamin, Adorno, Arendt, and Celan—those great non-German Germans" whose thought is fed by "emigration, dispersion and the impossibility of integration," philosophers of Exodus. See Lyotard, *Heidegger and "the jews,"* pp. 92–93.

58. This is undoubtedly a reference to the Trakl lectures which locate a more essential pain, beyond flesh and feeling, in the rift between Being and beings, in the "difference" itself. See *Poetry, Language, Thought*, pp. 204–205.

59. I am reminded of Luther's distinction between the *theologia gloriae*, which he said had become too much dominant in medieval scholasticism, and the *theologia crucis*, which he said is the true biblical idiom. Van Buren offers an illuminating discussion of the role this distinction played for Heidegger in *The Young Heidegger* (Bloomington: Indiana University Press, forthcoming). The pseudonym "de la Cruz" is of course a Spanish translation of *crucis* and Magdalena is a critic of the *philosophia gloriae*.

60. See *Glas*, p. 48a.

61. An early Christology, primarily found among Greek speaking Christians, which treated the figure of Jesus as a divine miracle man.

62. If your aim is to get beyond the plane of factical life, you may say you are going higher, which is the more modernist-Hegelian gesture (*Aufhebung*), or deeper, which is the Heideggerian step back or step in reverse (*Schritt-zurück*). But in a hermeneutics of facticity, we plant our feet firmly on the surface of factical life, dodging the bullets that sail by our head, unable to book passage elsewhere.

63. See Caputo, *Demythologizing Heidegger*, chapter 7, "Heidegger's Scandal:

Thinking and the Essence of the Victim," in which I further defend this line of criticism of Heideggerian thinking as a "phainesthetics" (*phainesthai* + aesthetics).

64. The expression is Lacoue-Labarthe's, *Heidegger, Art and Politics*, p. 102, which he says he attributes to the Nazis, but denies of Heidegger. But of course that only means that in Heidegger it recurs on a higher or deeper level, as a national phain-estheticism, where Being makes itself beautiful in Germania.

65. Or alternately, on Lyotard's version, all this aesthetics suffocates a higher an-aesthetic feeling, not of the beautiful but of the sublime. See Lyotard's *Heidegger and "the jews,"* p. 80.

66. Lyotard, *Heidegger and "the jews,"* pp. 79–94.

67. ". . . the essence of truth is the truth of essence." *Basic Writings*, p. 140. This critique of Heidegger holds whether you take "essence" nominatively or verbally. It makes no difference to the victims.

68. *Der Satz vom Grund*, p. 188.

69. Lyotard is misled and misleading when, as a part of his insightful critique of Lacoue-Labarthe—"under the authority and protection of him whom, under the name of Abraham, the young Hegel attacks with the well-known, truly anti-Semitic bitterness in *The Spirit of Christianity*"—he collapses the distinction between Derrida's "deconstruction" and Heideggerian *Destruktion/Wiederholung*. Deconstruction is contaminated through and through by these Abrahamic motifs, while *Wiederholung* attempts to purify itself of everything Abrahamic. See *Heidegger and "the jews,"* pp. 75–76, 81, 84.

70. E.g., the *Wesen* of man is nothing human (*Discourse on Thinking*, p. 58); the *Wesen* of technology is nothing technical (*The Question Concerning Technology and Other Essays*, p. 44); the essence of language is not a matter of human speaking (*Poetry, Language, Thought*, pp. 189ff.) See Caputo, *Demythologizing Heidegger*, chapter 6, "Heidegger's Essentialism."

71. *Poetry, Language, Thought*, p. 161.

72. *Poetry, Language, Thought*, p. 166.

73. The animal, Lyotard says, is a paradigm of the differend: unable to voice the damage done to it (it doesn't get a vote). *The Differend*, No. 38, p. 28 (LD, p. 50).

74. "Ackerbau ist jetzt motorisierte Ernährungsindustrie, im Wesen das Selbe wie die Fabrikation von Leichen in Gaskammern und Vernichtungslagern, das Selbe wie die Blockade und Aushungerung von Ländern, das Selbe wie die Fabrikation von Wasserstoffbomben." I follow the translation of Thomas Sheehan in "Heidegger and the Nazis," *The New York Review of Books* (June 16, 1988), pp. 41–43. The German text is found in Wolfgang Schirmacher, *Technik und Gelassenheit* (Freiburg: Alber, 1983), p. 25 where p. 25 of a typescript of the lecture is cited. See *The Question Concerning Technology and Other Essays*, p. 15, for the first part of the sentence. Heidegger is determining the "essence" of technology in terms of the *Gestell*. I have discussed this text in *Demythologizing Heidegger*, chapter 7, "Heidegger's Scandal."

75. The statement is accurate as far as it goes, Lacoue-Labarthe says, but it is scandalously inadequate. *Heidegger, Art and Politics*, pp. 34–35.

76. Lyotard, *Heidegger and "the jews,"* pp. 88–89.

77. "Only a God Can Save Us," *Philosophy Today* 20 (1976): 277.

78. Or rather it does make a difference: the "danger" would be even greater if there were *no* victims. In Heideggerian terms, it would be *worse* if nobody was murdered by means of technological instruments of destruction, because then the with-drawal of Being would be still more inconspicuous and so even more insidious. (Suppose people were murdered under the sky and upon the earth with handmade tools?) See Lyotard's discussion of Faurrison's historiography in *The Differend*, Nos. 2-49, pp. 3–33 (LD, pp. 16–58). Robert Faurrison is a French "revisionist" historian who has sought to cast doubt on the reality of the Holocaust by manipulating historical methodology.

79. *On the Way to Language*, p. 184. It is because everything that happens in a poem about war, or any other disaster for that matter, has to do with something "other" (*allos*) that I take Heidegger's reading of poetry to be fundamentally allegorical in which the poets supply the Thinker with allegories of the History of Being. That in turn is supposed to be what really listening to a poet amounts to. See John D. Caputo, "Thinking, Poetry, and Pain," *Southern Journal of Philosophy*, 28, Supplement (1989): 155-182.

80. Heidegger's "situating" (*Erörterung*) of Trakl's poetry of disasters seems to me more a deportation or exportation, which sends it off to another place (*Ort*). See *On the Way to Language*, pp. 159-161.

81. Derrida, *The Other Heading*, pp. 13-14.

82. *Basic Writings*, p. 105.

83. *On the Way to Language*, p. 184.

84. Derrida, *Glas*, p. 144a.

85. Mark 16:1.

86. Luke 7:37-38.

87. Sophocles, *Antigone*, trans. E. F. Watling (New York: Penguin Classics, 1947), p. 2.

88. *Antigone*, p. 29.

89. *Antigone*, p. 1.

90. *Antigone*, p. 15.

91. John 18:36.

92. *Antigone*, p. 28.

93. *Antigone*, p. 27.

94. *Antigone*, p. 28.

95. *Antigone*, p. 22.

96. A reference to Trakl's poem "Grodek," and an ironic insinuation about Heidegger; see *On the Way to Language*, p. 184.

97. *Glas*, p. 168a.

98. *Glas*, pp. 152a-162a.

99. *Antigone*, p. 24.

100. Magdalena now switches the trope: now the flesh is the law, the divine law, which Creon transgresses; but Creon's transgression is not a sacred anarchy, but rashness and the arrogance of power. In Sophocles's drama, the conflict is between two laws, two universals, which was a perfect invitation to a Hegelian *Aufhebung*, not between a universal law and the singular, which is the more Derridian slant given to it by Magdalena, who opposes the law (of the *polis*) to the anarchy of sensuous singularity (obligation). Hegel's concern is to exhibit the more encompassing role of the public and political and hence to offer a justification of Creon, while Magdalena follows Derrida's thematizing of the feminine operation.

101. "Even unto death." The Vulgate of Philippians 2:8. Jesus was obedient to his mission, and defiant of the Law, even unto death.

102. "To the tomb": a compact expression which resonates with Sophocles, St. Paul, and *Glas* (*tomber*).

103. John 20:16. Another woman tending to another contested, controversial corpse and another tomb. Magdalena now signs her own name to this text. She is speaking of her own namesake, Mary the Magdalene. The miscegenation of Greek and Jew intensifies.

104. Magdalena is trying to clear her namesake's good name. The woman mentioned in Luke 7:37 is unnamed and described not as a prostitute but only as a "sinner"—but then what other sin for a woman is there? She was for centuries conflated with Mary Magdalene—whence Donatello's magnificent if horrifying wood carving of a repentant Magdalene. That, the pseudonym seems to suggest, is a power play of the males who had come to dominate the Christian communities and

who were interested in distorting the memory of Mary and her importance as a disciple. On the history of the Magdalene legend see Marjorie Malvern, *Venus in Sackcloth: The Magdalen's Origins and Metamorphoses* (Carbondale: Southern Illinois University Press, 1974).

105. Jesus did wash the disciples' feet (John 13:5), but bending down before the man with the withered hand is strictly Magdalena's staging, an adaptation of both Kafka and Levinas; see above, "Before the Law."

106. For a discussion, see Tina Chanter, "Antigone's Dilemma" in *Re-Reading Levinas*, pp. 130–146.

107. *Beyond Good and Evil*, Preface, p. 13. "Supposing truth to be a woman—what? Is the suspicion not well founded that all philosophers, when they have been dogmatists, have had little understanding of women?"

108. *Spurs*, pp. 53ff. In *Spurs* the "feminine operation" is the *actio in distans*, the beguiling effect of women; cf. p. 51.

109. *An Introduction to Metaphysics*, pp. 146ff. Heidegger returns to *Antigone* in his 1942 lectures on Hölderlin, but with no better results. The focus of the discussion is still *to deinon* (*das Unheimliche*) and his discussion of the early exchange between Ismene and Antigone is directed at drawing Antigone herself into *to deinon*. He singles out Antigone's remark that she is ready to suffer what is terrible (*pathein to deinon*), which would be better than dying for nothing (see *Antigone*, p. 4). Antigone is not the protectress of the *oikos* but still another brother venturing out into the *Unheimlich*; the "feminine operation" is nowhere to be found. Her care for the *oikos* is allegorized by Heidegger into a care for the hearth of Being. See *Gesamtausgabe*, 53, *Hölderlins Hymne "Der Ister"* (Frankfurt: Klostermann, 1984), pp. 63-152, especially pp. 122–134.

110. *Glas*, p. 167a.

111. Derrida, *Spurs*, p. 97.

112. For all of his troubling of the Hegelian eagle, Kierkegaard's pseudonyms poetize profoundly masculine and aggressive figures: knights of infinite resignation or knights of faith, valiant Christian soldiers pressing courageously ahead, braving the fear and the trembling with manly valor, their hands set to the plow, pressing their forward repetition, and ready to fight the good fight of faith. It was this same militaristic quality that attracted the young Heidegger to Kierkegaard. His 1921 course on the phenomenology of religion was organized around a text in which Paul enjoins us to put on the helmet of hope and the breastplate of faith (I Thess. 5:1-8); see Van Buren, *The Young Heidegger*. This militarism and *Kampfsphilosophie* came back to haunt Heidegger with a vengeance in the 1930s and, as Magdalena shows, deeply informs "The Origin of the Work of Art" and *An Introduction to Metaphysics*. See Caputo, *Demythologizing Heidegger*, chapter 2, "Heidegger's *Kampf*."

113. Nietzsche, *Beyond Good and Evil*, p. 13.

114. For an interesting account of the exegetics and politics of suppressing Mary Magdalene's role at the very onset of the Christian tradition, see Elisabeth Schüssler Fiorenza, *In Memory of Her: A Feminist Theological Reconstruction of Christian Origins* (New York: Crossroad, 1986), pp. 323–334. The Magdalene was a primary apostolic witness and very possibly the "beloved disciple," which raises a sexual question that has disturbed the unconscious of Christianity from the beginnings to *Jesus Christ Superstar*. Of all the women authors of these discourses, this one I suspect may be using her proper name. My thanks to my student Laura Stevens for her interesting work on this issue from which I have greatly profited.

115. Magdalena may have been reading Jane Schaberg, *The Illegitimacy of Jesus: A Feminist Theological Interpretation of the Infancy Narratives* (New York: Harper & Row, 1987).

116. On this point, the older, unaltered ending of the gospel of Mark, the one that does not add the *coda* about the Resurrection, is much more interesting. It sim-

ply has the Magdalene and another Mary finding an empty tomb and running away afraid, saying nothing to anyone. That empty tomb has the ring of *différance*, its *glas*. Is the older gospel of Mark a jewgreek tragedy, a disaster?

117. *Glas*, pp. 64b–66b.

118. *Glas*, 165a-166a.

119. *Glas*, 171a. Innocence (*sine culpa*) is a dream of being without *différance*, however joyful (*felix*) and free of resentment it takes itself to be.

120. See Ernesto Laclau, "Community and its Paradoxes: Richard Rorty's 'Liberal Utopia.' "

121. *The Differend*, No. 197, p. 140 (LD, pp. 203–204).

122. The disciples who remained "faithful" to Jesus built a mighty totalizing *arche* in his name, a massive, male hierarchy, equipped with the power to burn, silence, and excommunicate everything Jewish and anarchical. What then is the difference between loyalty and betrayal, *traditio/tradere*? The little inserts in *Glas*, incidentally, are called "judas peepholes," in part because writing is betraying; see *Glassary*, 32c-33a.

123. *Concluding Unscientific Postscript*, p. 157.

124. *Concluding Unscientific Postscript*, p. 548.

125. Lyotard discusses the difficulty that Levinas has in writing about the ethical relation, viz., that writing levels the space between the I and the you and destroys their asymmetry; see *The Differend*, Levinas Notice, No. 4, pp. 113–115 (LD, 167-170).

126. Lyotard, *Heidegger and "the jews,"* p. 84.

127. Theodor Adorno, *Prisms*, trans. Samuel and Shierry Weber (Cambridge: MIT Press, 1967), p. 34.

128. *Poems of Paul Celan*, trans. Michael Hamburger (New York: Persea, 1988), "Deathfugue," pp. 60–63. The full text of this poem is presented here line by line in alternation with other texts and the commentary of Rebecca. "Todesfuge" by Paul Celan, from *Poems of Paul Celan*, translated by Michael Hamburger, copyright © 1988 by Michael Hamburger. Reprinted by permission of Persea Books, Inc.

129. Blanchot, *Writing the Disaster*, p. 41.

130. This and the next two texts alternating with *"Todesfuge"* are from *The Differend*, No. 168, p. 109 (LD, pp. 161–162).

131. The last sentence and the next two inserts are from Heidegger, *Der Satz vom Grund*, p. 188. *Es blitzt* is also Nietzsche's example of an action of the forces in which there is no separable agent. *Will to Power*, No. 548, p. 294. Morgenstern here runs the two views, Heidegger's and Nietzsche's, together, as in Sineculpa's cosmology of a cosmic game.

132. Hamburger correctly translates *spielt auf* as "strike up," but Rebecca wants us to hear the *spiel* (play).

133. Rebecca is suggesting an analogy of the *Todesfuge* and the *Seinsfuge*.

134. Lyotard, *Heidegger and "the jews,"* p. 94. Here the tone turns against Heidegger.

135. This criticism is directed against Heidegger's "The Origin of the Work of Art" and his opening remarks to the Trakl interpretation in *On the Way to Language*, pp. 159–161.

136. Johann Babtist Metz, *Faith in History and Society*, trans. David Smith (New York: Seabury, 1980), pp. 109–115.

137. Celan's acerbic rejoinder to Adorno, cited in Jerry Glenn, *Paul Celan*, Twayne's World Author Series (New York: Twayne Publishers, 1973), p. 35.

138. Levinas: others; Lyotard: *les juifs*.

139. Levinas, *Totality and Infinity*, p. 233.

140. Now the commentary begins to weave in *Todtnauberg*, the poem Celan wrote after his visit to Heidegger's *Hütte* in Todtnauberg. Heidegger too is a master—of

thinking—from Germany. "Todtnauberg" by Paul Celan, from *Poems of Paul Celan*, translated by Michael Hamburger, copyright © 1988 by Michael Hamburger. By permission of Persea Books, Inc.

141. Hamburger here translates *sein Auge ist blau* in the plural, as it appeared earlier in the poem. Rebecca, who sees even in the earlier instance "the iron eye of a gun," nevertheless follows Hamburger's translation here rather than the German text.

142. One thinks of the film *Shoah*, which was not a beautiful film, but which was no less a work of art.

143. See Hamburger's introduction to the *Poems of Paul Celan*, p. 22.

144. *Negative Dialectics*, p. 362: "Perennial suffering has as much right to expression as a tortured man has to scream; hence it may have been wrong to say that after Auschwitz you could no longer write poems." In *Aesthetic Theory* (London: Routledge, 1984), p. 444, Adorno praises Celan's poetry of horror.

145. Hamburger, *Poems of Paul Celan*, pp. 136–149. See Foti, *Heidegger and the Poets*, pp. 84ff. for an illuminating commentary on *Engführung*.

146. Again, I mention the basic thesis of René Girard and his critique of sacrificial religion.

147. There is an important thematics of the "date" in Celan as also in Lyotard, a way of recording the singularity of the event. See Foti, *Heidegger and the Poets*, pp. 104–107; Jacques Derrida, "Shibboleth," trans. Joshua Wilner, *Midrash and Literature*, ed. Geoffrey Hartman and Sanford Budick (New Haven: Yale University Press, 1986), pp. 307–347.

148. Foti, pp. 84, 100-104; Lacoue-Labarthe, *Heidegger, Art and Politics*, p. 46.

149. Foti, p. xix. For an opposing view of Heidegger's poetry, which sees it precisely as confronting the *Dichtigkeit* of life, see Gerald Bruns, *Heidegger's Estrangements* (New Haven: Yale University Press, 1989).

150. *Pace* Adorno, *Negative Dialectics*, p. 365.

151. Nietzsche, *Twilight of the Idols*, p. 55.

152. Nietzsche, *The Genealogy of Morals*, p. 44.

153. Nietzsche, *The Genealogy of Morals*, p. 45.

154. Nietzsche, *Beyond Good and Evil*, No. 259, p. 175.

155. Nietzsche, *Beyond Good and Evil*, No. 203, p. 109.

156. Nietzsche, *Beyond Good and Evil*, No. 259, p. 175.

157. Nietzsche, *Beyond Good and Evil*, No. 9, pp. 20–21.

158. Nietzsche, *The Genealogy of Morals*, p. 158.

159. Nietzsche, *Beyond Good and Evil*, No. 229, pp. 140–141.

160. Nietzsche, *Twilight of the Idols*, p. 54.

161. Nietzsche, *Twilight of the Idols*, p. 54.

162. Let justice be done, let the heavens fall.

Nine. Jewgreek Bodies

1. In §44 of *Cartesian Meditations*, trans. Dorian Cairns (The Hague: Nijhoff, 1960), Husserl explains the reduction to the sphere of ownness (*Eigenheitssphäre*) within which is included my own animate organism (*der eigene Leib, le corps propre*) as the region of nature in which I myself rule and govern. I am toying with that expression in order to differentiate my own proper agent body, which phenomenology valorizes, from the unbecoming, uncomely, embarrassing, improper body of the other.

2. Merleau-Ponty, *The Phenomenology of Perception*, pp. 126–127.

3. My thanks to Susan Krantz for her helpful correspondence on this point.

4. In *Totality and Infinity*, p. 134, Levinas speaks of the truth of hedonism; he

says that eating is directed at food, not at fuel for nourishment and growth; and he criticizes Dasein: "Dasein in Heidegger is never hungry."

5. See Jacques Derrida, *Cinders*, trans. Ned Lukacher (Lincoln: University of Nebraska Press, 1991), pp. 21 *et passim*. Derrida's essay is punctuated with references to Celan and to the ashen body of the Holocaust, all the holocausts.

6. " 'Eating Well,' Or the Calculation of the Subject: An Interview with Jacques Derrida," in *Who Comes After the Subject*, eds. Eduardo Cadava, Peter Connor, Jean-Luc Nancy (New York: Routledge, 1991), p. 113 and ff. Here, in this deconstructive context, the question of eating is taken with a seriousness unknown to metaphysics. For more on the politics of eating, see Carol Adams, *The Sexual Politics of Meat: A Feminist Vegetarian Critical Theory* (New York: Continuum, 1990).

7. Jacques Derrida, "The Politics of Friendship," *The Journal of Philosophy*, 85 (1988): 643-644.

8. On Levinas and the animal, see the contributions by Noleen O'Connor and John Llewelyn in *Re-Reading Levinas*, pp. 229ff.

9. Derrida, "Eating Well," pp. 113–116.

10. *Basic Writings*, pp. 202–204.

11. It was a reversibility effect—a confusion of head and hat—that Oliver Sacks was analyzing in *The Man Who Mistook His Wife for a Hat* (New York: Harper & Row, 1987).

12. For an example of reversibility in Derrida, see *The Truth in Painting*, pp. 267–273.

13. See "Eye and Mind," trans. Carleton Dallery, in *The Primacy of Perception*, ed. James Edie (Evanston: Northwestern University Press, 1964), pp. 159–190; and "The Intertwining—The Chiasm," in *The Visible and Invisible*, trans. Al Lingis (Evanston: Northwestern University Press, 1968), pp. 130–155.

14. Patrick Burke has shown convincing similarities between the philosophy of flesh and Schelling's idealist philosophy of nature.

15. See the critique of Merleu-Ponty's concept of flesh by Claude Lefort, "Flesh and Otherness," in *Ontology and Alterity in Merleau-Ponti*, eds. Galen Johnson and Michael Smith (Evanston: Northwestern University Press, 1990), pp. 3–13; and the rejoinders by M. C. Dillon, Gary Madison, David Levin, and Stephen Watson, pp. 14-48.

16. In *Discours, figur* (Paris: Klincksieck, 1971) Lyotard argued for a notion of the "figural" as a kind of disfiguration of the form which phenomenology valorizes. The mobility of the body enables the body to constitute a coherent form; but if the body is immobilized, it loses its constitutive powers. For an excellent account of these matters, see Bennington, *Lyotard: Writing the Event*, pp. 56–102, especially 74-75.

17. See Derrida, *Cinders*, pp. 39–43.

18. The English words *flesh* and *flay* both derive from the Sanskrit *pleik*, meaning to tear. The Latin *caro, carnis* derives from *ker, sker*, which also means to tear or scratch. See Joseph Shipley, *The Origins of English Words* (Baltimore: Johns Hopkins University Press, 1984), pp. 177–178 and 320.

19. Heidegger, *On Time and Being*, p. 78.

20. In Milan Kundera's *The Unbearable Lightness of Being*, trans. M. Heim (New York: Harper & Row, 1984), Tomas always showers after he has been with another woman, but Tereza can always smell the infidelity in his hair; see p. 142.

21. *Ecce Homo*, p. 126. See also Adorno's pungent reflections in *Negative Dialectics*, p. 366: "The man who managed to recall what used to strike him in the words 'dung hill' and 'pig sty' might be closer to absolute knowledge than [Hegel] . . . " and "[Culture] abhors stench because it stinks—because, as Brecht put it in a magnificent line, its mansion is built of dogshit."

22. *The Phenomenology of Perception* is the *locus classicus* of this work.

23. Of course pain is a vital sign or symptom of stress, disease, etc. But then it must be "read" by a second party, or one must oneself try to read it. That is different from inhabiting it, living through it, suffering it, in which case it lacks an intentional thrust and one succumbs to it.

24. Elaine Scarry, *The Body in Pain: The Making and the Unmaking of the World* (New York: Oxford University Press, 1985), p. 4.

25. Scarry, p. 30.

26. Scarry, p. 35.

27. Scarry, "Part Two: Making," pp. 161ff.

28. This is only superficially comparable to Heidegger's notion of the *Riß* between Being and beings as the origin of the poem, since the *Riß* is a mystifying allegory for factical pain. See *supra*, "Temples."

29. I am adapting here the argument of Hubert Dreyfus, *What Computers Can't Do*, rev. ed. (New York: Harper & Row, 1979): if the AI industry wants to build a computer to simulate a human being, it will have to build a human body.

30. For more on the phenomenon of sleep, see Levinas, *Existence and Existents*, trans. Al Lingis (The Hague: Martinus Nijhoff, 1978), pp. 69–72.

31. Camus, *The Myth of Sisyphus*, trans. J. O'Brien (London: Hamilton, 1955), pp. 114–115.

32. Although I have taken it entirely in the direction of a concept of obligation, I have found myself revisiting Sartre's distinction between flesh and the body in *Being and Nothingness*, trans. Hazel Barnes (New York: Washington Square Press, 1966), pp. 506–508.

33. For an interesting study of the historical fluctuation of the experience of pain, see David Morris, *The Culture of Pain* (Berkeley: University of California Press, 1991).

34. I take this excellent expression from Mark Yount's insightful study "Two Reversibilities: Merleau-Ponty and Derrida," *Philosophy Today*, 34 (1990): 129-140; see p. 138.

35. Of course, you can also torture animals, sometimes in the name of science, sometimes in the non-name of cruelty.

36. See Colin Turnbull's chilling account of the Ik people: *The Mountain People* (New York: Simon and Schuster, 1972).

37. Heidegger, *On the Way to Language*, p. 195.

38. For an eco-feminist approach to the flesh of the earth and animal flesh in terms of the feminine operation (without mentioning Derrida), see Andrée Collard with Joan Contrucci, *Rape of the Wild: Man's Violence against Animals and the Earth* (Bloomington: Indiana University Press, 1988).

39. Husserl, *Cartesian Meditations*, §§50-52.

40. Foucault, *Madness and Civilization: Reason and Unreason in the Classical Age*, trans. Richard Howard (New York: Random House, 1965), pp. 3–7.

41. *Discipline and Punish*, trans. Alan Sheridan (New York: Random House, 1977), pp. 3–6. " . . . [T]he flesh will be torn from his breasts, arms, thighs and calves with red-hot pincers . . . " (p. 3).

42. When Miss Temple marries and leaves Lowood, Jane Eyre discovers that "my mind had put off all it had borrowed of Miss Temple—or rather that she had taken with her the serene atmosphere I had been breathing in her vicinity—and that now I was in my natural element. . . . " Charlotte Bronte, *Jane Eyre*, 2nd ed. (New York: Norton & Co., 1987), p. 73.

43. Max Scheler is among the few philosophers to have employed the heart as an ethical category; see Peter H. Spader, "The Primacy of the Heart: Scheler's Challenge to Phenomenology," *Philosophy Today*, 29 (1985): 223-229.

Ten. Otherwise than Ethics

1. See also *supra*, chapter 5, "Judging Events."

2. You can hear the "minimalism" of "events" in the English expression "What's happening?" or the German "*Was geschieht?*" — particularly if you take it as an actual question and not simply a turn of phrase. Of itself, the question produces a stall, a momentary paralysis or freeze, which is a function of its vacuous (minimalist) open-endedness; and it invites an equally open-ended, vacuous, sometimes even slightly embarrassed response: "Not much." "*Nichts neues.*" The question needs a schema, a horizon or a framing, in order to get going.

3. Heidegger, *Being and Time*, §62, p. 358.

4. I argue this in "Husserl, Heidegger and the Question of a Hermeneutic Phenomenology," *Husserl Studies*, I (1984): 157-178.

5. Derrida, *Truth in Painting*, pp. 326–327.

6. Before knights of faith everywhere launch their assaults, let me hasten to assure such readers that I am not out to undermine faith but to set forth the parameters and uncircumventable limits within which practices like faith take root. As with everything else, *différance* is the condition of im/possibility of faith. I hope on another occasion to take up the question of faith in a postmodern setting. My impiety is hardly meant to exclude faith, I who am a heteromorphic lover of many possibilities, especially jewgreek ones, but to point to the possibility of an impious form of faith, one which is sensitive to the rights of those without faith, the others of faith.

7. See Levinas, *Otherwise than Being*, pp. 148–149, 150 ("I know not from where"); p. 156 ("apex"); p. 183 ("heartrending bustling"); 185 (he, *il*).

8. I have all along been running together Heideggerian "events" and Lyotardian "events" and the resources of the English word "events" in the hope of demystifying and demythologizing the *Ereignis*, of keeping both metaphysics and meta-metaphysics to a minimum.

9. See *Radical Hermeneutics*, chs. 6-7, for a more careful deconstruction of Heidegger's History of Being.

10. See *The Mystical Element in Heidegger's Thought*, ch. 2.

11. GA 65, *Beiträge*, p. 8 et passim.

12. This and the next three passages from Heidegger are taken from *Der Satz vom Grund*, p. 188 (my translation). Eng. trans. *The Principle of Reason*, trans. Reginald Lilly (Bloomington: Indiana University Press, 1991), p. 113.

13. The idea of an "epoch" of Being is itself a violent simplification, too forceful a gathering together of what happens into the unity of a well-ordered *legein* or *epochein*. It is impossible to believe that the complexity of what happens in an "epoch" can be so simplified. Such a notion is unadorned metanarratival mythologizing.

14. Heidegger, *Poetry, Language, Thought*, p. 4.

15. Foti, p. xix.

16. *Being and Time*, p. 271.

17. *Being and Time*, p. 435.

18. My thanks to Michael Thompson for bringing this feature of *Being and Time* home to me.

19. *Daybreak*, No. 130, pp. 129–131.

20. "For what are lacking, now and for the foreseeable future, are names, and most immediately 'sacred names', which in their various ways governed, and alone governed, the space (public or other) in which ethical life unfolded." Heidegger, *Art and Politics*, p. 33.

21. See Nietzsche, *Beyond Good and Evil*, No. 39, p. 50.

22. *Beyond Good and Evil*, No. 294, p. 199. Nietzsche was never so right as when he talked in terms of laughter. This is the most affirmative and benign version of the order of rank, in no small part because he was talking about "my" suffering, not the other's. The fault lies only in Nietzsche's intractable inclination to rank-order people, as if he had either the right or the means to do so, instead of letting people

be. To translate Nietzsche's point into an empirical example, George Colt records a case of a person who called a suicide prevention center and who upon getting a recorded message instead of a counsellor burst into laughter at the absurdity of the situation. That burst of laughter burst the tension and the crisis. The laughter was salvific. See George Howe Colt, *The Enigma of Suicide* (New York: Simon and Schuster, 1991), pp. 304–305. Colt offers a helpful, jargon-free, and comprehensive survey of the question of suicide which includes numerous and quite illuminating case studies of suicides.

23. For texts and an exposition, see Caputo, *The Mystical Element in Heidegger's Thought*, pp. 122–124.

24. Whence the recent controversy concerning "Dr. Death," a physician who has devised a technology to assist people in taking their own lives and the controversy surrounding Derek Humphrey's *Final Exit*. Humphrey is the founder of the Hemlock Society, a group dedicated to making information available on the means of committing suicide.

25. There is growing evidence of a correlation between suicide and an insufficiency of a neurotransmitter called serotonin; see Colt, pp. 203–205.

26. My thanks to Drucilla Cornell for "glamorized masculine anxiety" and "the lone phallus," formulations which I have neither the will nor the wit to improve. I can only add a little supplement, that when I was a child I thought it was "the long Ranger rides again."

27. See Hume's essay "On Suicide" in *Essays Moral, Political and Literary* (London: Oxford University Press, 1963).

28. Verena Andermatt Conley, "Communal Crisis," *Community at Loose Ends*, p. 68.

29. In my view, Levinas describes the dynamics of faith as well as anybody. Indeed, I think that what Levinas provides is above all a metaphysics of the religious, of faith, which organizes faith around the trace of the Infinite Other. I myself take the present work to be, among other things, a background for a possible account of faith and I take the notion of *différance* as a propaedeutic to a theory of faith; see chapter 2, note 21.

30. I am intentionally offering an alternate gloss to Heidegger's commentary on this poem in *Poetry, Language, Thought*, pp. 189ff.

31. I am at this point running Trakl's poem together with James Joyce's short story "The Dead" in *Dubliners* (New York: Penguin Books, 1967), pp. 175–223. I am intentionally running together Trakl with an Irish novelist much favored by Derrida.

32. *Dubliners*, p. 223. "One by one they were all becoming shades" (p. 222).

INDEX

JOHN D. CAPUTO is the David R. Cook Professor of Philosophy at Villanova University. He is the author of *Demythologizing Heidegger; Radical Hermeneutics: Repetition, Deconstruction, and the Hermeneutic Project; Heidegger and Aquinas: An Essay on Overcoming Metaphysics;* and *The Mystical Element in Heidegger's Thought.* He is coeditor (with Merold Westphal and James Marsh) of *Modernity and Its Discontents,* and (with Mark Yount) of *Foucault and the Critique of Institutions.*

CPSIA information can be obtained at www.ICGtesting.com
Printed in the USA
236290LV00001B/8/A